Wigs and Wherefores

A Biography of Michael Sherrard

Wigs and Wherefores

A Biography of Michael Sherrard

by

Linda Goldman

and

Michael Sherrard

Wildy, Simmonds & Hill Publishing

Wigs and Wherefores: A Biography of Michael Sherrard

British Library Cataloguing-in-Publication Data:
A catalogue record for this book is available from The British
Library

ISBN 9780854900305

First published in 2008 by

Wildy, Simmonds & Hill Publishing
58 Carey Street, London WC2A 2JB
England

Contents

Illustrations

Unless otherwise indicated, the photographs are taken from Michael's scrap-books. All thanks are due to the anonymous photographers.

FOREWORD

Michael Sherrard is such a good advocate that it must have been fiendishly difficult for Linda Goldman to cross-examine him. A modest and private man despite his natural charm and bonhomie, he is not one of those lawyers who wants to bore others with the minutiae of his life.

But the clients he represented and the cases he recounts are the stuff of legal legend — the drunken labourer ordered not to drink "even a teeny drop of sherry before dinner"; the generosity of colleagues towards a newly-called barrister in contrast to the appalling behaviour of Lord Chief Justice Goddard. And what must it have been like, "alone and without a leader", to have defended a man hanged for murder — in a case regarded for 40 years as a notorious miscarriage of justice?

In Michael Sherrard we find a man of great integrity and kindness, a man who has gained much from the law — but who has given back still more.

Joshua Rozenberg

September 2008

A FORETASTE

"Actually, the first murderer I ever met," says Michael Sherrard, "was Brian Donald Hume."

It was 1934 or 5. I was six or seven. Hume was about eighteen and working as an electrician on a building site near our house in Finchley. I was one of several children who gathered daily at the place where he was working, hoping he would notice us and offer a ride on his bike. We thought it was a great treat to be allowed to sit in the empty wooden tool box attached to the handlebars as he pedalled us, one at a time, up the slope of Chessington Avenue. Then he freewheeled down again, pretending that he was not going to be able to stop.

In October 1949, he killed Stanley Setty, a business acquaintance. The body was dismembered and various parts dropped from the window of a private plane that Hume had chartered from the flying club at Elstree. The headless torso was found in marshes near the east coast, having never made it to the deep sea at which, supposedly, it had been aimed.

The case came to trial in January 1950. My father showed me a news report about it in the local paper. "Look what that electrician's been up to," he said.

I remembered Hume at once from the photograph. As a very junior barrister, I had more than a little time to spare. I could not resist going to the Old Bailey to listen to the trial. It would be another ten or fifteen years before I found changing into robes a chore. For now, it was a wonderful opportunity to do so. Wigged and gowned, I made my way to Number One Court and sat on the end of one of the back rows of green leather seats. Although I was seated so that I could see him clearly, the aim was rather for Hume to have a good view of me. I stared at him intently as he sat between two warders. Not thinking about the rather long time that had passed since our last meeting, I wondered whether he might notice me. Rather stupidly, I thought that he would be proud to recognise me in my legal finery but he had other things on his mind than remembering building sites, bicycles and small boys.

1

When he gave evidence and was cross-examined by prosecuting counsel, Mr Christmas Humphreys[1], his answers became snappy and rude. He ignored counsel's request to moderate his tone. The trial judge, Mr Justice Sellers, was of the old school, known for his gentle manners and quiet voice. Affording the defendant a courtesy which was more likely to have been heard in an academic debate, in quiet, modulated tones he intervened to say, "Mr Hume, please don't take this personally." That was too much for Hume.

"They're trying to hang me," he retorted angrily, stabbing his finger at the judge as he spat out each word, repeating them for emphasis.

"Trying – to – hang – me! And you're telling me not to take it personally!! My life is personal!!!"

The jury could not agree a verdict on murder but convicted him of being an accessory for which he was given a life sentence. His parole came twelve years later. After his release, he admitted the crime – but the 'double jeopardy' rule then in force meant that he could not be tried again for the same offence[2]. Several years later, he killed a taxi-driver in Switzerland where he was finally convicted of murder.

To be strictly accurate, he was not yet a murderer in the Finchley days ...

[1]   Christmas Humphreys:1901 – 1983. QC 1959. Appointed to the Bench 1968. Retired 1974. Prosecuting Counsel in the Ruth Ellis case 1955.
[2]   The Criminal Justice Act 2003 provides for a retrial after an acquittal where new evidence has come to light.

CHAPTER 1

TO BEGIN AT THE BEGINNING

The childhood days were good training for the busy years to come. Michael did not have too much time to spend at the building site. He and his brother had more demanding roles to fulfill at home.

My younger brother, Barry, and I (still the best of friends) became Bengal Lancers when we were quite small. Aged five and seven respectively, we had seen *Lives of a Bengal Lancer*[1] at the local Saturday morning pictures. The film had an important influence on us. We thought that being a Bengal Lancer would be the ultimate in boyish sophistication: and that is how we came to be recruited. We received from the regiment direct written instructions as to our uniform. The clumsy lettering in which our orders were conveyed looked like our writing but, need I say, we were given oral dictation at HQ, the Orpheum Cinema, Temple Fortune. Later, we found a flyer advertising the film. The photograph was an invaluable guide to perfecting our appearance.

We dressed for the part using our pale blue fabric school scarves wrapped round our heads. We each had a broom handle as a makeshift lance. We took all this very seriously and could hardly wait to get home from school to go on duty. Day after day, we stood guard at the foot of the staircase at home as if outside Buckingham Palace, seated on our notional horses or holding them. The "Lancers" on duty would not answer when spoken to. We changed watch by taking it in turns to stamp-march up the stairs to the half-landing and down again. The Grand Old Duke of York had nothing on us. Our younger sister, Averil, refused to take part because "it's just silly." But what did she know about serious fun at the age of about 2?

Shirley protests that he should have confessed to this double life before marrying her. She asks, "Why didn't you join the Foreign Legion? Like Beau Geste?" Michael's answer is prompt and certain. "We tried the Foreign Legion, but it wasn't as good. The French soldiers were favoured and we were just left standing. And I didn't like the look of a white handkerchief under the back of my school cap."

---

[1] Starring Gary Cooper, 1935.

He goes on to explain how he and Barry came to be spies, allocated the task of monitoring the secret orchestra of the BBC which was conducted by Henry Hall whose greeting, "Hello everyone," roused their suspicions and prompted an important surveillance operation

The BBC Dance Orchestra played on the radio at tea-time every day when we returned from school. We copied Hall's clipped, flat voice to one another, using his catch-phrases. "Hallo everyone," "Goodbye everyone," and, "Here's to the next time." We were taken as a treat to some of the Orchestra's live concerts at the Golders Green Hippodrome. Our parents advised us that we should disappear into the audience and not reveal that we were really Bengal Lancers. But how could we be discovered? We were always careful to leave our uniforms at home.

I can still see Henry Hall in my mind's eye. A strangely placid figure, he stood perfectly still, scarcely moving his arm as he raised and lowered the conductor's baton. He had no obvious or perceptible influence on the musicians. I think he was asleep most of the time.

Barry started to learn the piano. His lessons disrupted our spying and meant that Henry Hall had to be turned off before he could volunteer to say "Here's to the next time![1]"

There was no next time as far as our regiment and our music were concerned.

[1] The programme began with the tune, "Hallo again. We're on the radio again." The closing tune, "Here's to the next time," reversed the order of the notes of the opening theme. In 1937, the BBC Dance Orchestra became Henry Hall's Dance Orchestra.

CHAPTER 2

SOME CHILDHOOD DAYS

When he was about six years old, Michael noticed that the clever children in his class wore glasses. He hoped to join their ranks by pretending that he could not see the blackboard. He must have put on a good show. He convinced the optician in Temple Fortune who diagnosed him as being short-sighted. Since then, he has rarely been seen in public without the glasses that he hankered after.

It turned out that they did not have the required effect of making him clever without any input from him, possibly because they made everything blurred. This was unfortunate as Michael was not interested in applying much personal effort to his studies.

When war broke out, Barry and I were on one of our frequent expeditions to the Express Dairy Farm in Allandale Avenue, a few minutes walk away from home. The farm-workers knew us well enough to allow us into the shop area so we could listen to the announcement with them. We were not surprised: our parents had been talking for some months, without coming to any conclusion, about what they would do if war came. Whilst we were listening to the discussion about who would be called up and whether farm-work would be part of the war effort, an air-raid siren went off, terrifying us. It seemed a good time to go home as quickly as we could.

There was the sound of a sudden explosion as we rounded the corner of Chessington Avenue. We ran even faster towards our house, believing that we were under fire. We were not. But the explosion turned out to have been caused by the first RAF casualty of the war: a fighter-bomber with technical problems had crashed into one of the houses in a neighbouring road[1].

As far as my parents were concerned, the war had arrived and we were in the front line. In the previous couple of days, the Government had been evacuating women and children to the country and was encouraging people who could leave the cities to do so. My father had been adamant that Finchley was not likely to be an enemy target. He had

---

[1]   Pilot Officer John Noel Laughton Isaac was killed in the crash.

been saying, "It'll take more than that *mamser*[1] Hitler to make me move. We're staying put."

The Mydat family of two parents and three youngsters in their late teens and early twenties lived next door. They had been packing for days. By the time we got home, Mrs Mydat was on her front doorstep, pleading with my mother to bring our family out to Aylesbury where they were going.

Until then, my mother had been assuring her regularly that we were staying in Chessington Avenue. But the aircraft being shot down, as we believed, almost on our doorstep was quite convincing evidence in favour of moving somewhere safer. We had nowhere to go but the two rooms the Mydats had generously offered us so, on the understanding that we could come back if things did not work out, we duly accompanied them.

Our sanctuary lasted ten days. It was better to be at risk in Finchley than cramped in Aylesbury.

My father was a fire-warden throughout the war. After I was thirteen, I was allowed to go with him on his fire-watching shifts, carrying hand-pumps and heavy buckets which were called into use when a local house took a direct hit from a German bomb. I also had to report incidents and make phone calls to emergency services when told to do so.

A bomb fell near Henly's Corner and destroyed one wall of a house in our street. The bedroom-occupant, who had miraculously slept through the event, woke to the draughty, chill feeling that characterises the loss of the entire side of one's home. My father shouted up to him, "Don't move – stay where you are!" Good advice, given that one more step forward and he would have fallen at least two stories into the bomb crater.

---

[1] "Mamser": Yiddish for "bastard"

CHAPTER 3

DOWN WITH DRUMS

It was somewhat annoying to have to bother with school when there was a war on. Further, to the despair of his parents, Michael knew that he would not need much formal education to be a jazz drummer. It was important to him to make plans for his future so as to be able to commit to the responsibilities of supporting a wife. He had proposed to Shirley in all seriousness at the age of fourteen. He had to wait eight years before her acceptance.

Some neighbours were more patient with the learning process than others. They needed to be. Their only respite from the relentless reverberation from the Sherrard house came in the all-too-short school days or the fire-watching shifts. A friendly listener across the way was a medical student who was also the leader of his band at St Thomas' Hospital: he urgently needed to recruit a drummer. Michael auditioned and was accepted, unmoved by his parents' anxiety when they learned that he would be expected to travel to the middle of London to provide the music for the staff dances. He used his fledgling advocacy skills to persuade them that the danger was negligible. The air raids were tailing off and the band would be travelling by ambulance, which was not only the safest vehicle that could be imagined but it also had enough space to carry the drum kit.

"I enjoyed the excitement of being part of the band," says Michael. "But I was a lousy drummer."

Before then and between what would now be called 'gigs', his interest in the law had begun in a vague way from leisure reading and films. A trip to the Old Bailey in 1945 put the musical career on permanent hold: the court visit was a revelation, a defining moment.

On considering the experience, Michael says, "It may be that the seeds of ambition were sown that day." He felt there was a goal to achieve in the law.

The occasion is preserved in a press photograph of the crowd waiting to go into the Old Bailey on Monday, January 16th, 1945. Michael is in the centre of the picture, the camera apparently focused on him. Instantly recognisable, he looks older than his sixteen years, wearing round

Some of the people who waited about today in the hope of being admitted later to the Old Bailey to hear the opening of the trial of the 18-year-old strip-tease dancer, Elizabeth Marina Jones, of Hammersmith. She and Karl Gustav Hulten, a U.S. paratrooper, are charged with the murder of George Edward Heath, whose body was found in a ditch near Staines.

Outside the Old Bailey with briefcase in hand, 16 January 1945

spectacles and formally dressed on a cold winter's day in an overcoat, ready for what turned out to be his first appearance at the Old Bailey. He carries a brief-case and stands in the queue outside the public gallery entrance to Number One Court to see the opening day of the murder trial of Elizabeth Marina Jones, an eighteen-year old strip-tease dancer, and Gustav Hulten, aged twenty-two, an American army deserter. They were petty criminals who, in October 1944, concluded their short, joint career by Hulten shooting George Heath, a taxi-driver. Unwisely, he had asked for the fare at the end of the journey. The press called the case "The Cleft-chin Murder" because of the dimple in the chin of the victim.

As I saw the judge take his seat, I did not even begin to imagine that, as a Recorder, I would one day do the same thing. I was absorbed by the excitement of being in the packed gallery, looking down on the court, listening to the solemn language and watching every movement. Although my view was mainly of the backs of the occupants of the courtroom, I admired the formality of dress, the dignity of the judge and the bleak grandeur of the process.

Jones was defended by John Maude KC, one of the "characters" of the Bar, who eventually was to lead me in a couple of cases. Later, after he became an Old Bailey Judge, I was to appear before him. He had a sonorous, plangent voice and spoke in a wonderfully laconic, theatrical way. His father, Cyril Maude, was a well-known actor. Perhaps that is where he learned his flamboyance. Not for a moment, as the trial went through the preliminary stages, did I think that each word he uttered was less than wonderful. I listened and learned. I thought, "That is what I want to be."

By the time I was established in my career, I came to realise how much more effective was counsel for Hulten, J.D. Caswell, who also became a judge. Maude was hyperbole: Caswell was moderate. He was also intellectually superior. His words were stirring but they were simple and his style was understated, going directly for the judicial jugular. He knew what the court wanted to hear. Steadily and reliably, he showed the jury the way home. When I was in practice, I was to learn that Caswell invariably achieved what he wanted in a case. But for the time being, for me, John Maude put on a very good show[1].

[1]   Both the accused were convicted of murder. Two days before Hulten was hanged at Pentonville on 8 March 1945, Jones was reprieved. Her sentence was commuted to life imprisonment. She was released in 1954.

CHAPTER 4

A CHANGE OF CAREER

The day in court led to a life-changing decision: Michael was spared a career in percussion. But to make the change, some rapid action had to be taken. The vague expectation that he would go to university now became a desire to read law. This suddenly required a great deal of academic catching-up which Michael felt could only be achieved by leaving school and having an intense course of private tuition. The same skills that persuaded his parents to allow him to join the dance band were applied to the finding of a private tutor who, in the eight months that remained before matriculation, would introduce Michael to the necessary elements of higher study which had been hitherto ignored as having no relevance to drums.

My father thought I was mad. He was a realist. My mother was a romantic. She, too, thought I was mad.

"In one huge step, you're leaving jazz for the law?"

I insisted that I could do it. I had no doubt about my interest in the subject but, although I would not admit it aloud, I privately doubted my capacity to complete the study required in the few short months before the exams.

"I really want to do this," I told him, "but I can't do it at school."

"If you can't do it at school," he said, "you can't do it anywhere."

"But I can," I assured him with a confidence I did not feel. "What I need is a tutor."

My father went to see the Headmaster who was amused at the thought of this indifferent pupil suddenly showing interest: too little, too late was his conclusion. As far as reading law was concerned, he thought that was ludicrous. He was certain that I had a bare prospect of success in the university entrance exams if I stayed at school and none if I left, tutor or not.

"Don't you think he can do it?" my father asked.

The Headmaster did not even bother to smile. He held out his left hand, palm upwards, tapping the palm with the index finger of his right hand. "When hair grows there, Mr Sherrard," he said, "that's when your son will get to University if he leaves."

The civics teacher who had sent me to the Old Bailey came to my rescue in two ways. I believe that she was instrumental in my being offered my university place by a letter she wrote to the Admissions Dean saying that I had started late but was shaping up well. That letter was only possible because of her introduction of Mr Cooper, my tutor, to my best ally, my mother. She persuaded her that I would do well if I was allowed to leave school and immerse myself in the sort of intensive coaching that could only be given by a private tutor.

Mr Cooper took over my life for the next eight months. There was much catching up to do but he made the tutorials so interesting. His enthusiasm for teaching made it easy for me to learn. Essays, previously a chore, became a joy to write and his constructive criticism underpinned the skills I would later use in legal analysis. I read Shakespeare for the first time and was lucky that my set play, *The Merchant of Venice*, encouraged my interest in the law. Getting to grips with French literature was no longer an impossibility. Even Latin came to life as a language through Mr Cooper's skill.

I was a hard task-master to myself. I had a strict timetable from breakfast to midnight: tutorials, essays, reading, learning – although I allowed myself an occasional visit to the cinema to see a Glenn Miller film. Even the joy of the ending of the war did not permit much of a break in study.

But the effort was rewarded in October 1945 when I became an undergraduate.

I chose King's College, London as it offered the best of all worlds for me: the Law Faculty had been evacuated to Cambridge during the war and was not expected to return to London until 1946. I had been looking forward to spending a year at Cambridge although by the time I started the course, the Faculty had returned to home territory in the Aldwych on the Strand. From the start, I enjoyed being a student. Although my degree was undistinguished, time getting it was well spent. I made some good friends, edited the student magazine and had a lot of fun as a member of the drama club.

11

The pace of work and the social side of student life were features of fundamental change. There were many facets to the settling-in period at the end of the war. One of the most significant was that the college population was not largely made up of youngsters in their late teens but a mixture of them and men and women of mature years returning from the battlefronts. There were many overseas undergraduates taking the benefit of the British Government sponsorship which provided university education to Commonwealth ex-servicemen.

In common with other Universities, London had problems arranging teaching cover for its courses in 1945 because many lecturers and professors who had been in the armed forces had not yet been demobilised. London University in effect amalgamated the law faculties at three main points: King's College, University College and the London School of Economics. The teaching of law was provided by the staff of all three places. Distinguished academics delivered lectures. Many still wore military uniform. There was often feverish activity while lecturers refreshed their memories, although most had managed to maintain high standards. I remember being present when Professor (Captain) Ronald Graveson arrived in full dress uniform at UC announcing that this was his last public appearance so attired. He then delivered a stunning lecture on public international law. The girls in the audience sighed audibly when he came in and were unfailing in their attendance from then on and often followed him about the college just to look at him. He had charisma.

The other academics were exceptional too[1]: Professor Jolowicz, Otto Kahn-Freund, Harold Potter, A J Kiralfy, Hughes-Parry, Wade, Phillips, Glanville Williams, Schwarzenberger, Keaton. The list of illustrious names in the one faculty was remarkable. Not only were they great lawyers, they taught with consummate skill. Glanville Williams' slim, memorable book, *Learning the Law* was essential reading for all of us. I believe it still is. Kahn-Freund was a brilliant, dynamic speaker whose lectures enthralled me – and everyone else in his audience. We some-

---

[1] John Anthony Jolowicz, later to become the co-author of *Winfield and Jolowicz on Torts*; Otto Kahn-Freund, 1900 – 1979, author and outstanding scholar in public and private international law; Harold Potter, Author of *Potter's Land Law*; A J Kiralfy, Co-Author with Harold Potter (1937): *Law of Personal Property*; Professor Ronald Harry Graveson (1911-1991), later Professor of Law, author of numerous works on private international law.

times applauded him, which was almost unheard of. I was mesmerised and could not take notes as he spoke. But his words stayed vividly in my mind so that I remembered them almost completely.

Most of my thirteen other fellow King's students of law went on to successful careers: the list of names reads like an advance flier for *Who's Who*. Roger Frisby was a young man of fearsome intelligence: many people thought his skills were wasted when he went to the criminal rather than the commercial bar. Bob McCrindle established a famous commercial practice: he would have made it to the Lords but he went off to an American firm in Paris. Joseph Jackson went to the family bar: he became famous as the editor of *Rayden and Jackson on Divorce and Family Matters*.

George Pelaghias was a sponsored ex-serviceman who had served in the Free Cypriot Airforce. He was characterised by the battered, slightly old-fashioned trilby hat that seemed welded to his head. He was to go into politics in Cyprus and become Foreign Minister in the Makarios Government. George introduced his friend, Glafcos Clerides[1], another ex-serviceman in the sponsorship scheme, into our social circle: his name became internationally known when he became President of Cyprus. George was fascinated by the occult and considered himself to have special, supernatural powers. In breaks from his studies, George would try to involve our group in his interest in paranormal, occult and psychic phenomena. We used to spend weekends at John Warnford-Davies' parents' place in Marlow. We spent some of the time swotting but after dinner, if other friends were there, we would spend hours talking about paranormal phenomena with George directing the conversation. Sometimes we would sit around the dining table and George would say, "Let us all link fingers and thumbs." Carried along by his enthusiasm and belief, we could feel something almost like electricity pulsing where our fingers touched. We could – and did – stand. With our hands circling the table, we could lift it from the ground.

---

[1] During World War II, Glafcos Clerides served in the Royal Air Force and was shot down over Germany, spending years as a prisoner of war. He was Acting President of Cyprus for four months in 1974 during the period of President Makarios' exile then President of Cyprus, 1993 – 2003.

John was utterly sceptical about these mystical processes. When George was conducting an experiment to prove a psychic phenomenon concerning our future which involved a long period of sitting still, fusing our thoughts, John had no hesitation in saying, "What a load of bunk this is!" George glowered at him. "You are asking for trouble," he assured him. "Do not mock the spirits. Do not despise what you do not understand."

Within an hour, John was in torment, fidgeting. Finally, he cried out, "I have to go and pee!" The spell, if there was one, was broken. George said sadly, "You must ask the spirit politely."

We had the joy of seeing John raise his hands in a supplicating gesture. In a respectful tone, he said, "Oh spirit, please – *oh, please* – may I go to the toilet?"

The ouija board spelt out, "Yes, you may." There was clearly an occult presence!

Stanley Clinton-Davis became a solicitor. His successful career in politics, including a spell as a European Commissioner, took him to the House of Lords. John Bowran also followed the solicitor route. He was the first Secretary-General of the Law Society. Michael Pritchard went on to be a Cambridge don.

In the final year, after the hiccup of referral in land law, Michael decided to take an important practical step to bridge the gap between a law degree and practice at the Bar. Against the wishes of the Faculty, at the same time as taking his degree, he sat Bar Finals. His preparation consisted of the use of Blake Odgers' "Civil and Criminal Procedure" and crossing the road from time to time to see what was going on in the High Court.

Of his proposed profession, he says that it was almost an end in itself. He had no notion of civil work, knowing nothing except what he had gleaned from Blake Odgers. If he had an idea of what he wanted to do, it was crime. He says, "I never saw myself as ambitious. It was almost enough to see myself as a member of the Bar. I was in a state of suspended excitement. But I can tell you this: I didn't know what I was letting myself in for."

Harold Potter, the land-law guru was Dean of the Faculty of Laws. He had his own view of what Michael was letting himself in for. He was highly displeased with the referral in his own subject and even more displeased with a student reading for the Bar when the degree should have been his only concern. He assumed that failure in both endeavours was likely. Bumping into Michael in the quad, he glared and pointed at him with something between disdain and disgust saying, "If you fire at two birds with one gun, you miss them both. Two birds with one gun, Sherrard, two birds with one gun..."

But Michael's main interest was the Bar exams. On 29th June 1949, the day the results were to be published, his father went to Leicester Square in the early hours to buy the first edition of The Times so that they would know the outcome as soon as possible. "The results are there," he told Michael cheerfully, without saying what they were. After anxiously searching the list, he found his name. He was through! The degree results, posted at Senate House some time in August, were – literally – of academic interest. Having a degree was a bonus at a time when the only essential requirement for being a barrister was a pass in the Bar Finals.

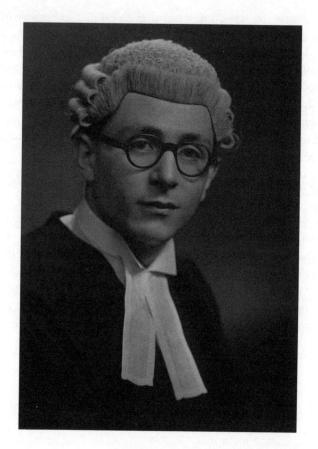

Call day, 1949

CHAPTER 5

CALL DAY

Middle Temple Hall has been the heart of the Inn since it was completed in 1573. Its magnificent hammer-beam roof encloses the 100-foot length of the hall, soaring almost 60 feet into its apex. Its smoke-darkened structure has looked down on generations of earnest students, sometimes relaxed diners and revellers, arching over panelled walls, portraits of kings, queens, important figures in legal history and the coats of arms of holders of high office in the Inn. The strength of the hammer-beams prevented the total destruction of the building when a bomb destroyed the South wall in May 1941. While waiting to have its wounds healed, the Inn carried on its business in the adjacent, undamaged Great Rooms, including the Call to the Bench ceremony in 1944 of Queen Elizabeth[1]. Throughout the war and until the Hall was repaired[2], students prepared for their Call by "paper dining". This ingenious system of "let them eat paper" maintained the tradition of learning by compulsory dining during term-time. Students signified attendance at non-existent dinners by signing a book in the library, a temporary Nissen hut in the area that is now Brick Court.

Within a few days of the Bar Finals results, the young Sherrard, slight of frame, dark of hair, sporting round glasses (square lenses did not appear until the 1950s) and wig and gown, was Called to the Bar, bowing to Her Majesty the Queen, the Royal Bencher. He remembers how good it felt to be wearing his robes. "There were about fifty of us, mostly people in uniform. The Queen wore her silk Bencher's gown."

He bowed, with the fears common to all who wear the wig: will it fall? – can it be held on? In the event, the answer to both being, mercifully, "No."

On 4th December 1996, on the occasion of Family Night[3] as Master Treasurer of the Honourable Society of the Middle Temple, he recol-

---

[1] Her Majesty had been the Royal Bencher since 1944. She was Called in what is now known as the Queen's room".

[2] Repairs to the building were completed by 1949 with the generous assistance of the American and Canadian Bar Associations

[3] Family Night is so called in tribute to the Royal Bencher.

lected the events of his Call in proposing the toast to the health of Master Her Majesty Queen Elizabeth, the Queen Mother,:

"Your Majesty, it is with the greatest pleasure and sense of privilege that I rise to offer a double welcome to you on behalf of our Inn ...

"May I be permitted to strike a nostalgic personal note? I had the immense good fortune to be one of those you Called to the Bar during your year as Treasurer in 1949. You stayed after the ceremony and took tea with us, and I have never forgotten the occasion. It was a wonderful start to a young man's career... I need hardly say how honoured I am to have been at your side this evening.

"A little further research led me to find a record of your Call to the Bar by that great advocate Serjeant Sullivan when he was Treasurer on 12th December 1944. It was indeed a grand occasion, despite the wartime conditions. We hope that this evening's meal has been pleasing to you and that the menu contained some of your favourite dishes. In 1944 the records show that you had a war-time regulated "five-shilling meal". It was relatively simple: clear soup, roast turkey, apple tart and cheese and biscuits. However, the great tradition of our wine cellars was maintained even then. The wine served was a Chateau Margaux 1924.

"Serjeant Sullivan's address is also on record and I should like to quote briefly from it. He said:

"Again a Queen Elizabeth comes to the Middle Temple, but she comes not as a stranger guest, but as our comrade, the first daughter of Domus to take her seat at our Board. She comes filling the deficiency under which we have laboured for so many hundreds of years, with the charm and grace of a lady in our midst. And by her advent Domus becomes a home indeed – for it the woman who makes the home."

"I should like to develop the theme of Home. Home is where you are: and you have never confined it to Domus itself. Let me explain. For the last two and a half years, I have been privileged to lead the student weekends at Cumberland Lodge. St Catherine's Foundation, of which you are such a treasured Patron, will celebrate its golden anniversary next year. The debt that we, and countless other student groups, owe to you is inestimable. For the Middle Templars, however, there is an extra abundance of gratitude for your personal hospitality at Royal Lodge itself – your home. You have so often been gracious enough to invite

Masters of the Bench and groups of students to pre-luncheon drinks on those very special Sundays. You can, I hope, imagine the thrill this is for the young – and the not-so-young. They regard this visit as the highlight of their student lives. Throughout the Commonwealth, too, there are students who will never forget your hospitality, your kindness and your warm interest in them.

"So, from the bottom of so many hearts, we thank you very much and will always remember that you found so much valuable time for us.

"Your Majesty, I invite your fellow Benchers, to rise now and toast you (for this year and last year). We wish your Majesty many more years of good health so that you may long be able to visit us for this Family Dinner: the high-spot of our Calendar."

Her Majesty instructed her personal secretary, Sir Alastair (Master) Aird, to write to Michael, saying how pleased she was by the speech.

***

Michael was set to follow the traditional route of pupillage but, having been called that summer afternoon, there was something else that he simply had to do.

With HM The Queen Mother,
December 1996

19

CHAPTER 6

A TOE IN THE COURTROOM WATERS

The morning after his call, Michael could think of nothing but trying on his wig and gown again. This time he wanted it to be a real experience. He hesitated to go into the High Court. He spoke to his university friend, John Hazan, who had just completed his pupillage.

"Where can I go to get the feel of wearing my robes?"

"London Sessions," was the unhesitating reply. "Just go and sit there."

"Where?" I was a North Londoner. I had no idea what he was talking about.

"Elephant and Castle," he told me. This was just as great a mystery but I managed to resolve it and eventually arrived. There was no-one in the robing room. I put on my collar and bands, my wig and my gown. I did what John said and, gripping the edges of my gown, found two court-rooms. Peering through, I could see that both were full of barristers, all waiting for something, I knew not what. I decided to go into Court 1 to see what was happening and made my way in. Several barristers were sitting in the front row. I joined them and watched what was going on from my vantage point at the end of the line.

After a short time, four defendants appeared with warders in the well of the court. The gate through which they passed clanged shut. The Clerk addressed them in time-honoured, solemn tones of officialdom.

"Are each of you possessed of the sum of not less than two pounds four shillings and sixpence so as to be entitled to a dock brief?" There was a muttering of assent. "When I call your name," said the Clerk, "turn round and, from Counsel sitting in court, you may choose who you would wish to defend you. You will later pay them the said sum of two pounds four shillings and sixpence."

As it happened, the prosecutor, a very senior barrister, was in court. The first Defendant turned and promptly chose him: a good choice on appearance but of course he was not eligible. The second choice stood up, bowed to the judge and went off with his new client. This was not very interesting to me so I started to leave but, before I knew it, I heard a gravelly voice say, "I'll 'ave *'im*." Defendant number 2 had picked me! I was taken aback. I turned to the chap next to me. "What do I do?"' I whispered.

"Bow," he snapped. I bowed. My wig slipped but I managed to keep it from falling. "I only came to try on my wig and gown!" I whispered.

"Go and find the prosecutor outside before you get another dock brief," he hissed.

I managed to leave the court, remembering my new client's name and not much else. I found someone who looked as if he could help. He turned out to be the prosecutor who had been in court a few moments earlier. He was Maxwell Turner[1]. He looked and sounded very much like the actor, Robert Morley. I introduced myself. "I'm Michael Sherrard," I said. "I'm looking for someone who is going to prosecute Robert Stephens."

"I haven't had the pleasure of meeting you," he said.

"No, sir."

"Don't call me sir," he said wearily. "Call me Max, if you must, or Maxwell Turner."

The niceties were over. "I'm not really supposed to be doing this one," I said, suitably chastened. "I only came to try on my wig and gown. Is there someone else who could do the case?"

"How long have you been called?" he glowered down at me.

"18 hours."

"Oh, dear!" He seemed to think about it for a moment. I was in too much fear to know what I was thinking. "This is a rather serious case," he said at last.

"What's he done?" I asked with a dry mouth, half-deafened by the sound of my heart pounding.

"He's charged with living on the immoral earnings of 2 schoolgirls and he's jumped bail."

My legal training suddenly felt somewhat inadequate.

---

[1]   Maxwell Turner was later to become an Old Bailey Judge.

"We never did immoral earnings," I told him earnestly.

"I don't suppose you did," he said. "Would it be convenient to you if I could persuade the judge to postpone the case until 'not before 2 o'clock' tomorrow?"

I thought about this. Most of all, I thought that would give me enough time to get to Calais and carry on travelling out of the jurisdiction as far as I could. He went on, "I'm supposed to hand you my papers. Here they are. Go and see the defendant, don't forget your £2 4s. 6d. and do not forget to see if there's a plea."

"A what?" I was mystified.

The prosecutor clearly took pity on me. "He might plead guilty. He's got form." This was something I could understand but the information was not helping me to deal with the problem of representing Mr Stephens.

As it happened, Maxwell Turner was second senior prosecuting counsel at the Bailey. That he was at London Sessions was an indication that 'my' case must be very serious.

In a fog of nerves, I managed to make my way to see my client. I remember that he said, "I'll plead if you get one of the girls out of this." I was more interested in why he had chosen me and could not resist asking him when perhaps there might have been more relevant questions. He said, "You was wearin' 'eavy 'orn-rimmed glasses – that means brains."

I did thank him for that before hurrying back to Maxwell Turner, elated by the news. "He'll plead guilty to the offence with only one girl," I said.

"Right," said Turner. "I'll see if we can amend the indictment. You do a plea in mitigation."

Defeated, I had to ask, "What's that?"

How did he have such patience with me? Without turning a hair he said, "You address the judge."

"But what do I say?"

He thought about this for a moment then said, "You tell me what he's told you and the reasons why he did it and I'll dictate the plea I would make if I were you. I'll put the prosecution case. All you have to do is go and learn your part off by heart. But really by heart – you must be eyeball to eyeball with the judge. You will not be able to read a word of it."

I realised that I had been saved. But I did not know that there was a still more serious hurdle for me to surmount before taking up my client's case. Maxwell Turner then told me that the judge, Eustace Fulton, suffered from a neurological condition similar to St Vitus' Dance.

"What's that?" I asked. Turner gave me a brief demonstration of the condition. Arms and face twitching and grimacing respectively.

"You're joking." I did not believe that my nightmare could be compounded any further. I could only imagine myself bobbing up and down to keep the required eye contact.

"Oh, no," he assured me cheerfully. Fulton had been appointed to London Sessions as Chairman on a permanent basis despite his condition. "But what you could do," he told me, "is simply look at the Royal Arms above his head. Keep your eye on them. He'll think you are looking at him. I hope you don't mind me telling you this?"

"I'm so grateful," I said. It was an understatement. I did not know then that, in one of life's curious coincidences, Shirley was being taught acting at RADA[1] by Mrs Maxwell Turner, the actress Fabia Drake.

He wrote what I felt was a marvellous speech beginning, "Sir," and explained that this was the mode of address to the Chairman of the London Sessions. I would be spared the embarrassment of saying "My Lord," or "Your Honour", which would have marked me out instantly for the novice that I was.

Armed with my notes, I went to the cells to see my client. Feeling slightly more confident, I told him that one girl was off the indictment.

He grinned. "See. I said you was clever."

---

[1] The Royal Academy of Dramatic Art.

I was alarmed that he was so pleased. "You're not hoping to walk out of here after this, are you?" To my relief he said, "Nah – not with my record! Just do yer best."

Somewhere during the next minutes or hours, the indictment was amended and the prosecution asked for the case to be put back to the next day marked 'not before 2'. The judge must have agreed.

I travelled home feeling more than a little dazed and almost guilty, as if I was a schoolboy again, getting into trouble. I half expected my mother to be annoyed. She would wag her finger at me and say, "See, I told you not to go to court!" And that would only be the beginning of it. My father, if asked, would have said sadly, "I knew he'd get himself into trouble." I wanted to show them how grown-up I was by coping on my first day albeit that I had identified the prosecutor and nothing else.

As it happened, my father was away on a business trip in America. Only my mother was at home when I arrived. I described the events of the day and the impossible nature of the task I had called upon myself by the urge to go into court, stressing that I had not expected to make an appearance. There was not much time to go into detail, except that I told her enough for her to get a feel of the thrill of the events of the day: the journey to the court, the dusty, smoky smell of the robing room, the smell of wax and sweat in court. In telling her about Maxwell Turner, I visualised him as being considerably larger than he really was and I felt considerably smaller than I knew I was.

My mother's first thought was that Calais was a good option, as long as I carried on as far East as I could. But the long and short of it is that she and I were up half the night, she directing and rehearsing me until it sounded as though it might be all right.

***

The next day begins. The robing room is empty as I robe up. This time it is because I am the first one there. I go to the court and somehow, before I know it, we start. The defendant is in the dock and Fulton is twitching at me with his curious, upward-looking grimace. I am sick with excitement. Maxwell Turner gets to his feet. He starts. The case sounds terrible. It is terrible. A crime amongst crimes. Soon, too soon, he sits down.

It's my turn.

"Mr Sherrard," the judge says to something situated towards the ceiling at the back of the room. I get to my feet. I deliver a less than polished performance, gazing at the coat of arms above the judge's head. The neurological twitch is working away. I say what Maxwell Turner had prepared.

He – I – said, "He was having sexual intercourse with a girl younger than sixteen but, Your Honour" – *did Maxwell Turner flinch?* – "he did not know ..."

Turner sat at the end of the row, listening intently as if he had never heard a word of it before. Everything I said seemed to come as a total surprise to him.

I got through it in five or six minutes. Before I had my bum on the seat, I heard the judge say, "Seven years preventive detention."

I was aghast. While I was digesting what seemed to be a catastrophe, Turner leant across, smiling. He whispered, "You'll be all right – you'll get your name in the *News of the World*."

And so I did – they didn't get my name quite right but there it was: Mr A. Sherrard! My first press report, probably because of the seniority of my opponent.

Subconsciously, and eventually consciously, I realised that what Maxwell Turner had done for me that day convinced me of the truth of the words, "A wonderful profession is the law."

By the way, I got my £2 4s. 6d. for the first of my two dock briefs.

CHAPTER 7

SECOND STEP

Michael was offered pupillage by Charles Du Cann, otherwise known as "the Duke", a member of the chambers of A.A. Gordon Clarke[1] in Dr Johnson's Building in the Temple. The Duke had been John Hazan's pupil-master and John had effected the introduction. The pupillage was to start after the Long Vacation. It would enable Michael to gain experience in a rather more structured approach to the Bar than stumbling into dock briefs. He would develop written skills through drafting pleadings, preparing opinions and carrying out legal research. A successful pupillage would give him the best chance of becoming a tenant in chambers.

There was no structured Vocational Bar course then. There were voluntary twelve month pupillages (for which the pupil paid the pupil-master a fee of fifty guineas for each six months) but these were not regulated or inspected. The notion of the first six non-practising months and the second six of supervised practice did not start until 1965. Some pupils in crime would boast of seeing their pupil-masters only once in their six months. They expected to be in court every day, learning on the hoof.[2] Even when pupils entered the modern twelve month form of pupillage, it was the usual practice to have one day – if they were lucky, more usually one hour – of advocacy training in chambers, then off they would go to court.

On my first day in the Law Courts as a pupil, the Duke introduced me to Hartley Shawcross[3] whom I admired greatly. Hartley asked, "What do you want to do, practice-wise?"

"Crime," I said.

"Think about it very carefully," said Hartley. Some years later, I was able to tell him that my practice had become about 60% civil. "Good

---

[1]   A. A. Gordon Clarke used the pseudonym of Cyril Hare as a crime writer.
[2]   The General Council of the Bar itself took no part in training of barristers. The first advocacy requirements were imposed by the Inns but they were unstructured ritual dances.
[3]   Hartley Shawcross (1902-2003) Attorney-General 1945-1951. He was Chief Prosecutor for the United Kingdom at the Nuremberg Trials. Founder member of 'Justice', 1957.

thinking," he said. "Knowing civil work is an advantage in crime too." I was some way off discovering that for myself.

Although my pupillage was not due to start until October, I was permitted to attend chambers and did so through the Long Vacation sometimes going to court with one of the tenants or dealing with paperwork. I thought I had learnt the lesson to avoid future dock briefs[1] from my trip to Inner London and managed to keep busy out of court, but my blue bag was always with me, stocked with my wig, gown, bands and starched collars. One dark night in those very early days of my career, as I walked home with it slung across my shoulder, I was stopped by a police officer near my house in Finchley. He looked even younger than me. He thought that my blue bag looked remarkably as if it was carrying swag and I had to show him its contents to prove that I was a barrister. "Not many of them about in Finchley, sir," he said. Which was a little different in tone and content from his beginning words of, "Oi! You! Wassat you've got there?"

I was always ready to go, bowler-hatted and dressed in a dark three-piece suit and white shirt with stud-attached collar. Earlier than I can remember, I was introduced to an arrangement with Tom, the robing room man at the High Court who ensured that all his gentlemen looked the part. He starched collars to a rigidity that can only be compared with ivory. Tom was your best mate. He did your laundry. He called you 'Sir' even if you were knee-high to the Law Courts' legally aided grasshopper. He was a big man. Many years later, a group of barristers arranged his retirement dinner at the Cock Tavern in Fleet Street but he collapsed when he rose to make his speech. Two strong members of the Bar managed to lift him, help him down the stairs and take him to Barts Hospital by taxi. It appeared that he had had a heart attack brought on by the emotion and stress of the occasion. He couldn't believe these Lords, these gents, were honouring him – he was overcome. His successor, the 'other robing room man' was probably Bill but I always thought of him as Jerry.

---

[1] Dock briefs ended in the 1960s when Legal Aid became fully established. The £2 4s 6d fee covered the entire proceedings, whether a full-blown trial or a plea in mitigation.

I had my Tom-starched collars ready in my bag when I arrived at chambers one morning to be greeted by the clerk.

"Got your robes, sir?"

My robes? Of course! They went with me every day. I held the bag up.

"Step down to the Bailey, if you please, sir. Court 4. The Recorder of London. They'll call Simpson on – 'e's the client. The judge is prepared to adjourn it to 2 o'clock if we make an application. All you've got to do is say, "Would Your Lordship adjourn the case until 2.00 p.m. OK?"

I was delighted. My first appearance at the Old Bailey! I rehearsed the words in my head all the way there, over and over.

I had not yet learned from my pupil-master to stay out of court until my case was called.

I found a place on the bench where two other barristers were seated in Court 4, waiting for their cases to be called. While I was waiting for my turn, I learned a little more about my chosen profession. The origin of the 'cab-rank' rule is usually related to the dock brief because barristers could be likened to taxis on the rank: available for hire. I was concentrating very hard on the tone of voice and imagining the stance I would take when it was time for my thirteen syllables so I barely noticed a prisoner being escorted into court and observing me on the cab rank. As it turned out, this was the arrival of my second dock brief.

The words, "I'll 'ave him," entered my consciousness. I had caught Johnny Startup's eye before I had spoken a word of my application.

My application for the adjournment to 2.00 p.m. succeeded. Instead of going straight back to Chambers, I used the expertise acquired from my first case and went to acquire the papers from the prosecution and to see my new client. He was going to plead guilty and my task was to plead in mitigation of sentence in a couple of days' time. Shirley wanted to hear me in court and this was going to be the perfect opportunity. Came the day, I told her how to get into the public gallery and went off to see that justice was done. I only hoped my performance was polished enough to impress.

Although Startup, a scout leader at some stage of his non-criminal life, had the appearance of innocence with his round face and metal-rimmed spectacles, his character was not entirely unblemished. He had developed a method of enhancing his income by using a realistic-looking toy gun to hold up elderly people collecting their pensions. If he did not have the gun about him, he would resort to the use of a lemonade bottle. Once caught, he had the deepest regrets about his shocking behaviour. He told me that he had resorted to slashing his wrists as a manifestation of his remorse. This was appalling. I could not imagine how bad he must have felt. He told me that he was schizophrenic and I immediately took the view, to be expressed in mitigation, that his split personality needed care, not prison.

The Recorder of London, Sir Gerald Dodson, was the Judge. His hobby was writing operas. He had poor eyesight and would screw up his thin, papery face to focus on the object of what was usually his displeasure. He had some form of emphysema so that his voice was reedy and querulous at best. He used the noise of his breathing, the asthmatic technique, as a signal that he was not pleased. He would throw his head back, take you in his sights and inhale with a mighty wheeze which would distract you, as it was intended to do. So you knew things were not going well.

A police officer, Sergeant Virgo, was there for the prosecution. No-one told me to check with the police to see what would be in their evidence. There was no Maxwell Turner present to guide me through this next phase of my career. If there had been, I might have found out that Startup was inclined to drama when he was upset and would simulate suicide as a diversionary, hysterical tactic. When he was in a good mood, he helped his neighbours, as a good scout would, in various useful ways.

The sergeant went into the witness box. This was my first chance to cross-examine in a courtroom. The drama of the situation was exciting in prospect. Shirley was up there in the public gallery with an excellent view of the back of my head and possibly my shoulders as well. But I was about to learn that things in the hand were not as good as in the mind.

"The Defendant has shown the greatest remorse," I put to the officer. It was not a question and with a slight rustle from his throat, the Recorder muttered, "That's not a question."

Virgo answered it as if it was. "I wouldn't say that."

"What!" I exclaimed. "He who has slashed his wrists? You can't say that is not remorse!"

The Recorder muttered the same words again, adding a shake of his head. Virgo carried on.

"Well, sir, I will say that my information from those who know him is that your client has been known, when in difficulties, to make superficial cuts on his wrists."

I was not pleased but decided that the statement should be treated with as much contempt as I dared to muster.

I heard a voice. It said, with a disdain that was, unfortunately, outweighed by the spoken words, "Scuperficial scuts!!!" My voice. There could be no retraction. I can still hear the words reverberating through the courtroom. Scuperficial scuts is what I was sneering about.

The Recorder of London drew in a great wheezing sound as if filling dusty bag-pipes. His eyes rolled. He might well have been controlling the urge to laugh but to me he looked as if he were in a state which included an unhappy mixture of boredom, rage and asphyxia. If he was not laughing, I believe there were several in the courtroom who were.

I glared at the witness and recovered what passed for composure. I could not even get it right the second time. "Scuperficial scuts, indeed!" I had to do something dramatic before there was any further hint of laughter. Seizing the moment and without asking the judge's permission, I turned towards the dock and ordered the accused to raise his arms and show his wrists.

He did so at once.

It was clear for all to see: they were superficial cuts indeed. I heard the officer say, "As I said, Sir – superficial – no lasting injuries."

The Recorder exhaled asthmatically and sat back in his chair so that he could focus better on me. Was he smiling? Whilst considering this, Virgo said primly, "I have nothing to add."

The Recorder waved Virgo away and said to me, "Is there anything else you wish me to hear?"

I tried to recover my dignity and embroidered heavily on the information that I had.

"... schizoid ... a split personality ... potential suicide risk ... (and, for extra effect) Dr Jekyll and Mr Hyde ... the good outweighs the bad ... hospital not prison... treatment not punishment... help and support – "

Whatever I said, there was little more to do than to attempt to soften the inevitable blow. Above all, I was hoping that Shirley would not have left the court, forever suffering the memory of my discomfiture. I might never see her again. As I pondered these matters, I heard the Recorder clear his throat and saw him look down his nose towards me, flicking the occasional glance towards my client.

When he had his breath he said, "Startup, you frightened those old people with what looked like a gun. Your use of a bottle was potentially more dangerous. Your learned counsel, Mr ... Mr .... Mr .. er ... has said everything that could be said on your behalf and some that could not. He suggests that you have a split personality [wheeze], a Jekyll and Hyde; that there are two sides to you, one good and one bad; that you need treatment. For this outrageous attack [wheeze], where you are going, you'll get the treatment, if any, which you need – both of you. [Wheeze]Three years."

In the back of the court, waiting for his case to come on was a well-known barrister, Harry Leon. He was sitting in the Bailey, noting all this. This story is mentioned in the book he wrote under his pseudonym of Henry Cecil, *Brothers in Law*.[1]

So, I had two important observers for my last dock brief.

Shirley had not disappeared. She kept to the plan of meeting afterwards at Counsel's entrance to the Old Bailey. Very tactfully she said,

---

[1] Cecil, H: *Brothers in Law* pub. Michael Joseph 1955, pp 158-159: *'This, too, was the Court where the man who was said to have been a sort of Jekyll and Hyde, had stood to receive his sentence. "Counsel has argued eloquently on your behalf," said the Judge, "that you are really two people, one very good and one very bad. As to that, all I can say is both of you must go to prison."*

"With a difficult case like that, I think it was a jolly good notion to inject some humour. I thought the Judge was grateful to you."

CHAPTER 8

COUNSEL'S FINKIN'

The Duke was to be led by Cyril Salmon KC[1] in the Divisional Court. The main point in the case was whether, in the light of legislation in relation to brothels and bawdy houses, the Defendant was entitled to elect jury trial rather than be judged by a single magistrate. But it turned out there was a clash of hearing dates: the House of Lords, which took precedence over the inferior courts, listed one of the Duke's cases on the same day. He would not be able to go to the Divisional Court. Michael was delighted but had to step straight into the Duke's shoes!

How could this happen? The Duke was blithely confident. "You know what to do. Just go to the library, prepare a chronology, and draft a note on the law." He whose forte was that an ounce of fact was better than the weightiest point of law! With measured haste, he left chambers, saying, "You get in touch with Cyril Salmon – tell the clerk – OK?"

I had to phone Cyril Salmon. King's Counsel, no less. My fingers froze in the dial. I did not know what to call him except that I remembered from Maxwell Turner not to call him "Sir". I tried to envisage calling him "Salmon". But, I thought, he doesn't know me. I ended up introducing myself but calling him nothing.

"Good morning," I said. "I'm Michael Sherrard, Du Cann's pupil. He's going to be in the House of Lords next week and I'm going to be your junior. Do you want to see me? Is there anything you would like me to do? I've already prepared a note on the law for you."

"So kind of you to call," he said. "I'm very familiar with the point on jury trial but I don't know about brothels. I'm sure you'll be able to give me adequate assistance." I mulled his words for quite some time.

He gave an elegant performance from the first moment that we arrived at court. Watching him robe had to be seen. The routine was always the same. He had his own hanger in his locker in Tom's robing room in the Royal Courts. He would stand with lifted elbows to shrug his jacket into Tom's waiting hands. He would tug his waistcoat into place

---

[1]   Cyril Salmon KC (1903-1991). He became Lord Salmon of Sandwich. He was from the catering family, Salmon and Gluckstein.

then stand with his head slightly bowed as Tom lifted the gown onto his shoulders and helped with the collar studs and immaculate bands. When he was satisfied that his wig was in exactly the right position, he would go into court and arrange the contents of his waistcoat pockets at the side of his lectern, starting with his gold-edged diary. The gold Parker pen followed, then his other impedimenta, including several perfectly sharpened pencils. From the other side of his waistcoat, he produced a cigar case and placed it beside the other items. Every article was placed neatly with barely a flourish but with the utmost grace. Each movement was as if choreographed and impressed me greatly. There was, perhaps, more entertainment value than learning in the experience but I had enjoyed preparing the case and he told the Duke that he was pleased with what I had done.

In addition to the impressive performance, he was also a very good barrister and, in time, very good as a judge. I appeared in front of him once or twice, watching his graceful movements as he arranged his writing instruments before the case started.

***

Soon after this first experience of working with a silk, Michael had a legally aided case handed down to him by the judge in the court where the Duke had sent him to make an application. It was a particularly shabby fraud that had been perpetrated by an unpleasant man called Rosefield who had the Midas touch in reverse. His grandiose schemes all turned to dust which is just as well since they were based on lying, cheating and confidence trickery.

Rosefield's system was to cream whatever spare cash they had from refugees from Europe on the pretext of starting them in business in a non-existent branch of the cosmetics industry. He had been sentenced to eight years and wanted to appeal although, given the seriousness of what he had done and the havoc he had wreaked with already damaged lives, the sentence seemed modest even to my inexperienced eyes.

This was my third case in pupillage. I quickly learned that the system of appeals was regimented so that one applied for leave to appeal on the first Monday in the month. The decision on whether or not to grant leave was made on the third Monday. I appeared before Lord Goddard, Mr

Justice Hilbery and Mr Justice Hallett. They granted leave in response to my less-than-convincing argument. I sat there, very surprised.

As soon as I could, I got on to John Hazan.

I told him about the case and the sentence and explained why I had called him. "I've got a reservation about this," I said.

"What are you worried about?" he asked.

"Could they increase the sentence?" I wanted to know.

"That's just what I was thinking," he said, "but I didn't want to put you down."

I went to see Rosefield when he was brought up to London for the appeal. I told him that I thought there was a serious risk of the sentence being increased.

"I don't think I'll get more," he said with the same confidence that he used to trick his unfortunate victims. I assured him even more seriously that the risk was too great to take. With his extensive past experience of the criminal legal system, he was able to say with some authority that I might not be allowed to abandon the appeal. And, if I changed my mind about my advice, I would need leave to abandon the abandonment!

Eventually I got his signature in agreement to abandoning the appeal. When I got to court, the Duke was already there. He was junior to David Maxwell-Fyfe[1] in a first conviction appeal. Their case was before mine. However, I was called first because I had received leave the previous week.

Any appearance before the Court of Appeal is a momentous occasion. Still wet behind the ears, I was on my feet before three of the most senior judges in the land. As I began to open my mouth without any sound emerging, the clerk handed up my notice of abandonment. Lord Goddard, seated in the middle of the three, looked at it with disgust or disbelief before passing it to the other two with a quick whisper to each of them.

---

[1]   David Maxwell-Fyfe, later Viscount then Earl Kilmuir, 1900 – 1967. Lawyer and politician. Deputy Chief Prosecutor at the Nuremburg Trials.

"Mr Sherrard," he said in a voice tinged with a mixture of horror and disdain yet overwhelmingly patronising, "we give you leave to abandon the abandonment."

I found the courage to stand my ground.

"I am not asking your Lordships for leave."

"Think about it," he said. It was an invitation to withdraw the notice accompanied by a short adjournment for me to consider the position.

David Maxwell-Fyfe said, "You really must accept." But the Duke disagreed. "Don't trust them," he advised me.

The usher called out for the court to rise. The judges solemnly resumed their places high above the well of the court. I was breathless with fright as I prepared to be defiant. I glanced towards the right and saw Mr Justice Hilbery, seated to Lord Goddard's right, arch his fingers and place the fingertips together in front of his sash. His eyelids drooped a fraction. He gave an almost imperceptible shake of his head.

Rightly or wrongly, I believed he was encouraging me. I found my voice. "I do not proceed with the appeal."

Lord Goddard glared at me. He suddenly snapped at Rosefield.

"Rosefield, yours is the most disgusting fraud. Your counsel is your angel of mercy. We would undoubtedly have increased your sentence to the twelve years you deserve. The public needs all the protection it can get. Take him down."

Michael returned to Chambers, hoping to talk this through with John Hazan, who was by then a junior tenant at Brick Court. His telephone rang. It was his clerk, telling him that the Attorney-General was on the telephone.

Of course, I knew it was John Hazan.

"'Allo John," I said, affecting the Cockney accent which was the usual way that we carried on our informal conversations.

A strange voice responded. "Michael Sherrard?"

I thought: this is not John.

It was indeed the A-G, Hartley Shawcross.

36

He said something like: "David Maxwell-Fyfe came to see me just now. He told me how disgracefully you were treated by Lord Goddard."

I was so shaken, I barely knew what else he said. It had seemed to me, at the age of 21 (and I looked it) that Rosefield, who had lots of form, might have expected the Court of Appeal to have more sympathy with me, and therefore with him, because of my appearance.

I think that this case was one of the reasons that Hartley remembered me later.

I formed a much better relationship with Malcolm Hilbery in the years to come. It was so good of him to give me the nod.

When Sir John Gielgud pleaded guilty to soliciting in a lavatory at an underground station, his conviction and fine were headline news. "It makes you ashamed to share your K with a blighter like that," Sir Malcolm is reported to have said. However, walking back from the Old Bailey he was known to raise his hat (a topper, in those days) to the Holborn Viaduct public lavatory. In his time at the Bar, he had earned a good few twenty-five guinea fees prosecuting – and defending – soliciting offences that had happened there.

Michael was some way off being part of that higher membership of the Bar where renowned cases linked to famous names. Having made his foray into the Civil Courts, he faced the more usual level of work for a pupil: he was given his first brief in the magistrates' court.

The court was to be asked to make a maintenance order against my client, a young, recently married husband. I was to have a conference in chambers – my first conference! – when the solicitor would tell me about the case. The conference was to take place in the pupil's room which meant careful moving of papers to give the impression of being tidy whilst preserving the appearance of being very busy. I cleared space for the client and solicitor to sit and posed several times at the desk to be sure of presenting the right air of authority when the conference took place. This required several placings of the tips of the fingers so that each hand touched in a grave yet understanding way. I also dealt with the practicalities of ensuring that my pen was full of ink for taking notes and was carefully placed on the newly-papered blotter for immediate access when needed. After several rehearsals, I felt confident that I could move gracefully from being grave but sympathetic into practical mode.

I greeted the solicitor and my client in the waiting room and took them to my allocated space. The solicitor, an elderly man, sounded like a rough diamond and looked like a survivor from a Dickens novel. He wore a long, black overcoat to his ankles and a bowler hat which he unceremoniously removed and placed on my blotting pad. Somewhere under its greasy rim, my pen was concealed.

The lay client husband, a lanky, shy young man, whose name was Simon, was unsure whether to sit down. Still concerned about the position of the hat, I could do no more than nod towards the arm-chair, so recently divested of several briefs.

The solicitor looked around the room then noticed the client hovering anxiously. His gravel-rough voice barked at the young man.

"Siddahn, Slimey."

Simon sat down. If he was offended by the tone of voice or the name, his face showed no dismay. I arranged myself behind the desk as Simon perched on the edge of the seat, sitting forward so that he could see me arranging my fingertips into the chosen arch-shape. The solicitor wandered around the room, reciting the history of Simon's case without looking at either of us. I found a pencil at the side of the blotter and started to take some notes from the endless stream of hoarse narrative.

There came a time when the hitherto silent young man ventured to make himself heard.

"Can I say ..." began the timid voice.

The solicitor stopped moving, fixed Simon with a forbidding stare and imprinted these words on my memory: "Shut up, Slimey! Counsel's finkin'!"

Serious and even sad moments, or any gaps in conversation are now filled with these words. "Counsel's finkin'" is, after all, what Counsel does.

CHAPTER 9

A NEW AREA OF WORK

Michael had been called for about nine months. He was not busy but his practice was developing satisfactorily. One morning he came into chambers, ready to see what the day had to offer. His clerk greeted him with the words, "Here's a smart brief for you. You're going tomorrow to the Mayor's and City of London Court in a salvage case."

"Salvage? What's that?"

The brief was handed over, fat, with a neatly tied pink ribbon. It was marked up for me personally and was quite a coup, being from a well-known City firm of solicitors.

"Something to do with goods being lost on barges. Lightermen get a percentage of what they salvage. You just need to look it up."

To say I was all at sea puts it mildly. I did my research into Admiralty matters. Barely understanding the principles but with a grasp of the facts, I set off for the court to see what faced me. The judge was Ralph Thomas, an admiralty expert with a fine line in expressing controlled rage.

"Could Your Lordship look at the plan?"

"Chart!" snapped His Lordship.

"I'm most grateful." I collected my thoughts. "On the left – "

"Port!"

"I'm so grateful." A moment's pause and I continued, "Towards the front – "

"Prow!"

" – and in the container area is a sort of buttress –"

"Bulkhead!!!"

It went on like this. It was a new language. The few people who were in court were all lightermen interested in the outcome of the case. They sat together where there would normally be a jury. They thought it was hilarious. They were silently mouthing each correction that the judge made.

Somehow, the case ended and, as my first and last foray into the Admiralty Court, remained as a discomfiting experience, not be forgotten.

In 1978, at a time when he had been in silk for about ten years, Michael was a guest at an Amity dinner given by the Council of the Law Society. He introduced himself to the member sitting next to him.

"I've often thought of you since you did a small admiralty claim for us," said the fellow guest.

"Do you remember it?" the guest asked.

"Very well," Michael answered. "It was the only one I ever did."

The guest explained, "Our managing clerk recommended a young and able junior with a name something like yours. The name got lost in translation through the secretary finding the address."

At least Michael understood how it had come his way but realised that the impression made on the court that day had been long-lasting when the guest finished the reminiscence saying, "Oh yes, we've laughed about it so much over the years."

***

After the completion of his pupillage, Shirley and Michael became engaged She and Michael had been friends since the summer of 1942. A mutual friend introduced them in the gardens of Avenue House, Finchley, a favourite meeting place for local youngsters. She had been appropriately impressed by his most prized possession, a splendid red sports bicycle and it was an early sign of commitment that Michael was prepared to surrender the opportunity of riding it home in favour of walking back to Temple Fortune with Shirley.

Shirley's aunt, Stella Bagrit, regarded me as the most eligible suitor for her niece. She gave a large dinner party one evening. All the family were there. I realised later that it was a set-up but my main concern was whether I would be in a financial position to marry, even though my practice seemed to be developing.

Stella came up to us and said, "Well, Michael and Shirley – can we announce the engagement?"

This was embarrassing. When I was fourteen I had told Shirley I would marry her, she had laughed at me and carried on laughing about it.

"Well?" she pressed on.

"Not quite yet," I said.

"What!" Stella was amazed. "What are you waiting for?"

"For me to see myself making a living," I said.

That was not a good enough answer for Stella. And, strangely, Shirley was not putting her off or disagreeing with her.

So we announced our engagement.

CHAPTER 10

HARE COURT

As Michael's pupillage in Dr Johnson's Building was coming to an end, he began to anticipate tenancy. On the whole, he had done well. Although there was likely to be room for only one tenant from the various pupils, he was optimistic. He had done a wide range of work and had good relationships with other people in chambers. But it was not to be.

At the time, David Maxwell-Fyfe was the Attorney-General. He was looking to help a member of his family, Peter McNair, a young barrister who had lost an arm at sea in the war. He needed a tenancy. Maxwell-Fyfe got in touch with Gordon Clarke who felt he really had to offer the tenancy to the protégé.

Although I heard about it before Gordon Clarke told me, it was still disappointing to hear it from him personally, even though I could see that the tenancy would go to a meritorious applicant.

Gordon Clarke was plainly relieved that I was understanding. As I left he said, "Don't worry. I'll find a good home for you to go to."

And he did.

He travelled from the country daily and during the commute fell into conversation with the Head of Chambers at 1 Hare Court, Walter Raeburn, KC, who had recently taken silk. He agreed to see me.

I learned that the chambers was principally civil. He explained to me that I would find a very different atmosphere in his chambers when compared with the criminal set where I had been for almost a year. He said that what he would like me to do was to spend six months with Morris Finer[1] (of whom I had never heard). He said, "Finer has a reputation as a bright young chap. He has never had a pupil but, if you can persuade him to take you, so be it."

I eventually saw Morris. He had a very large room on the top floor with a double-partner's desk, smothered with civil papers. He had a powerful intellect and, in today's language, was 'laid-back'. He was certainly casual in his manner. He said something to this effect: "Can't for

---

[1]   Morris Finer QC (1917-1974), QC 1963, appointed to the High Court in 1972.

the life of me think why you would want to be my pupil. I don't know what you do with a pupil. So you'd better sit there." He pointed to a small, mercifully empty, desk at the other side of the room.

I asked if he minded if I finished the last month of my pupillage with the Duke. I think he was relieved at the postponement of the responsibility of having a pupil.

"Good idea – you, at least, will know something about crime – come back when you're ready."

I think it's fair to say I did not immediately recognise that Morris Finer was going to be the most powerful and long-lasting influence on my professional life. Our meeting was the beginning of a profound friendship that lasted the rest of Morris' life and remains as a series of affectionate memories.

When I told the Duke that I was going to Morris for a second pupillage, his response was a mirror reflection of what Morris had said.

"Well, at least one of us will know about civil work, and it won't be me."

I had a certain sadness leaving my pupillage with the Duke. From him I learned as much about jewellery and snuff-boxes as I did about the law. I learned about antiques and literature and cherish to this day the copy of *Marie Donadieu* by Charles Louis Philippe which carries the Duke's inscription:

"For Michael Sherrard – a tribute to his docility as a pupil, his industry as a helper, his ability to exceed the speed limit in both starting and continuing to talk, and his excessive enthusiasm for our common profession as legal gladiators and mercenaries."

Another of my prized possessions is a copy of the Duke's book, published in 1960[1], *Miscarriages of Justice*.

Changing pupillage would mean the end of early morning calls about a new treasure that the Duke had found or was hoping to buy. A classic example is the telephone call at 6.00 a.m. The excited voice: "I've tracked down a signed, first edition of *The Ballad of Reading Gaol* and I'm going to make a bid for it. We leave from Waterloo at 7."

---

[1] Du Cann, C. G. L. *Miscarriages of Justice* (London, Muller, 1960).

***

The first pupillage came to its designated end and I moved on to Hare Court. Morris' room was much as I had last seen it. Papers were piled on the chairs and scattered on the floor. His desk was littered with documents taking up most of the space. A typewriter, however, had pride of place. To my dismay, he passed me a loosely-tied bundle of papers for an opinion on a bankruptcy matter, a topic of which I knew next to nothing.

I knew that I would be unable to get to grips with the problem in the chaos of the room. I could not work like that. I summoned up the courage to ask him, "Will you be offended if I go somewhere else to do this?" I suspect that he was relieved not to have to watch over his first pupil and was happy to let me go to the library. I found a corner on the third floor where, for several days, I grappled with a problem which was as incomprehensible to me as if it had been written in Japanese. Knowing that my pupillage would probably come to a rapid end when I confessed my inability to deal with the piece of work, I nevertheless had to face Morris and confess my ineptitude.

I went to see him.

"Hello," he said. "Where've you been?"

I wanted to tell him that I had been on another legal planet but opted for the truth.

"Over in the library."

"Good," he said. "What's the upshot?"

"I only have a downshot, I'm afraid. It was like going into a maze. I thought I'd found my way out three or four times, but I was only getting more and more lost. I'm afraid I need you to take me through it." I felt that it was probably unforgivable to ask a pupil master for help.

He took the bundle from me, glanced at the instructions and flipped through the papers that the solicitor had provided. Now was the first of many times that I was to see him lean back in his chair, rub his eyes and temples then flex and close his fingers before stretching them over the keyboard of the typewriter. I was ready to begin my first lesson as his pupil.

Morris was one of the very few barristers who could not only type but deigned to do so. This greatly increased his efficiency. He was able to keep up with his heavy case-load because of his colossal breadth of knowledge and amazing ability to apply it to the problems of his clients.

Sheet after sheet of paper went through the typewriter as Morris' fast fingers tapped away. He handed the final, twelve-page document to me and went through the eye-rubbing routine again.

"There you are. Now you'll know what it's about."

I turned away, ready to leave. I was wondering how I could get out of being his pupil if he was not so disappointed as to be deciding how to get rid of me. I must have looked dejected.

"Don't worry," he said, as if reading my thoughts. "You'll get over it."

And I did. But once a pupil, always a pupil. Years later, by which time I was in silk, when the Board of Trade Inquiry into the John Bloom companies was not published for legal reasons, the then Attorney-General, Lord Elwyn-Jones[1], was reported to have said, "Morris Finer's pupil has managed to put an insurmountable obstacle in the way of the publication of the Report."

***

Another discovery in my first week with Morris was that he was also a journalist[2]. It was his regular Friday task to write the light-hearted Saturday leader for the *Evening Standard*. This knowledge came to me when he came back from lunch on the first Friday and said, "Give me a topic for Saturday's leader." I was flattered to be asked and in times to come, he would occasionally pursue one of my ideas.

The six months with Morris involved me in a huge amount of work and I gained invaluable experience: chronologies, research and opinions were all subject to his expert blue pencil. One way or another, he must

---

[1] Frederick Elwyn-Jones QC (1909-1989), Baron Elwyn-Jones of Llanelli. Labour MP 1945 – 1974. Attorney-General 1966, Lord Chancellor 1974 – 1979. He was a member of the British prosecution team for Nazi war crimes at Nuremberg under Sir Hartley Shawcross QC.

[2] Morris Finer was appointed Chairman of the Royal Commission on the Press a few months before his untimely death in 1974.

have reported to Walter Raeburn that he thought I was good enough to be kept on as a tenant. It is an understatement to say that I was happy and relieved to have become a member of chambers.

I was given a place in John Stuart's room. He was charming, good-looking and very clever. He married Suzanne Norwood who later became a criminal judge.

John was a brilliant D-I-Y expert and, in the weeks and months after the euphoria of achieving tenancy faded to the realisation that, unless I received instructions, I would starve, taught me how to be a handyman in the many spare hours that we spent together. We also honed our skills at canasta and developed a neat trick of concealing the cards so that, if anyone came into our room, all that would be seen was two young barristers in earnest conversation. Suffice it to say, we had a good deal of spare time.

I thought John was infinitely more skilled than I was and more likely to succeed. But the contrast between our paper-free room and the stacks of work piling up on Morris' desk left me anxious. There was no pressure of work for me and, like many others at the Bar, I wondered why on earth any solicitor should send me instructions. Why should anyone send me a brief? I didn't know anybody on the civil side.

Luck was with me. Briefs started to come in and I became busy enough to sustain a degree of optimism that I might make a living. But, whilst we were together, I felt uncomfortable that my practice was flourishing while John's was making no progress. Solicitors would accompany me to court and hear me but not him. I became busier and my little practice began to grow. John improved his skills at solitaire. He seemed unable to attract much in the way of work. We used to talk about it as it would have been too painful not to have exchanged sympathies.

"I wish I had your luck," John would say. But he harboured no grudges and was generous in offering ideas to help me run my cases.

Luck was indeed the one thing that was missing from his otherwise perfect life. He was an unfortunate young man in many ways but the worst thing was that he died very young, while we shared the room. He developed cancer and died within eighteen months.

CHAPTER 11

SOME TALES OF THE FIFTIES

Michael and Shirley married on 6th April 1952 with a reception at the Savoy Hotel. John Hazan was the best man, the speeches were good and the send-off wonderful. The few days of honeymoon over the long Easter weekend would be a welcome break from both their flourishing careers.

As Shirley was well known as a broadcaster, wedding photographs appeared in the press. The bridal couple was recognised on the Golden Arrow, the train to Paris, and fêted by staff and passengers alike.

My marriage did nothing for any reputation I may have had for competent elementary tax law. The married couples' tax allowance would be lost if we married at the opening of the tax year – 6th April – rather than on the last day of the previous tax year, 5th April. Friends and family thought the loss was very droll, but I did point out that synagogues knew not tax legislation and 5th April fell on a Saturday that year.

The five-day honeymoon started with the opening of a wedding present. On arrival at customs at the Gare du Nord, the gendarme asked in a sort of Peter Sellers accent through a puppet-like crack in his face if we had "any sing" to declare. At least he could speak English. "Nothing," we said.

"Are you carrying any dry goods of any kind?"

"A wedding present," we told him. "We don't know what's in it."

"Please open it."

Packed within the beautifully gift-wrapped box was every imaginable and unimaginable kind of contraceptive device, and in vast quantities. As the wrapping came off and the box opened, they spilled over the customs bench and on to the floor. Everyone could see. The customs officer turned up the corners of the crack in his face and may have been laughing, like the other people around us.

"Please shut it up," he said. But the damage was done and a few of the thoughtful gifts remained scattered on the floor of the customs hall as we made as dignified a retreat as possible.

The honeymoon came to an abrupt end as the train pulled into Victoria and they were greeted by Michael's clerk who managed a polite greeting to Shirley before putting a brief into Michael's hand. "Honey-moon's over. Marlborough Street Magistrates, sir. Tomorrow."

During the Fifties, case followed upon case, many of them being re-ported in the newspapers. Michael's reputation grew to the public as well as to the profession. He was so busy, he did not manage to be with Shirley for the birth of their sons. The news that the second baby had been born was made to him at the end of a lengthy hearing at Old Street Magistrates' Court. "We got the call an hour ago, sir," the usher said as he caught up with Michael, who was about to leave the building, "but I didn't want to interrupt you."

A change in career beckoned in 1955.

I did some broadcasts for the BBC in 1955, shedding light on legal issues in a light-hearted way as the filler between two halves of concert broadcasts. As the live audience went off to buy their drinks in the inter-val, the radio listeners had the choice of turning off their sets or listening to my wit and wisdom. Some time later, someone at Granada television thought that I was one of three people whose style might translate to the small screen whose programmes were to be interrupted on a more pro-fessional basis. By commercials.

I was in competition with Robin Day[1] and Ludovic Kennedy[2] for the role of anchorman-newsreader. History shows that I was a runner-up to Robin, as was Ludo. He went on to a successful career as a writer and journalist but I stuck to the day job as a member of Walter Raeburn's set at Hare Court.

Robin Day was later to apply his interrogating skills to me when we held an "Any Questions" session at Middle Temple. He informed me that I was in the highest paid league at the Bar and had recently undertaken the first million pound brief. I told him that I was flattered and looked forward to moving into such elevated financial ranks but the reality was quite different. The number might apply to the occasional brief in Singa-pore dollars but the arithmetic was a far cry from pounds

***

---

[1] Robin Day (1923-2000). Called to the Bar 1952. Knighted 1981. He brought an aggressive, cross-examination style to television interview programmes.
[2] Ludovic Henry Coverley Kennedy (1919-) Knighted 1994.

Back in the real world that was my working life, I was aware that Walter's extensive practice as an eminent junior ground almost to a halt after he took silk. Inexplicably, he was not popular as a leader although I pushed as much work his way as I could.

Walter was a striking-looking man with piercing, hypnotic eyes. He was born into a Jewish family. During World War I, he had a vision and converted to become a passionate Christian. During the course of his career, he was appointed Recorder of West Ham. He sought to help those who had done wrong to reconstitute their lives. When sentencing he would say, "You are eligible for a prison sentence of three or four years. However, I am giving you this opportunity to join the army where you will stay for four or five years …" This caused offence, not only within the judiciary, but in the armed forces. The press articulated the general sense of outrage. How did this judge dare to equate four years in prison to a career in the army?

Walter led me in the defence of a married man in his forties who had allegedly raped his elderly landlady. The unfortunate victim was built like a gun-emplacement, a massive block of a woman with a sturdiness that belied her venerable years. My theory was that she had made up the story as a means of getting rid of the defendant and his wife who were sitting tenants in her house. I told Walter that I thought there was a way that she might be vulnerable to cross-examination. Part of her evidence was that she had bruises on her arms which she said had been caused by the Defendant when he gripped her arms. I believed that she could have gripped her own arms and caused the bruises herself. I expounded on the theory in Walter's room in chambers when I set about demonstrating how it could have happened.

I rolled up my shirt-sleeves and crossed my arms across my chest and showed him where self-inflicted gripping marks would be made. "Quite different from the marks made by an assailant," I said. "Now you grip my arms and see where the pressure points are." I lay across the desk so he could lean over to complete the experiment.

Then our clerk came in. We looked up at his stunned face. "Sir – oh, sir," was all he said. If there was a plausible explanation, it did not come immediately to his mind.

The experiment proved my point: the marks were in a different place from those that the victim described.

Walter was also prepared to follow a line of questioning to our client's wife to show that, not only was he not capable of such a vicious crime but that there was no need for him to commit the offence, being a happily married man with a regular married life. Word came that she had arrived. "She's here. She's here."

"Go and see her," Walter said as he set about establishing that the landlady had not called the police for twenty-four hours after the alleged attack. Her overbearing physical presence did not encourage the jury to believe her evidence that she was too upset at the time.

I left Number One Court of the Old Bailey accompanied by our instructing solicitor. We went into the great cavern that is the central meeting area. Billowing across one of the benches in an alcove was the wife: a carbon copy, perhaps slightly younger, of the landlady. The jury might well take the view that, even if he was happily married, the defendant might have had a certain taste in women. One glance might be enough to start some conjecture about his particular likes. The wife's appearance alone would damage his case, a point not lost on our instructing solicitor.

I returned to court.

"He's on his own," I told Walter. Our experiment on the bruises had to be enough to save the day. And it was.

***

Walter led Michael in the defended divorce of Gilbert Beyfuss, a matter which was likely to be of some public interest as Gilbert was the leader of the Divorce Bar.

Gilbert Beyfuss was an outstanding barrister nicknamed after Sergeant Buzzfuzz in the *Pickwick Papers*[1]. His most notable physical feature was a facial tic which resembled an exaggerated wink. When he spoke, there would be a pause as the tic took over, his eyebrow lifted, the eyelid drooped, then his eye closed. Speech would resume as his eye

---

[1]   Famous for his peroration at the trial of *Bardell v Pickwick* a fictional breach of promise suit.

opened. Every judge in the PD and A[1] knew him very well. They were all aware of this problem which, in some circumstances, appeared to be used to his advantage. For example, he would rise to cross-examine an errant husband.

"When did you stop loving your wife?" was a typical question. The wink, unbidden as it certainly was, always threw the witness into confusion.

"You did sleep with the au pair, didn't you?" And then the wink.

Walter and I were concerned about acting against a fellow member of the Bar. We were advised to write to Gilbert to tell him that we had been instructed for his wife. He wrote back:

"It would be a scandal if my wife were represented by any less eminent counsel.

Yours ever,

Gilbert"

He capitulated. His unpleasant wife got her divorce. The Bar and the public were deprived of the scandal that a contest would have caused, *The Evening Standard* merely announcing who the parties were and that the divorce had happened. From Walter's career perspective, this was not enough to improve his flagging fortunes.

***

Soon after the Beyfuss divorce, better and larger premises for Chambers became available. Most members were keen on making the move. Walter was not. The only solution was the amicable split that took place: Walter and some others stayed at Hare Court. The new set at the recently built 2 Crown Office Row was born. The members were Eric Falk, Peter Pain, Brian Capstick[2], Campbell Hackforth-Jones and Morris Finer who was to be Head of Chambers. Hare Court was not a reliable shop window for Morris whose commercial career was developing rapidly. Walter could have moved over to Crown Office Row but there was no realistic possibility that he would be any better off there or that he would be, in effect, anything more than a visitor.

[1]   Probate, Divorce and Admiralty Division of the High Court
[2]   Brian Capstick (1927-2005). Appointed as an Old Bailey Judge 1987.

Eric Falk was an interesting character. He was a very senior man who had a parallel career as an art and music critic. He made his living at the Bar on regular forays to Northampton appearing before the Commissioner in about a dozen undefended divorce cases at a time. The single fee of twenty guineas, multiplied several times, made this a lucrative line of work.

At about the time of the Chambers split, the President of the Probate, Divorce and Admiralty Division of the High Court, Lord Merriman (a former resident in 2 Crown Office Row and in whose bedroom I set up my practice) took the view that it was not healthy for undefended cases to go through the sausage machine in this way. He decided, on one of Eric's appearance days, that he would preside over the court. Eric took this in his stride although it was unheard of for such a senior judge to take part in proceedings at this level and he was concerned about the change that this might presage.

Eric set out his usual stall, "The husband ... the petitioner ... I shall call the enquiry agent ..." Merriman suddenly interrupted the mundane flow of the set-piece.

"What's your authority for that," he snarled, as if Eric were making a complex legal argument instead of merely dealing with uncontested facts.

Eric's temper was ignited. He glared at Merriman, whose interruption was pointless and, arguably, a nuisance. He snapped, *"Rylands v. Fletcher*[1]." He maintained his glare. Merriman backed off. Palms facing outwards, he said, "I only asked!"

***

Licensing cases were often dull but they were a reliable source of income. Butty Sugrue's case was more interesting than most of the others. He ran an all-Irish drinking club at Maida Vale. The clientéle would leave in the early hours of the morning, tripping, falling and occasion-

---

[1] *Rylands v Fletcher* [1868] LR3 HL 330. The defendant's contractors constructed a reservoir on their land. They failed to close off disused mine shafts on the site so that when the reservoir filled with water it escaped into the plaintiff's mineshafts on the adjacent land. The defendant was liable for the escape of water which constituted a nuisance. Not a great deal to do with the law of divorce.

ally having energetic, often physical, arguments. They were known, from time to time, to leave souvenirs such as vomit on the pavements or in the gardens of nearby houses.

Butty applied for a new licence. The local people thought it would be a good opportunity to get rid of the club. Michael was instructed to oppose the licence application.

Butty Sugrue spoke up for himself. He said that his clients rarely slipped and never made a sound when they left the club. I put to him: "The complaint is that you are not a fit and proper person to have a licence of this kind."

"God bless you sir, your honour!" he exclaimed in an Irish brogue that was so pure, it sounded as though it had never been tainted with any English dialect over the thirty years or so of inhabiting the hinterland of NW6. "I am the man for that licence, I surely am!"

Various members gave evidence for him. To each one, it was put that Butty was not fit to run the club.

"Not fit!" was the horrified response of each of them, all managing to keep the tones of Galway even in those two short syllables. One elaborated, "I consider he is … immaculate."

The final witness defined fit for Michael. "Fit – fit is it? Him who pulled a tram up Ballymeeny High Street with his teeth! That's fit, that's what it is!"

He lost his application.

***

In 1958, the impresario, Bernard Delfont, opened the spectacular nightclub, The Talk of the Town, in the former London Hippodrome Theatre. He put on dinner-show combinations which lived up to the name of the venture. It was set to, and did, attract the rich and famous and anyone else who wanted to enjoy stunning entertainment, good food and lavish surroundings. He had the good luck to be able to persuade Princess Margaret, her future husband, Anthony Armstrong-Jones and six of their friends to come to the opening event. They were given the best table, overlooking the cabaret area. The next morning, Michael received an emergency telephone call from the well-known solicitor, David

Jacobs. He came to see Michael with the managing director of a well-known, nation-wide employment agency.

There had been a spot of high-class bother. David explained, "They have had a problem with a temporary waiter they provided to the Talk of the Town."

The events involved a very senior waiter who had been appointed to serve the royal table. It seems he had taken a relaxed view of the importance of his assignment. He had not been acquainted with the views on protocol held by the Princess. Instead of offering the menus in the classic style to which her Highness was accustomed, he dealt the menus like a hand of poker. He then compounded the employment death wish with the words, "Hands up – who's for chicken?"

The Princess let her displeasure be known. Bernard Delfont communicated the compounded shame and embarrassment of his organisation to the agency who, via David, wanted to know how to rescue themselves from this calamity. If the story was anything like true, it was essential not to feed the interest of the press. I think that the advice I gave was the briefest of my career.

"Settle it," I said. "Whatever it costs."

The shoulders of the managing director sagged with relief. "I've been saying that all morning," he said wearily.

***

Some cases involved travelling about the country. For example, a time came for heading North.

The Magistrates' Court in Consett, County Durham, was at the top of a mountainous road. I reluctantly accepted David Freeman's instructions to represent a steelworks although I was due in the High Court in London the next day. After our business was done and as we were preparing to leave the courtroom, the chairman of the magistrates spoke to us.

"Mr Sherrard, I have to tell you that, since starting this case, we have been snowed in. The only vehicle that will be leaving Consett today is the Black Maria. I am sorry you did not have notice of our weather but my wife and I would be happy for you to stay. A colleague will put your instructing solicitor up, if that would be convenient for you."

David and I went into a huddle.

"What time is the next Black Maria?" he asked the usher.

Although grateful for the chairman's offer, within ten minutes we were sitting in the back of the window-barred van in the company of a couple of prisoners on their way to HM Prison, Durham. The chairman had made an order that the doors of the Black Maria were to be left open at all times, as long as we were sitting in the prisoners' cubicle. There was no mention of whether our travelling companions posed a risk. I decided then that anything out of the way (in England, at any rate – as it turned out) was not on.

But there was a case in the Far West...

A case I did with David Freeman involved a former schoolmaster in a large private school for boys. He had been sacked after a scandal involving his friendships with the pupils. He turned into a Vincent Crummles character, straight out of Dickens but with added Micawberesque qualities.

He took a theatrical touring company into a town about ten miles from Swansea. It was a big show and very well organised. Advance arrangements, costing a huge amount of money, had been made for individual lodgings for the principals with the chorus and stagehands in dormitory-style accommodation. Many local people were seriously affected when their bills for providing digs for the company were not met.

We needed to get this case knocked out at the magistrates' level rather going to trial at the local assizes.

The whole town was affected. If you hadn't lost money yourself, your father, wife or other relatives knew someone who had. The ripples of the economic disaster spread wide: jobs were lost as the affected landlords laid off staff as they could not afford to pay wages.

We got off the train. The police were there to meet us. "There are too many people involved," they told us. "The hearing is going to be at the concert hall in the local town council building."

When we arrived, the podium had been set up for the magistrates' bench with space for lawyers and witnesses on a lower platform that would probably have been used by the orchestra for the musical performances which must have been the more usual use of the hall. The public were in the body of the hall. There was not a spare seat.

I pitched in.

And, of course, most of them were hopeless witnesses, remembering things as they should have been, not as they were, asking one another for help – "That's right, ennit, Mrs B?" – and relying on hearsay to an overwhelming degree.

I made a long submission of 'no case to answer'.

During the justices' retirement, David said, "The mob is going to lynch you if this comes off."

"We'll have a word with the police," I said. I was not confident that they could or would help: they, too, had sisters, cousins and aunts who had suffered losses.

The justices came back. They dismissed the charges. In the same breath, the police officer (probably not a man with local roots) said, "Follow me."

At the back of the theatre was a car with outriders at the ready. We had a hair-raising journey to the station.

***

There was an organization in Hampstead which did medical research in the 1950s using live cats. The thieves who were paid to bring in the animals had to be defended.

I used to get hate mail when I defended these cases. The thefts occurred mainly in East London which meant that they usually came up for trial at the Magistrates' Court at Stratford. During one of the hearings, defending, as it happened, Mr and Mrs Hooker of Hackney, an old lady came charging through the court at me. She must have been the model for Grandma of the Giles cartoons. Dressed in black, she brandished a large, furled umbrella which she used to deal me a generous whack across my shoulders.

"You wicked man!" she shouted.

I was absolutely stunned. Court officials were equally taken by surprise but moved up as if to stop her as she seemed to be squaring up to deliver another blow.

I looked at the bench. The wing members had pursed their lips and were shaking their heads in disapproval. I hoped it was of the old lady's actions, not of my part in the case.

"Madam," said the chairman, "you must not behave in this way and allow your emotions to get the better of you. If you do that again, we will have to take steps to punish you ..."

***

In the late 1950s, Michael's political career started. Stanley Clinton-Davis invited him to a political rally at Portsmouth Docks. Stanley was the key speaker and it would be interesting to see him in action.

I arrived at the appointed time and place. There was a vast, wire-enclosed area between huge warehouses. It was packed with dockers and warehousemen who had come to hear Stanley's speech. I was greeted at the gateway by a local Labour party official.

"Mr Sherrard?"

"Yes." I was pleased that someone had been looking out for me as I was not sure whether I was supposed to join the rather angry-looking crowd or sit on some sort of dais, which was not immediately apparent.

"I'm here to look after you. Stanley's been held up. He's asked for you to start the meeting and hold the fort until he gets here. He won't be long."

"But how long is he going to be? I don't know what he's going to say! I don't know what these people are expecting! I know nothing about politics! Why can't you just tell them he'll be late?"

"Stanley says you'll be fine: if anyone can do it, you can. Just talk to them about anything." He was steering me towards a large gantry which I had not noticed before although it stood about sixty feet high with a platform hanging out over the crowd milling below.

"You don't expect me to go up there?" I asked, knowing what the answer was going to be. He stood behind me, grabbed my hands, one of which was occupied with holding the handle of my brief-case, and placed them on the metal poles at the side of a vertical stepladder that stretched upwards, seemingly endlessly.

"Good luck."

I needed it. I held on to the briefcase as a sort of life-line even though it was more of an impediment. "Don't look down," I heard my looker-after say. It was looking up that was the problem. There seemed to be, quite literally, no way but up and the sky was getting closer.

I reached the top and scrambled inelegantly on to the metal grid that was the platform. The chairman of the meeting was there, speaking into a microphone. "We are very lucky to have – " he turned to me anxiously with a questioning look. I told him my name. He turned back to the audience, "Michael Sherrard. He is a – ". Another questioning look.

"Barrister," I whispered.

" – barrister who is – ". Another anguished look. I said the first thing that came into my head. I told him my age.

"Twenty-seven."

He turned to me again. "Where have you come from?"

"Court. I've just finished a murder trial."

"He's fresh from doing a murder. He would like to speak to you and wish you all good voting. Don't hesitate to ask him your questions."

He tugged me over to the microphone.

A voice boomed out from the crowd below.

"What's your party's intentions with regard to the docks and with regard to aircraft production?"

The truth is, I had no political affiliation and I hadn't the faintest idea what were the intentions of Stanley's party.

I said something and, for my pains, my voice was immediately drowned out by jeers and shouting. "Speak up," – "Go home," – "Where's Stanley," were some of the politer words that reached me.

I tried harder. Then I heard a clear shout, "You don't know nothing about the docks." I was saved from having to respond by Stanley appearing and taking over. It was the end of my political career.

CHAPTER 12

DR STRANG

On 9 October 1954, Michael was listed to prosecute a theft at Bow Street. The principal witness was a CID officer. It was with regret that he therefore he had refuse the urgent request at 7.00 a.m. from David Freeman to go to West London Magistrates' Court. Freeman was in a state of agitation when he phoned. "Harley Street doctor – shot a policeman – I want you to get him bail."

The client was Dr Robert Philip Strang, a 43 year-old dermatologist who stood charged with attempted murder. He had been keeping company with a Miss Fay Thompson, coyly described in the press as 'a former Windmill girl[1]'. She occupied half the front page of the Daily Express on the day that the story was first reported because the shooting took place in her presence. Michael describes her as "all legs and mini-skirt on roller-skates".

The flat where Dr Strang had set her up had been burgled the previous evening. In his fears for her future security, the doctor had acquired a pistol so as to be better able to protect Miss Thompson if there were any further intrusions into the property. Unfortunately for Detective Sergeant Anning, whilst carrying out his investigations in the early hours of the morning, Dr Strang mistook him for a burglar and shot him in, what he was to argue later, was the use of reasonable force. It would have been a wonderful case for Michael but the theft had come first.

Because Michael could not be there, he did a Maxwell Turner for David. "This is what you say." He dictated words to be used, which were to have the required result of securing bail, and set off to do his appointed work at Bow Street Magistrates' Court. On arrival, he went to look for the officer in the case.

"Oh, you won't find 'im, sir," a court official told Michael. "'e's in 'ospital. 'E was shot last night ..."

The bullet had missed DS Anning's heart by a centimetre, otherwise the charge would have been murder. The officer recovered and eventu-

---

[1]   The Windmill Theatre in Soho, London, was famous for its tableaux of naked women, forbidden by law from moving.

ally became chief of police in Hong Kong during the time when I had a busy practice there. But that was far down the line. In the short-term, by this remarkable coincidence, I would be defending the doctor at the Old Bailey. Because of the importance of the case, David Freeman asked me to recommend a silk. My suggestion of Bill Fearnley-Whittingstall, was accepted.

Bill was a great advocate. If you'd not met him previously, you might well have ignored him because he looked like a drunk pulled in from the night before. He had twitchy eyes and was a total neurotic. But he was a brilliant speaker and made one of the three greatest mitigations that I have heard at the Bar.

The judge was Mr Justice Lynskey, renowned in the 'blood-and-guts' area of the law. Because the policeman survived the shot, Bill got intent knocked out and managed to get murder reduced to grievous bodily harm. Bill knew that the judge would take a hard line in this very serious crime. He told the doctor to expect about fifteen years behind bars and went off to prepare his mitigation overnight.

Shirley and I were living in Shepherds Bush at the time. At 5.00 a.m. the phone rang. It was Bill in a state of some distress. In a sad, tremulous voice, sounding very much as if he were holding back tears, he said, "C-can y-you c-come to the C-Carlton C-Club right away. It's v-very important." I shot out of bed and hastily dressed so as to be ready to go straight on to court to take Bill's place which, from the sound of his voice, was likely to happen. I reached the Club in record time. There was Bill, fully dressed in his usual scruffy outfit, not looking distressed at all. Looking the worse for wear was usual for him and did not bear comment.

"What are we going to say in mitigation?" he asked, sounding quite cheerful. This could not have been the same person who had phoned me in what seemed to have been the middle of the night.

"Is that what you got me out of bed for?" It was. And he did not need any help from me. He just wanted the moral support of someone around.

His mitigation was brilliant. You couldn't add a syllable except to applaud, which had to be avoided by sitting on your hands. He had a difficulty with presentation, however. He was distracted by noise. My main task as his junior was to ensure, by overt glares and frowns and other subtle gestures, that no extraneous sound was made by anyone in the court. He could just about tolerate the judge's pen moving on paper but seeing the movement of writing put him on the alert for a sound that no-one but he could hear.

Mr Justice Lynskey was very fearsome indeed. He had a red face which seemed to portray pent-up fury that was about to be released. The redder his face, the nearer he was to erupting in rage. He had bushy white eyebrows that contracted in what appeared to be anger. He had eyes that bored through you.

Bill could weather this style of judicial disapproval. He performed his marvellous mitigation. The judge said, "Fifteen months." The doctor fainted. He thought it was the fifteen years for which Bill had prepared him.

Lynskey was moved by what Bill had said and the way he said it. He might have been persuaded to a shorter sentence but for the fact that it was an officer on duty who had been injured.

Strang was imprisoned at Wormwood Scrubs. He wrote a paper on conditions affecting wardens and men while he was in there with the full co-operation of the Senior Warden who found him a cell which could accommodate his research papers, desk and so forth. He had the run of the prison. By the time he was released, he had a major effect on cleaning it up. He came back to the prison every day for three or four weeks after his release to finish his research.

The Fearnley-Whittingstall approach to any kind of noise when he was speaking is reflected in a murder trial in the mid-1960s before Austin Jones LJ.

Bill Fearnley-Whittingstall was in the old timbered courtroom at Lewes. The jury box consisted of two rows of six seats. The members entered it through a half-door that, once they were seated, was kept in place by a small brass ratchet lock.

Bill opened the case and as he spoke, the noise started. He was predictably distracted. A juror was fiddling with the brass lock. Tk – tk – tk. This was his Achilles heel. Tk – tk – tk. Tk – tk – tk. The noise continued, rhythmic, noticeable. After a while, it became the only noise in the room. Oblivious, the juror continued. Tk – tk – tk.

Bill waited for a very long moment indeed. Tk – tk – tk.

"If you don't fucking stop, I'll fucking do for you," he said, in a loud, menacing tone that belied his shabby, diffident manner, looking directly at the offending juror. The juror stopped. Everyone in the room held their breath.

Austin Jones' eyebrows shot up into his wig.

"Really, Mr Fearnley-Whittingstall!"

"Really!" said Bill. "These were the words of the accused, uttered as threats to his wife."

Of course.

CHAPTER 13

DANDY KIM

In 1960, Michael Caborn-Waterfield, then aged 30, was known to the public as "Dandy Kim". He was short, like a jockey, and very good-looking. He was quite a hit with the ladies and virtually invented jet-setting before jets were even in commercial use. He had a specialty of wooing heiresses and nearly marrying them. One was the daughter of Jack Warner, the film magnate. In 1953, in what was to be the final stage of their romance, the pair agreed between themselves that she would get the family jewellery, later valued at £25,000, from her father's safe in their home in the South of France. She would then hand it to Dandy Kim who would take care of it in the course of their proposed elopement. They were to leave Nice Airport on separate flights. Miss Warner indeed handed over the jewellery and took the 13:30 but whether or not Dandy Kim took the 12:30 as had been planned, he did not make their rendez-vous. The degree of her heartbreak was second only to that of her father. He reported the theft to the police.

The French police went into action if not at once, at any rate by 1956. They issued a summons for Dandy Kim to appear before the magistrates on a date which, in the same way as the Warner romance ended, he failed to keep. The French court sentenced him in his absence to four years imprisonment for failing to attend the magistrates' hearing and, eventually, informing the English authorities that they sought his extradition. The offence was "par contumace".

For a time, this did not particularly curtail his activities. He was a bit careless and very identifiable so it was very likely that the English warrant for his arrest, requested by France, would be served on him. The inevitable occurred and Dandy Kim was arrested in England on 12 January 1960. He found himself behind Brixton bars awaiting his French fate.

Michael was called in shortly after his new client had made his whereabouts known to his solicitor. A photograph of him coming out of court, accompanied by Dandy Kim with all his immediate wordly possessions (a pullover) tucked under his arm, shows that the first objective was achieved. Sarah Skinner, 22 years of age, stood bail for him. Dandy Kim was sprung. The second objective, to ensure that he stayed free, was going to be a harder target, as the French Government would not want to lose face and would pursue the course on which they had embarked, to ensure that the needs of French justice were served.

After carrying out some basic investigation into the legal position, I went to see Dandy Kim with his solicitor in conference to discuss the future conduct of the opposition to the extradition request. The solicitor agreed with me that the matter was of sufficient importance to warrant the use of a QC. "Who do you want to lead you?" she asked.

"There is only one man," I answered, "Fred Lawton[1]." He was a great scholar and bilingual. Although I made the correct choice, I should have remembered advice given to me in pupillage by Du Cann: never to say "There is only one man." Several years later, I was to assure James Hanratty that there was only one man who could defend him. When that man was not available, the only one man turned out to be me. But for this case, I chose Fred and he saw the case through. I set about preparation.

A little research in Middle Temple Library, which required the cutting of folded vellum on a hitherto untouched copy of the extradition treaty, confirmed my view that *par contumace* was not a concept in English law. Fred agreed with me that this was therefore not a matter for which a person could be extradited. The only lawful basis for extradition would have been an allegation of theft.

When it came to the hearing, Fred found volumes of French law to support his argument, all of which went with us to Bow Street Magistrates' Court where we were opposed by Maître Koenig of the English and French Bar. He looked as though he was an actor dressed-up to be a lawyer with his immaculate clothes and perfectly-trimmed goatee beard. He appeared discomfited as he stood alone against the two of us.

An hotel chambermaid provided a written statement which enlivened the dry legalities. She swore that she had seen, in Dandy Kim's bag under the bed "certaine jouaillerie ..."

The legal arguments were prolonged and profound. Fred Lawton had sifted through the Napoleonic Code and the relevant decisions based on it. For three hours, he read to the court from textbooks, translating the learned arguments as he went. The magistrate bravely gave the impres-

---

[1]   Later appointed to the High Court and then a Lord Justice of Appeal.

sion of following every word. The essential point was that Dandy Kim had not been charged nor convicted of the offence of theft and the matter revolved around the technicality of extradition to France to serve a sentence for an offence that was not known in English law.

Fred finished his submissions. The magistrate was looking at the note-book on his desk, holding his pen. Before Fred could draw breath and as he went to take his seat, the magistrate's pen touched the paper. As he wrote, and without looking up, he said in a flat, expressionless voice, "I prefer the evidence of the chambermaid. Order granted."

Fred was enraged by the almost nonchalant decision. "Michael," he said, "get an appeal going. I want habeas corpus on the road as soon as you can. He has to be taught a lesson."

Two weeks later, we were in Lord Chief Justice Parker's Court. Maître Koenig was there for the French Government. The Attorney-General, Sir Reginald Manningham-Buller, represented the Home Office. He said to me, "Are you Sherrard?" I said that I was. "What a ridiculous point," he said dismissively. "This won't take us long to dispose of."

"We'll see," I said.

The Lord Chief arrived with the two other judges. They took their seats and we waited for the indication that the hearing was to start.

Parker leaned forward and said to Manningham-Buller, "You can't hold this extradition order, can you." He sounded friendly, almost conversational. "What is this *par contumace*? It sounds very French. Not known in English law, is it?" These were sweet words for the Dandy Kim team.

Manningham-Buller attempted to justify his arguments for about twenty minutes. The court did not require Lawton to say a word. A few days later, a complicated judgment was handed down in which it was held that Dandy Kim had the right to have the extradition warrant set aside.

Later, we gave some advice to Dandy Kim which he heeded for a while. "Keep your head down and watch out." However, his liberty did not last for long. Within a few months, he was stopped for a driving offence in South London. He was almost begging to be noticed in his powerful sports car. This time, the French were slightly better organised and had proper grounds for his extradition. The arresting officer, perhaps helped by seeing the name on the driver's licence, greeted him with the words, "I have reason to believe that you are Michael Caborn-Waterfield. There is a warrant for your arrest and extradition to France." And indeed there was.

This time there was nothing we could do because they were going to try him in France. Like the gentleman that he set himself up to be, he pleaded guilty and did the two years required of the four-year sentence meted out by the French court.

I acted for Dandy Kim several times over the next few years in civil matters. By then, he had married Sarah Skinner.

Leaving court with Dandy Kim, January 1960

CHAPTER 14

SOME JUDGES AND JURORS

In 1965, Treasury Counsel John Buzzard had the task of prosecuting a very complex indictment at the Old Bailey alleging serious frauds by, let us say, Mr A and Mr B against a series of victims. Morris Finer led Michael for Mr A and Sebag Shaw[1] defended Mr B.

The selection of the jury called for considerable care. The case required a high level of literacy and numeracy on the part of each juror. The judge was the ring-master. His role in empanelling the jury was crucial.

He indicated to us that in view of the likely length of the trial, quite apart from the mass of commercial documentation, he intended to make a detailed statement to the jurors-in-waiting, warning them what was in store and that they should consider the personal consequences for them if their names were drawn from the box.

As we watched the crowd of potential jurors being brought into the court-room, Morris whispered to me, "All I can say is: anybody who doesn't know how to get off this jury after listening to what this judge is going to say isn't fit to try a case of such complexity."

One after another of the 100 or so jurors-in-waiting took their places, some to be rejected on sight, others after a moment or two's hesitation. It took the best part of the afternoon to sift through them because the judge (who regarded the jurors as spectators to admire his performance) wanted to impress them with his firm control of the proceedings and admirable skill with words.

He started by greeting the mass gathering almost as if he were the Pope, waiting to bless them. Resting his elbows on the desk-top, he turned his hands so as to frame his face and smiled benignly. He was obviously enjoying the musical sound of his rather high-pitched voice explaining the procedure whereby he would decide whether to release or excuse them.

---

[1]   Sebag Shaw QC (1906-1982), appointed to the High Court 1968 subsequently Court of Appeal.

"Ladies and Gentlemen, I am told the case we are about to begin may last upwards of six months. No-one knows better than I the privilege of undertaking jury service. But it must not be an instrument of oppression. If your name is drawn, you must tell me of any hardship you might endure were you to be selected to serve."

A small, limp flourish of his right hand.

"Let me give you some examples of the sort of difficulties that might affect you. If you have a holiday booked and have paid for it – or paid a deposit – you must tell me. If you are a one-man firm employing up to two workers in, say, a foreign field and would be unable to continue your business commitments, you must tell me." He had several other examples. Each was suffixed by the exhortation that he must be told if anyone applied to be excused.

One after another, did they tell him!

It came to the turn of a man who announced he was an electrician's mate. Before he could say anything more, the Judge aimed something akin to a blessing at him, palm of his hand facing him: "You need say no more! Things electrical cannot wait indefinitely."

"But, Your Lordship, I'm fascinated by the law and I want to serve!"

The judge's hands went flat to the desk. A small judicial frown. "If you are not seeking to be excused and – " a slightly pained smile " – you are not challenged by either side, you will be able to serve."

The jury was eventually put together. It consisted largely of blue-collar workers and included the electrician and the caretaker of a block of flats who was either so nervous or so illiterate he could hardly read the oath. Morris muttered to me, "How on earth will they understand the implications of offshore accounts?"

"Don't assume the judge won't have some of the same problems that might let him excuse himself," I whispered back, just catching the judge's eye as he beamed happily towards the wider audience.

When we were in the robing room at the end of the day, John Buzzard, the most formal of men when in court, expressed his anxiety.

"I knew it was going to happen. You were warned about jurors understanding. I don't like to say so but I think our judge has the same problem! We'll have to do something about it."

But there was nothing to be done. The case plodded on for three or four weeks. It was difficult to know who looked more puzzled by the technical evidence, the judge or the jury. Eventually, Buzzard came unstuck with a witness who purported not to know what he was there for. His evidence concerned a minute that had allegedly been taken at a meeting on 17th January which simply had not happened. The judge decided it was time to come to the rescue. Addressing the witness, he said:

"Pay attention to me. What Mr Buzzard is trying to do (not very successfully so far) – " (we sensed Buzzard's silently borne outrage) "- was to have your evidence about the commercial procedure at this company. I think I may have more success if I describe what stage we have reached in that process and invite you to tell us whether I have got it right … you can nod or shake your head."

The judge then proceeded, literally, to give evidence for the witness in some detail without actually going into the box. John Buzzard could contain himself no longer. Enraged by this improper conduct, he rose, protesting that it was not for the judge to give the evidence.

The judge was astonished and, in a quick change of role to naughty schoolboy said, "I was only trying to help!"

Tartly, Buzzard reminded him that what was happening was quite irregular and brought the interchange to an end in formal terms. "My Lord, can the jury take a break?"

Almost disappointed to be stopped while he was in full flow, the judge nevertheless agreed. In the adjournment, Buzzard, who was still clearly upset, said, "I'm going to ask him to discharge the jury and start all over again. There must be another twelve people out there who can count up to ten."

Sebag said, "He's not going to start again. He's not understood a word so far. Now is the time to for a plea to a lesser count and do a deal."

The jurors were sent away for the day and the usher came to tell us that the judge wanted to see us in his room. We duly assembled there.

"Hello chaps!" said the judge, as if we had come into a children's tea party. "I think I may have gone a little far this time but I've been very impressed by the reality of this case."

He addressed himself to John Buzzard. "You said in opening that the central allegation is in Count 1."

"Actually, the essence is set out in Count 3."

"Oh, of course!" He slipped into a comfortably relaxed position in his rather grand chair and after a moment or so said, "Now, if these defendants were to plead guilty to that count, it may be that I could be persuaded to treat it as being at the lower end of the scale…"

Morris and I did not dare to look at one another. He said, "Would you agree that there should be no sentence of imprisonment? We could discuss the financial implications."

"Oh, no," the judge smiled. "There really would have to be a short term – "

"There should be no question of custody." Morris was firm.

"Well. I'll have the jury back tomorrow and think about this over-night. Let's bring them back at 3.00 p.m."

The next day we arrived at court at 2.00 p.m., allowing plenty of time to be ready for the afternoon's proceedings. The judge summoned us again. This time, he looked serious, and even dropped the pitch of his voice a notch or two. "I think I can avoid a sentence of imprisonment. You've got to crack these complex cases, you know."

The truth was he would not have known how to sum up. John Buzzard was beside himself with mute disapproval. We left him fuming as we went to see our respective clients who were, by then, prepared for fines in the region of £50,000 that would enable them to walk free. On that basis, we told the judge that we would plead guilty to Count 3. It was a specific allegation and we only hoped he could cope with that.

Count 3 was put to the defendants again and they pleaded guilty. The judge prepared to enjoy himself.

"Well, members of the jury, this case comes to an end many months before expectations. You'll no doubt be interested in the outcome, so do come back tomorrow when I deal with sentence."

We were dismayed. There was no need to postpone sentencing since it had already been decided. Perhaps this was another judicial idiosyncrasy.

"Bail as before?" said Sebag.

"Oh, there's no question of bail," the judge said. "Oh no! In custody."

"All rise," said the usher as the defendants looked as though they were about to faint. Our clients were in a state of shock. Why would someone be remanded in custody unless they were going to be sentenced to imprisonment? They thought they had been assassinated: tricked into the guilty plea. Everything that had looked so good before now looked dreadful. They were taken down to the cells where we went to see them. The fact that we could only encourage them to believe it was to be for one night was no comfort to them: if one night was possible, so were many, many more.

We saw them next morning on their return from HM Prison, Brixton. They had visibly aged: gaunt and unshaven, hollow-eyed from lack of sleep. Mr A was trembling uncontrollably. "Do you know what happened, to me? TO ME?"

We shook our heads, dreading what was to come.

"I'm put in a cell – a CELL! – and it's DARK – and there's NO LIGHT – and suddenly, I'm aware there's someone else in there with me. I can hear him panting and then I can see the whites of his eyes looking at me. He's looking at me! And these huge arms go up in the air and he says –"

We drew breath, waiting for the denouement.

"and he says, 'Don't you come near me – I'm only here for wife-debt – I'm not a criminal!' To ME he says THIS!"

Messrs A and B were released with a great speech from the judge about how serious were their offences but they were, after all, at the lower end of the scale.

As we were making our way out of the Old Bailey, when we were in the part that is called the City Lands where town planners meet, one of the jurors, the caretaker, stopped Sebag and said, "I thought the case was very interesting."

Sebag, his arms full of papers, was like the wedding guest to the juror's Ancient Mariner.

"You know," the juror continued, unstoppable, "we knew what the truth was about that minute of the January meeting. Because the prosecutor totally missed the point, when we were sent out of court on all the short adjournments, we used the time to do a little analysis for ourselves."

I echoed his word. "Analysis?"

"We thought Mr Buzzard had missed the point and you gentlemen didn't seem interested in pursuing it, so we made a schedule –

"A schedule?"

"- a schedule of his overseas trips and the travel agent's bills and the stamps in his passport – "

The jury had pieced the story together to show that, on Jersey's national day, the banks were closed and, if that was the case, other meetings could not have happened when the prosecution said they had. Morris and I had not dealt with this point yet in the presence of the jury. We were waiting to see what happened when Buzzard reached the issue. Our feeling was that he was in for a surprise. It did not occur to either of us that the jury would have someone among their number who could help them to sort it out for themselves.

Two things: Morris' *bon mot* about getting out of jury service for the case did not hold up; and it is sometimes unavoidable to hear how the jury works, even though they have not had to come to a decision.

***

Sometimes it possible to conjecture what might have been in the jurors' minds. Turn back a couple of years to a case from the late 1950s.

The defendant (hereinafter referred to as 'the defendant') used premises whose demise was a ramshackle cellar under an anonymous, brick-faced building. It was, literally, in the bowels of Wardour Street. The entrance to the stairway down to the cellar was through a door decorated by flaking strips of ancient paint. The door was secured by a lockdown iron bar and the bar was locked in place when the room was in use. In another life, the room might have passed as a cinema for the enjoyment of pornographers who did not have their own pornograph. What it had was an elderly domestic movie projector, a fairly large screen supported on an easel and a stock of blue movies. Perhaps blue does not sufficiently indicate the depth of the colour of the films which attracted a viewing public drawn from the ranks of the dirty raincoat brigade who would frequently assemble for early afternoon cut-price showings.

On the day in question, the defendant had no notion that at least three members of the audience had borrowed their grubby mackintoshes to disguise themselves. They were police officers waiting for a suitable moment whilst the film was running to make the announcement that they had raided the premises and no-one should move.

The defendant was not affected by this order, which came at a critical moment, because once he had the projector creaking along, he decided to visit the barber shop just across the road. He left his makeshift cinema and made sure that no-one else could enter by locking the door with the security bar. He looked at his watch and calculated that the programme had forty minutes to run: plenty of time for a haircut.

The police plan went into effect at the appointed moment. When the officers told their literally captive audience not to move, they realised that they themselves were just as much affected by the order. Within the allotted forty minutes, the defendant returned, unlocked the door and was promptly manhandled by the police. They were very upset, not so much because they wondered how the film would finish but because of how long it would now take to collect the addresses and details from identity documents. They gathered the information they required, including a large cardboard crate of pornographic films.

The senior officer, an Inspector, had been particularly enraged at the defendant's cavalier attitude to the safety of his customers.

"You didn't give a toss whether we would die – and we almost certainly would have done if there had been a fire. An old projector like this piece of Meccano – it could have ignited at any minute."

The defendant was arrested and taken to Savile Row police station.

I received instructions to advise on the defence, if any. I said that if the charge related to the nature of the film, we might be able to say something to the effect that it would not corrupt and deprave. My pupil suggested that we ask to see the film, in the interests of justice.

Our instructing solicitor had applied for bail and I was to meet him to discuss the options after the film had been shown to us.

The police station at Savile Row was infinitely more salubrious than the underground cinema but somebody said that the film was going to be shown from the projector that had been seized in the raid. This was alarming, given the level of police concern about its safety.

My pupil had insisted that I went with him to see the film. He did not mind too much when, after a short time, I said, "That will be enough." The lights were switched on and I looked about the room. There were six or seven men there. One of them was obviously my client, easily identifiable by his rough clothing and miserable expression. I approached him and told him who I was. Although I felt sure that he had figured out for himself that the prospects of an acquittal, based on the few minutes of the film that I had seen, were slim, I said to him quietly, so as not to be overheard, "This is hopeless and a very serious and dangerous background will do the case no good. You'll have to plead. It will be my job to make the best of it but it's not going to be easy."

He nodded. "I quite agree," he said, "but I'm not your client. He's no doubt gone for another haircut somewhere. I'm Inspector Ponsonby. The papers are at Scotland Yard for the charges to be drafted."

No doubt in anticipation of a plea of guilty at the Old Bailey, the prosecution were content to bring charges based on an alleged obscene performance. The prosecution were, however, going to make plain that the gravity of the offence was to be considered in the context of the extreme danger of locking people into the cellar room. The case came before Judge Rogers who reluctantly directed the jury to see the film before the opening speech. Neither the prosecution nor I took any objection to that course being followed.

The all male jury largely struggled to maintain solemn faces but walked soberly to the projection room behind the court. Within five minutes, the judge looked at his watch and said, "That will be quite sufficient. We'll have them back to court and start the trial."

I had little difficulty in detecting the disapproval of the judge but sensed that the jury were disappointed: they thought Judge Rogers was a killjoy.

The trial was short. I called no evidence. The prosecution did not want to make a closing speech. The judge summed up briefly, as was his wont, and the film was not shown again.

The jury returned within half an hour and the foreman with the po-est of po-faces but tight-lipped, eyeball-to-eyeball with the Judge said, "Not guilty."

For the first time, the jury smiled, all twelve of them.

CHAPTER 15

A WINDSOR KNOT

Junior barristers spend a great deal of their time waiting in court for their cases to be called. Sometimes there is something of interest to be gleaned from watching earlier cases.

In the early 1960s, there was a day when I had a 'nuisance and annoyance' case, last on Henry ("Harry") Leon's list in Windsor County Court. As a judge, he looked severe but under the serious facade, his alter ego as a humorous writer often had him on the brink of bursting into laughter.

The case before mine was of the same genre: a domestic drama brought under the Rent Acts which provided that, if protected tenants were guilty of nuisance and annoyance, the landlord might apply to the County Court for an order that the tenant should lose the protection and be obliged to vacate the premises. These cases tended to take an inordinate length of time to try with seemingly endless evidence in chief as to what the parties were doing to each other. A common feature of many of them was hammering in the night. What could so many bad tenants/landlords find to build when darkness fell? In essence, the landlord would have to show that it was intolerable to live under the same roof as the tenant. Because the hearings would be so burdensome, it was usual to put them on for hearing at the end of the list. Lawyers involved would get used to sitting in court waiting with dogged patience to the preceding cases. There was the slimmest chance that something interesting might happen.

There was nothing for me to do but sit and listen. The afternoon crawled on until eventually there was only one more case ahead of mine. The Plaintiff, a heavily-built, lugubrious Nigerian, was represented by a local solicitor whose plummy, pessimistic voice had earned him the title, "Solicitor-General of Windsor." He was a large, flabby man who was always in such a hurry, he did not have time to change before he came into court. In winter, he wore an overcoat and a scarf under his solicitor's gown and would always leave court with his yellowing bands still attached to his collar. Sarcastic rumour had it that he wanted to be ready to leave quickly if he were to hear that his office was burning down.

The case was essentially a claim for damages for assault but the solicitor had wisely advised the Plaintiff not to bring a private prosecution in the magistrates' court because there was a statutory provision which would prevent him bringing this civil action to recover damages as well.

The defendant landlord, a very small man, was white. He was a medical doctor. He occupied the ground floor of the house. The Plaintiff and his cousin were tenants of the top floor. The kitchen was on the middle floor and was shared between the occupants of the upper and lower floors. A timetable had been devised at some time in the past which regulated who could use it and when.

Discord arose when the doctor intruded on the upper-floor tenants' time zones. Finally, an incident occurred on which the current litigation was based. The Plaintiff and his cousin were on their way down to the kitchen at their designated time. The cousin was carrying a frying pan and a bowl of eggs when the doctor came up from his quarters and was alleged to have provoked trouble.

I found that this case was beginning to be interesting: the puny doctor against the giant counterpart.

The Plaintiff went into the witness box, towering over it, to give evidence.

Windsor's "Solicitor-General", in his characteristic voice, went through his examination-in-chief.

"Did you go into the kitchen?"

"No, sir."

"Why was that?"

"The Landlord, sir. The doctor. He was standing in front of the kitchen door with his arms out, like Jesus Christ, sir." The Plaintiff spread his massive arms wide to demonstrate. " 'You not going in here,' is what he said, sir."

"What did you do?"

"I said to the man, 'I'm going to take you to the Rent Tribunal'."

"Did that have any effect on the Landlord?"

"Yes sir! He put down his arms and gets hold of me by the – by the ...." The witness had a problem finding or remembering the right word.

"Where did he get hold of you?"

The Plaintiff took a deep breath. At the risk of offending the court, he said, "By the ... by the ... by the b-b-balls, sir." He looked at the Judge whose eyes were fixed on the notes he was writing intently. "I had a terrible pain," he added. "I could not go to work because of this pain. I lost my wages."

I could imagine that to carry out this act, the doctor could no longer have been barricading the door.

"While this no doubt excruciatingly painful event was taking place, did anyone else see what was happening?"

The Plaintiff said that the cousin was there.

In due course, the frying-pan-holding cousin was called. He was a strange-looking man with probably the most pronounced lantern jaw since the Hapsburg dynasty. He had no hesitation in describing what he had seen. In heavily accented but perfect English he said sternly, "He got hold of my cousin by the – by the – ah – person, sir."

Again, the judge did not look up as he took a careful note.

The "Solicitor-General" asked, "Did you do anything?" There was the sort of silence in court that means every listener has held his breath for a moment, waiting for a frightful denouement or an unpleasant description of what happened next.

The cousin looked at his hands. We could imagine them holding the heavy iron pan. The court hung on his words.

"Well, sir – I said to myself, this is the time to fry them eggs. So I did."

The anticlimax was terrible.

The judge could barely contain himself. Judicial control did not quite go out of the window but it is a fair description to say that he was absolutely creased.

I returned to chambers in due course and, needless to say, I told the story. The sentence went into history, only slightly truncated as, "This has got to be the time to fry them eggs." It became a catch phrase in chambers for many years, guaranteed to lift the heaviest of moods.

Many months later, I appeared in front of Harry Leon at his new base in Willesden Court. It was a rather dull road traffic accident case. The witnesses were dull, my opponent was dull, the mood in the court was – dull. It soon became clear that my client had been in the wrong and we were going to lose the case.

My opponent asked the witness, "After you got out of the car, did you say something?"

Leon leaned forward, stony-faced. "I will check my notes," he said. Then, "Yes. My record is, 'He said to me: This is the time to fry the eggs.'"

My opponent woke up. "There has been a fundamental misunderstanding, Your Honour. Nothing like that was said."

"Mr Sherrard?" Leon looked at me, po-faced.

I pretended to look at my note. "Yes, Your Honour. I have certainly heard words to that effect before." I pointed to lines in my note-book. "This is the time to fry the eggs."

The opponent was rightly enraged. The judge said, "I will see you both in my room." He left the court. The opponent was furious. "F… him," he said, "I don't know what's going on here. I'm not going!" But he did.

The judge was still laughing when we went into the room. "I'm sorry," he said when he could draw breath, then burst into laughter again. "I couldn't resist frying the eggs – Michael, tell him the story!" I was laughing when I told it, Harry's laughter was so infectious. Within a couple of minutes, even the opponent joined in.

Harry Leon was, of course, going to find against me and he would certainly have done no injustice to the hapless Plaintiff. I knew that I had lost as soon as he referred to his "note".

CHAPTER 16

JOHN MAUDE

At the Old Bailey, the judges are guests of the Lord Mayor of London[1]. Ancient ceremonial involves the Lord Mayor, the High Sheriff or an Alderman, dressed in full regalia to see judges into court. The traditional sound of a gavel striking outside the judge's door signals that he is about to enter: almost like Morse Code there is one tap followed by a long gap then two short, staccato taps. The City representative sees the judge to his seat. At least once a year the judge is presented with a nosegay as part of the tradition of remembering both the need to be protected from the foul odours of the Old Bailey's predecessor, Newgate Prison, and to commemorate the occupants of the tumbrel-cart taking them from the cells to the gallows at Tyburn. The judge accepts the nosegay, bows and takes his seat. The dignitary leaves and goes to accompany the next judge. The combined simplicity and grandeur was, and remains, something that is truly remarkable.

From John Maude's first day as an Old Bailey judge, he perfected the drama of the occasion and made a grand entrance. He waited as the Sheriff or Alderman knocked at the door. Everyone in court rose. The dignitary entered and took up his position but Maude held back. The general public held their breath in the gallery, waiting for something to happen. It was like this every time from then on. Maude would choose his moment to emerge from the doorway and sweep into the courtroom. There would be another palpable pause before, drawing his gown about him, he made a slight shift of the shoulders, to be taken as a bow to the dignitary followed by a gesture with his hand, a deprecatory wave, signifying that he considered the escorting duty completed. He would then take his seat and, with what seemed to be an innate rather than a practised flourish, flick back the trailing sleeves of his robe, place his elbows on the leather desk-top, press his arched finger-tips together and exhale, "Nnhh-ye-e-e-essss…" as his signal that he was ready to hear the sound of his own voice.

The speech tones that resonated through his nose and characterised his court performances must have been practised intensely from the time his voice broke: it was impossible for there to have been any precur-

---

[1] The Common Serjeant and the Recorder are officers of the City of London.

sor in the form of a childish treble. The voice was used for dramatic purposes, occasionally enhanced by a sneering downturn of the corners of the mouth accompanied by an intense flaring of the nostrils or an approximation of the eyebrows. The resonance increased with each dramatic emphasis.

His peculiar turn of phrase together with the extraordinarily nasal delivery made mimicry, a talent which I recognise I have, not only easy but almost essential. It was with delight that I could, many years later, recite the sentencing remarks he made to two young men convicted of indecent behaviour: "You dirty beasts [*nnhyow dhuuurrty bnheasts*...] – misbehaving yourselves [*nnnhyhoursyelves* ...] – and under one of London's loveliest bridges too ... A moment of madness it has been called. I am not going to send you to prison – now go away and pull yourselves together ..."

And again, there was the utter pleasure of being able to repeat the speech he made to an itinerant labourer convicted of malicious damage (drunk and disorderly for the umpteenth time). He had smashed glasses and mirrors and wrecked tables in yet another pub – "...it's the dusty work, sor, it gives you the thirst, sor..." pleaded the defendant, begging not to be sent to prison again.

"It's all very well for you to say you won't do it again but we can't have the inn-keepers of London under repeated attack from people like you ... I take note that you are hard-working and have managed to hold down a job in spite of this disgraceful behaviour. But this must not happen again ... I'm going to give you a chance. I'm going to put you on probation."

"God bless you, sor!"

"But there must be conditions."

"Ah yes sor, anything you say, sor!"

"To protect the public, we must keep you dry for three years, do you understand?"

"Sor, I do! Dry, sor." Hysteria and relief.

"You will not touch alcohol in any shape or form." Utterly sincere.

"I'll do it sor, I will. I'll do it!"

Over his half-moon glasses: "Yes. Seriously. Not even a teeny drop of sherry before dinner."

"God love ye, sor!"

A disdainful wave of the hand.

"Nnnnhtyake hyimm dyown."

***

Despite his precious mannerisms, John Maude was well-liked at the Bar. There are tales of his *bons mots* which justify recording for posterity.

A young Spanish student was a witness to a brutal killing in a lodging house in London. His statement to the police was to the effect that, hearing a violent voice threatening to kill, he had rushed from his room and, looking over the stair-rail, found that he was close enough to see what had happened. He was expected to give evidence that a man lying on the floor was bleeding profusely from the chest. Unfortunately, no-one had mentioned to prosecuting counsel that the witness' reaction to the sight – or memory of the sight – of blood was to faint. Two or three times, the witness was brought gently to the vital point, only to turn deathly pale and collapse in the witness box. Judge Maude to the rescue!

"Usher, I want you to stand close behind Mr Gonzalez and if he appears about to faint I want you to catch him as he falls." He drops his usual languid demeanour and turns to address the witness. "Do please listen to me while together we try to help you tell the jury what you saw. Now, I am going to read my note of the evidence to the point where you collapsed. I want you then, very quickly, to tell us what you saw."

Gonzalez nods and gives a slight moan. Maude rattles off the evidence to the crucial point then commands him, "Now tell us, right away, what you saw. Now! Now! Now!"

The witness moans again and falls silently into the usher's arms. Maude sighs and signals to the usher with an outward flick of the wrist to help Mr Gonzalez from the witness box and out of court.

The ensuing silence is broken by Maude addressing the jury thus:

"Poor, poor fellow!" A longish, thoughtful pause. "How he must *detest* bull-fighting."

To Reggie Seaton, his rough-diamond sparring partner in chambers before he was appointed, the voice was a weapon in the class war that characterised the post-war years. While Seaton was still smarting from word having got out that he had spent most of a recent night waiting in his parked car at a farm gate (having believed it was a level crossing that was taking rather a long time to open), he was invited to Maude's house in Eaton Square. He arrived early. Whilst waiting for his host to come down to greet him, he passed the time looking at a large aquarium set into an alcove. As John came into the room Reggie said, "What fascinating fish! Where do they come from?"

A nasal sigh. A pause.

"Harrods ... "

It was all in the voice.

And the voice nearly got Michael into trouble. In the early 60s, Michael was defending one of the accused involved in a six-handed affray, an unpleasant business that had taken place outside a cinema in Stamford Hill in North London. John Maude was the trial judge. The sneer was a fixed feature on the judicial countenance and the voice was frequently put to use as he took every opportunity to interrupt, putting in the boot whenever he thought that the prosecution had not been sufficiently aggressive.

My client is being cross-examined. John Maude has a deadly question, the answer to which is certain to sink the defendant without a trace. I try not to huddle into my gown and am glad that its folds hide my shoulders as I hold my breath in almost unbearable anticipation. I await the response with dread. I can feel it coming.

But the answer turns out to be breast high in favour of the defence! No-one is more surprised than I am. Except the judge!

The feeling of elation must be concealed as much as the preceding fear. John Maude's eyebrows have met in the middle of his forehead but I can breathe again.

I beetle off to the shorthand-writer during the adjournment before closing speeches. "There is a short part of the transcript I need from this morning," I tell her. "Would it be possible for me to have a copy before I make my closing speech?" Somehow, I break the standard "No" barrier. I have the words, straight from the judge's mouth.

I go through the basics of what has to be said on my client's behalf. The jury pays polite attention. Then, holding the transcript, and looking directly at the most interested juror, I say, "Wiser words than mine – if I may say so, a wiser head than mine – " (a slight inclination of my head towards the judge). " … you may remember His Lordship's question …"

I read from the transcript. I am entranced by it as the judge's words flow. Unfortunately, although it is me speaking, it is also, without me being aware, his voice. With every vocal mannerism as perfect as if uttered by him. Every "nnnh", every extended vowel. Although looking at the script, I am able to glance towards the jury occasionally and am aware that they are more than usually alert. In the background, I begin to notice a tap-tap-tap sound from the bench and look up to see the furious, fully flared nostrils almost trumpeting at me.

"There will be no more of that, Mr Sherrard," he says, in a perfect imitation of himself, every word more nasal than the last. A glare. "No more of that!"

I am a millimetre away from a reprimand. Yet I hear the tones of his voice escape from my lips.

"Not if I can help it, my Lord."

"Nhhlets ghet orhn."

***

Years passed and John Maude retired. At his chambers retirement party, an old friend toasted him. He lifted his glass and said, "Well, John, I want to state publicly that there is no justification for saying that you were a judge given to the occasional flashes of silence.

GOING—to jail. Constance Smith.
Waiting for her—Rotha film parts

Constance Smith, 1961

CHAPTER 17

BLOOD AND GUTS

Blood and guts were not Michael's stock-in-trade. The escalating order of criminal brutality is not reflected chronologically in his career. Very serious matters, such as murder, cropped up at a relatively early stage although there was often an undercurrent of luck for victims in other cases who had managed to survive horrific attacks.

It never ceased to surprise Michael that some people who are convicted of crimes of violence simply do not appear to be capable of brutality.

In 1962, he defended a beautiful young actress, Constance Smith, who had stabbed her lover, the film director Paul Rotha[1]. The case attracted huge, international press coverage because of the combinations of sex, violence, fame and beauty.

Although Rotha was married, he and Constance lived together in a small flat in Clifford's Inn. In 1960, whilst he was making what was to become one of the most important documentary films about Adolf Hitler, Constance accompanied him to Germany where she visited Dachau concentration camp. She became overwhelmed by the horror of what she saw and learned. She fell into a depression which increased as the work on the documentary progressed. Her mind was filled with the images of Nazi atrocities as she watched the films from which Rotha drew his material and listened to descriptions of the obscenities and tortures endured by the victims. While she was in Germany, she began to see every person about her as Nazi storm-troopers or camp guards. She felt as though she was living in a graveyard of innocent victims. Back in England, in the claustrophobic atmosphere of the tiny flat, the images in her mind became overwhelming. A terrible tension built up between the lovers. Rotha's wife became ill and Constance became torn between her wish for him to tell the wife about their affair and her desire for secrecy about it. She was well known as a film actress and lived in fear of the press photographing her coming and going from the flat. She took to going out in disguise but finally stopped going out at all. For six months, she stayed in the tiny flat and twice attempted suicide. On the night of December 15th 1961, she slashed her wrists with a knife and daubed the

1   Paul Rotha (1907-1984) was an outstanding documentary film-maker.

walls with her blood. When Paul Rotha returned, he did not take her attempt on her life seriously. She lunged at him with, of all things, a cheese knife. It pierced an artery in his groin: the wound was life-threatening. The lurid – but accurate – description in the press was that there was so much blood, there was enough to paint the walls of the flat. Much of that blood was Constance Smith's. But she saved Paul Rotha's life by calling for an ambulance. She was charged with attempted murder but pleaded guilty to unlawful wounding. A dignified plea in mitigation resulted in a three month sentence.

***

Another unlikely candidate for violence was Israel Small. He had been sentenced to 15 years, but it could have been the death penalty if his victim had not, miraculously, survived. I had not defended him at his trial but was called in for the appeal. I remember going to Wandsworth to discuss the case with him. He was so gentle, mild and contrite. It was very difficult to picture him using a bayonet to hack off the hand of his gypsy boss.

***

If motive is considered in crimes of violence, jealousy is a prominent feature, usually that of the wronged partner or spouse. Many years on in my career, I was asked to defend an Indian woman in Singapore on a charge of attempted murder. I thought of it as the case of the jealous mother-in-law. Her son's wife was astonishingly beautiful but the king-pin of the prosecution case was she was not to my client's liking. Some months after the marriage, a man called at the young couple's house to deliver flowers. He also delivered a jet of sulphuric acid onto the bride's face and body. She was left blinded and cruelly disfigured but she survived the attack.

The mother-in-law denied any involvement in the crime but during the course of our consultations, it became apparent that she did not like the questions that I had to ask her. She did not think that I was persuaded that she had a good case. This led, in due course, to my suggesting that she should not be inhibited from seeking someone else to represent her. And that is what she did. Stanley Clinton-Davis became the solicitor. He brought Gilbert Gray out to take over my role. He marshalled his considerable skills and she was acquitted

As my career as a junior progressed, I began to have leaders to suit my practice as much as my client. I asked for Ted Eveleigh, later Lord Justice Eveleigh, to lead me at the Bailey in a murder that had been committed in the Panama Canal when the defendants, two lads, about 19 years of age, were alleged to have pushed the gay cook out of a porthole. Our client was a clean-cut but sulky-looking youth who slouched with his hands in his pockets when we met him in the cells for the conferences before the hearing.

Ted had our man give evidence. No more sulky slouching. He was all earnest attention and polite responses. Butter wouldn't melt in his mouth. He stood smartly to attention in the witness box. I said to Ted, "He'd make a good guardsman."

"I told him to stand like that," he answered.

"Why?"

"Then his hands will be down at his side."

The evidence against them was overwhelming but they were acquitted. The trial was in an era when homosexuality was abhorrent. It was likely that the jury would have found it unacceptable for a homosexual to be allowed to work on a boat where there was a predominantly male crew.

After the acquittal, as we said our goodbyes to him, I saw our client's knuckles. Tattooed across them was the word "HATE".

***

I did quite a bit of work with Ted. His chambers were beneath mine in Crown Office Row. He always called me Michael when we met. He became a High Court Judge. High Court Judges could – and did – sit at the Old Bailey. I appeared before him in 1973 acting for one of the defendants in what has since become known as "the Bertie Smalls case". This was the first of the "grassing" cases and has become the synonym for an informant. Bertie gave evidence against his accomplices in a bank robbery in exchange for a non-custodial sentence: his subsequent unpopularity with the criminal brotherhood cannot be overestimated. Ted was going through the list of counsel for an informal directions hearing.

At the hearing, he went through all the defendants, taking note of counsel's name. Finally, he asked, "Who is defending King?"

I stood up. He recognised me instantly and in the same instant, he froze.

There was a twitch. His lips pursed for the "M" of Michael. Had he been able to remember my name, he would have said, "Yes, Mr Sherrard. But he couldn't.

"Michael Sherrard," I said. "Yes!" Ted replied with a lot of relief crammed into the one syllable.

***

All murders are shocking crimes but some murderers stand out more than others. In 1980 I prosecuted Paul Brumfitt, a chap who looked like a matinee idol. At the Old Bailey, he admitted his guilt to a charge of manslaughter of an Essex tailor and the murder in Denmark of a bus-driver. The judge, Ralph Gibson, heard of the shocking circumstances of the crimes and accepted the plea of diminished responsibility. Ralph said that Brumfitt suffered from "a psychopathic disorder which had resulted in a permanent disability of the mind." But parole was inevitably granted. He was released in 1995 and went back to his previous pastimes. And killed again: four years later he murdered another young woman, Marcella Davies. He dismembered her body then burnt it. I was interviewed by the press about this case in February 2006 when the news broke that over 30,000 prisoners had been released early from prison without supervision. The obvious question arose: how much of a risk is posed to the public when a person serving a life sentence for murder is released early? When I was asked that question in an interview, I said, "It was clear to me in 1980 that Brumfitt had all the hallmarks of a serial killer. I am horrified that he was released and it has all happened again."

CHAPTER 18

JAMES HANRATTY

BBC News, 23rd August 1961[1]

Police have launched a murder hunt after a man was found shot dead and his companion seriously wounded in a lay-by in Bedfordshire. The couple were found by a police patrol in the lay-by on the A6 at Deadman's Hill, near Luton, at 0645 BST today.

The dead man, who has been identified as physicist Michael John Gregsten, 34, had been shot twice in the head with a 38-calibre revolver. His companion, 22-year-old laboratory assistant, Valerie Storie, had been raped and shot five times in the chest. She was taken to hospital in Bedford where she underwent surgery for her injuries.

Police believe the couple, both employees of the Road Research Laboratory near Slough, were confronted by a man with a gun as they were parked on Dorney Common in Berkshire yesterday evening. They were ordered to drive to Deadman's Hill, where the attack took place.

The murderer left the scene in Mr Gregsten's grey Morris Minor which was found abandoned in Ilford, Essex, this evening.

Detectives and tracker dogs have spent the day searching the surrounding area and so far two cartridges have been found. House-to-house inquiries have also been carried out.

Miss Storie's mother said: "Michael came here last night and had tea with Valerie. They then left and took with them maps and other things to organise a car rally being held at their office this weekend.

"Valerie has worked at the laboratory since she left school five years ago and she has known Michael for a long time."

Mr Gregsten's body was tonight identified by his wife, Janet. He leaves two sons, aged seven and two.

Shirley and Michael Sherrard taking a break from Bedford Assizes,
February 1962

James Hanratty, 25 years of age, was arrested on 9th October 1961 and convicted of the murder of Valerie Storie's lover, Michael Gregsten at Bedford Assizes on February 17th, 1962. His appeal was dismissed on March 13th, and, despite a petition signed by 28,000, he was hanged at Bedford prison on April 4th. He avowed his innocence to the end. His execution was one of the last three before capital punishment was abolished three years later.

***

The Bootleg Theatre Company was run by two actors who wrote and presented a play based on a conversation between Hanratty and Alphon, the other suspect. It explored rather than answered the questions which, at the time of the trial, were unanswerable.

During the writing of the script and throughout the rehearsals, they occasionally wrote to Michael about the trial and ultimately invited him to the play. He went with Shirley. It was an extraordinary sensation for him, seeing the two men come to life, casually having a conversation that went to the root of all the anomalies in the evidence. It brought back to him how difficult it was to curb the optimism of Hanratty and his family given the lengths to which the police were prepared to go to secure a conviction. It was only recently confirmed that the presentation of the police evidence was deeply flawed: at the time, the defence dealt with what they had. In the end, the case for Hanratty was just not strong enough to persuade the jury. There were flaws all over the place, and not only from the police. But listening to the play was like living the case over again, with its painful mixture of doubts and hopes. Sitting in the theatre, Michael was like an eavesdropper, hearing the voices from the stage.

"... what did you say you did about that?"

"I told the solicitor but he couldn't be bothered with it. He didn't care."

"Did you tell your counsel?"

"Yes – that Mr Sherrard. He was a real gent. He took it very seriously."

Michael felt uncomfortable about the complimentary reference to him, as if it had been forced, even though it reflected Hanratty's confi-

93

dence in him through all the stages of the trial, the appeal and the plea for clemency. The play added to Michael's concerns about the outcome, rather than easing them.

Ted Kleinman, a solicitor who was also a long-standing friend, instructed me to deal with the committal proceedings. Hanratty was not unfamiliar with criminal court procedure. His previous convictions for car theft and other petty crimes had left him in one form of custody or another for much of the previous seven years but he was now in very serious trouble.

The case was committed for trial from the Bedford Magistrates. It had been touch and go whether they would find that there was no case to answer but the huge press interest in the horrific events meant that they must have felt that the world was waiting for the outcome of a full trial. The seriousness of the case compounded by intense local interest and the risk of bias enabled me to persuade them that the case should be remitted to the Old Bailey for trial.

I advised Hanratty that I wanted a leader. I wanted Victor Durand. Hanratty was almost in tears about that. "Why can't you do it?" he asked.

I assured him that I would still be there throughout. Even today, I am morally certain that Victor would have secured an acquittal. He was hugely admired by his clients, solicitors and the Bar. He had a big practice and had much success with juries. He was the natural first choice. I knew his style very well. He had led me many times but in nothing as weighty as this.

In persuading Hanratty that a leader was needed, I forgot my pupil-master's advice never to say, "There is only one man … "

So I told Hanratty, "There is only one man. Victor Durand. He is very good."

He was not convinced.

I said, "He is better than me. He is a star. He is a Recorder at Bedford Assizes so he has local knowledge. He really is the best." I still mean it. Because I was so fully committed to Victor's excellence, I managed to convince Hanratty that no other would do.

This gave me some difficulty when Victor was suspended from practice and could not take the case.

Victor Durand had been instructed to defend the Commissioner of Police in a civil action involving false arrest and malicious prosecution. It was a jury trial before Mr Justice Milmo. The officer who was the cause of the complaints had been demoted in internal disciplinary proceedings from Inspector to Detective Sergeant. By addressing him or referring to him as "Mister" throughout, Victor avoided the jury knowing about the demotion. The judge sent the jury out and summoned Victor to his rooms where he told him, "Your conduct is reprehensible. You and I both know that the jury may have been misled because they are not in possession of all the information they should have." The matter was brought to the attention of the Benchers of Inner Temple who suspended him for a year. It was over ten years before Victor recovered his status sufficiently to be appointed to the Bench.

Victor Durand would have conducted the Hanratty case in his own way. For one thing, he would have maintained his dour stance and been more distant from his client. I think that he would not have gone down to the cells every day as I did after the court rose. That might not have given Hanratty the chance to change his alibi. He may have been able to influence him so as not to have given evidence, particularly as, at the time, the jury was not allowed to draw any adverse inference from the silence of the accused.

Without Victor, there was no persuading Hanratty to have another leader. If there was only one man, as far as he was concerned, it was Michael Sherrard. As far as the Bar was concerned, I was very young to have such a case. I was 33 and my areas of serious crime to date without a leader had previously been commercial fraud. I was not on entirely unfamiliar territory but my previous murders had been with leaders or where my client was one of several defendants.

Having persuaded the justices at committal that a trial in Bedford would be likely to deprive Hanratty of the fair trial that could only be achieved in London, it was something of a shock when, a matter of two weeks before the case was to be listed, we appeared at the Old Bailey before the Recorder of London, Sir Anthony Hawke, who greeted us with the words, "I'm told that there is a convenient day for the hearing to start at Bedford on January 17th 1962." Graham Swanwick[1], counsel for the prosecution, had not even opened his mouth.

I was left with suspicions that there had been manoeuvring behind the scenes for the trial to take place in the court where the prosecution was most likely to succeed. No matter what my views were, the decision was not negotiable.

So we transferred.

This caused an unexpected difficulty: as a member of the South-Eastern Circuit, I required permission of the Midland and Oxford Circuit, of which, coincidentally, Graham Swanwick was the leader, to appear in the Crown Court at Bedford. I also had to rely on them to assign a junior to me. Graham resolved the problem promptly: I was permitted to lead the case and my junior was John Ellison[2]. Graham's junior was Geoffrey Lane[3].

On the day the trial began, I gave up smoking cigarettes, although small cigars remained in evidence for several more months. I hoped that God would take notice of this gesture but he may have been preoccupied.

The tale unfolded before a jury called from the Burghers of Bedford – or something similar, according to the criminal bar. They turned out to be exactly as described to this novice: all male, middle-class, white, property-owning gentry. From the outset, they appeared to be all too likely to live up to the Bedford reputation of being of the notoriously hard-nosed hang-'em, flog-'em school of justice. We were together for over four gruelling weeks, then the longest murder trial in English history.

The gloom of the situation was alleviated by the knowledge that we had been given a delightful judge, Mr Justice Gorman, to take the trial. He was a Liverpudlian who was later to become a Treasurer of Middle Temple.

There was enormous press coverage of the trial, given the horrific circumstances of the attack and Valerie Storie's consequent plight. The *Sunday Pictorial*, for example, took a not entirely accurate interest in

[1]   Later a judge at the Old Bailey
[2]   Later to be the Attorney-General of Bermuda
[3]   Geoffrey Lane, subsequently QC, Lord Chief Justice 1980 – 1992

matters peripheral to the main events. It reported that "the dark-haired Shirley, niece of the newly knighted Sir Leon Bagrit, was in court every day, flashing Mr Sherrard a confident smile as the other lawyers in the court admired his Perry Mason style …"

When not being dazzled by Shirley's smile, the press was fascinated by the cut and thrust of cross-examination, reporting it almost as if it were an entertainment. But it is fair to say that histrionics are out today: the tough approach and the skilful use of language on which the press enjoyed elaborating is no longer the style. The magic has gone out of words.

The *Sunday Pictorial* maintained its lack of reliability to the extent that Shirley's grandfather was rather upset to learn from one of its articles that she was expecting her third child. In fact, he was blazing mad. He rang her as soon as he had read the story, demanding to know what was going on.

"Why wasn't I told first? This is a terrible shock to think that you would rather tell a newspaper and not your own grandfather!" He was distraught. He would not believe Shirley when she said, "It just isn't true. I'm not pregnant – of course I would have told you."

"If it's in the papers, it must be true," he insisted. She handed the phone to me. I explained, "Look, sometimes the newspapers make a mistake. Do you remember when they wrote that Shirley has blue eyes? You know she has brown eyes. So that is a mistake."

"Blue eyes? You're right – but how could they make such a mistake? How do I know if they haven't made other mistakes?" We left him with his faith in the press shaken.

***

The trial progressed slowly. After two or three weeks, it was getting near to the time when the prosecution case would end. I went to the cells on my routine visit

"I want to go in the box, sir," Hanratty insisted. I was not happy about that. The law did not require him to do so. The only thing I was concerned with that he could contribute sparked from his blank denials of any part in the crime. There were questions that would arise about this alibi which hinged upon him being in Liverpool and meeting three

97

men. He would be asked who they were, their names and why he was visiting.

I said, "Look, Jim, you'll have to explain why you were in Liverpool. You'll be asked these questions and you will have to reply."

"I can tell that, sir," he answered. Then he looked down and said, "Well – actually, I wasn't in Liverpool."

My whole case preparation from the moment that committal proceedings had begun had been based on his presence in Liverpool. After a time, I realised that I had probably been holding my breath. That was the only way to account for the perfect silence in the cell after he had spoken. Hanratty's gaze remained fixed on the floor. He began to explain what was to become "the Rhyl alibi", a new account of his whereabouts at the time of the murder. Ted Kleinman immediately took a new statement from him, had it typed up and arranged for a clerk to deliver it to my hotel room in Bedford. I had been waiting for it to see how I was going to dig myself and my client out of the gaping chasm that it had created.

Late that night, there was a knock at the hotel door. The clerk had arrived with the statement. Or should have arrived with it. As he greeted me saying, "I expect you'll be pleased to be able to get to work on this, sir," he put his hand into the inside pocket of his jacket to retrieve the statement. His smile quickly changed to a frown and then a look of horror.

"My God," he said. "I've lost the bloody statement!"

"You can't have!" I did not believe it could have been lost. It had to be there. "See if it's in your coat pocket." It was a freezing night and he was wearing an overcoat with two deep pockets. He dug into those, to no avail.

"Take the jacket off," I said. "See if there's a hole in the lining!"

But there was not.

"I must have dropped it somewhere," he said. I thought he was going to faint.

"Look," I said, "just retrace your steps. Hurry – go back to where you collected it and just keep your eye out for it. It must be somewhere."

I helped him back into his jacket and coat. I opened the door to see him out only to find a nice policeman standing outside with his hand raised, ready to knock. Smiling, he said, "I think you've dropped something." He handed over the long, manila envelope and gave us back Hanratty's new attempt to save his life.

The police were in Rhyl before I had finished reading the statement...

The judge worked very hard to reduce the consequences of Hanratty's introduction of a new version of his whereabouts on the night of the murder. He said, "He does not have to prove his alibi. The failure or otherwise of the alibi does not make him guilty. You do not have to rely on it." He gave the jury a perfectly good direction.

He was bursting himself to indicate to the jury that he did not think the case was strong enough. His summing-up, in his high-pitched voice, was a model of fairness, emphasizing that the jury had to be sure and making points that I would not have dared to do had I been in his place.

Graham and I had been invited to several lunches in the Judge's Lodgings throughout the long weeks of the trial. The guests included the Leader of Circuit, the High Sheriff of Bedfordshire and the Director of Public Prosecutions. Our last invitation was to tea during the ten-hour wait for the verdict. Part of the waiting time was spent drinking the whisky brought by the DPP. At one point, a note came in from the jury. We thought it was a question about the evidence but it was their own request for tea. The judge was outraged. He calmed down after a couple of minutes then resumed polite conversation.

"Well, Michael," he said, "I think I've looked after you pretty well." Had I known what the verdict was going to be, I might have said, "Too well." A smile was the only possible response at the time.

We waited and waited. The jury were out for nearly ten hours. I convinced myself that being out for so long meant that there would be an acquittal. But the Foreman said "Guilty," and that was the end.

The donning of the black cap as the precursor to the sentence is chilling beyond belief, the words of the sentence freeze the mind and heart.

"... that you suffer death in the manner authorised by law and may God have mercy on your soul ..."

Going down to see him in the cells after the verdict was very hard. What do you say to someone who has been sentenced to die within a matter of weeks? When I came to the last step at the bottom of the stairway, he was facing me, each hand cuffed to a warder on either side. My first thought was, "He looks so young."

I approached him and whilst I was trying to think of something – anything – to say, he reached out to me. The warder's arm followed the gesture in a grotesque shadow. He took my hand and said, "Don't you go upsetting yourself, sir. You've done everything you could. We'll appeal."

My voice an echo: "Yes. We'll appeal."

The journey back to London was a combination of self-recrimination and future planning for the start of the appeal process. The whole balance of the case had been altered by the late alibi, the subject of fearsome prosecution criticism. The bulk of the cross-examination took place on that topic. It was much easier for the prosecution to destroy a vulnerable alibi than to rely on circumstantial evidence presented by dubious witnesses. Hanratty himself was a likeable, articulate character, a Cockney sparrow, quite up to the mark on repartee whilst maintaining a reasonable demeanour before the court. He did not do that badly on the alibi but perhaps he was lucky not have been cross-examined by Geoffrey Lane. I had not wanted him to give evidence, but it was his choice and he would afterwards not have had any regrets about failing to take part in what was a matter of his own life or death.

There was no going back on the events of the trial. The next stage was planning who should lead me in the effort to save Hanratty's life. The first thing I did when back in chambers was to secure, with considerable effort, Gerald Gardiner QC[1] to conduct the appeal. Within days of the verdict it had become plain there was a groundswell of heavyweight protests. Views were expressed by Lord Russell of Liverpool, Paul Foot and Louis Blom-Cooper: they all believed that there was something wrong with the conviction. This might have influenced Gerald, the most highly-respected silk on the cab-rank, to agree to take the case. My mood lifted at once.

---

[1] Gerald Gardiner QC, Lord Chancellor, 1964.

I went to see Hanratty as soon as I had the news. We were given a cell for the conference. He was brought in, handcuffed to a warder. As the cuff was being unlocked so that he could talk to me in relative freedom, I started to tell him what was happening.

"Good news," I said. "Gerald Gardiner can do the appeal!"

Hanratty looked down, in much the same way that he had when I had told him that we had to have a silk for the trial.

"He is outstanding," I assured him. "He's just what we need for the Court of Appeal."

He continued to stare at the floor. "I don't want anyone else."

"I need someone!" I could hear myself pleading with him.

The handcuff was now undone. He squared his shoulders back and, after a long moment, looked at me directly. "If I'm going down," he said, "I'm going down with you." He spoke politely but there was no arguing with him. That was the way he wanted things to be and as far as he was concerned, that was that. I was on my own again, bearing an unimaginably heavy responsibility.

In spite of Hanratty's confidence, Michael's arguments failed to persuade the Court of Appeal.

Another visit to the prison. Another expression of confidence from Hanratty. The only hope now was to visit the Home Office to see if the Home Secretary, R A Butler, could be persuaded to grant a reprieve.

The visit to the Home Office was like a scene from "Yes, Minister" except that it turned out to be a "No, Minister" scenario.

The Head of the Civil Service, Sir James Cunningham, rang about the appointment. He was totally on top of it. They had evidence of remarks made by Hanratty on remand, things that, on the Home Office view, only he could have known if he was the true murderer. The Home Office was frustrated that these matters had not been used fully in the trial. Nor could they have been. But, although inadmissible to the jury, the Home Secretary was entitled to look all the inadmissible material, whether from the prosecution or the defence. He was particularly interested in the story of the prison hospital officer, Alfred Eatwell, who had reported hearing a prisoner, Roy Langdale, describe a conversation with Hanratty including details of the crime before the trial had taken place. Hanratty had denied the story and, more to the point, as I was assured by friends, I had totally destroyed Eatwell in cross-examination. Nevertheless, Sir James pointed out that the Home Secretary would be influenced by the full information made available to him.

The atmosphere was not promising during that long afternoon at the Home Office as Sir James watched me, unconstrained by the rules of the English courts, pace about the room as I went through the written argument that I had set out as the basis of my petition for a reprieve. Finally, there was nothing more to be said. I returned to the uncomfortable seat that I had been offered. He said, "Drop of sherry before you go?"

This was the sign that our business had been concluded and we could now be sociable.

"You will let us know if anything else occurs to you, won't you?" It might have been a conversation about a business plan.

"Of course," I said. It was the only thing to say under the circumstances.

Sir James became quite affable. "May I say, I think you've put up a very good show." He smiled. "Another sherry?"

The response came from the Home Office on April 2nd, 1962.

"Clemency is refused."

Ted Kleinman, my instructing solicitor, wrote to the Hanratty family. The family sent a telegram to the Queen. Her Majesty replied that the telegram had been forwarded to the Home Secretary.

It was the end.

The warders were in tears when they heard. They had got to know him and liked him.

I went to the prison and said goodbye to Hanratty, aware more than ever of the irony that his life would end, as did Gregsten's, because of the events on Deadman's Hill.

The High Sheriff attended: he was still unconvinced by the evidence.

It was my wedding anniversary on April 5th, the day after the hanging. We were too sad to celebrate.

***

It turned out that evidence was retained, frozen, to await the new technology that was eventually used: Valerie Storie's knickers; Hanratty's handkerchief. When the 2002 forensic results came through, confirming that there was a 1:2.5 million chance of the DNA on the handkerchief and knickers not being from Hanratty, one of the actors from the Bootleg Theatre Compnay telephoned Michael.

"So, do you think he did it?" he asked.

Michael gave him the only answer he could. "I think the court is going to think so."

"What shall we do?" he asked. Michael was puzzled. He could not think that these DNA results would affect the actor.

He explained, "All our livelihood is in the play. We thought it would run forever."

Perhaps they had to change the ending.

Whatever its final outcome, the play made me think again about what must have been in the jury's collective mind as it went through its deliberations during the long hours which gave us hope that there would be an acquittal. Had the jury speculated on why Gregsten and Storie had gone to that particular country field in the first place, if not set up to it, perhaps by his family, wanting to frighten her off? Had they wondered why so many shady characters turned up as witnesses, having suddenly become good citizens, ready to deal with the police in a way that hitherto had not been their custom? And what would they have made of the police fiddling with witness statements, had modern forensic hand-writing tests been available to them? Hanratty would have been proved to have been telling the truth about much of what had been altered. Things like that would not have turned back the DNA-test-clock, but …

The "buts" are and were many in this extraordinary matter.

In the end, the Court of Appeal did not think it was necessary to decide about how the evidence was presented and whether, as modern tests indicate and as was part of Hanratty's case, it had been tampered with. The fact of the DNA results does not vindicate their methods. But ...

Detective Superintendent Oxford, eventually knighted, was the number two man in the investigation team. I formed the opinion that he was a very subtle operator. People who met him – including the jury, no doubt – could not help but be impressed with his personality. The comparison with the dour, almost clumsy style of the other important player, DS Acott, was like that of the proverbial chalk and cheese. In the run-up to the recent appeal process, he was to be asked about the integrity of the police notes. But he had a heart attack and died. His explanation for the forensic findings of alterations will never be heard.

There has been a suggestion that Hanratty was a hit man and that police were investigating other offences in which they believed he was implicated. He was alleged to have said, in the car in which he was arrested, "I've done the lot." I treated the words as a boast that was easily explained by his criminal CV. He had, indeed, done the lot: Borstal, corrective training, prison, preventive detention. The prosecution took the line that he was a small-time burglar who had not "done the lot" until now. Graham Swanwick and Geoffrey Lane simply used the evidence provided by the police. The closing speech was scrupulously fair. "Let's consider the best version for the defendant," Graham said, something along the lines of describing Brutus as an honourable man.

The evidence that confirmed Hanratty's guilt, so far as the appeal process is concerned, is the DNA. But who would have thought that, for 31 years, the police would have kept, on ice, Valerie Storie's knickers and the handkerchief that wrapped the gun? Or exhumed him for DNA matches?

Perhaps modern techniques would have changed the way that the evidence was presented and there would have been a clearer understanding of the way that the jury came to its conclusions.

Perhaps.

CHAPTER 19

DS CHALLENOR

The story of Detective Sergeant Challenor[1] has become synonymous with corruption in the police. He was ultimately detained at Her Majesty's Pleasure pending his recovery from mental illness, so never stood trial for the charges of conspiracy to pervert the course of justice which were brought against him. In 1964, the Government commissioned a judicial enquiry "into the circumstances in which it was possible for Detective Sergeant Harold Gordon Challenor of the Metropolitan Police to continue on duty at a time when he appears to have been affected by the onset of mental illness." He was found to have been suffering from paranoid schizophrenia from April 1963 but it will never be known whether this or overwhelming zeal was a reason for the planting of evidence on at least twenty-six of those he arrested.

Challenor had an outstanding service record in World War II. As a member of the Special Air Services, he was the only survivor of a ten-man unit parachuted into Italy. He was captured, tortured and sentenced to be shot but he managed to escape and was awarded the Military Medal for his activities with the partisans. After the war, he joined the police. In 1962 he was stationed at West End Central Police Station in London, dealing with the maintenance of law and order in the Soho district. His system of dealing with the people he arrested was simple: he brought them back to the station and if they were empty-handed, he would produce a weapon, actual or improvised. He then thrust it at the accused saying, "That's yours. Sign for it."

In August 1963, Michael was instrumental in Challenor's downfall.

Queen Frederika of Greece was a political pariah of the left in London. She was followed by protesters with banners everywhere she went, including the theatre. Sgt Challenor was put in charge of her safety and arrested a great many protesters who had allegedly harassed her. The conviction rate was high.

Stanley Clinton-Davis had briefed me in a different case which had nothing to do with the protest. He rang me to say that our case at Marlborough Street Magistrates' Court might be delayed because of the long

---

1 Harold Challenor MM 1922-2008.

list of cases involving the most recent protest against Queen Frederika. His idea was that we should meet in the court lobby to see whether we might be transferred to another court.

He went ahead of me to the cells to speak to our client. After I had had a few words with the Clerk, I went to meet Stanley in the cell area. He beckoned to me to go with him to the space at the foot of the stairs leading from the cells to the courts above. He looked anxious.

"What's the matter?" I asked him.

"I've just had a rather worrying encounter. I saw our client and told him that there would be a delay. As I left him, I heard a man sobbing in the group of prisoners waiting to come up. It sounded so pitiful. He was a middle-aged man, sitting on the bench with his head in his hands, in real distress. I asked him,' What's your problem?'

"He said, 'I was arrested last night. I can't believe what's happening to me. I've been framed by a policeman. I can't get in touch with my family. It's a nightmare …'

"What exactly does he mean – 'framed by a policeman?'" I asked.

Stanley said, "I asked him what happened. And this is what he told me. 'I was walking along the street carrying a protest banner. A police officer grabbed hold of me and marched me up the road to Saville Row police station. He took me into a room, opened a locker and took out a brick. He smashed it on a window ledge and put one of the two chunks into my hand. He said, 'This is down to you – offensive weapon!' The next thing I know, I'm here and that's the evidence that's going to be used.' He broke down again, so I only managed to find out that he is Donald Rooum, a political cartoonist. Would you see him? I'd like to help him but I need to have your view."

I was intrigued by the story. If it was true, it was shocking. A grave miscarriage of justice could take place if the court were to rely on the police evidence.

Stanley introduced me. I started our meeting by telling him that I was a barrister and that I, too, would like to help him. The sobbing came under control. His shoulders sagged. His relief that we were interested in helping him was almost palpable.

"I understand that you have explained the events to Mr Clinton-Davis," I said, "but I need you to start at the beginning of the evening in question and tell me everything that happened before you were locked up for the night." I went on, "Mr Clinton-Davis and I both think, from what you've told us, that the police officer will stick to his story in court and say he found the brick in your pocket so we think it will help if you can describe as much of the detail of the events as you can remember."

We learned from his description that the brick was most likely to be of the variety called Marston Valley but it was also clear that, whatever size or make of brick it was, Donald Rooum's trouser and jacket pockets were too skimpy to accommodate a portion of brick which might be described as being an offensive weapon.

I looked in his pockets and confirmed for myself that there was no trace of brick dust. Stanley Clinton-Davis knew of an experienced forensic investigator who would be able to help. I felt that we were off to a fine start.

Rooum was still worried. "How are you going to prove that I didn't have the brick?"

"I'll ask the magistrate this morning to order you to get out of your suit and put on a white boiler suit. " I explained that the court kept that sort of clothing for use when the defendants' own clothing might be needed in evidence. "Mr Clinton-Davis will take your suit to an expert forensic scientist, Ferdinand de Keyser. He'll make a report very quickly but you may have to wait here in the cells until the end of the day in court."

I persuaded the magistrate, Mr St John Harmsworth, to authorise the change of clothing and make an order for bail effective at the end of the afternoon or sooner if the suit was returned. Donald Rooum actually smiled when the magistrate fixed an early date for the trial.

Mr Harmsworth was also the sitting stipendiary magistrate on the day fixed for the trial. We arrived at court, complete with the forensic report which gave us a great deal with which to attack the police officer. I was looking forward to the trial but Challenor did not appear. Mr Harmsworth put the case back for a week. Just as we were leaving the court building, Challenor arrived, out of breath as if he had been hurrying to get there. Naturally, we thought we should go back into court and said so. He looked as keen as we were to see the matter through.

"Oh no," Challenor said. "I'm off! See you next week." And off he went.

We were back the next week before a different magistrate, Edward Robey[1]. His previous career had been as a prosecutor with the DPP. One could only hope that he would not be too sympathetic towards prosecution deficiencies!

The public gallery was full: mainly members of Rooum's family and his supporters. A large number of reporters were also there.

Challenor went into the box for the first time to lay the charge. He was quite lively, even cocky, and seemed to be doing a little tap-dance. Mr Robey, who at the best of times, had a detached air in court, seemed not to mind.

Rooum pleaded not guilty and was allowed to sit down in the dock.

I now had the forensic scientist's report. There was not a scrap of brick-dust in Rooum's pockets, just the usual detritus, dust and fluff. Nothing brick-coloured at all. Brick is particularly friable and would always leave its mark.

During the cross-examination of Challenor, I put the allegation of the "frame-up" to him. The silence in the courtroom as I spoke was as if everyone present, save for Challenor and Robey, was holding their breath.

"You planted this brick on Mr Rooum by putting it into his hand, didn't you?"

The charged atmosphere, and probably the question as well, seemed not to have entered Robey's consciousness. He seemed not be concentrating on the proceedings at all.

"No I never," said Challenor, smiling as if I had said something amusing. "I found this brick in his pocket, pulled it out, then put it in his hand. 'What's it doing in your pocket,' I asked him. 'What do you want this brick for?' He just laughed. I said, 'Soon get that laugh out of your skin.'"

---

[1] Son of the stage and music hall star, George Robey.

I continued. "This was a deliberate frame-up by *you*, wasn't it?"

"Who? Me?" snarled Challenor through his now rigid smile, quite unnoticed by Robey. He was gripping the front rail of the witness box as if to restrain himself. There began to be something hysterical about his demeanour and his eyes were dancing as he glanced about the court-room.

"Do you see anyone else in the witness box?" I asked.

"Who else," I said again, fascinated to see a look of fear come across Challenor's face as he took the question literally and turned his head, looking about him in all directions towards the canopy and sides that enclosed the stand as if to see who else might be there. Then he said something that sounded like, "Just a minute," turned his back on Mr Robey and peered around to the entry steps.

I glanced at Mr Robey, expecting some reaction, although he had not been interested enough in the witness' demeanour to look up from his notebook for the past two or three minutes. He seemed not to notice what was going on. He was like a wax-work, although not as lively.

"Who else do you see?" I said. But there was no answer, only Challenor looking around, now in apparent terror.

Challenor was about to step out of the witness box, my point having been made by default even before turning to the expert report. I thought at this point that Robey would have been satisfied that there was at least a reasonable doubt so that he would not need to hear any more from me. But learning that Mr de Keyser was in court waiting to give evidence in support of the defence, Mr Robey, with a sigh of apparent reluctance, asked in a flat, bored tone, to look at the report and put it to Challenor.

I noticed that Mr Robey was handling the piece of brick on his blotting pad, the severed portion that Rooum had described to me. It was the first sign that he was interested in the trial. I waited. I was much encouraged and began to think that he might – as he could have done – acquit there and then. Eventually, much to my surprise, he indicated that he would hear me. "Yes," he said, without much enthusiasm. "Oh yes, I want to hear you."

I stated my case, telling the story that Rooum told me. The brick was broken by Challenor and planted on Rooum by putting it into his hand.

Now he was interested.

An expression of distaste formed on his face. He drummed his fingers as I spoke. Finally, he said in tone of cold outrage, spitting out each word as if reminding a naughty schoolboy how to behave, "Policemen don't behave like that!"

"I'm not accusing *policemen*," I said. "I'm accusing *this* officer. You have been witness to his behaviour just a few minutes ago."

Then I noticed him fiddling with the brick. There was a line of red dust on the blotting pad in front of him.

"Forgive me drawing you directly into this matter, sir. But you have brick dust scattered from just a minute of touching the brick on the blotter. It is not conceivable that there could be no trace of brick-dust on or in the defendant's clothes if the brick had been in his pocket."

There was a sigh from the bench.

"I suppose you are right, he said reluctantly. There is a doubt about it ..."

***

Outside court Stanley said, "What do you suppose he did with the other half of the brick?"

***

The other half has a story of its own. A young Greek Cypriot called Apostolou had been hauled up in South-Western Magistrates' Court in Wandsworth, charged with possession of an offensive weapon. He had been accused of involvement in the Frederika protest. It turned out that 'his' brick fragment fitted the Rooum part. The lad had been convicted. Stanley instructed me to conduct his appeal on the grounds that the piece of brick had been planted. The appeal succeeded. Successive magistrates involved in the first instance trials and the appeals made telling observations based on Apostolou's half-brick fitting the part forced on Rooum.

We soon learned that there was a string of similar cases in which several defendants had also accused Challenor in open court of planting weapons on them. But another magistrate was angered by the accusation and said that it was a disgrace for legal aid to be so misused as to support people who made such outrageous allegations against the police!

Public outcry about the miscarriages of justice caused by Challenor's efforts led to an internal police enquiry. This revealed that his activities were known to other officers who had colluded with him. In 1964, Challenor was one of four policemen who were charged with conspiracy to pervert the course of justice. Challenor became too sick to stand trial. The remaining three were convicted, despite the best efforts of their counsel, Victor Durand QC, by then back in harness.

They got a couple of years each from Fred Lawton. In sentencing them, he said, "Honest police officers are the buttress of society. But dishonest, perjured officers are like an infernal machine ticking away to the destruction of us all."

Privately, he always mentioned that I was responsible for bringing the other cases to light which led to the conviction of the police officers.

A public enquiry followed the trial, conducted by the Recorder of Derby, Mr Arthur James QC[1], and two other silks. All interested parties could be, and were, represented. Observers commented that it was more like an inquisition than an enquiry with the victims of Challenor's efforts being subjected to harsh cross-examination.

The turn of events at the Rooum trial was not in itself sufficient to bring Challenor's infamous career to an end. The peculiarities of his behaviour finally impressed his superior officers. He was put on sick leave on 6 September 1963. Although he appeared in the dock at the Old Bailey with the three other officers, he was found to be unfit to plead. He went off to an institution. On 2 July 1964, the Home Secretary, Mr Henry Brooke, announced that Challenor's "excessive devotion to duty and overwork in the police service" had precipitated a mental breakdown. He stated that there were twelve cases in which gross injustice

---

[1] Later Lord Justice James.

had occurred and that five free pardons had been given. In fact, there were fourteen more cases which Mr Brooke forbore to mention.

Challenor recovered after what a number of commentators thought was a less than 'respectable' period of time. It is said that he took up a new career as a security officer.

CHAPTER 20

A TASTE OF TRAVEL

Gerald Gardiner QC led Michael in the representation of Frank Cradock, a businessman, as the affairs of his company were being investigated. Gerald's role was largely advisory and it was hoped that charges would not be preferred. However, the investigation revealed matters which were to lead to an indictment for fraud.

Several police officers arrived at Cradock's flat in Central London as dawn was breaking on an autumn day in 1964, intending to give him the early morning call that ends with the words "… you have the right to remain silent …" And so on. In the event, a sleepy and surprised Mrs Cradock opened the door: her husband was away from home.

While Mr Cradock was making his way from his overnight business affairs to his office in Piccadilly some time later, he saw the billboard for the early edition of the *Evening Standard* pronouncing "City tycoon arrested". Wondering who, of his competitors, had the misfortune to be the subject of the news, he bought a paper and was surprised to see, as he walked freely down the road, that the person arrested was none other than he. It appears that someone had helpfully, albeit prematurely, leaked the news of the arrest to the press.

Tucking the newspaper under his arm, he walked briskly over to the Café Royal where he pondered the situation over a cup of coffee. He tried, but was unable, to get hold of the solicitor, so he telephoned me. I said I would call Gerald and I did. He thought it was hilarious, saying: "Oh, how piquant!"

He agreed that it could hardly be a mistake to go to Great Marlborough Street to strike a blow for justice by being the first off the mark. The three of us met at the Magistrates' Court. We walked into the courtroom. Gerald and I quietly seated ourselves on Counsel's bench and Cradock took a place in the public gallery.

The stipendiary magistrate, the amiable and always helpful St Harmsworth noticed – and recognised – us. He raised his eyebrows and pulled his register towards him.

"Pause there," he said to a pale young barrister who had been saying something earnestly in favour of a shabby-looking defendant who was standing in the dock, looking thoroughly miserable.

Harmsworth checked through his list of cases to see if he could detect anything serious enough to attract the services of Leading Counsel. Unable to find any reference to case of sufficient weight to bring this distinguished advocate to his humble court, he asked, "Mr Gardiner, Mr Sherrard – what case are you in?"

Gerald stood. "We don't really know, sir, but it looks as though there is going to be one before the morning is out."

"I see," said Harmsworth, although quite evidently he did not and, indeed, could not.

Gerald said, "I wonder, sir, whether it would be convenient to particularise the reason for our being here?"

Harmsworth seemed to have forgotten that there was someone in the dock. The pale barrister took the opportunity to sit down as Gerald explained the situation.

"I'm not sure if you can call it a case, sir. I represent a gentleman named Francis Cradock who has, in fact, not been arrested but if you believe what you read in the papers, he has been."

The stipe could see the funny side of this.

"What do you want me to do?" he asked.

"I am concerned that he should get full credit for his prompt response to the threatened proceedings since the news of his "arrest". What I'm truly concerned about is that the police should be summoned at once to come to court, arrest him and charge him – unless the newspapers have got it totally wrong and the arrest, having not happened when they said it did, is not going to happen now. I will suggest that his totally proper response should earn him bail free of restrictions."

In those days newspapers would carry a column called "Laughter in Court" and there was quite a bit of it in Great Marlborough Street that morning.

Mr Harmsworth asked whether Gerald had brought his client along with him. Indeed he had. "Could you stand, Mr Cradock, and made

114

yourself seen to the court?" Gerald asked. The sad defendant in the dock turned, with everyone else in the room, to see the defendant-in-waiting rise.

"Good morning, Mr Cradock," said the stipe. "I'm going to ask Mr Gardiner whether it would be convenient to him and to you if I put this situation – hardly a case yet – back to 1.00 p.m. and we'll see if the arresting officer can make a better job of finding our court than he has so far of you."

Gerald said that would be an admirable idea. "I will return to chambers and risk leaving the case in the hands of my admirable junior, Mr Sherrard."

Off he went, and off I didn't.

Normal business resumed. The pale barrister took up his speech again and the defendant looked sadder than before, unrevived by the temporary diversion.

Charges were soon brought but there were delays in the committal proceedings in the coming weeks, at one point because there was a shortage of magistrates. Between hearings, I was in the course of general case preparation when Gerald Gardiner phoned me. He had been rewarded for his diligence and something more than talent exhibited throughout his career. He said, "I'm going to have to let you down – I've been appointed to the Lords ..."

I said, "Many congratulations. It's a hard life! I shall have to struggle on without you."

But the weight of the case meant that I should not struggle on alone. In the short term, I was in need of a leader. Gerald recommended Jeremy Hutchinson[1] who had taken silk a couple of years before.

Cradock and his co-defendant, a tubby man who was appropriately named Taubman, stood trial before Judge Bernard Gillis and a jury at the Old Bailey on charges of having committed company frauds involving large sums of money. The judge gave no indication of noticing Jeremy fulfilling his reputation of being a man who relied more heavily than

---

[1] Jeremy Hutchinson was elevated to the peerage as Baron Hutchinson of Lullington in 1978.

most on his junior's preparation. In this case, he very much needed to: this was a complex fraud and we were lucky that he had been able to step into Gerald's shoes. Because of his heavy case-load, Jeremy had not had enough time to work up the detailed cross-examination I had planned. Although he was helped considerably by the colour-coded system I had developed for identifying documents rapidly[1], he needed help with the specific questions that had to be asked. His cross-examination was carried out through a series of sotto voce prompts from me, masked by the drape of his gown as he leaned elegantly backwards, holding his arm away from his body across the upper rim of the seat back-rest. Having arranged himself in that way, creating a perfect screen for me, he waited for my whisper. I stretched as far as I could while maintaining what I hoped was a nonchalant stance, leaning over counsel's table to get within his hearing range. It was a posture designed to create back-trouble. Jeremy's part required gymnastic skill almost as much as advocacy.

Sherrard: You then acknowledged the letter.

Hutchinson: I suppose you acknowledged the letter.

Sherrard: Can you remember to whom the letter was addressed?

Hutchinson: Please help me. To whom was the letter addressed?

And so it went. The junior for the other defendant was the only one who could see what was going on.

The witness eventually crumbled.

The case against both defendants collapsed.

Jeremy and I had a long-running joke about being ventriloquist and dummy. I was not quite sure if he knew who was which.

I phoned Gerald to tell him that the case had been slung out. I gave him a little summary of what went on. He made interested sounds. I never found out whether he knew that, even as we spoke, Cradock was

---

[1]   Pink indicated documents in the prosecution case that were in favour of the defendant; livid, 'highlighter' yellow indicated favourable defence documents. Where evidence converted what looked like an adverse point to a favourable one, the relevant documents would be photocopied on green paper. The whole thing looked like a fruit salad. Where does blue come in? In two-handed cases, pale blue was used for relevant co-defendant's documents.

being given advice by someone that the police were unlikely to hang around before picking him up for something else. He understood that he was not to go anywhere near Piccadilly or Great Cumberland Place.

To be on the safe side, as there seemed to be other matters which might cause a repeat performance on different charges with no guarantee of the same outcome as in round one, Cradock caught the first plane to Beirut where he had substantial business interests. Which is where I found myself with my solicitor, Leon Stirling, within the next couple of weeks having a long conference with him – to discuss, purely in the abstract, what would happen if a new case were to arise and on what sort of evidence it would be based and how it could be defended.

I had never been to the Middle East before. Beirut was wonderful: it was a beautiful, cosmopolitan city with all the best qualities of the Italian and French Riviera. My heart bled in later years as the city was systematically destroyed by war. But at the time, there was the thrill of not only having to go abroad suddenly but to somewhere that was exotic and glamorous. The client was something of a playboy and made sure that we were entertained lavishly as well as working.

I heard no more of Frank Cradock. Perhaps the quality of life in Beirut as it was before it became a battlefield tempted him to stay there. In that case, he must have had a surprise lately ….

CHAPTER 21

ANNIE RICHMAN

Annie Richman was a lady bookmaker. She had a younger brother whose son with severe learning difficulties although in his early twenties had a mental age of less than ten. He lived with her in Baker Street and she devoted her home life to taking care of him. She died suddenly. The nephew managed to telephone Annie's older brother who came to the flat as quickly as he could and even more quickly, made his way to Annie's wardrobe from which the nephew saw him plunder her jewellery and money from its hiding place. To say the least, the brother was a very nasty man.

As it happened, the nephew was the main beneficiary of Annie's will. Despite his disability, he managed to tell the executors that he had seen his uncle taking her possessions and they believed him. They brought an action against the uncle to recover the money and the jewellery. Morris Finer led me in the case for the estate.

Lewis Hawser was for the defence. His premise was pretty impudent: he set out to show that Annie had fallen on hard times, largely due to the recent relaxation of the gaming laws which now permitted betting shops on the high street[1]. The competition was unprecedented. The will was accepted but it had been made when things were better for Annie's business. A particular feature of the defence case was that, in recent times, Annie had been obliged to – and did – live off her savings and sell all her jewellery to make ends meet. Thus, there was nothing left to steal.

The nephew was a pivotal witness. In an artless, childlike way, he described his uncle going to Annie's wardrobe and pulling away the bottom shelf below which, as the family knew, was a deed box containing cash, kept as a necessary float for paying out the clients' winnings, and valuables. It was also known in the family that Annie mistrusted banks and preferred to keep as much control as possible over her portable property.

During preparation for the trial, we had used an enquiry agent to obtain evidence to show that Annie was not in financial difficulties. We had all but given up hope that he would be able to help but a message

---

[1] The Betting, Gaming and Lotteries Act, 1963.

reached me as the nephew was completing his evidence that the agent had arrived with his report and a witness in tow who would be able to corroborate our case. We were taken by surprise as much as the defence team.

The witness was an elderly Jewish lady from the heart of London's domestic jewellery trade, Black Lion Yard in the East End. She had a strong Eastern European accent and unmissable, unrealistic red hair. Do I imagine it, after the passage of time, that she entered the witness box, trailing her varicose veins behind her?

Morris took her through her evidence in chief, relying on the notes provided by the enquiry agent. After she referred to Annie by name, she added a Yiddish phrase which, in her pronunciation, seemed to come out as "Oliver Sh ..."

"I'm sorry," said Mr. Justice McKenna. "Oliver who?"

"*Alava sholem*," she enunciated clearly. "It's Yiddish. It means her soul should rest in peace." The judge looked puzzled. "It applies to men too," she said reassuringly.

Morris Finer explained further. "She was injecting the vernacular, My Lord."

Steering her back to the subject, he asked her if she knew anything about Mrs Richman's jewellery. The witness' face lit up.

"She had such a diamond!"

Morris asked her to describe it. She raised her left hand and made what appeared to be a thumb's-up sign to the judge.

"Like this," she said, tapping her right index finger against the thumbnail. The judge made a note. Spectators in the court were suitably impressed that a diamond could be the size of a thumbnail.

Morris' next question was, "Did you have anything to do with that diamond?"

"Anything to do?" She was quite indignant. "I sold it to her! It was a very important sale for me," she assured the judge, nodding her brilliantly coloured head for emphasis. Then, sadly, "She was a very good customer for me and I was very sad to hear that she passed on. Very sad."

She then spoke about the time and the event of the sale and how she liked Annie.

Morris pressed on. "Could you describe her?"

"In Black Lion Yard from where I'm coming, she was like the late Queen Mary, *alava sholem…*"

"What do you mean?"

"She was wearing a toik."

The judge interrupted. "A toik?" he asked, the hint of an Irish accent competing with the idiosyncracies of the witness' pronunciation.

She waved her hands around her head to demonstrate what we gradually began to understand, given the reference to her late Majesty, was a toque.

"She was like – *unbeschrier* – like Queen Mary. She always wore a toik. And a white scarf – a cravat. Over the scarf, from her neck to her ankles, she was wrapped in mink." A long look at the judge to make sure he understood. "*The. Best. Quality. Mink.* She was like – like royalty!"

Morris asked, "When did you last see her?"

"I didn't know it was going to be the last time but when I saw her she was fine – a lovely woman – it was before Christmas last year – I was coming along the street in Piccadilly and there she was – like Queen Mary – she looked as wonderful as ever – who would know? To die – such a terrible thing!"

Morris allowed a moment's respect for the dead. "What was she wearing?"

"It was a very cold day. Bitter, bitter cold. She wore the mink coat, down to her ankles. Like royalty! I noticed the ring and I remembered it – in fact, I was very proud of it – which I sold from my best collection." She stopped for a moment and, as if taking the judge into her confidence, she leaned across the ledge of the witness box and whispered to him, "I have to say, the diamond had a flaw in one facet. Which you wouldn't notice unless you was an expert." She pursed her lips, lowered her chin and pointed a finger at her chest to show that an expert stood before him.

"Did you see any signs of financial difficulty or anxiety when you met her?" Morris asked.

"Definitely not," was the firm reply.

Lewis Hawser began his condescending cross-examination. He looked at his fingernails and managed not to yawn. "Tell us again. The last time you saw Annie Richman?"

She repeated the description of the meeting in Piccadilly.

He went on, "You haven't been asked about her gloves. You remember that you said it was a bitterly cold day. Are you telling the learned judge that she wasn't wearing gloves?" He bowed his head, relishing the lethal question.

She took a deep breath. She leaned forward, across the edge of the witness box.

"Young man," she said patronisingly, "Bol-ieve me, when you're wearing such a K-nacker – bol-ieve me – *you don't wear gloves*!"

Morris had no re-examination.

When it came to the defence case, the brother sat looking smug as his respectable bank manager gave evidence about whether the bank had been asked to lend Annie Richman money: this would have been consistent with her business having been short of cash.

The issue was whether, on a visit to the branch to discuss opening an account for the nephew rather than keeping the money at home, a conversational remark had been made to the effect, "If you need any help, let me know." This was not consistent with her having a money problem.

It was necessary to examine bank records. It became apparent that an additional file was required and it had to be brought from the branch by messenger. Because I was sitting in the second row, I had a better view than anyone else in court of the ledge of the witness box. I could see exactly what was happening after the bank manager received the file. As he was being taken through his evidence in chief, I believe I was the only person to spot him looking down at his hands and quietly removing some pieces of paper and slipping each one under the file. There was something furtive about the gradual, barely perceptible movements and the careful way that each paper seemed to be hidden. I was sure that he was deliberately concealing something. I leaned forward to let Morris know what was happening. A slight tap on his back. A slight dip of his shoulder indicating that I had his attention. A whisper.

"Morris, he's hiding papers under the file. Ask him why he was at such pains to conceal those documents."

When Morris started to cross-examine him, he said in a conversational way, "You haven't been hiding documents, have you?"

The manager looked startled. "Why would I do that?"

Sitting behind Morris, I could not see his face but I could hear the smile in his voice as he said, "Now, that's what I was going to ask you! Would you hand down your file? With *all* the papers? The usher will bring them to me."

The file was handed down with the 'hidden' papers in a separate pile beneath.

"Thank you," said Morris. He looked at the loose papers and quickly saw that they included notes that the bank manager had made at appointments with the brother expressing his concerns both about his probity and cash-flow problems. One of the documents was plainly consistent with Annie Richman's financial health. Morris handed the whole bundle to the usher to take back to the witness box.

"Perhaps you would like to show His Lordship how you carried out your little conjuring trick?"

At that point, the judge rose and the court rose with him, not knowing quite what to expect. He hoisted up his robe, thrust his hands in his pockets and walked over to stand behind the witness box.

"Mr Finer," said the judge when he was in a position to see every movement that the witness made, "Would you repeat your question?"

So the game was up. Documents had been concealed that put the brother in a bad light. The judge took the pragmatic view and simply allowed the bank manager to leave the court. As he was stepping down from the witness box, the judge quietly clapped his hands one on the other several times and frowned at Lewis.

"Yes, Mr Hawser. Are there any more witnesses?"

We won our case. There was judgment against the defendant in favour of the estate for such sum as another judicial officer would determine at a later hearing. Annie Richman's nephew would have the financial security that she wanted for him.

CHAPTER 22

DR GOSWAMI

During the 1960s there were strict currency controls in the United Kingdom which affected business transactions abroad. Effort and ingenuity went into ways to circumvent the restrictions in what would be known nowadays as money laundering. A syndicate devised a scheme ultimately prosecuted as a conspiracy to evade the control laws albeit that it depended on an ostensibly legitimate procedure using sterling in cash to purchase gold in the sterling area. The gold would then be brought into the UK to be sold to bullion dealers. The system depended on the reliability of couriers.

One courier was Dr Goswami. Independently, he formed an idea to circumvent the syndicate's procedures by buying the gold in India in the belief that no-one would be the wiser. Part of the process involved getting his local bank manager to permit him to withdraw £25,000 in notes for his planned transactions. This roused the bank manager's suspicions. He telephoned the Home Office who put him in touch with Customs and Excise who set up a greeting party for him at Heathrow. An officer stepped forward.

"Are you Dr Goswami?" Upon the doctor agreeing that he was, he was asked to "step this way."

In a room off the Customs Hall, Dr Goswami asked if this would take long as he was about to catch a flight to India.

"You may have to take another flight, sir. Where did you begin your journey?"

"Muswell Hill. I live there."

"What's in the bag?"

"Books – pyjamas – gifts – a little money for other business."

The customs officer pointed to several pieces of luggage that were piled in the room. "Which bag is yours, sir?"

"This bag." Dr Goswami pointed to a large holdall.

"Please open it, sir."

"But it only has my pyjamas," Dr Goswami assured him.

"Let's see, sir." The customs officer pushed the bag in front of Dr Goswami who, after a few more explanations about its contents, opened it. Underneath the pyjamas and a spare shirt were packet upon packet of £5 notes which bore no relation to the description of 'a little money'.

"Is that your money?" the officer asked.

Dr Goswami considered the question. "Well, yes – in a way. But in a way, not."

"Where were you going with it?"

"To Delhi."

"Are you still intending to go there?"

Dr Goswami answered promptly. "No. If you'll excuse me, I'd like to go back to Muswell Hill."

The officer shook his head. "We are unable to excuse you, Dr Goswami."

While the doctor was in custody, he was helpful to the police. In what amounted to a confession about his activities, he referred to the syndicate's scheme, Byzantine in complexity, involving the import and export of notes of the realm which related to the purchase of gold.

The members of the syndicate were charged with conspiracy. Goswami pleaded guilty. He was represented by Sir Ian Perceval QC, later to become the Solicitor-General. The defence silks for the syndicate included Jeremy Hutchinson, Lewis Hawser[1] and Michael Havers[2]. We had a wonderful conference with all the leaders and juniors at Lewis' chambers in Garden Court to consider the evidence needed to prevent Goswami's confession 'infecting' the defence of the others and to show that there was nothing illegal about taking money out of the country if the same money was brought back in. The defence was based on the simple premise that, for all its complexity, the scheme was lawful.

---

[1] In 1974, the Home Secretary asked Lewis Hawser QC to review the Hanratty case. His report in April 1975 concluded that the convictions were safe.

[2] Robert Michael Oldfield Havers QC (1923-1992), Solicitor-General 1972-1974, Attorney-General 1979 – 1987, Lord Chancellor 1987.

Lewis said, "The transactions can be shown to be legitimate but I wonder if it wouldn't be a good idea to translate this into real life because we need some more evidence to see where the sterling is actually going and how it gets back home."

He had the idea of sending someone abroad to change a £5 note for local currency then buy it back with local notes. Whoever did the deal would record where the transaction happened so that a jury could understand that this was perfectly legitimate. Michael Havers instantly saw the possibilities of this style of case preparation and responded enthusiastically.

"Admirable idea! It's an absolute winner. I'll make arrangements for my clerk to do it."

But somehow it came about that it was the clerk who made the arrangements for Michael Havers to do the trip. He went to Singapore and Hong Kong for the first time. He was six weeks on the case coming back via the Bahamas and Bermuda. He just kept on buying and selling the £5 note.

When Michael came back, we were like children. We all said, "Tell us about your adventures."

***

Dr Goswami's confederates were acquitted. The doctor, however, paid the penalty for developing his private initiative.

At the end of the trial, we were all invited to a dinner given by the members of the syndicate at a large house in Temple Fortune in North-West London. The house was elaborately, if not alarmingly, adorned with fountains and gnomes in the gardens and dark, plush wallpaper and carpet merging into one another inside. We learned that the wife and the maid had been up all the previous night, making the most delectable food. After polite greetings, we were seated at an enormous table but, to our discomfort, the family remained standing, each positioned at various points against the walls, watching us. It was rather difficult to enjoy the food whilst under scrutiny. There was no way of being able to draw our hosts into conversation. We quickly learned that turning to talk to the nearest observer resulted in nothing more than a nod or a shrug or hands flapping us back towards our loaded plates. Our job was to enjoy what was offered and their job was to oversee the process. The only way to get through the evening was to eat as quickly as possible and leave to catch up with the suddenly-remembered preparations for court the next day.

***

When Michael Havers became Lord Chancellor, he visited Hong Kong where, after the Goswami case, he had worked when at the Bar. I asked him how he had got on while he was there.

"It was better the first time," he said.

During the course of the trip, he had been invited to open a new court but when he opened what he thought was the door, he found himself in the broom cupboard. This was taken to be an undignified manner for such a high officer in the British Government to conduct himself.

"I can identify that broom cupboard," I said. "It is next to Court 13."

CHAPTER 23

DAVID JACOBS

Michael's career brought him many famous, as well as some infamous, clients. Stage and film actors came to him, mainly from the well-known solicitor, David Jacobs[1]. The idea of most show-business people was for someone to wave a magic legal wand and save them going to court.

David Jacobs had a fantastic practice. Many of his clients were actors or entertainers. He was something of a socialite but he had a wretched personal life and eventually committed suicide. But at the time he was instructing Michael, he was successful, popular and in demand.

By 1963, when David instructed me to help her, Judy Garland had managed to establish herself as being the most unpredictable star ever to play the London Palladium Theatre. Heavily dependent on prescription drugs, her moods fluctuated without warning depending upon how much alcohol had been used to get her through the day. She had a particularly disconcerting habit of treating a live performance as a rehearsal: she would stop the orchestra and make them start again if she felt like it. But the audience loved her even though she sometimes looked somewhat the worse for wear when she came on stage.

In March 1963, David telephoned me and said I had to see Miss Garland urgently to advise her in a dispute she had with the impresario, Val Parnell. He had made a public statement that he was considering taking her off the bill for her much publicised show at the Palladium. There were heavy hints that this was because of the effect of drinking on her behaviour. My understanding was that she was much wronged by the slur on her reputation.

That afternoon, I met her at chambers. She was carrying a small basket covered by a gingham cloth. "Do you want red or white," she said, drawing back the cloth to reveal two half-bottles of wine and a corkscrew. Although she was smiling, she was clearly very uptight and stressed. There was no doubt that she was a drinker and living up to her reputation even at our meeting.

[1]   David Jacobs (1912-1968).

We gave an undertaking and no more was heard of the matter. She remained on the bill and the audience loved her.

In January 1966, I was led by Desmond Ackner, representing another impresario, Emile Littler, known to us as 'Plus Petit', in a libel action against Bernard Levin. Bernard was one of several theatre critics who had accepted Emile Littler's offer of a pair of free tickets to attend the opening night of a new play, "The Right Honourable Gentleman." The theatre programmes were issued free but it appeared that there were not sufficient to go round. Bernard Levin's critique of the play the next day was less than kind and, to add insult to the injury of not being entertained, he had not even been able to buy a programme. His article included an accusation against Emile Littler of having rationed the programmes and criticised his theatre management. It appears that the proprietor of a theatre can live with bad reviews but it is intolerable to be accused of being ungenerous with programmes.

The Evening Standard carried the headline, "First Night Libel." Leon Brittan[1] represented Bernard Levin. It ended with an apology and an undisclosed sum of money being accepted by Emile Littler. It would have been cheaper for Bernard to have bought a programme, had there been one available.

Not long after that, David sent Kim Novak to see me. I was so dazzled by her beauty, I cannot remember what problem she had. Whatever it was, I would have gone through fire for her.

Michael represented Trevor Howard, another of David Jacob's drinking clients.

Trevor Howard was a wonderful actor and a very nice man. It is no secret that he had a great liking for booze. I defended him on drink-driving charges at the Guildhall, led by Christmas Humphreys, by then in silk. The jury was bursting itself to acquit him. They all knew him as the broken-hearted gentleman who loved and lost in Brief Encounter. But justice prevailed and, on the evidence he was convicted.

And then there was Sid James.

---

[1]   Leon Brittan: called to the Bar 1963, QC 1978, Home Secretary 1979, knighted 1989 and appointed to European Commission

Sid James had committed a driving offence that required some legal expertise to save his licence. After I had done the necessary, Sid invited me to the studios where one of the Hancock's Half-Hour episodes was to be recorded. His warm-up was even funnier than the programme. Perhaps he was in a good mood because he knew he was going to drive himself home after work.

Michael acted for Bruce Forsyth in a civil matter in the early 1960s.

He turned up for a conference at chambers. People recognised him wherever he went and the staff all wanted to see him. There was a noticeable number of barristers loitering in the lobby as he waited to be brought through to my room. As he was leaving chambers, I told him that I was bringing my son, Nick, and some of his friends to see his show at the Palladium. He invited me to bring them backstage to meet him. This was going to score quite a lot of points for me with the children. I was delighted to accept on their behalf.

On the day of the show, we were approaching the theatre. As we passed Liberty's, we happened to meet the gaoler from Marlborough Street Magistrates' Court. He saw the crowd of little boys in tow. He asked, "Are these all yours?" I explained that one was, the rest were friends.

"Do you think they'd like to look at the cells?"

There was enough time for a visit so went along to the court where he showed them around the cells. He put handcuffs on them but, even though he immediately lost the key, their hands were small enough to slip through. They were delighted to be able to escape. We went on to the show, which they enjoyed greatly. After the final curtain, we took up Bruce's invitation to visit him in his dressing-room. He had arranged for biscuits and soft drinks to be brought and was on good form, even greeting them with his catch-phrase which was guaranteed to crease them: "Nice to see you – to see you nice!" They nodded solemnly and barely responded to his jokes.

I was mystified. They were not usually shy and they had been looking forward to this so much. Bruce tried harder, "Is there anything you'd like to see while you're here?" They looked down at their feet. Definitely shy.

"Go on, tell me – what would you like to do?" Bruce asked. "I'll see if I can arrange it."

Faces lit up. "Can we go to the prison again?"

***

David Jacobs had a lovely house in Hove. In the summer of 1963, he gave a Hawaiian party in honour of Sophie Tucker[1] who was in England for what was to be her last performance at the London Palladium. He invited an immense crowd of people to meet her and had arranged for her to receive guests whilst enthroned in a large, intricate Rattan chair. This had been arranged on a pedestal in the vast area which, although called a garage, was more of a closed arena in which he normally kept several of his cars. On this night, all signs of vehicular occupancy had been eradicated in the process of decorating the building to recreate a pretty realistic Hawaiian beach scene.

There she sat, looking … well – huge! We lined up to pay homage. As I waited my turn, Shirley Bassey was singing her heart out to entertain the guests, even though about nine months pregnant. Waiting was no hardship. Canapés were brought around, more lavish than a banquet, yet they were to be superseded by a buffet of even more wonderful food. Famous faces milled about, everyone happy and enjoying the atmosphere.

David Jacobs stood by Sophie Tucker's chair like a royal equerry. When it came to my turn to be introduced, he said (ignoring the fact that I was some years off silk), "Sophie darling, this one of the greatest Queen's Counsel in England."

She looked at me appraisingly.

"Well, honey, you look just like an ordinary Yiddishe boy to me."

The party was unforgettable. The house and gardens were decorated with artificial trees and tropical flowers and fruit. The mixture of colourful lighting, candles and lamps created a glow which enhanced the beautiful displays of food which was sensational in variety and quantity. There were bowls of caviar, platters of foie gras and a seemingly limitless supply of champagne.

---

[1]   Sophie Tucker (1884-1966), vaudeville entertainer, actress and singer.

David Jacobs loved to entertain but he did not have any close friends. He was gay at a time of social hypocrisy and intolerance. This placed a strain on his personal well-being. He developed a persecution complex which was dreadful for him and his colleagues.

Several years after the Hawaiian party, I was in the middle of the Rolls Razor committal proceedings in the RAF Building in Kingsway. My clerk came in and passed me a note. It said: "Mr Jacobs must see you urgently." I could only see him at lunch-time.

He turned up at the entrance to the building. He looked haggard, not himself. His eyes darted side to side as he looked about him. He put his forefinger to his lips, making a shushing sound as I started to say hello. He motioned away from the steps towards the road then flailed his arms wildly to flag down an approaching taxi. He steered me towards it, opening the door with one hand, the finger placed on his lips again, showing me that I had to remain silent.

Inside the cab, he told the driver to carry on in the same direction then turned to me as we moved away from the kerb.

"You know how they're after me," he said. "The only way for us to talk is in a taxi picked at random." He looked around as if to check that no-one else was in there with us. "It has to be at random otherwise ..."

His voice tailed off as "otherwise" was too awful to contemplate. The taxi drove us around in circles while David told me what he wanted to say. His words were so intermixed with his paranoid fears that it was impossible to understand what he was talking about. I told him that I had to get back to court but that we should meet later that day so I could give the problem better attention. He seemed to calm down but within days, he took his own life.

He hanged himself in December 1968 in the garage building that had been decorated with such splendour.

CHAPTER 24

FINERY

Morris Finer was one of Chambers' leading lights and, indeed, was the first member to take Silk.

1963. All of us in Chambers were delighted that Morris had been awarded Silk. We looked forward to seeing him in the elaborate robes and full-bottomed wig. The afternoon before the swearing-in ceremony at the House of Lords, we were in Chambers. He came to my room and asked me to come to his. Of course I agreed. When we were in his room, he closed the door and pointed to the usual disordered array of papers on his desk, on top of which he had spread his wig. The tail coat, waistcoat and Silk gown were spilling out of a large, tin deed box perched precariously on the edge of the insufficient space that had been cleared for the purpose.

Morris went over to the deed box and was fishing in it as I told him how exciting I thought it was to be so close to the ultimate in fine robes. He was not paying much attention to me as he continued his search. After a moment or so, he produced a pair of black silk stockings.

"I have a problem with these," he said.

"Well, I'm no expert," I said. "Are they the wrong size?"

"No." He flapped them at me. "I can't keep them up."

I considered the problem.

"Have you tried garters??"

"Yes, but they still slip down and out of my breeches." Clearly, he must have given the idea a try to be so sure that it would not work.

This was a serious problem. Taking part in the procession with his stockings trailing behind him was not to be contemplated. We discussed alternatives, one of which was a pair of tights. But even if either of us knew what size he would need, neither was willing to go out to a ladies shop and buy them.

"Can't we ask somebody who knows?" I suggested.

"Good idea!" Morris looked relieved that there would be someone who could help. "Mark Littman will know. He's been in silk for a couple of years." Morris made the phone call and asked the question. The eager expression on his face faded and was rapidly replaced with a look of despair as he listened to what Mark had to say. He put his hand over the receiver and, whispered to me, "A suspender belt!"

A suspender belt! That would be even worse than getting tights. I was imagining what would be the protocol for calling in the clerk to take the necessary measurement when I notice that Morris had cheered up. I saw him smile broadly and heard him thanking Mark. "Thank you so much. Really, I can't thank you enough."

Mark was going to lend Morris his suspender belt. Morris did not ask how he had acquired it.

Within an hour, a flat, square box arrived at Chambers, tied with legal tape. Morris opened the box and found a note pinned to the discreetly unadorned black satin garment.

"Greater love hath no man than this, that he lay down his suspender belt for his friend!"

Thus was Morris able to stride forth confidently in his finery. We never found out his hip size.

CHAPTER 25

A FATHER'S SON

Michael's father died in 1965, the penalty of a lifetime of smoking. In the last days, Michael was in the Court of Appeal enduring Mr. Justice Melford Stevenson presiding.

He was enjoying himself in his usual way, making pointless jokes and trivialising the entire proceedings. I ploughed on with my case, thinking, "My father's dying. At the back of the court are the appellant's mother, father and older brother. I have a job to do here."

Melford Stevenson had, in his own opinion, made a wonderfully droll remark, He was nodding and smiling at Fred Lawton for approval.

I said, "My Lord, no doubt you will be unable to forgive me, but do you really think that schoolboy quips and howlers are going to ease the agony of the family of this appellant?"

Melford Stevenson got up, wrapped his dressing gown sleeves around him and marched off the dais through the door to the left. The other two ensured that he came back. Lawton muttered over his shoulder, "Look old chap – come on back." There were some questioning glances between the two judges who had the grace to remain seated. After a long moment, he returned, hands in pockets. You could see the elderly version of a naughty schoolboy. I thought he would turn the tables on me and say, "I suppose you are going to apologise." And I do not think that I would have done so.

But he did not say anything. A slight nod and I completed my submissions. For once, he had a sixth sense that something must be terribly amiss for me to say anything that could amount to a breach of court etiquette.

The usher came to me as I was collecting my papers together.

"Lord Justice Lawton would like to see you."

"Good," I answered, but really thinking that there would be another delay before I could get home.

In his book-lined room, Fred was waiting for me. He said, "I do apologise – he really does overdo it – it's so embarrassing – robs the court of its dignity. It's not just for you, you know."

I said, "Thank you. I'd rather have a public scolding and a private apology."

Fred said, "Don't take it to heart."

I was thinking that my heart had a different sort of pain at that moment. I said, "I shall always be more careful with Melford."

He said that I would do well not to take him seriously. No, I would not. There were really serious things on my mind. It was kind of Fred to call me in for the reassuring talk but I only wanted to be at home.

Some weeks later, after his father's death, Michael was a guest at at an Inner Temple function. Melford Stevenson made a bee-line for him. He said, "That little escapade of ours really was quite fun!" Was that an apology?

CHAPTER 26

CARTOONS IN COURT

Michael discovered that he could produce case-sensitive cartoons with a real likeness to the characters. The talent became manifest during a trial in which he was being led by Leonard Caplan, who rarely let his junior get to his feet to conduct part of the proceedings. There was little need even for the junior to make a note of the evidence because transcripts were delivered to the homes of all counsel. The cartoons began as "doodling", but those sitting behind him told him that the drawings were really very good, so he began to add some witty punch-lines. He produced one or two drawings a day which he deemed fit for publication to the select audience that made itself known to him in court.

The case came to be known as "the Roselodge Diamonds Affair."

A colourful gentleman called Harry Rosenberg ran the Roselodge company, principally through a jewellery shop in Hatton Garden in the City of London. He imported diamonds from Antwerp for use in the manufacture of high-class jewellery. All the incoming stones were covered by Lloyd's insurers. Customs and Excise officers were regularly on duty in the Hatton Garden area and traders co-operated with them. As a matter of law, they were entitled to inspect precious stones and traders were used to being stopped and questioned.

Because Saturday was the Sabbath for Mr Rosenberg, Sunday became a routine working day for him. On Sunday, 31st January 1965 at about 7.30 p.m. he was in his car on his way home when he was waved down by two men in blue. This was not an unusual event and he complied with the direction. He pulled over to the kerb and rolled down the window of the car to speak to them. He was asked whether he had any fresh consignments of diamonds. He said that he had a newly arrived parcel and was asked to produce it for inspection. He did so without hesitation. When they had the small hand-case containing the package, one of them produced a gun, pointed it at Mr Rosenberg and advised him not to raise an alarm until they were out of sight. As soon as he dared, he rang for the police.

The loss of the diamonds in cash terms was about £300,000 and in due course, he put in an insurance claim. Lloyd's refused to pay and the Company put in a claim for an indemnity from them. The Lloyd's nominated "name" to act for the defence was Mr Arthur George Castle, an Underwriter.

The trial judge was Mr Justice McNair, the Senior Commercial Court Judge. The case lasted for something over 35 days. *The Times Law Report* for April 26th 1966 was headlined "Diamond Cases are For Ever" but there was not a single secret agent in the whole case!

The defence alleged fraud against Roselodge: that there had been no robbery as alleged by Mr Rosenberg. But the judge, after reviewing the other evidence, let it become obvious that he was not impressed by the defence, which then proceeded to press other more technical strategies. At a late stage, leave was sought to amend the defence still further by alleging that there had been material non-disclosure of the fact that Roselodge had for some years employed a man who had served a sentence of imprisonment in America for smuggling diamonds. The judge was not impressed by this allegation and referred to "yet another defence". He pointed out that one item after another of the original defence had hitherto been abandoned. He declined to allow the late amendment 25 days into the trial.

Without the amendment, the defence had little hope of succeeding. They took the unusual step of appealing the refusal to the Court of Appeal while the trial itself was still in progress and achieved a ruling in their favour on the ground that, albeit late, the amendment was directed to a legitimate ground of defence.

But the case for Roselodge was doomed to failure when the judge found that on the evidence it was established that there had indeed been material non-disclosure. The judge made it plain that he regretted the validity of the late amendment because he was satisfied that Mr Rosenberg had been robbed and had been telling the truth. The employee at the heart of the final amendment had, as the judge found, played no part whatsoever in the robbery or any other material aspect of the case.

Acting for the defence was the formidable team of Patrick O'Connor QC, Robert McCrindle QC and Michael Ogden. It seemed to me to be a pleasure opposing them and both sides were distinguished by their good nature and respect for the other's expertise.

Save for the excitement generated by the appeal, I was required to do virtually nothing except think. There was only so much thinking that could be done. That is where the doodling began. First it was caricatures of the plaintiff. He was an exceptionally tubby man whose outline began as the shape of an egg, He eventually became a Russian doll. The nominated defendant was always characterised by a paper Christmas crown, depicting him as king of the eponymous castle. Other characters in the court rapidly followed. I scribbled away, thoroughly enjoying the diversion.

The defence team noticed what I was doing. They encouraged me by telling me that the drawings were very good and it was obvious from the head of steam that they generated that people did indeed find them amusing. Bob McCrindle suggested that, if I agreed, their side would copy the cartoons on a daily basis and deliver them after assembling at Court the following day. I agreed and the cartoons became the main feature of the case and were, I believe, circulated within Lloyd's.

We jogged along in good faith until, quite near the end of the trial, the judge's clerk came into the well of the court to speak to me before the day's proceedings began. He had a very solemn face.

"Mr Sherrard, could I have a word with you?" he asked.

"Of course," I said, wondering what he could want of me.

"Sir, I assume you are aware that photographing in court is not allowed. Indeed it would be a contempt of court."

I felt the hand of fate hovering over my prospective application for Silk as he spoke.

"There is little doubt that sketches in court would also be a contempt."

I had to agree.

"To be blunt, sir, it has come to the attention of the judge that you have been making cartoons … without his leave." He glared at me.

The game was up and there was no point in arguing the toss: there was not much to toss. I saw my career prospects fading as the clerk continued that he had spoken to Mr O'Connor in similar terms.

I found my voice. "It had not occurred to me it would be contempt of court. I assure you that it will not happen again."

"That might not be enough." Of course it would not be enough.

The clerk's next words interrupted my melancholy thoughts. "The judge is very upset. But he is about to celebrate a significant birthday. Perhaps the cartoons could be used to soften the blow, if any, of the event."

I was somewhat gloomy after the conversation. Needless to say, my pencil stayed put. At the end of the day, I told Leonard Caplan what had been said and he agreed that we should have a word with Pat. He suggested that it seemed that the judge would like to see the cartoons and we could present a set of them to him. Pat was delighted with the idea. He could hardly conceal his excitement and suggested that I draw a suitable cover sheet and he would draft a message.

I drew a respectful cartoon.

The next morning, the judge took his seat as usual. Pat rose slowly, holding in his hand the bundle of cartoons.

"My Lord," he said in his most sober, sonorous tone of voice, "I apologise for the number of applications with which I have to worry your Lordship during the course of the trial but there has been a development overnight in this case. Now, once again, I have to draw to your Lordship's attention a bundle of documents which have come to light at this late stage."

The judge frowned. The Court of Appeal decision overruling his judgment on the defence amendment still appeared to rankle.

Pat held the bundle at arm's length so that the usher could pass the bundle to the judge. It contained all my cartoons under a cover page bearing the words, "Roselodge -v- Lloyds." The judge took it and gazed at the cover sheet and the birthday greeting. I was delighted to see the frown disappear to be replaced with a warm smile as the judge turned the pages and saw my handiwork.

Then in a solemn tone, he put the bundle to one side and said: "I don't think this bundle needs an exhibit number. I will keep it safely." Then, "Thank you all very much. *I* am getting on. Shall *we* now get on?"

I could just see the judge's clerk discreetly and silently clapping his hands out of the line of sight of other people in court.

The case lasted almost as long as *The Times* had predicted in their "For Ever" Law Report headline. Mr Rosenberg, vindicated on the essential merits of the claim, rightly in my view, decided that there was no prospect of succeeding on an appeal and bowed to the judgment.

The judge became one of my sponsors for silk, but not before I had managed to lose a couple of cases before him.

CHAPTER 27

PUPILS

Taking a pupil is a barrister's contribution to the next generation of the profession. Quite a few pupils applied to be with Michael before he took silk. Sometimes two pupillages overlapped. He kept them pretty busy. They had to learn to keep papers meticulously tidy and never to have two sets of papers open at the same time. They had to learn to eat and walk as the only time for a snack during the day was when they were hurrying between court and conferences. Most made a useful contribution to Michael's work as well as preparing themselves for practice. They went on to good careers in the law, some breaking away to become solicitors but Michael's friendship with, as he puts it, those who have been good enough not to die, flourishes. Among their number were several from Hong Kong and Singapore who kept in contact with Michael and worked with him when his career developed in the East.

Michael used to insist that his pupils never allowed more than one set of papers relating to a case to be opened at a time. He demanded absolute confidentiality and that papers should be kept in chambers unless being taken to court. He had a horror of things going amiss since the occasion when a chambers' typist accidentally sent the discretion statement of one of Morris Finer's clients to her estranged husband in a contested divorce.

The first pupil was Leah (now Harris). She chose to sit at the back of the room as she did not want her facial reactions to the clients' sorry tales to be observed. She was succeeded by Carolyn who became, and still is, a senior law reporter, now married to Judge John Toulmin, CMG QC, a fellow Bencher.

Let me tell you about some others.

I went back to chambers during a short break while the Winn Committee was sitting. There were large amounts of papers to deal with on a daily basis. On the way to my room I noticed a middle-aged lady sitting in the hallway.

"Is it your mother, sir?" my clerk asked. He knew that it was not, but she could have been the same age, at a glance. "Who is she?" I asked. "Has she come to see me?"

"She wants to be your pupil," he said. I thought, "How am I going to get out of this one?"

But I did see her. She made herself a place by moving a pile of papers from one chair to another, keeping the new pile separate from the old and, before she left, put them back where she had found them. She was completely at ease as she described how she had come to me on an introduction from Morris and Edith Finer. She had had a career in business with her sisters-in-law. More recently, she had written an up-dated version of Lamb's *Tales from Shakespeare*[1] which sold well enough to be published in 17 languages. Irene's stunning *c.v.* showed that she had outstanding ability but I did not see her as a pupil. She patiently conducted the interview, trying to persuade me that she was a suitable candidate but there was no way I was going to take her. I tried to tell her politely. My concern was that older pupils seemed less likely to stay the course. I was remembering one pupil in his early sixties who didn't make it. The clerks called him my grandfather. One day, his little pencil-case was missing from the pupil's desk and he was gone.

Irene insisted that she wanted to come to the Bar.

I almost pleaded with her. "It's not for you," I told her. I said, quite frankly, that I was a couple of years short of silk. My work was frantic. I was up and down the country. But there was something both determined and pleasant about her. She nodded her fiery red head at everything I said, agreeing with how difficult was my life but disagreeing, with a slight downturn of her eyes, about her ability to follow me.

The telephone rang from somewhere in the mass of Winn Committee papers on my desk. She leaned forward and moved the right pile so that I could answer it.

My clerk was at the other end of the line. "Could you have a word with the Attorney?"

"You're joking," I said.

"No," he assured me. "It's the Attorney-General."

I took the call, feeling as if I should be standing to attention.

---

[1] Buckman: *Twenty Tales from Shakespeare* (London: Methuen, 1963).

"Hallo, Michael," Elwyn-Jones said, after introducing himself. "I hope you don't mind me calling you out of the blue. I'm sending a very dear friend called Irene Buckman to see you about a pupillage. I hope you feel flattered. She is –" he paused then went on, "a senior lady. I will say no more, except to assure you that she is not relying on patronage. This is more of a reference in case you need one."

There must have been some form of social nicety that ended the conversation but my recollection is only that it was important to me that someone at the Attorney-General's level should think so highly of this remarkable lady.

She became my pupil. Other barristers teased me at the start. The standard joke was, "What's your mother doing in pupillage?" But the last laugh was on them: she was a brilliant lawyer who was indefatigable and able to cope with everything that was thrown at her. But I did make some concessions for her. Knowing that she had a family and a home to run, I told her that she could work from home in the evenings to get her work done. Provided we did not have a late conference, she could leave by 7.30 p.m.

After completion of her pupillage, she became a tenant and went on to be my junior in many of my cases[1], including those of John Bloom and Rolls Razor. We became quite well-known as a team. Her husband, Bernard, became a good friend to us and later gave our younger son, Jonty, a job as his assistant, travelling to the international locations where his business was conducted.

Irene's legal career was founded on her son's lack of interest in the law. Jack Jacob and Elwyn-Jones had come to dinner at her home to try to persuade Peter to come to the Bar. The stories of courtroom successes and intrigues abounded and the guests entertained one another enormously. The conversation resolved Peter's doubts. "After talking to you," he told the guests, "I have no doubt: the Bar is not for me."

Irene was dismayed. "How can you be so ungrateful," she demanded. "I'd give my right arm to be a barrister!"

---

[1] She went on to become Treasury Counsel and a Deputy County Court Judge.

Elwyn's wonderful Welsh voice interrupted what looked to be the start of a parental tirade. "Well, would you? I think you'd be splendid. I'm putting your name down tomorrow to become a member of Gray's."

***

After independence, William Chan developed into a fine lawyer. He practised for a while and I led him in Hong Kong. But, as the eldest son, he had to abandon the law to take on the responsibility of running the family business.

Allen Yau established a substantial practice as a solicitor-advocate in Singapore. He eventually transferred to the Hong Kong Bar and practised for a while in the chambers of Dennis Chang QC. I led him on several occasions. Indeed, while I was in Singapore, amongst the other juniors, I led one of Morris Finer's former pupils, David Marshall: he went on to be the First Minister of Singapore after independence.

***

At the time I was up for silk, I took Ian Brownlie as a pupil. He was a don, the Vinerian Professor of International Law. I was told that he had to have a pupillage otherwise he would no longer be able to represent the Pope. The Bar Council agreed that six months was sufficient, given his legal eminence.

"I will take you," I said, "but I do not want to be a party to a charade. If you come to me, you are a real pupil." He wanted to come for two days per week, which would have taken him rather a long time to complete the required six months as he would not have any concessions from me. But from the outset, he was hooked on the work we were doing. He ended up staying for twelve months, living most of the time in a house owned by Irene and her husband.

He was a tower of strength to me during his pupillage. His knowledge of law was encyclopaedic and, as I often reminded him, nearly as good as mine.

He had a habit of clearing his throat if there was a contribution he wanted to make. I would hear his "Hmm, hmm …" and know that there was something useful to be said. If he disagreed with what I was saying, there would be a slight shake of the head. That would be my clue to change tack or ask him if he had anything to offer on the point. And what he had was usually invaluable.

Taking silk put an end to the era of pupils.

CHAPTER 28

SILK

Taking silk identifies both skill and seniority. The process has a significant psychological impact as the barrister develops the realisation that he attracts a calibre of work that requires a special degree of experience and expertise. There may be years of being ready and indeed wanting to move up to the next rung of the ladder but there is also the uncertainty of the effect that there might be on the barrister's practice. Although solicitors may hint at giving instructions in more important cases when a barrister has taken silk, it is widely reported that all too often work can dry up completely.

By 1965, the larger part of Michael's practice was civil. He had become quite well known, with much of his work in the High Court. At the time, personal injury cases comprised as much as seventy to eighty percent of the litigation in the Queen's Bench Division. In common with many other lawyers, he was appalled at the delays inherent in bringing the claims to court. Plaintiffs often suffered great hardship waiting for procedural hurdles to be overcome and battling against the difficulties of getting evidence to substantiate liability for their injuries. The public had a huge interest, whether it was aware of it or not, in procedures being improved. When claims succeeded, the level of damages was not generous and by the time cases came to court, the awards were often too little and too late.

One day, in the robing room, I met a man who was disabled. He had been affected by polio. Now he was having quite a struggle getting his gown on. I helped him. Rodger Winn introduced himself as the Treasury Devil, expressing his gratitude for the assistance.

Six months later, Rodger was appointed to the High Court and rapidly moved to the Court of Appeal where, in 1966, he was to hear an interlocutory appeal in the Roselodge case. Lord Scarman, the first Chairman of the Law Commission, had persuaded the Lord Chancellor, Gerald Gardiner, to set up a Committee whose remit was: '*To consider the jurisdiction and procedure of the courts in actions for personal injuries.*' He appointed Rodger Winn to the Chair and asked him who he wanted to assist him. The six members were to effect what was to amount to a revolution in the way that personal injury litigation was conducted, making interim payments the norm in serious cases and imposing compulsory disclosure of police evidence. Rodger Winn invited me to be on the Committee. This was an important stage in my career and a crucial part of my progress towards taking silk.

I would not have been invited to join the Committee without someone like Winn asking the Lord Chancellor for me. Winn was an excellent barrister who managed to overcome serious disability to achieve an outstanding career at the Bar and then in the judiciary. One of his memorable sayings was, "Why lie when the truth can be so misleading?"

Rodger was a man of integrity. When he was Treasury Devil, a senior civil servant went to see him to twist his arm to give advice that would benefit him personally. Rodger considered the request, glanced at the papers that had been brought, quietly put the tape on the brief and flung it at the head of the civil servant as he rose from his seat.

"Don't forget to pick that up as you leave," he said.

The invitation was a great honour and was likely to lead to advancement of my own career. However, I knew that the Committee would make substantial demands on my time. Indeed, the Committee was to sit through 1966 and would continue into 1967. The members of the Committee represented different interests in personal injury litigation. We used to meet in one of the courts of the Court of Appeal after normal working hours for two or three hours a day.

Rodger and I sat on the raised dais and would have given the appearance of being judges to someone who just happened to drop into the room without knowing what was going on. Indeed, when any point was raised, Rodger turned to talk to me as if I were a judge. I was in discomfort. I felt like teacher's pet and thought my relationship with the Committee was suffering. It gave me an unfair advantage when it came to the arguments. I asked one evening if I might sit with the boys. Permission was granted.

Eventually, I managed to sit by myself in a room along the judicial corridor on the grounds that I was swamped by papers and could make better progress on my own. Rodger would still ask me first about any tricky point. To save him moving about, he would send for me. Before I had a chance to say hello, he would wave a piece of paper on which he had scribbled notes in the margins. "What do you think?"

In general, I thought, along with those of us who were concentrating, that the form of the report was unwieldy. I was worried about how hard-hitting it would be. During the long vacation of 1967, Jack Jacob, a veteran author of civil practice textbooks, and I drafted the report. It was hard work: tedious but timely. We achieved more on our own than if the Committee had checked every stage. We took advantage of Rodger's absence on a cruise. The others played along: they needed a break as much as he did. We were pleased with the result and looked forward to showing it to Rodger. He would undoubtedly want to tweak it but the body of it was there.

When Rodger returned, we met. He told me, "I've got a present for you. I drafted the report while I was on the cruise."

The final report[1], published in July 1968, is a combined version but he would have been quite happy to have gone ahead on his own.

***

People in the know realised that the two juniors who were on the Committee would be likely to take silk. Perhaps the same people had been asking Michael to start thinking of when to apply. He was not convinced that taking silk would help his practice. He had seen Walter Raeburn's thriving practice shrivel when he became a KC.

I came round to the view that the invitation to join the Winn Committee was a real indicator that I should apply for silk. I was not yet 40, so there was little prospect of immediate success. Logically, the application was somewhat premature. However, membership of the Committee was bound to lead to advancement of some sort. Indeed, after its publication[2], of the other members, Judge Mais was promoted to the High Court bench, Lord Winn was himself awarded a further honour and Jack Jacob

---

1   Cmnd 3691, July 1968.This procedure was innovative because we published interim findings so the public were informed regularly of our progress. Our recommendations were designed to fill the gap left by textbooks yet to be published on the subject. The improvements effected by the Report speak for themselves.

2   The publication lists the members of the Committee (p.3) as: The Right Honourable Lord Justice Winn, CBE, OBE, Chairman, His Honour Judge Mais, Vice-Chairman, Mr P A House, Master I H Jacob, Mr Raymond Kidwell QC, Mr Michael Sherrard QC, Mr Robin Thompson. John Churchill, Secretary to the Committee, serves honourable mention.

became the Senior High Court Master. The other junior barrister also took silk. But that was in the future, and nothing would be achieved unless we put in our applications.

What I did – and Raymond may have done this as well – was to apply during the currency of the Winn Committee which was a signal to the Department that I would take silk the next year, after the report had been published and the most likely time for the goal to be achieved. In the event, it happened before publication.

Anyone who wanted silk required sponsorship. There was known to be a rush for the most popular sponsors. Rodger Winn tipped me the wink that he would support me. He told me to see the broadest-based members of the judiciary.

Fred Lawton, by then in the Court of Appeal, said yes. Willy McNair, the Senior Commercial Court Judge, said yes. I knew Jack Simon (head of the Probate, Divorce and Admiralty Division[1]) thought well of me, but there was no need to go to him. He sent me a letter the night before the list came out saying, "There's no need to ask me."

Then there was Lord Justice Leslie Scarman[2], at the time Head of the Law Commission. To my surprise, he telephoned me and said, "I'd like to see you in silk." I met him and he spent a full hour with me.

I went up to see the Lord Chancellor. He was very serious and spent an hour interviewing me. He made notes and seemed to be doing calculations as I was talking. I was not sure if he was paying attention. Seeing his concentration apparently turned away from me, although I had been ambivalent about applying, I thought, with something like panic, "My God, he's going to turn me down." At that moment, it became very clear to me that membership of the group of Queen's Counsel was a club that I very much wanted to join. After what seemed a very long time, he turned towards me and looked up from the frame of his hands, palms facing each other, fingertips touching and tapping.

---

[1] Jocelyn Edward Salis Simon (1911-2006), QC 1951, Solicitor-General 1959; President of Probate, Divorce and Admiralty Division 1962; elevated to peerage, Lord Simon of Glaisdale 1972.
[2] Leslie Scarman (1911-2004), 1961: High Court Judge of the Probate, Divorce and Admiralty Division, Law Lord 1977.

"I was a little troubled," he said, as I had the immediate thought, "Was! That doesn't mean 'is'!"

"I was a little troubled about your age." Some more finger-tapping. "But I'm going to back you. Someone has got to let the Department know the things you have told me."

Now I knew I had a really strong backing team. But I was still unsure about getting silk. I was 38. That was considered to be very young then and could have been a major obstacle, far outweighing the value of a solid contribution to the profession.

The wait for the outcome of the application seemed very long. On the Tuesday before Maundy Thursday[1], Shirley and I went to see our favourite opera, *Tosca*. This was the Zefirelli production[2] at Covent Garden with Otakar Kraus[3] as Scarpia. We later met him and his 'constant companion', a singer. If I didn't get silk, this would be a consolation prize. If I did, it would be a celebration.

Recently, I had finished a defended divorce before Jack Simon. I was against the husband who was acting in person. I had to stop him where necessary. The judge would not have taken too kindly to me being heavy-handed.

In the interval, I met Jack Simon coming down the stairs towards the Crush Bar. He smiled at me. "I've just written you a letter," he said. I spent most of the second act wondering what he would have written to me about. As Scarpia was murdered, I was thinking, "It must be about the case."

Shirley's uncle was the Chairman of the Friends of Covent Garden, He had invited us along with three or four other guests to dinner at the Mirabelle after the opera. William Rees-Mogg[4] was one of the guests. He was a close friend of theirs as was another guest, Harold Schonberg, the music critic of the *New York Times*[5]. The meal was probably won-

---

[1] Maundy Thursday is the day when the list of new silks is published.
[2] The last performances of this production were in 2004.
[3] Otakar Kraus (1909-1990), The Czech-born English baritone. In 1973, he was made an Officer of the Order of the British Empire.
[4] William Rees-Mogg, Baron Rees-Mogg (b. 1928), journalist and politician. Editor of *The Times* 1961-1981. Life peer, 1988.
[5] Harold Charles Schonberg, 1915 –2003. Music critic of *The New York Times*

derful. The company could not have been better but I was in such a jelly because I had not yet had the announcement.

The next day was the day before Maundy Thursday. I had gone back to Chambers with Shirley and found that Jack's letter had arrived, delivered by hand. It read, "My Dear Michael, I could not have been more pleased than I was this morning when I saw the shortlist. I was so impressed with how you handled the case before me ..."

This was a very nice way of finding out that my application had been successful. He knew that he was not allowed to tell me when we met at the opera. It was his way of giving me a very strong hint. Even so, I was delighted to see the announcement in *The Times*. One of the others who took silk at the same time as me was one of my former university tutors, Glanville Williams.

There was quite a family turn-out for the ceremony in the famous Moses Room of the House of Lords the day I took silk in 1968. The Lord Chancellor, Gerald Gardiner gave orders for a large dining table to be brought in for children to be seated so they could see over the heads of the adult members of the audience. My sons, Nick (later to become a mathematician – one of the first forensic accountants) and Jonty (whose career in advertising awaited him) were there. My sister Averil, whose career as an artist and sculptor was far removed from the law, brought her children. They were to go on to become distinguished lawyers. My six-year-old nephew Lewis asked me, "Can I do this one day?" When he took silk in 2002, I gave him my full-bottomed wig with its large, barrister's black and gold metal box. His older sister Alexandra is now a well-known solicitor and sits as a Recorder.

In common with other new silks, I believed that, from now on, I would be alone in making all the decisions in running my cases. However, there were several occasions when I was in "double-harness", either with a more senior silk, or being more senior myself.

Waiting for silk had been demoralising. It was a dangerous game in which there was likely to be serious financial consequences. I knew that many new silks often found that achieving the goal led to an empty diary. For me, as with others, there was a risk that the mere fact of moving up

---

1960-1980. 1971 Pulitzer Prize.

In silk, accompanied by his clerk, 1968

the ladder would not be sufficient for some solicitors. The age-old question remains to this day: is a new silk better than a senior junior? After all, apart from the expense of a QC, when the chips are down, the client only wants to have the better cross-examiner, regardless of the stuff of which his gown is made even though not every jurisdiction requires the cut and thrust of the art of the advocate on which the Bar is perceived as relying. Indeed, it has to be said that the Chancery Division judges were long perceived as not believing in advocacy at all. Even audibility was regarded as an affectation according to Sir Sidney Kentridge QC, the great human rights lawyer.

Although I had led other juniors many times, there was always the possibility of taking a leader in the more complex cases. From now on, I was at the highest level of leadership in the profession. The taking of silk puts a barrister into a lonely position in terms of responsibility. It puts the art of the advocate under the microscope of the profession, the client and instructing solicitors. Not knowing when and if your first brief will come in as a silk is usually the most worrying thing. This was resolved for me by David Freeman, solicitor to John Bloom.

CHAPTER 29

JOHN BLOOM

The cheerful, apron-wearing housewives depicted in the advertisements and films of the 1950s were, in real-life, subjected to the dreary demands of housework, assisted by very little in the way of gadgetry to ease their domestic lot. Household washing was a time-consuming and physically demanding chore at a time when ownership of a washing machine was largely confined to the more affluent members of society.

Enter John Bloom, a young entrepreneur with a flair for publicity and sales gimmicks.

He made a fortune by freeing many thousands of housewives from wash-day drudgery. Starting in 1957, then aged 22, he used a direct sales technique to bring the cheap, reliable and virtually indestructible Electromatic twin-tub washing machine from its Dutch manufacturer into homes all over the country. The small profit margin kept the prices low. His customers, who had no realistic hope of buying one of the well-established brands of machine, flocked to bring in the articles Bloom was prepared to accept in part-exchange for an Electromatic – old copper boilers, bird-cages – anything they could carry to the collection point.

By 1959, the Dutch company could barely cope with the demand. Bloom looked for premises in England in which to assemble the product. The key to his success was the low cost of his machine. If he could save on his import expenses, he could cut prices even further and maintain his advantage over his competitors. His search led him to the dying Rolls Razor Company in Cricklewood, North London. In a complicated deal in early 1960, Rolls Razor sold him a large number of its almost worthless shares and bought his Electromatic Company.

Bloom retained control over the manufacturing process and Rolls Razor came back to a new life, initially assembling, but eventually producing in their entirety, the washing machines. The name "Rolls" replaced the humble "Electromatic" giving the machines a style and cachet that boosted sales even more.

As his wealth increased, he led an increasingly flamboyant lifestyle and his circle of celebrity acquaintances grew. The press maintained a relentless interest, in which Bloom appeared to revel, in the lavish par-

ties he gave at home and abroad, his visits to expensive night-clubs, his yacht, his gambling and the occasional scandal. Indeed, he had to go into hiding in 1962 after being hounded by reporters, eager to have him explain his involvement with a young woman, killed by her jealous husband at the Blue Gardenia Club in Brighton.

In 1963, an enormously successful advertising campaign and ready access to a simple hire purchase scheme put over 200,000 of his twin-tubs into customers' homes. John Bloom was reported to have become Britain's youngest millionaire.

As high as the sales of the washing machines could climb, so could they fall. The main-stream manufacturers, irritated for too long by Bloom's inroads into their profits, suddenly brought out cheap, fully automatic machines. The twin-tub was obsolete. Orders fell. Production dwindled at the Cricklewood factory. By July 1964, Rolls Razor had gone into voluntary liquidation with debts of £4 million followed by a Board of Trade enquiry. The police became interested in 1966. Their investigations continued for nearly two years. In January 1968, Bloom was arrested and, together with fellow directors, was charged with fraud.

John Bloom:

Count 1: On 5th December 1961 as a Director of Electromatic Washing Machines Limited, with intent to defraud, you were concerned with omitting £28,940 liability for advertising charges and £39, 457 liability for Purchase Tax from the Balance Sheet and accounts for 1959 – 1960

***

Count 2: … with intent to deceive shareholders, you made or concurred in making what you knew to be a statement of accounts in the Balance Sheets for 1963 which was false …[2]

Count 3 …, 4 …, 5 …

Bloom was regarded as being quite a character in the business world, although somewhat naïve about financial technicalities, relying entirely on professional help, which ultimately contributed to his downfall.

Soon after Rolls Razor was geared to take up assembly of the erstwhile Electromatic, the Dutch manufacturers backed out of supplying him. In the weeks before the Cricklewood factory could be geared up to producing an entirely new product, there were numerous complaints from customers about machines not being delivered. The press refused to publish any further advertisements from Rolls Razor unless they were satisfied that all was well on the production line. An inspection visit was arranged and Bloom was alleged to have gone to extravagant lengths to create the impression of the factory appearing overwhelmingly busy. The main shortage was of mechanical parts; but there were plenty of machine cases on display and he devised an ingenious system to make the actual 75 finished machines in stock appear to be many hundreds. The visitors to the Rolls Razor building saw an apparently bustling shop floor and, having been suitably impressed, agreed to continue accepting Bloom's advertisements. The lifeblood of the business was assured and it was not long before production was going ahead full-pelt.

Bloom impressed himself as much as his visitors with the grandness of his office on the first floor. The main purpose of his numerous gadgets was to display affluence. A favourite was an item that appeared to be a precursor to the digital twenty-four hour clock: a flap would click down at intervals, revealing a number. At meetings, as each flap unfolded, Bloom interrupted whoever was speaking to call out the number. "3753". Click: "3754." Each number was supposed to show that another machine had come off the production line. He went through the routine when I was in his office. He asked, "What do you think of my numbers gadget?"

I said something about electronics being marvellous these days.

"What electronics," he said. "No, look at this."

He showed me a string connected to the gadget which went over the back of the desk and through a hole in the floor, passing through to the workshop below. As the factory controller walked back and forth, he tugged on the string, causing the number flap to turn over. It was possible that nothing was happening below, except for the show.

The doors closed in July 1964. The Board of Trade appointed Morris Finer QC and Sir Henry Benson (a chartered accountant and head of Coopers Lybrand) as inspectors to investigate and report on the events which led to the collapse of Rolls Razor. Because of the outcome of proceedings in the courts, the Report, although highly praised by the Attorney-General, was never published.

Initially, I had been advising on the criminal side and was involved at the earliest stage when it began to look as though criminal charges were likely. However, led by Arthur Bagnall QC, I also became involved in the civil litigation that characterised the fall of Bloom's commercial empire. The creditors of the insolvent Rolls Razor were, like most creditors, always nagging the liquidator, in this case Kenneth Cork[1], to get results. He instructed senior lawyers on the Chancery side to allege maladministration and misfeasance but it was obvious that there would be a delay until the outcome of the criminal proceedings.

One important matter which had a life of its own concerned the dividends due to the shareholders of Rolls Razor. The funds were held by Quistclose, a Rolls Razor company, and deposited at Barclays Bank, which had the negative privilege of providing a loan facility to Rolls Razor. Barclays viewed the Quistclose funds as being a useful way of recouping some of its losses. The logic was simple: the Bank had made loans to Rolls Razor; £209,219 of which had been transferred to Quistclose. The Bank therefore argued that it was entitled to have the Quistclose balance repaid to fill the gaping hole left by the Rolls Razor collapse. Arthur Bagnall argued that the Quistclose money was held in trust for the shareholders and was not liable to be otherwise drawn down.

Shortly after the Board of Trade investigation was concluded in early 1967, the High Court ordered the funds in the Quistclose account to be paid to the the Bank as part of its recovery of previous loans to Rolls Razor. This order was challenged by way of appeal, ultimately to the House of Lords[2]. Barclays could not have been pleased when the appeal

---

[1] Kenneth Cork (1913-1991), later knighted and Lord Mayor of London,1978.
[2] The case was finally resolved in the House of Lords: Barclays Bank v Quistclose Investments Ltd, 1970 AC567. The directors of Rolls Razor Ltd declared a dividend payment. Because it had insufficient funds to pay, they borrowed money on the condition that the funds would be used to pay the dividend. The borrowed funds were paid into the Quistclose account opened specifically for the purpose. Before the dividend could be paid, the company went into liquidation. The House of Lords held that the loan gave rise to a trust to pay the dividend and the lender had an equitable right to see that the funds were used for the stated purpose. However, because the purpose could not be carried out, the funds were held to revert to the

decision was upheld: the Bank was held not to be able in law to use the Quistclose funds.

Although Bloom felt comfortable with the Court of Appeal decision, the criminal investigation continued. Within hours of being assured that no charges were forthcoming, he was arrested on 29th January 1968 on two major allegations of fraud. The several defendants included Bloom's brother-in-law and Richard Reader-Harris, the Conservative MP for Reading, who was a director of Electromatic. All the defendants were represented by silks and the prosecution was led by David Croome-Johnson QC.

I had worked on the case and prepared for it as a junior since 1965. But when it started, on 24th April 1968, I had just taken silk.

The committal hearing was before a stipendiary magistrate at Victory House in Kingsway. The operations of an ordinary court would have been brought to a halt by its length – a record-breaking 115 days – and the vast number of documents as well as the seemingly endless procession through the building of the 127 witnesses involved. The evidence was technical and difficult to understand. There was not much light relief. Bloom even took to bringing office paperwork with him so that he could keep up-to-date with his other business affairs as the case ground on.

One filthy, rainy evening during the committal, the doorbell of my home rang. On the step stood a befraggled Bloom.

There were no social niceties. "Freeman's given me some papers to look at and bring to you."

"Come in!"

"They said you wouldn't want to speak to me."

This was our first and (apart from an accidental and brief encounter years later in a restaurant that he was running in Majorca in his 'life-

---

lender on the resulting trust. Now you see me – now you don't! The original idea was to secure the shareholders. The making of the loan itself gave rise to the trust. But the trust could not be activated because of the insolvency of Rolls Razor. A trust all dressed up and nowhere to go.

after-Rolls-Razor') only meeting outside court or chambers. It was unusual to see him out of context in an almost social setting.

"Nonsense – come in." We sat in the lounge. He said. "There's something about this place … Is there a balcony upstairs?"

"There is. On the first floor."

"Can I have a look at it?"

When the rain eased off, we went to the driveway and looked up at the first floor windows.

"I dunno," he said. "It's just that this place looks sort of familiar."

"We haven't lived here long," I said. "We bought it from a solicitor – a chap called Felix Nabarro." We had moved in so recently that we had just given a drinks party to introduce ourselves to our neighbours. It was a fairly pointless exercise: we had invited the Nabarros as well and most of the guests assumed that they were the hosts, thanking them profusely for the hospitality as they left!

"Do you know Felix?" I asked.

He smiled. "That's it! Felix put me up here when I was hiding from the press when they were chasing me!" He put his hand to the side of his nose. Speaking confidentially against his palm, he said, "The Blue Gardenia..."

I remembered the case: the press had pursued Bloom relentlessly for his account of his relationship with the unfortunate Mrs Holford during her husband's trial for her murder, prompted by his jealousy of her affair with a "well-known millionaire" during a six-week stay on the French Riviera. During the course of the trial, which ended in Harvey Holford's conviction for manslaughter, Bloom's name was mentioned several times. Holford had alleged that it was Bloom who had killed her because she had given him up. The police did not take this seriously but Bloom had to cope with the overwhelming attentions of the press until Felix offered him sanctuary in Burgess Hill.

As long as there was nothing more than rumour, the reputation of Rolls Razor would not be damaged by Bloom's connection with the case. As it turned out, the company would have far more serious problems than coping with the alleged dalliances of one of its directors when Bloom had his own trials to face.

Bloom noticed me talking to another silk in court on a day during the committal when there were some complicated issues that had to be resolved. The silk was a curious-looking man with sloping shoulders that barely supported a jacket. He had hollow, drooping eyes and sallow, sunken cheeks. In truth, he looked as though he had stepped off the Munsters' film-set. Although he looked more as if he were haunting the court than representing a client, he was a very nice man who would come over to chat if, as was usual, I remained in the court through the lunch adjournment to make sure everything was ready for the afternoon. At this particular time, Bloom was sitting to one side of the court. He looked up and saw me involved in a conversation with the barrister. He called me over.

"I don't like that man." He nodded in the barrister's direction. "I'd rather you weren't seen talking to him." A sniff of disgust.

"But why not?" I expected to hear that there was some past involvement in litigation that involved them both and that Bloom had suffered in the experience.

Bloom shook his head and sighed in resignation before spitting out these words with supreme authority as if dictating them to someone hard of hearing:

"Be-cause," he articulated both syllables clearly, "that man is a *po-ten-shall ex-Nazi war crim-in-al*!!!"

The conversation, of course, ceased in my client's presence.

The outcome of the hearing was that Bloom was committed for a trial at the Old Bailey, likely to start in May 1969 to run for nine to twelve months although the more realistic estimate was up to two years. That would amount to an intolerable delay for Kenneth Cork to achieve the 'revenge' he was seeking for the creditors through civil proceedings. Rolls Razor, through the liquidator, claimed over £300,000 lost as a result of the way the sale of the Electromatic company was structured. The claim was against Bloom personally, his brother-in-law and one or two others. It was to be heard in the Queen's Bench Division in the High Court.

At a directions hearing for the criminal trial at the Old Bailey, Judge Carl Aarvold, the Recorder of London, said, "Let's get the summer out of the way and start in September."

That meant that, in spite of the convention that crime is tried first and the usual dance of words in which the parties go on the record to say how upset everyone is about the lack of progress, there was an unrealistic opportunity for the civil trial to precede the criminal case. I learned on the grapevine that Mr Justice Fisher would be the trial judge in the civil case if it were to be brought on first. He was one of the best judges in this class of case and my team, which included my former pupil Irene Buckman, thought we would be fortunate to have him.

Our preparations for the directions hearing included a critical consultation with Bloom. I told him, "I think we can make the liquidator neutralise the Crown's case. We have a superb judge. I'd say there's a very good chance he'll throw out the civil case. The criminal charges are based on the same facts. How could the DPP then hope to overcome the finding that, even on probability, they failed? The prosecution has to prove its case beyond reasonable doubt. They'll be in a terrible jam. Putting it bluntly, under any circumstances, the criminal case will be tainted in our favour by the civil proceedings."

Bloom said, "I'll leave it up to you. If you want to do it, I'm willing to go along."

The hearing for directions was before Mr Justice Blain. Murray Stewart-Smith was for the liquidator.

He said, "It's scandalous that we are being prevented from pressing for a civil judgment."

The judge said, "What do you say, Mr Sherrard?"

There was more than a ripple of excitement when I took the line that had been agreed with my team. My surprised opponent heard me agree. And I was compliant with the proposed timetable for starting the civil case before the Old Bailey trial. "Mr Bloom is anxious to clear his name as soon as possible," I assured the judge. The years of preparation by then behind me meant that I would have been ready if he had said we would start the next day.

"There you are then," said the judge, obviously delighted with the meeting of minds. "I'm not giving any directions that might delay the hearing. We can start on the date fixed, in two weeks' time."

Then the liquidator's team recognised their problem.

"But – " someone bleated – "none of the leaders in the civil proceedings are up-to-date!" Indeed, they were not. There were 115 days of committal proceedings and all the relevant papers. The situation was daunting if not wholly impossible for the liquidator's team whereas I had the advantage in that I had been working on the case for three years by then and much of the material overlapped between the civil and criminal matters.

In spite of what seemed so obvious, the liquidator went ahead and instructed a team of silks to get to grips with the case quickly. Their leader told me, darkly, "There will be no going back." I took that to mean that they were serious in seeing the action through.

I agreed. "That's what big decisions are about," I replied, equally darkly.

There must have been frantic efforts in the opposition camp with much burning of midnight (and, come to that, midday) oil. In the event, they took it to the brink. It was not until the evening before the hearing was due to start that I received the anticipated phone call from one of the liquidator's silks.

"We should have asked for an adjournment of the civil …"

Without irony, I asked if he was now seriously asking me to agree to an adjournment until after the Old Bailey trial.

"We thought it would help," he said.

"Well, why don't you go back to the judge and ask him for a postponement?" I asked. "Then in open court we can let the press know that the liquidator now appears to be unready …" There are times when it is better to tail off rather than go into details.

"We can't do that!" Shades of forensic horror were apparent. "Kenneth won't hear of it!"

There was no application to adjourn. The civil case began. It was almost enjoyable to hear the Plaintiff's Counsel stumble through the preliminary stages with much shuffling of papers, turning to each other, to juniors, to solicitors and referring to the judge like children who have not done their homework, hoping that teacher would help them.

The judge lived up to his reputation. Everything I had ever heard of him was amply justified. He had been reading ahead. Apart from our team, he may have been the only one in court who was fully prepared.

As the days went on and it became clearer than ever that no realistic case was being made out, I made the decision not to call Bloom as a witness. I took the line that the only course of action was for the judge to throw the case out. "Not only is there no criminality," I said, "but there is no case even on the civil standard of proof. This is a huge embarrassment."

Indeed, there was only a very limited case. The judgment handed down on 30th July 1969 was that John Bloom was liable only for the non-disclosure of Electromatic's possible liability to purchase tax. Mr Justice Fisher rejected claims for breaches of warranty concerning servicing of the washing machines, advertising, stock and bad debts. He made it clear that the case only concerned breach of contract and no allegations had been made against John Bloom of dishonesty, fraud or impropriety as a director of Rolls Razor.

It was a pleasant walk back to Chambers that summer afternoon, after Mr Justice Fisher gave his judgment. There were bound to be interesting repercussions on the criminal side sooner or later – in fact, sooner.

David Croome-Johnson and Michael Corkery were due to prosecute at the Old Bailey in September 1969. Whoever they had sent to the Royal Courts would doubtless have given them the news quickly. We waited to see how they had taken the news.

David telephoned me. "Michael, can you meet me at the post-box at King's Bench Walk? We could go for a walk around the garden."

I replied, "You're up the creek, not the garden!"

However, I met him and during the course of our six-times-round-the-garden stroll he said, "Look, the liquidator's action has sunk us. You were on a terrific gamble."

I considered this. I did not agree. "No. Your problem is that you've got a very weak case. We had a very good judge."

And there was the interest of the Attorney-General, Elwyn-Jones. Arthur Bagnall wrote to him suggesting a *nolle prosequi*[1].

He said, "The A-G wants us to drop the case in return for some pleas."

I was suitably indignant, despite my affection for Elwyn-Jones. I could not offer him the courtesy of considering a guilty plea.

"No way! We won't plead to anything that involves impropriety or dishonesty." David looked so disconsolate. I decided to give him a chance to have his spirits improved. "If you can think of something under the Companies Act," I said, "that might be different."

His solemn rejoinder was, "But the public interest must be served. Be realistic."

"I'm not paid by the public," I told him. "You are. I have to do my best for John Bloom."

We learned that the trial judge was to be Bernard Gillis. I thought that he would need some persuading that the case should not proceed. The following Monday, the Judge suggested that a meeting should take place at Court over the next three or four days to deal with procedural matters but then the DPP stepped in: it was clear that Bloom's reliance on flawed financial advice was not sufficient to support the allegations of criminality. By the time we appeared before him, the Judge knew that a *nolle prosequi* had been mooted.

He scowled at us from the high dais in Number One Court at the Old Bailey. "Are you telling me," he asked the prosecution in a tone of incredulity, "that you are going to drop this case in the public interest? *Because of what a civil judge has said?*" He was outraged.

I said, "With great respect, the Attorney-General and the Director of Public Prosecution are both of the view that the case will be almost impossible to try in the light of the findings adverse to the liquidator. We support the application."

---

[1] Nolle prosequi means "unwilling to pursue." It is the term applied to the prosecution's application to discontinue criminal charges before trial

165

There was a short adjournment. We identified a possible offence under the Companies' Act relating to failing to keep proper books of account. Eventually, after several days' discussion with us in his room, Judge Gillis capitulated to David Croome-Johnson's suggestion. Of course, he could not have gone on in the light of the Attorney-General's indication. The criminal case would end with a fine for contraventions of the Companies' Act. In chambers, the judge mentioned that the likely fine would be in the region of £50,000. That was a huge amount of money and I felt myself wince as he said it. I pointed out that Bloom should not be punished for the wider offences that were no longer sustainable and that the actual 'value' of the Companies' Act breaches was closer to £30,000. That still hurt but not quite as much.

It is an understatement to say that there was great rejoicing in the Bloom camp. The guilty plea to the lesser matters was an honourable outcome to the years of legal 'torture' to which he had been subjected.

I prepared a blistering mitigation which was, to put it mildly, critical of the accountants. One of the audit managers had admitted knowing that accounts were not properly kept at Rolls Razor and that he had done nothing about it. Another audit manager had admitted to the Inspectors that he had made a false note: he discovered that he had chosen to invent a false memorandum of a meeting with Bloom on a date when he was not even in the country but was, as a matter of fact, in New York. I knocked on the head the notion that Bloom had secret assets stashed away and made sure that the court – and the public – knew that the punishment was, at root, for the offence of taking bad advice.

Judge Gillis fined John Bloom £30,000.

The press did not convey that there was any difference between the alleged fraud, for which there was no evidence, and the technical nature of the admitted Companies Act offence. The reports referred to the fine and the Crown offering no evidence on five of six charges.

Outside the court, Mr Bloom spoke to reporters. He was quoted as saying, "I was too cocky … but don't worry, I can always make a living."

***

Because the Rolls Razor case ended after days rather than months, I had time to take a holiday.

CHAPTER 30

OF MEN AND BOYS

In the 1960s, holidays abroad were taken in the sterling area because of the £50 limit on the amount of foreign currency that could be bought. When Michael finished the Rolls Razor trial early after the prosecution case collapsed, he found himself with three clear months on his hands. He had worked 18 months without a break. Now was the time to take a well-earned holiday abroad. A tour group travelling to Cyprus and then on to Malta, both within the sterling area, was an attractive proposition. Michael's old college friends, George Pelaghias and Glafcos Clerides, had long since returned to Cyprus. The principal friendship had been with George but letters had gradually petered out over the years and eventually communication had become limited to an annual Christmas card. It was going to be interesting to try to see him again and renew the old friendship.

George would figure large in the Cyprus part of the holiday although Malta was set to be exciting as well: Jack Jacob, now a Queen's Bench Master, had introduced me by cable to the Chief Justice, Sir Anthony Mamo, who, by virtue of his office, was Acting Governor of Malta. He went on to be appointed Governor and was subsequently its first President. When I told Jack about our trip, he got busy and suggested we met for dinner. "Dinner" was to be an understatement.

We arrived in Famagusta with our tour group. They were a nice bunch of people who were politely interested in my plan to find George. I had some of his last known address, Avenue Major Poulios, but I did not know the house number. I had a phone number but could not get a reply. In the end, I called virtually every Pelaghias I could find in the telephone book but in vain. The tour group heard about every failure and began to think that either it was a fool's errand or, perhaps, there was no such person.

There was time between the telephone searches for sight-seeing. We were able to visit Kyrenia, in the Turkish part of the island, travelling in a marked United Nations car which actually had the effect of making us more nervous than re-assured. En route, we made a deliberate detour to the village where Laurence Durrell had lived and worked. We saw his house at Bella País and the 'tree of knowledge' at the side of the village square where he would sit and read recently completed passages of his current writing to the local residents, several of whom featured by name or description in his novels. We went to see the gardens tended by Kosta Collis. We saw a citrus tree, a miracle of grafting, lovingly carried out over the years by him. It bore an abundance of oranges, grapefruit, lemons and limes as if that was what nature had intended.

We were delighted to meet Mr Collis. Shirley told him how much she enjoyed the Durrell books and congratulated him on the part he and the villagers had played in their development. "You must be very proud," she said.

There was a long pause. Mr Collis shuddered. "Proud?" he asked.

At first we thought he had not understood the word but he continued. "Proud? Proud of *him?* I *spit* on him! I throw tomatoes at him – eggs _"

He shook his fists in the air as we wondered what we had said to upset him so. All was to be revealed.

"Everyone helped him! He ate our bread. He drank our wine. He promised everyone a copy of the book with his name. As soon as it was published – he was gone. We heard no more from him at all!"

The village had been insulted.

Shirley was later to write a fictionalised version the story for Blackwood's, the great literary magazine of the time.

We stayed on the Greek side for our next expedition. Shirley and I hired a car to take a drive over to Nicosia on a road terrifyingly constructed from a combination of old railway sleepers and tarmac. If a car came the other way, you just halted and let it make its way past, probably veering off the track. By a combination of slow driving and flinching, we reached Nicosia, parked and started to walk.

The name "flash storm" speaks for itself: it was to lead to a torrential downpour of intensity that I had never experienced before. We dived for the nearest doorway but we were soaked to the skin within seconds. Shivering and wretched even though we sheltered by a porch, we both noticed at the same time the brass name-plate at the side of the door.

"George Pelaghias, LLB, London."

I was astounded by this stroke of luck. I rang the bell.

The door was opened by a butler wearing a morning coat. No doubt his training prevented him from looking askance on the bedraggled couple standing before him.

"Good afternoon?" It was a question rather than a greeting.

"I am a friend of George's, from London," I told him.

"Please come in," he said. "You are getting wet."

We waited, dripping on the black and white marble squares of the spacious hallway. A stranger came to greet us. It was not the person I was looking for. Nor was I anyone he knew. But the wrong Mr Pelaghias, coincidentally a graduate of University College, was at least able to help with my search.

"I think I can find the George Pelaghias you are looking for," he said. The butler brought some paper and a pen and he wrote down a telephone number for me. It was not anything like the numbers that I had found in Avenue Major Poulios.

We were too wet to accept his offer of hospitality or enjoy an afternoon in Nicosia. We left our unexpected host and made our way back to Famagusta along the road which had been made even more dangerous by the rainstorm. I greeted the tour party with the information that I now had George's number.

"Oh yeah," they said, signifying a degree of disbelief that dented my optimism somewhat. Still, it was worth a try.

I dialled the number.

A familiar voice answered after a few rings.

"George?" I said.

Without a moment's hesitation he said, "Michael Sherrard!"

"Did you know I was coming?" I asked him.

"No," he said. "But I've been hearing about you and reading about your cases."

He had the better of me. I knew nothing about what he had been doing.

"George, I don't know what you've been up to – are you married do you have children – tell me what's been going on."

"You didn't know!" He sounded surprised. "Well, I," he said, pausing slightly for the effect his words were certain to have on me, "I am the Foreign Minister."

I was stunned. I thought, "If he can be Foreign Minister, anything is possible." I congratulated him but expected that the next thing he would say was that he was joking. "That's marvellous, George!"

"Look," he said, "it's a bit of a rough time at the moment. I'm working at the Palace of President Makarios but you've found me because I've just come home to leave my laundry. We are heavily engaged politically but we've got to eat. I'm sure Makarios would love to meet you. Why don't you come over for supper?"

It was with real regret that I had to refuse, after having spent all these days trying to track him down. "I'm so sorry – we've just eaten and we have to leave really early tomorrow. We have a 6.30 a.m. start." The excuse was genuine but part of my reluctance was the awareness that Makarios was receiving bad press in England and, as a new silk, it might not be advisable for me to be on social terms with him.

"What flight are you on?" he asked. I told him. "I'll be there at the airport," he assured me.

I reported to my fellow travellers. "He is real," I said, "You'll see for yourselves tomorrow."

Our group arrived at the airport as planned. There was no sign of him. I began to think that, although the voice was familiar and the words were right, I had been fooled. The group were looking at me with something like pity.

Then, from the main doorway we all saw white motorcycles approaching, their headlamps blazing. They were carrying uniformed outriders escorting a flag-bearing Daimler. Sitting within and wearing the unmistakeable homburg hat was George. An attendant opened the door of the limousine and George stepped out, arms wide to greet me and Shirley. The tour party now believed that he existed.

Within moments, he took our passports and whisked us off to the VIP lounge for Byzantine coffee. While we were there, he gave muttered instructions to his assistant who nodded and went off to fulfil George's instructions.

We caught up as best we could in the short time that we had together. He told us that he had married Chloe, the girl he had met at college, that they had a home in the Nicosia area and had a son, Christopher. There was not enough time for more than the barest outline. Our flight was called and, even with the VIP concession that we had achieved through George's good offices, we had to board our aircraft. We then learned that the message to the assistant had been a request from George in his official capacity for him and his honoured guests to meet and inspect the flight crew. We crossed the tarmac from the airport building to where they were waiting for us at the foot of the steps. As George introduced us, I could not help noticing the smiling faces of our tour party at the windows of the aircraft. Indeed, George saw them as well and raised his battered hat to them.

As it turned out, they were not smiling for us but laughing at us: the result of our grand connections was that we had not taken part in the seat allocation process so we had to sit apart for the flight to Malta in the only two seats that were left. I made up my mind to tell George about this. He would have seen the funny side.

***

The second part of the trip deserves more than a mention.

When we arrived in Malta with our tour group, we were greeted by an official from the Governor's office. After the George experience, the tour group thought we must – collectively – be "somebody". We certainly enjoyed being fussed over, especially after drawing the short straw on the seating arrangements on the plane. It turned out that the official was one of a group who, to all intents and purposes, had camped out at the airport to meet the flurry of dignitaries who were arriving for the dinner that had been so casually mentioned to us by Sir Anthony: if you were on the list, you were assumed to be have some sort of high status that not only merited but probably demanded an official greeting.

At the time, ambassadors to Rome were *ipso facto* ambassadors to Malta. They carried out their diplomatic duties largely by attending the annual dinner hosted by the Governor or, in this case, the Acting Governor.

By the time we reached our hotel, we understood that we were invited to attend Malta's most important social event of the year. The guests were to be in full regalia. We could expect and, eventually saw, the lot: tiaras, gongs – all the trappings of diplomatic and aristocratic splendour.

Shirley had travelled with a little black dress. The dress was elegant. But it was short. Her principal memory is that hers were the only visible legs that evening. I had planned less well. I had a sports shirt and slacks. Something had to be done.

"Is there a Moss Bros. in town?" I asked the concierge. In London, Moss Bros. was synonymous with the hire of formal dress. It turned out to be internationally known, at least as far as Malta.

"Sir," he said, "There is not a big choice. You must go now or someone else will get the suit."

I found the outfitters where clothes-hire took place in the far corner of the shop. I tried on the suit that the concierge had mentioned. The staff dealt admirably with my dismay. In what remained of the day, they altered the trousers by letting out the waist and shortening the legs. They shortened the jacket sleeves. The result can only be described as remarkable.

"You look like a gangster," Shirley said. "I'm going to pretend I'm with someone else."

The party was very grand. And the broad-shouldered, short-sleeved, long-jacketed, baggy-trousered look must have had some advantage. If appearance is anything to go by, the Mamos must have been sufficiently impressed – or forgiving – to continue their friendship with us subsequently.

They visited us over the years when they came to London, particularly in the period after our Malta trip while their son, John, was at Oxford. John Mamo came to stay with us one weekend. His fellow student, Michael Crystal[1], dropped him at our house in Burgess Hill on a Satur-

---

[1]   Michael Crystal: called to the Bar 1970, QC 1984, Master of the Bench, Middle Temple 1995.

day morning and collected him the following day. We were not good hosts: Shirley had flu and was confined to bed. Poor John had to fend for himself. However, he was the perfect guest. Before starting back to Oxford, he asked Michael Crystal to stop at a florist so he could buy Shirley some flowers. The florist was less than enthusiastic about the sale as she was just in the process of closing the shop. Nevertheless, she grudgingly produced a handsome bunch of lilies and parted with a card for John's message. Shirley, who has always loathed lilies, still keeps the card: its black border cheered her immensely in her recovery.

***

Although George did not get in touch with us for some time after the Cyprus visit, he eventually let us know that he was coming to London and we were able to arrange to spend an evening together. At his request, we took him to see *Jesus Christ Superstar*. He enjoyed it immensely. In the interval, without a trace of irony, he said, "Makarios would love this."

I asked, "Would he accept a gift of the music?"

"He would be so pleased."

So we bought the President a tape of the music which, apparently, he did enjoy, even though it was perhaps not strictly in the Cypriot Orthodox tradition.

***

After some years, George Pelaghias cropped up again.

In 1974 I was thrilled to be invited by the Foreign Office to go to Larnaca to relieve the resident High Court Judge of the Sovereign Base. I was told there were not too many cases but there was a wide spread of work including family, crime and civil. Shirley was invited to accompany me. The outgoing judge would stay for three days to show me the ropes in preparation for the take-over. This was an unusual and exciting opportunity. We were nearing the completion of our not insignificant preparations for departure on the specially commissioned RAF flight from Northolt when in early July, without advance warning, we had a visitor from the Foreign Office who announced apologetically that the situation in Cyprus had become very serious. The Makarios regime was likely to come under attack. The present judge would stay on for the time being but other British nationals were being evacuated, particularly those with families. He left promising that when things settled down, which they did not, the Foreign Office would be in touch. If it has to be done in a single word, disappointment is the only one to express how I felt as I watched him walk away.

***

Whilst the situation was becoming increasingly troubled in Cyprus, we learned years later that George's son, Christopher, had had a dream in which the Turks came to their house early one morning and shot his father. The boy, who was then about 19, was upset by this dream and truly afraid for his father's safety. He was passionate in urging his mother to persuade George to leave the country. George would have been impressed by the psychic phenomenon of an apparent prophecy coming through the message of a dream. The son's efforts succeeded: arrangements were made for George and Christopher to go to Lebanon immediately. They stayed in a casino hotel where they gambled, watched floor shows, ate and slept. When they arrived at the airport for their return journey, they picked up the news that Makarios had been deposed in a coup supported by the mainland Greek regime and had fled the country.

I tried to get in touch with George and phoned the Foreign Office for news of him when we could get none from Cyprus but they could not help. There was nothing more that I could do. Shirley and I took advantage of the unexpected gap left by the cancellation of the Cyprus appointment. We took a brief holiday. Whilst we were away, we heard of the coup and when we returned, we saw a clip on the television news of 19th July 1974 showing Makarios arriving at the United Nations building in New York to state the case for the lawfulness of his regime and to put forward his protest that the Greek coup was a breach of international law. Because of his close links with Makarios, we were looking for sight of George and were relieved when we saw them together. Somehow, he had managed to get to New York from Lebanon. However, worse was to come for Cyprus: Turkish troops invaded the next day. The island was partitioned and, after a few days of a puppet Greek presidency, Glafcos Clerides became the acting constitutional President of the Greek Cypriot part during Makarios' absence.

We took a family holiday in December, 1974, staying at the Grande Bretagna, a large hotel in Athens. Its decaying grandeur was reflected

175

in the standards of service which extended to changing the bathroom towels every third day. Its catering standards confirmed my opinion that, save for a sesame bun on a stick, the best Greek food at the time was served in the Cypriot restaurants in London. We ate most of our meals at a nearby Chinese place.

Work was to intrude slightly on the holiday as I was to meet a client who was flying in with Allen Yau for a consultation far from what he perceived as the prying eyes of Singapore. We were passing the time pleasantly enough on the terrace waiting for the meeting. As I looked around to see if there was any sign of the client or Allen, I could not help but notice a bedraggled figure heaving himself up the steps from the gardens below.

"Shirley," I said. "Do my eyes deceive me? Is that George?"

It certainly was George but he was bareheaded, unshaven and looking very much the worse for wear in shabby clothes. He was wearing fishing boots which, in addition to their incongruity, looked far too big for him. Worst of all for George, there was no sign of the hat. I went straight over to him and said, "George! What's happened?"

He glanced at me without a flicker of surprise that I should be in this place at this time. "I had to leave in a hurry," he gasped, looking and sounding as if he were still fleeing. "On a boat – had to get to Athens – been hiding on a boat."

He drew breath and looked about him as if becoming aware of where he was. "Here I am," he said. He made a small gesture with his hands, palms upwards. "I have nothing. Only the clothes I stand up in."

He came to our table and we ordered coffee and cake and then more and more. He was famished. Between mouthfuls, and looking about him to see if anyone was watching or listening, he told us a little of the horror of the Turkish invasion and the terrible casualties that had been suffered in spite of United Nations intervention. I asked him, "What about Glafcos Clerides – is he in trouble?"

"I don't know," he said. And, almost as an afterthought, "He's the president now."

George left us after a time, hinting that he was to meet people who had come to Athens to rescue him. It could not have been more than a few days until Makarios was restored to power, although Cyprus remained and remains partitioned. However, we never found out what forced George to flee at this time, leaving everything.

Some years later, I heard of his untimely death. I wanted to get hold of Clerides to talk about George and share some memories. I did not manage to get in touch and as each day passed, the need decreased. After a while, I convinced myself that he would not have remembered me anyway.

***

We met Chloe in London after George had died. Over dinner she asked, "Do you remember when the Turks invaded Cyprus?"

"Yes, of course," I said.

"They turned up at our house at 5.30 a.m.," she told us. "I was watering the plants. I have always been an early riser."

I could immediately visualise her on the wide gravel paths in the bright-flowered, leafy garden which we had seen in photographs that George had shown us.

"A lorry came," she went on. "Six Turkish soldiers jumped down from the back. Their officer shouted across to me and demanded that I produce George. They didn't believe me that he was not there. I told them to go and search the house. They did. They wrecked the place. They left no stone unturned."

She told me that the reason George had remembered me at once when I phoned while we were on the Cyprus trip was because he had been reading English newspaper stories about the Rolls Razor case and was delighted with what he saw as a great adventure for me in court.

CHAPTER 31

A BOXING DINNER

Not all the trappings of silk are to do with litigation. Sometimes there are speaking engagements as a spin-off of advocacy skills. Michael has always been known as a mimic and raconteur, which may be why he was invited to speak at a dinner hosted by the British Sports Writers Association at the Café Royal. He prepared something moderately light, based on research from a pamphlet about the rules and regulations related to pugilism, drawing the information into the way the sport was conducted in modern times. He would make respectful references to the improvements effected by proper controls.

A priest stood next to me in the lift going up to the reception floor. He introduced himself.

"I'm Martin O'Sullivan, Dean of St Paul's. I'm speaking at the dinner tonight."

I told him who I was and that I too was speaking.

"It's an enormous do," he told me.

"What do you mean 'enormous'?"

"It's the whole of the roof area of the Café Royal. five or six hundred people, so I'm told."

I was alarmed. I had expected a formal dinner and assumed that the guests would be numbered in dozens rather than hundreds. My idea of a cosy after-dinner chat was not at all what was required. Whilst I was trying to assemble my thoughts on how to amend my speech to address a huge audience, Tommy Farr[1] stood at the head of the reception line. He might have thought he was shaking my hand with his huge fist but to me it felt as though he was lifting me bodily into the air. He seemed quite unaware of his enormous power. An indefinable bond forms with a man who has, to all practical purposes, dislocated every joint in your arm as his greeting.

---

[1] Tommy Farr (1914-1986), British and Empire Light Heavyweight Champion, 1937

I did not have to say very much as I was introduced to other boxing dignitaries, many of whom were either as strong as Tommy or compensated for lack of power in their arms by loud voices. Nursing my injured hand, I made my way towards my place at the dinner table, re-jigging my speech between bouts of jolly and boisterous conversation. This was hardly the sort of do for a discourse on "Rules and Regulations …"

I found myself seated next to the Chairman of the British Board of Boxing Control. "It's our turn to host the Sports Awards Dinner," he said. "I hope you don't mind being on TV?"

"TV??"

"Presenting the most promising boxer of the year[1] with his belt. We're beaming the programme to Sydney. We don't know what they've got in mind. They might want you to sentence him!"

I began to wonder if they'd called on the wrong person. What would someone of my standing be doing at such a prestigious ceremony?

I knew that I had to do something that was out of the ordinary and inspiration came, not a moment too soon. The plan was to wait for the toastmaster to call me in the usual way. I would not get up. This would lead to a bit of a kerfuffle. I knew that I would be called again and it would not be long before the toastmaster came over to see if I was all right. I had enough time to scribble down some notes for him to read when he reached me. I would then hand him the paper and whisper to him to read it. He would say, "And now for round three! Speaking from the red corner, weighing in at 13 stones with an unblemished record fighting for the law, Mr Michael Sherrard!" I decided to tell him, "And I want to hear the bell ring."

As the dinner proceeded, I learned that I was to be the first to reply on behalf of the guests. The Chairman leaned towards me and said, "Don't worry if it doesn't go the way you've planned. It'll be all right."

The first speaker was called. The toastmaster banged his gavel for silence. He spoke.

"My Lords, Ladies and Gentlemen, in the right-hand corner, the lightweight speaker …."

[1] Joe Donovan: 1968, Australia's most promising boxer

I looked in the direction gestured by the white-gloved hand. I saw the Dean of St Paul's beginning to rise from his seat … Not for the first time, I found that I had to put together a new version of a speech to deal with unexxpected circumstances.

CHAPTER 32

TALES FROM THE CENTRAL BANK OF INDIA

The Central Bank of India instructed Michael in several cases in the 1970s, mainly commercial matters. However, one case gave him the pleasure of obtaining an injunction to prevent the loss of the original (and priceless) 7' high bronze statue known as the Shivapura Nataraja. This statue has been widely reproduced in every imaginable size ranging from full-scale replicas to miniature medallions. It shows the elegant limbs of the god Shiva in womanly form intertwined with those of Nataraja, Lord of the Dance.

Someone who knew India very well was driving near Horsham in Surrey. Whilst sitting in a traffic jam, he noticed at the side of a house something that looked remarkably like the great sculpture. He saw the representation of the source of all movement within the cosmos being constrained by the space between neighbouring walls. This troubled him. When he arrived in London, he told a colleague at the High Commission what he had seen.

It transpired that the original sculpture, an important work, both of art and of holy significance, had begun to suffer damage by corrosion and rust. It had been sent to experts in Bombay to be cleaned and protected. In due course, glossy and restored, it was to have been replaced in the shrine from which it had been removed. Behind the scenes, the people in Bombay had been persuaded to sell the statue so that it could be copied. To the naked eye, the copy was to be indistinguishable from the restored original. The shiny, new appearance of the forgery was precisely what had been expected after the restoration and did not cause suspicion or lead to trouble.

An American gallery was involved in the acquisition of the original sculpture which remained in a sorry state at the time it came into their hands. They sent the statue to the principal expert in the care of Indian artifacts and objets d'art. She happened to live in Horsham where she set about dealing with the corrosion. She started the cleaning process, seen from the traffic jam, by immersing it part by part in a bath of acid outside her house. She had no idea of that there was any plan to copy the statue and was totally innocent of any part in the conspiracy.

My instructing solicitor told me the facts. "Can't we get moving?" he asked, "I need to get that statue back to its owners. We have to do something now."

I could not manage 'now' as I was in court that day but at the end of the morning list, I asked the judge in chambers to release me for 15 minutes so that I could apply for an order for return of the statue to its lawful owners. In fact, we went for a more practical solution: the restoration expert would complete the job she had started and agreed that the statue would not be moved from her property until collected by an authorised person so that it could be taken back to India to replace the convincing fake that stood in its place.

There never was a trial. The Americans were anxious to avoid one. It was their case that they had acted in good faith. They knew the statue was an important piece but they had not known it was *the* Shivapura.

I became the hero of the day to India but I did not deserve the praise that was awarded to me. The real hero was the man in the car.

***

And there was the defence of Noshir Mistry, acquitted on 13 November 1972, of the charge of possession of forged bank-notes.

In happier times, Mr Mistry was the manager of the Bombay office of the Central Bank of India. He had been the chief prosecution witness in a £1 million fraud case against a previous London manager of the Bank who was ultimately sentenced at the Old Bailey to seven years imprisonment. Now it was Mistry's turn in the dock. His defence to the subsequent charged of possession of forged £5 notes was that the notes had been planted on him as a vicious personal vendetta arising from the evidence he had given in the fraud trial.

There was a strong suspicion that the evidence that the police used to bring the charges against Mr Mistry had indeed been planted. As a result, Henry Pownall, who prosecuted the case, formally offered no evidence against him. He was acquitted but he had powerful enemies out there.

There was strong Indian government influence in the management of the Central Bank at the time Mrs Gandhi was in power[1]. One of the

---

[1]   Indirha Gandhi was Prime Minister of India 1966-1974 and 1980-1984

managers was replaced when he fell out of political favour. I went to his farewell party at the family's Kensington home when the London posting finished. The younger of his two teenage daughters took me rather by surprise when she came up to me and without any preamble asked, "Will you be my uncle? Can I write to you? Will you write back?"

This was not a matter to be negotiated. I agreed. Over the years, we maintained correspondence and I was to learn of the development of her interest in the law and of her subsequent legal studies and qualification as a solicitor.

The former bank manager was head-hunted for a job in Dubai which he took in the interests of his family, and particularly the daughter's career, the progress of which was difficult for her in the current social conditions of India. Some years later, when I was often working in the East and the route to Singapore included a transit stop in Dubai, I was invited to visit them. They were a lovely family and I was tempted into accepting the invitation by the prospect of the opportunity of breaking one of my long journeys together with the chance of exploring Dubai properly rather than simply looking round its airport lounge. Shirley was unwilling to go to Dubai. She thought we might be shot, or something. We arranged things so that I left England first and I would join her on the connecting flight to Singapore.

My host met me at the airport, apologising for his straightened circumstances. He warned me that the family now lived humbly, contrasted against the opulence of the London house. Perhaps he thought his Cadillac should have been a Rolls-Royce!

Early next morning a drive in the desert was proposed. It seemed like a good idea at the time. I had not imagined that for something like three hours, we would drive through mile after mile of endless banks of grey sand piled on either side of the road. While trying to stay awake, I suddenly saw, like a child's pop-up book, the facade of an enormous green and white edifice. I woke up sharply.

"Is that a mirage?" I asked.

"No. It's the Palace Hotel at Jebel Ali, a very interesting place." And only three hours from home, plus another ten minutes or so to negotiate the driveway through the sudden lush greenery of the gardens surrounding a colossal palace and then walking through the vast entrance to the building. I was absolutely bemused.

"What do you think of this?" said my host, not attempting to conceal his pride.

"Do you really want to know?"

"Yes!" He beamed at me.

"If I was the sort of man who had a mistress, this is where I would bring her." I was thinking of the gaudy anonymity of this outrageous monument to kitsch and the sort of men I had known who had taken women to places barely as tasteless.

Suddenly, I heard a voice.

"Hello, Mr S. What are you doing here?"

It was Perla Racousier, an antique dealer who I knew well from Hong Kong. After what I had said, what would my friends think about me being there?

"Good God, Perla," I heard myself say. "What are you doing here?" Then, it occurred to me that perhaps she had been brought here by – but before I could complete the thought, she said, "I'm giving a dinner party."

Not entirely relieved, I said, "Who for?"

"The Sheikhs."

All was not clear.

"Come and see," she said. I looked to my host who nodded me away, agreeing to release me from the duties of friendship.

She walked off, leading me about half a mile across the lobby toward the dining room. It was garish, stupendous and marvellous all at the same time.

"I'm entertaining all the Sheikhs," she explained, not needing a megaphone to reach me as the acoustics were so good. "After the dinner, we auction everything down to the dirty laundry – they want it because someone else does, for face's sake."

She became very rich…

184

We went back to Dubai. My expectations had been low but the realisation was significantly greater. The Soukh was wondrous: shelves and shops and stalls piled with gold, silks, trinkets, people milling, singing, shouting, food and drink everywhere and barely any room to move as the crowds pressed you along. I could hardly believe that I was there.

And a few hours down the road, the vast emptiness of Jebel Ali and the Palace Hotel.

***

On the Thursday before going to Dubai, I was lunching in the Benchers' apartments. Tom Denning came in. The custom is that the newcomer sits on the nearest available seat.

"You still travelling?" he asked me. I nodded, dealing with a mouthful of hot soup.

"Where?"

With my palate scorched from the sudden gulp needed to cope with essential conversation, I managed to tell him "Singapore – tonight – going to spend a few days in Dubai – no extra cost – spend a weekend with friends." As my mouth soothed to the beginnings of a blister, I described my correspondence with the remarkable young daughter of the family and her interest in the law.

"Nice young woman," he said. "Very clever from what you tell me. What gift will you take her?"

I had that day bought one of his books for her. I told him so.

"Where is it?" This was more a command than a question. I left my soup, hurried to chambers where the book was still in its paper bag on my desk. I was back to the table with it before the soup had a chance to cool down. He spent the next ten minutes or so covering the frontispiece in his careful handwriting with his inscription, a message to all our Commonwealth lawyers. It ended, "I hope you will accept my affectionate greetings."

CHAPTER 33

SAVUNDRA

In 1963, anyone who had £50 million capital could set themselves up in the motor insurance business. That was the year when Dr Emil Savundra[1] took advantage of the arguably lax system to invest money from goodness knows where to purchase an insurance business that thenceforth traded as the Fire, Auto and Marine Insurance Company. He set about attracting trade by offering premiums which drew a large number of unsuspecting customers into his net. However, Savundra's propensity for spending the company's money rather than using it to pay out claims led to its collapse in 1966 with debts of £1.4 million. Kenneth Cork was appointed as the liquidator but that was of no assistance to the policyholders, many of whom faced financial ruin as their claims remained unpaid.

Even if Savundra did not make a fortune in the insurance business, he certainly spent one. He enjoyed expensive cars and clothes to match and he travelled widely, always staying in the best hotels. Depending on your taste, he lived in an ostentatious or magnificent mansion in the Millionaire's Row of North-West London, The Bishop's Avenue. Even when the company was failing to meet its obligations to its customers, it managed to pay Savundra's 'wages' and 'expenses'. Daily press coverage of the hardship of the policyholders and third parties fanned the flames of public interest in the scandal. Savundra was displeased with what he regarded as unwarranted attacks on his character. He approached the television personality, David Frost, with a request to appear on his programme. The aim was to charm the 'national' audience into liking him as much as he liked himself.

Several of the affected policyholders gathered in the BBC television studios on 5th February 1967 to watch the Frost interview and to ask Dr Savundra questions themselves.

Frost's interrogation was thorough, so much so that Lord Justice Salmon later warned that trial by TV should not be tolerated in a civilised society. Savundra was not unnerved by the questions. He displayed an arrogant indifference to the plight of his clients and refused to be

[1]   Emil Savundra (1923-1976)

drawn into discussion with them, saying, no doubt with the best of intentions, "I do not want to cross swords with peasants."

Soon after the broadcast, he left the country, assuring those who were interested (and there were many) that he would return.

I was involved with Savundra's machinations because, at the time of the company's collapse, David Freeman had instructed me to act for Kenneth Cork, to find a route to recover some of the Company's losses from Savundra's personal assets. I proposed that proceedings should be commenced against the Company and Savundra should be made a personal defendant to get his back to the wall on disclosure of documents: he would then have the right to represent himself. It was light relief compared with the Normansfield enquiry which had been going on at much the time that Fire Auto and Marine was being bled dry.

The Frost programme seemed to act as a catalyst in the prosecution of Savundra for fraud but no step could be taken when he was abroad. We knew of his boast that he would return and that, according to him, as a man of his word, he could be trusted to do so. But the police had information that, if he kept to his plan, he would only be passing through Heathrow between undoubtedly first-class flights. The police knew about my part in the civil proceedings and thought that I would be a useful contact for them. They wanted to see if there was any legal assistance that I could give to the criminal team in light of the absence of the potential defendant. A small posse descended on my house in Burgess Hill on the Saturday after the Frost programme to see what charges should be preferred against Savundra and how he could be brought to justice. Shirley said good-bye to what would have been a family weekend and left us in the dining room to grapple with the problem.

One of the officers said, "It's a pity he's not even staying overnight. Goodness knows when he'll be back again."

Another said, "He'll be back when the money runs out. Then he'll have to take in lodgers – there's room for 43 of them."

While they were discussing the interesting proposition that taking lodgers would pay the bills after running an insurance company into the ground, I was thinking about the pity of Savundra only being in transit. I believe that I went into "Counsel's finkin'" mode. I realized that it made no difference whether the stopover was long or short. As soon as the plane landed, he would be in the jurisdiction. He would be ours. It was almost too simple. I told the visitors my idea: that he should be arrested as soon as he came down the aircraft steps or into the Terminus. They were pleased: it had been worthwhile for them to give up their weekend as well.

"Could you draft the charges?"

I could. I did. A magistrate was found out of hours to endorse the warrant for his arrest.

The smiling, affable man-of-his-word arrived at Heathrow. He had said he would return and he did. Of course, he returned for somewhat longer than he had anticipated. In 1968, he was convicted of fraud and sentenced to 8 years in prison. He was also fined £50,000. He conducted his appeals against sentence and conviction in person, complaining that he could not have had a fair trial because the television programme had prejudiced the outcome. His appeals did not succeed because criminal proceedings were not under way at the time of the broadcast.

My next part in the Savundra cases arose through the liquidator's interest in how he had managed to finance his palatial home in one of the most expensive areas of London. My main objective was to prevent him removing his assets from the country and to recover the money, which had gone astray. There was a slight chance that could be achieved by suing Savundra as well as the Company and enforcing the judgment debt against the property. It turned out to be a good chance: the judge did what I thought was improbable: he gave leave to do just that.

In 1972, Savundra, serving time on fraud charges with his appeals to the Court of Appeal and House of Lords dismissed, was not in court to hear the news that meant he would have to lose his house but his current situation did not stop him taking his case to the Court of Appeal who upheld the judgment. The next step for him was to petition the House of Lords for leave to appeal to the highest level. Kenneth Cork told me that he would not have enough time to come into the Lords for the hearing. However, he wanted as much weight as possible. He felt that an eminent leader would convince their Lordships that the right place for the value of Savundra's home should be in the depleted coffers of the insurance company. Morris Finer led me. Savundra's funds, for once, did not run to representation.

For the occasion, he was allowed out of prison. I saw him for the first, and only, time when he appeared at a Committee Room of the House of Lords. Dressed in an immaculate white suit and accompanied by two warders, he seemed to be quite at ease in the formal surroundings where Lord Hodson presided over the panel of three Law Lords. Savundra stood at the podium as if it were a soapbox, pounding the lectern to make his many, lengthy points. He was better dressed than any of the lawyers in the room. His wife, Pushpam, sat at the back watching steadfastly. She was the one with most to lose: Savundra had a roof over his head, courtesy of Her Majesty. When this appeal failed, Pushpam would have none.

I sat back and listened to him address their Lordships in a heavily accented tone that combined indignation and pomposity. He complained, "I am sitting here in this calumny." Morris' submissions were dismissed as nonsense. "This poop-in-jay," he sneered, stressing each distorted syllable as he waved his perfect cuff at him in disgust.

When he had finished his diatribe, their Lordships looked at one another for a little telepathy. Lord Hodson spoke.

"Thank you," he said kindly. "Their Lordships are not disposed to give you leave to appeal."

Savundra was furious.

"You may not give leave," he said, stressing the "you" scornfully, "but I will go to the Court of Human Rights at Strasbourg."

Hodson turned to each of the other judges as if the threat were being taken seriously.

"Yes, indeed," he said gravely.

Savundra's moments of freedom were over.

CHAPTER 34

PETER HAIN

In 1950, Peter Gerald Hain was born in Kenya, the son of South African parents whose activities in the anti-apartheid movement of their home country led to them being made "banned persons". The family fled to England in 1966 where the son became a dedicated campaigner against the hated apartheid regime.

The effect of apartheid had ramifications into sport[1]. Hain would have been very much aware of the 1968 scandal concerning his fellow ex-patriate, Basil D'Oliveira. "Dolly" was a brilliant cricketer whose talents were being suffocated in South Africa because he was of mixed race. He had migrated to England where he became an outstanding member of the English cricket team. After a stunning contribution to the test match against Australia, the MCC excluded him from the subsequent South African tour, apparently because of his race.

Peter Hain was part of a pressure group which saw links with South Africa through sport as legitimisation of the political regime. He was chairman of the "Stop the Seventy Tour (STST)" campaign whose aim was to stop exclusively white South African sports teams from competing in England and raise public awareness of a regime which excluded black or 'mixed-race' sportsmen by reason of their race. The ultimate goal was prevention of the official cricket tour planned for 1970. From 1969, organised disorder interfered with a Davis Cup tennis match and the unofficial Wilf Isaacs XI tour of England, a private team whose members were largely drawn from the ranks of former and current South African Team players. The campaign continued with demonstrations on the rugby field during the official Springboks' tour that winter. It was clear that there would be serious disruption of the 1970 cricket tour even if the STST campaigners acted within the law and eschewed violence. The MCC tried to maintain a non-political stance and, to show that it was not intimidated, set about barricading selected pitches with barbed wire. Despite its well-prepared defences, it eventually bowed to the Labour Government's request to call off its invitation to the South African team. The MCC then reviewed its position and decided not to resume relations

---

[1] Changes did come to sport and were followed by those of the political system, culminating in full democracy in 1994.

with South African cricket until non-racial team selection had been established[1]. The aim of the STST had been achieved.

Peter Hain's book, "Don't Play with Apartheid[2]" contained details of the campaign of disruption, including his leadership, which formed a critical plank of a private prosecution brought against him by a barrister, Francis Bennion. The substantial cost of the exercise was funded by subscriptions raised in South Africa. The case against Hain was founded on the ostensible confession in the book to his leading role as chairman of the STST in the alleged conspiracy to prevent the exclusively white South Africans competing with British teams.

Regular demonstrations against apartheid took place in London, mainly outside South Africa House near Trafalgar Square. There were frequent arrests, often of the same people, on charges of some sort of breach of the peace (chanting anti-apartheid slogans), criminal damage (knocking a policeman's helmet to the ground), obstructing the police (refusing to move on) and resisting arrest (as one would). As a junior, I was one of many barristers, sympathetic to the principles of the demonstrators, who ensured that they would have a reliable defence or mitigation offered on their behalf as they appeared time and again at Bow Street or Great Marlborough Street Magistrates' Courts. I believe that I came to the defence of Peter Hain because of this background. The equally sympathetic Brian Capstick was my junior.

What was obvious was that Hain had probably been singled out from thousands of anti-apartheid demonstrators because his name was known to the public. A more sinister interpretation was that he had to be punished so as to stop opposition to the South African government's inhumane policies.

In the fortnight preceding the trial, which ran between 24th July and 22nd August 1972, we took stock of the options. We agreed that we should move to quash the indictment as being objectionable as a rolled-up conspiracy. If that did not succeed and the trial were to continue,

---

[1] Many other sporting bodies around the world followed the MCC's lead.
[2] Don't Play with Apartheid: Background to the Stop the Seventy Tour Campaign: Peter Hain, 1971; Allen & U; ISBN 0043010318. The title succinctly describes the content. The allegations of conspiracy arose more from phrases in the book than from any hard evidence.

Peter realised that he would be vulnerable to cross-examination through the content of the book. Further, if he did not give evidence, although the jury would be instructed not to draw any inference from his silence, there might be a perception that his failure to go into the witness-box was self-condemnatory. Brian and I forecast that Peter would be in a better position if he did not give evidence but were to seek to make his points in a closing speech to the jury. He could do that if he were to take over his defence at half-time. We decided to review the situation towards the end of the prosecution evidence but we had the strong feeling that Hain would wish to end the case by taking over his own defence to complete his political agenda.

The prosecution team was led by Owen Stable QC, with Mark Potter[1], the real strength of the team, as his junior. Owen had little half-rim glasses whose purpose, perched at the end of his nose, was to be looked over rather than for use as a visual aid. He always dressed in pepper and salt trousers, spats, a black waistcoat and a black, hacking-style jacket with pockets edged with silk. He wore a black bowler hat and invariably carried a furled umbrella, using it as a walking accoutrement with a certain flourish, not at all as a walking stick. Certainly, it was never put to use in the rain. He earned the title, "Racing Correspondent for the Church Times." This covered his passion for horses combined with his devotion to religion.

You can tell when the other side is panicking. You see the leader scratching a hurried note for the junior or turning to whisper to him to send him off to look belatedly for a crumb of legal hope in textbooks outside court. You sense the solicitor coughing quietly or tugging at the junior's gown to try to catch his attention with some idea of his own about how to deal with an impending crisis in case counsel had not noticed that flak was falling. I saw Mark Potter hurrying out of court time and again as the obvious signs of panic set in on the prosecution side. After much whispering and deprecating half-smiles towards me as I paused to let them have the benefit of a little chat about what on earth they were going to do next, Mark would be sent scurrying off to research each new point that I made.

---

1   Sir Mark Potter is now the President of the Family Division.

It was thought by some that my other opponent was the Judge: Bernard Gillis. There was a perception that the memory of what he had seen as a disappointment in the John Bloom matter might rankle. However, you take your judges as you find them. The law has to be above judicial vindictiveness. Judge Gillis listened to my argument preceding the trial that conspiracy is a non-offence. Apparently taking the prosecution by surprise, judging by junior counsel's series of disappearances, I submitted that there cannot be a criminal offence to conspire to stop a cricket tour: you have to conspire to commit an offence that would stop the tour. The point was based on the cartwheel principle: you could not allege conspiracy at common law to commit offences and have a revolving danger that anything that cropped up then might be an offence and would, *ipso facto*, be caught by the allegation of conspiracy. I argued this at great length, over several days, as I recall.

Perhaps he did have Bloom memories. Gillis would not have any of it. Much later, my arguments were reflected in the law which recognised "contingent conspiracy". But that is legal argument. We had to crack on with the facts.

After three and a half days of legal arguments there was a day and a half of Owen Stable opening the case to the jury and evidence began on the following Monday.

First, there was sub-poenaed evidence from a local press photographer about the damage caused by demonstrators at the Parks Ground in Oxford. The next witness was Wilf Isaacs.

Michael's cross-examination was based on the well-grounded premise that Isaacs was a supporter of the current South African regime. He began with questions about Isaacs' personal involvement in the case. Isaacs confirmed that he had come to England for the committal proceedings in the Magistrates' Court and had been cross-examined there. The law provided for such evidence to be read but Isaacs said he had been asked by the prosecution to attend the trial.

In cross-examination, I asked Mr Isaacs whether he had contributed indirectly to the prosecution fund by agreeing to pay his own fare to attend the committal hearing. He sidestepped the questions by saying that he "took advantage of coming to England at the time on holiday and on business". He responded to the suggestion that the prosecution had been inspired by South Africans who wish to sponsor racialism in sport by blandly assuring the court that he was here representing a private team in a private capacity and happened to be here at a time that was convenient to him as a regular visitor to London.

As he had told the court that a non-white person would play for his team I pressed him on the point. I asked, "Are you telling us that you are now allowed to include as a player in your team any African, Asian or person of mixed race? Someone who is actually going to be allowed to play cricket?"

And what did Mr Isaacs say? He said, "I'm not saying that."

Of course he wasn't. I continued, "Don't you think you ought to make it plain that if you wanted to bring a team from South Africa comprising mixed races, you would have to have the permission of the government to do so?"

The judge intervened to ask if it would mean the government having to authorise who should be in the team or whether I was concerned with passports and visas. I meant more than that: documentation would not be issued to people who would not be allowed to play. I continued the cross-examination.

"Mr Isaacs, I suggest that you could not bring from South Africa a Wilf Isaacs touring team comprising white members, Asian members, Indian members, Africans, Chinese, travelling together to play together as a team." I asked the rhetorical question, "Would the government give you permission to do so?" And answered myself, "I think not."

Wilf Isaacs' explanation that he had not had to seek government permission for any arrangements for his private team was an invitation to ask the question, "Have you ever sought, as an anti-racialist, to include in your team, travelling abroad, during all these years, a single, non-white player?"

His answer seemed to echo in the courtroom. "I have not."

Other witnesses gave their evidence. One was Dawe de Villiers, the Springboks' captain. Within days of giving evidence, he was at home in South Africa, declaring himself as a candidate for the Nationalist party whose electoral platform was the continuance of apartheid.

194

Brian Capstick and I had, of course, foreseen that there were dangers ahead for Peter. We were fast approaching the end of the prosecution evidence and the crucial question whether he should give evidence had not been raised. Peter had reached his own conclusion as to what he should do. In his very readable book, *Sing the Beloved Country*[1] he puts the dilemma into perspective: "taking my own defence was daunting."

Once Peter had made up his mind, I had no option but to make the announcement that Brian and I would be retiring from the team and watching the game from the pavilion. The judge said words to the effect that he had "seen this coming". As Peter describes it, he tried to get him to change his mind. There was some satisfaction for me to hear Judge Gillis assuring my client that his defence was in capable hands. But we all had a glimpse of the tenacity that would see Peter Hain through his future political career. He was determined to see it through on his own.

I popped into court over the final days to see him presenting an articulate and sensible case. The jury could not agree on three of the four charges (the judge ordered acquittals) but a majority of 10:2 found him guilty of conspiring to disrupt the Davis Cup tennis match. Judge Gillis fined him £200. A curious feature of the way the case ended was that both sides thought they had won. I had the pleasure of being recalled to the case to argue successfully against a costs application by the prosecution.

***

A couple of years after the 1994 collapse of the apartheid regime Peter Hain launched "Sing the Beloved Country" in South Africa House. His parents telephoned me to make sure I was coming and to ask if I had a copy. If not, they would make sure I had one.

When I arrived, I was welcomed by a man I recognised. I had defended him several times in the series of demonstrations some twenty years previously.

"It's the first time I've been inside here," I said. I did not feel entirely comfortable and perhaps it showed.

---

[1]   Peter Hain, *Sing the Beloved Country: Struggle for the New South Africa* (London, Pluto Press, 1996).

"It's not quite my first," he said. "But I still hesitate sometimes when I come in, in case they won't admit me. Then I remember that now I'm the High Commissioner."

Peter wrote a dedication in my copy of his book. We had a chat and after a time, I left.

I thought no more about the changes in the fortune of the High Commissioner with the change of regime until I went to South Africa a couple of years later as part of a lecture tour, including advocacy training. Our group was shown around Parliament House, a magnificent building, all the more impressive for no longer being home to a disgraceful system.

The Minister of Justice, a qualified doctor, was our guide. She came to speak to me, starting with greetings and a few general comments. Then she said, "You don't recognise me, do you?"

I looked more carefully.

"Your face is familiar," I ventured, without coming up with any positive identification.

"You've seen me in court quite a few times," she said. "You defended my husband." I still looked politely blank. "My husband," she repeated, "the High Commissioner in London. We have always been so grateful for what you did."

My status in the group went up.

The former Prime Minister, now Leader of the Opposition, Fredrik de Klerk[1], went to the despatch box. To see him, a white man, defer to the black Speaker was very moving. I felt humbled by my small part in the process that had made this possible.

***

Some post-scripts:

1   *The Court of Appeal dismissed Hain's appeal against conviction. The Daily Telegraph of 23 October 1973 reported the Court as saying that his conviction was 'fully justified' and quoted Lord Justice Roskill as saying that Hain had not elected to give evidence, adding 'He*

---

[1]   Winner of the 1993 Nobel Peace Prize

gave no explanation of his part over the incidents with which he was charged'.

2   *Peter Hain was subjected to another trial in 1976, charged with a bank robbery in 1974. Two witnesses identified him at an identification parade. He was allegedly framed by South African intelligence agents. Lewis Hawser QC defended him. He was acquitted.*

3   *Peter Hain is an MP and has held high office in successive Labour governments.*

4   *12 July 2006. Ashwell Prince, aged 28, was appointed South Africa's first black cricket captain.*

.

CHAPTER 35

A BOMB AND A BLONDE BOMBSHELL

Thinking back from the tragic events of 7 July 2005 when terrorist bombs brought death and destruction to London, there are memories of the IRA's campaign on the British mainland, principally from the 1960s onwards. On the afternoon of 8 March 1973, a car parked near the Old Bailey roused police suspicions that it might contain an IRA bomb. Their suspicions were well-founded. Shortly after the successful evacuation of the people in the nearby "George" public house, the car exploded, wrecking the pub and causing damage to the West front of the Old Bailey. Flying glass and debris caused injuries to 174 people, some of whom were leaving the court when the bomb exploded. One man died.

During the course of the morning, I had been in the Old Bailey representing the singer, Dorothy Squires[1]. She was facing corruption charges with Jack Dabbs, a BBC record producer. It was alleged that in February 1970 she treated him to holidays abroad in return for his assistance with her flagging career by playing her records, including 'My Way'[2] on the popular programme, *World Wide Family Favourites*. In fact her career received a kick-start when she hired the London Palladium later that year for a come-back concert: it was sold out and much enjoyed by her faithful fans. But the police continued a leisurely investigation and, in early 1973, the corruption charges were brought against both of them: her for allegedly offering the bribes, him for allegedly accepting them.

Dorothy was well known as an entertainer. 'My Way' illustrated the much-publicised ups and downs of her life. She had certainly loved, laughed and cried and, as a vexatious litigant, had had more than her share of losing. Her sense of humour stayed with her, so she probably did find amusing, in the long run, to have done "all that" her way.

One of her claims to fame was her short marriage – and its stormy ending – to the film-actor Roger Moore, later to become known for his role as James Bond. She was also an enthusiastic litigant who acted in

---

[1]   Dorothy Squires (1915-1998).
[2]   "My Way", 1967: Paul Anka.

person[1] in several libel actions. A criminal trial was a very different situation.

After Dorothy had been bailed, prosecuting counsel, James Caesar Crespi, was left with a hole in his diary for the rest of the day but this was filled when Scotland Yard instructed him in another case. This meant that he had to cross the courtyard between the Old Bailey main building and the annex to reach the court next door to the George Pub. As he made his way out of the main building, the bomb went off. Injured by flying glass, he was photographed by the press being led away from the smoke and debris by uniformed officers. The pictures of him in his bloodstained shirt with the makeshift bandage covering his eyes are a harrowing reminder of terrorism on London's streets.

I went with a mutual friend to visit him in Barts Hospital. We arrived filled with sympathy for his plight and admiration for his dignity and courage. But it was difficult not to think how funny James looked, propped unhappily against his pillows, spattered with shrapnel, successfully imitating a lugubrious, human version of a Spotted Dick. A big man with a well-earned reputation as a trencherman, James' main discomfort was the thought of his impending encounter with hospital food.

"We've come empty-handed," I said, stating the obvious. "Can we get something for you?"

"There's a restaurant at the end of Old Bailey," he said sadly. "They do the most marvellous paté…"

We took this as instructions and went off to the restaurant. The owners knew James very well. We bought the entire paté and brought it back to the hospital wrapped in cling film. He got through the whole lot in four days.

***

---

[1] Her forays into the law ended in 1982 when, after losing several cases, she was declared a vexatious litigant But she won a case against the *News of the World: Moore v News of the World Ltd.* [1972] 1QB 44: the paper published an article about her marriage, attributing authorship to her. The Court of Appeal (Lord Denning presiding) upheld the jury's award of £4,300 for libel and £100 for false attribution of authorship.

As far as Dorothy's case is concerned, she and Jack were on bail for eighteen months pending the trial which started on 4th November 1974. The prosecution evidence was clearly inadequate. I put forward a submission of 'no case to answer.' On the third day, Judge Neil McKinnon directed the jury to find both defendants not guilty.

He did not quite say that she done it her way, but he refused to award her costs. It rankles to this day that a person should have to bear the cost of defending a case when there is insufficient evidence to support a charge.

CHAPTER 36

BROWN'S BLOOD

On 12 September 1973, the newspapers had a field day reporting the spectacular crash of Lord George-Brown's Jaguar into the wall of a garage forecourt in Maida Vale, London. As the Foreign Secretary in Harold Wilson's Labour Government five years previously, he counted as a celebrity. Then as now, the misdemeanours of a public figure were very likely to catch the eye of the press. The interest here arose from his Lordship's response to the garage attendant having the temerity to point out that he was not fit to drive. For his attention to detail, the attendant received a well-placed punch on the nose from the ennobled fist.

The court was told that both a qualified mechanic and a police officer confirmed that the car had suffered brake failure. It was said that the brake pedal sank to the floor without any pressure whatsoever. The prosecution accepted this evidence. But whatever was the mechanical state of the vehicle, the attendant's first impression may well have been reasonably accurate. Lord George-Brown's blood was alleged by the police to have contained 150 mg of alcohol per millilitre, considerably exceeding the legal limit of 80 mg. The press were delighted.

I challenged the use of the type of container and method of analysis when Stanley Clinton-Davis instructed me to defend Lord George-Brown on drink-driving charges. The trial took place at Inner London Crown Court's temporary accommodation. The courtroom had formerly been Lady Astor's bedroom. Suzanne Norwood was the judge in the full-scale jury trial which fed the media for days. My junior was an enthusiastic assistant, Michael Hill. We were a happy team and, in years to come, he and I became the leading lights in organising advocacy training for newly qualified young barristers[1].

Donald Farquharson QC was prosecuting. The press could not help but notice that a drink-driving offence should be prosecuted and defended by an unusually high number of legal luminaries. He wanted to talk to me about a plea.

---

[1]   Michael Hill QC (1935-2003), pupil of Morris Finer; silk, 1979; founder of the Criminal Bar Association (1972) with Basil Wigoder, Lord Hutchinson, John Hazan and Richard Lowry.

"I can't talk to you about anything. The whole thing has become a publicity stunt. I will confine myself to whether the blood sample results were correct. If I win, you offer no evidence." Neither of us was going to allude to the post-accident event on the forecourt. The point was that if the police analyst's certificate was not in order, there could be no basis for continuing the prosecution.

In the absence of the jury, we spent two or three days at Inner London going through the chemistry of the blood tests to determine whether the police evidence concerning the sample was admissible for the purposes of the road traffic legislation. When the blood was taken, it was contained in three capsules, one of which had been retained by the police. Lord George-Brown was offered the choice of one of the remaining two. The defence tests had been carried out on that sample and provided the basis for my argument that the analyst's certificate must be flawed.

The premise was that the fabric of the sample container increased the chances of making the blood clot. If the sample contained clots, the residual blood plasma would show a distorted, high level of alcohol. The judge heard evidence from experts – and we had a small army of them – on whether an accurate result could be obtained from clotted blood which had been reconstituted by whizzing ball bearings through the sample or by macerating clots with plasma. We heard some astonishing statistics: in 1970, 49% of samples were contaminated by clotting; in 1972, the figure was as high as 80%. In the end, Judge Norwood said she was satisfied that the preliminary point had failed: Lord George-Brown's driving days were about to be heavily curtailed.

The jury were called back. They were directed by the judge to find the Defendant guilty. There was a stir in the jury box, some muttering and then a juror stood up. His principles had overcome his natural diffidence. He cleared his throat and said, "There's no way that I'm going to find him guilty. I admire the man!" There was a sense of approval from the jury.

The judge took a deep breath. She closed her eyes briefly, then looked up to the ceiling. She folded her arms on the desk surface and turned her head slightly towards the jury. She sighed.

"Let me explain," she said sternly. In terms which rendered any dissent prohibited, she made it clear what was required of them. On the direction of the judge, the verdict of guilty was duly entered.

I made a plea in mitigation in which I told the judge that, as a citizen and a legislator, he profoundly regretted that he had contravened the law. He admitted to having consumed what he perceived to be a minimal amount of alcohol on the day of the crash. He found that his brakes were not working properly and pulled into the garage forecourt to prevent an accident. The only way to avoid an oncoming vehicle and to stop his own car was to swerve into the wall. There was no question of his Lordship actually being drunk, nor of him driving dangerously.

"You are fined £75 and £250 costs," was the immediate judicial pronouncement, with a twelve-month period of disqualification. "Lord George-Brown, I am reluctant to have to pass a prison sentence on you in default of payment but if you can pay now, I will not have to. Have a word with your counsel."

"Very thoughtful," I managed to say. I turned to Stanley. "Have we got any money?" It appeared that the defence team was strong on credit but low in cash. George had a few hangers-on in court. They effectively passed the hat round. The vocal juror put in £5.

George-Brown asked the judge, "You're not on Amex are you?"

"No."

There was laughter in court when he said, "Don't they accept cheques here?"

We were given the luncheon adjournment to see if we could come up with the required amount in cash. Stanley made a telephone call to organise what was needed and we left court and walked up the road to L'Ecu de France where he had had the foresight to book a table for lunch. In the lobby, we met Harold Wilson[1] and Gerald Kaufman[2]. Harold Wilson loathed George-Brown. It was mutual.

---

[1]   Harold Wilson (1915 – 1995). Prime Minister 1964-1966, 1966-1970, February-October 1974, 1974-1976
[2]   Sir Gerald (Bernard) Kaufman (1930-), junior minister in the 1974-1976 Government, Shadow Foreign Secretary 1987-1992, knighted 2004.

"Hallo, Stanley," Wilson said, ignoring George-Brown.

"Do you know Michael Sherrard?" Stanley introduced me.

"Yes," said Wilson, "Didn't we meet at …" He tailed off somewhat, and flicked a glance in George-Brown's direction without actually looking at him. He certainly knew about the trial. "If there's anything I can do to help," he continued in his lugubrious, Northern drawl, "like giving him a character."

I accepted the irony of this. George Brown had too frequently embarrassed his colleagues, often through his fondness for non-political parties. His white tie and tails were given frequent airings. At one large party where he had consumed the great deal of alcohol which was his norm. The small orchestra encouraged dancing. George noticed a very elaborate and highly coloured dress which it pleased him to admire. He made his way towards the flowing mauve garment.

"That's a superb dress," he said. "Would you like to dance?"

"Grazie! I am the Papal Nuncio and I do not dance …"

***

During lunch, George-Brown went to the washroom. He did not come back. After a very long time, Stanley Clinton-Davis sent the maître d' hôtel to look for him. He came back, head slightly bowed to indicate a hint of deference or tactfulness in a difficult situation.

"Sir, he cannot come back. He has broken the zip in his trousers. He would like you to telephone Lady George-Brown to send him a spare pair of trousers by taxi. Please can you also postpone the afternoon court hearing. He cannot appear with an open fly."

An adjournment was out of the question. Further, it would have been a serious contempt of court to have appeared in a partially dressed state in Lady Astor's bedroom. The problem was resolved by the strategic use of a large serviette provided by the resourceful maître d' hôtel who had wrapped it around the affected waist to form an impromptu cummerbund secured by two safety pins. Harold Wilson knew what was going on. He dealt with the potentially embarrassing situation with sibilant "Ttts, tts" noises which resounded quite well between the discreetly placed tables throughout the room. Together with a practised, rueful shake of his head and a couple of upward rolling movements of his eyes, it almost seemed as though sympathy had overtaken dislike for the time being.

CHAPTER 37

IMPRESSING THE JUDGE

Michael's path crossed frequently with Elwyn-Jones who was a very gregarious chap. He was the nicest of colleagues. Even as Attorney-General, the Leader of the Bar, he took a real interest in the factory floor of the profession. He would even pop into Michael's Chambers to pass the time of day. His office would telephone, looking for him, to be told that he was in consultation. Loosely translated this meant having a cup of tea. His introduction of Irene Buckman to Michael led to her becoming his pupil. Irene and her husband were close to Elwyn and his wife, Polly. The group of friends included Paul Sieghart[1], a leading liberal lawyer who brought human rights to the forefront of legislation.

When Paul was at the Bar, his head of chambers at 3 Hare Court in the early days was Sir John Foster, a charismatic, dynamic sometime Conservative Minister who led me several times. He looked like a craggy, bronze Michael Ayrton[2] bull. Members of our chambers were very much on social terms with Paul and Jack Jacob, later Master Jacob.

My relationship with Paul was semi-professional. He was quite distinguished as being an appallingly bad driver. I defended him – unsuccessfully – on each of the numerous motoring summonses that dropped through his letter box. He would bring a test case at the drop of a wig. He believed that some magistrates thought it would not be good for them to have their decisions challenged where Paul had anything to do with it!

Paul's energy was a byword. Alas, it was to be defeated by a developing cancer, masked initially by the urgency of his practical ideas for reform.

Just before he died, aged 62, there was a tribute dinner for him in light of his outstanding roles as a lawyer, politician and jurist. The créme de la créme of the judiciary came and paid him homage. He wore his achievements like jewels in his crown. For me, his outstanding achievement was securing the foundation of "Justice", an all-party watch-dog of legal processes and political reform. I was invited to join the Council and

---

[1] Paul Sieghart, barrister and law reformer (1927-1989), founder of Justice and the International Commission of Jurists. Father of the writer, Mary Ann Sieghart.
[2] Michael Ayrton (1921-1975), Sculptor and artist.

I was, for many years a member of the Executive Committee. My niece, Alexandra Marks, a solicitor, retired recently as Chair of the Executive Committee. In its early days, Tom Sargant ran the organisation from a very small room, scarcely more than a cubicle with a cupboard, in Chancery Lane. Tom and Paul were powerful voices in law reform and human rights legislation. I felt privileged (and certainly better informed) to have been an active member of *Justice*.

But back to Elwyn-Jones, friend and colleague. He was heavily reliant on junior counsel for his case preparation. Sometimes, they laboured over every word of his speeches. Michael, as junior, prepared virtually everything that Elwyn said, adapting his script with his elegant timing and modulation.

In the early 1970s, some years after I had taken silk, I had one of my most unpleasant experiences during a case in which Sir Elwyn was leading. We were acting for a solicitor charged with fraud. His trial was to take place at St Albans. Elwyn lived in Gray's Inn (to which he was devoted) but he also had a place in the country. During the trial, as his wife, Polly, was at the country house and I was going to drive up every day to St Albans from Hampstead, Elwyn would come to my home by taxi, have breakfast and travel with me to court. He became used to spending time in our house: while Polly was away, he occasionally came to us for supper and chatted to our boys while helping with the washing up.

The case was due to last for two weeks. John Stocker QC (shortly to become a judge of the High Court), was to prosecute and Mr Justice Thesiger was the trial judge. He was of the old school: totally in charge, regarded as a tough tribunal. His formidable physique matched his reputation. A no-nonsense man.

The case proceeded at a fair pace for the first week. On the Friday, Mr. Justice Thesiger sent a message inviting Elwyn, John and me to lunch the following Tuesday. The Lodgings were some miles away, near Luton. We were to travel with the Judge, all of us fully robed, to and from court in a limousine led by two motor-cycle police outriders on white motor-cycles. The Judge's Clerk sat next to the uniformed driver.

The weekend passed with a review of the evidence in the case. I had a slight headache on the Monday morning. It cleared up and we finished the cross-examination of the principal witness.

Elwyn stayed to supper that evening. Before he left, he reminded me that we were to lunch with the judge the next day and we would be travelling with him in the limousine.

"Don't forget to wear your full morning coat and waistcoat," Elwyn said in his lilting Welsh accent. "He would not approve of 'the shorty!'" This was a reference to a waistcoat with sleeves, a cooler outfit by far. "He's going to rise twenty minutes early and we're to meet in his room."

The next day, the headache had worsened and I felt like staying at home but Elwyn encouraged me to carry on. He assured me that I looked fine, that I would be all right and that he had confidence in my driving.

I managed to get us to court and to keep awake for the morning but there was no doubt that the headache was about as bad as could be. On the way to the judge's room, I seriously considered making my excuses and said so quietly to Elwyn. He was not persuaded. Rather, he seemed determined not be left alone with the judge.

"You'll be all right. You look better now than you did this morning." Having told me I looked fine! Although I said nothing, my disquiet must have showed in my face. He added, "You don't have to talk – he'll do all the talking. And you need do no more than play with your food." The tune of his voice persuaded me, against my better judgment.

We made our way to the judge, who led us to the limousine. I dare say that passers-by would have thought it a colourful procession or an advert for a circus!

The motor-cyclists were warming up. The smell of exhaust fumes swept into my head, magnifying whatever had been going on inside it before. The Judge's Clerk held the door open for the judge who clambered aboard and set himself down, billowing across the near-side seat. Elwyn followed and sat next to the judge, John Stocker sat on the "dicky" seat which had been folded down in front of Elwyn. After the clerk had done the same with the second "dicky" seat, I took my place. The headache had heightened my sense of smell. I was aware of exhaust fumes in the car, leather, polish, the warm wool of the judge's robes, scarlet and ermine, tobacco on someone's clothes. My head was throbbing and my eyes were watering. Truly, I was not well. In fact, I was quite ill. The only relief was to be sitting down.

As the car started off towards the lodgings, I heard the judge engaging Elwyn in conversation. John Stocker was a quiet man and he sat silently, looking out of the window. I had nobody to think about ... but me.

We must have been on the road for about ten minutes when I felt the presence of an alarming symptom. I began to feel distinctly nauseaous. I realised that the fumes given off by the motor-cyclists who were leading us were the immediate cause of my heightened discomfort. I half-turned towards the passenger window in the hope that it would make me feel better. It did not.

The smell of diesel, or my awareness of it, persisted. The gentle movement of the car did nothing to improve my situation. I had to turn my head away from the front of the car. I did just that, to be confronted by the large, red-robed lap of the judge. It was like the car, moving gently, rhythmically, draped between his sturdy knees.

There was a sudden shudder as the car turned left into the grounds of the lodgings. I could feel bile rising. I was silently praying, "Please, please, dear God, don't let me be sick in the judge's lap ... it can't be far to the lodgings ... please don't let me ..."

I caught Elwyn's eye. He tightened his lips severely and shook his head at me. A wishful command.

The tyres crunched noisily on the gravel and the car came to an abrupt stop, with the sort of lurch that made a fragile stomach feel as if it had been hurled against a wall. The clerk was very quick to leave the car. He threw open the door to let me out. Indeed, I had to get out so that the judge could do so. As I stepped down, only praying now that I would not be sick where I stood, I caught sight of an attendant near the front door. Afterwards I learned he was the butler. I stumbled towards him. With immaculate understanding, having seen my colour, he said, "First door on the right, sir." The directions were to save me the anticipated disgrace as I found myself in the sanctuary of an old-fashioned loo.

Although there had been no alternative to jumping out ahead of the judge, under normal circumstances, I would not have run headlong into the Lodgings ahead of him. I spoke to Elwyn later about my apparent rudeness, saying that I hoped the judge had not been offended by my behaviour. He assured me that the judge had not noticed. I told him that I felt so ill that the alternative would have meant me being sick in his lap. "Oh, he'd have remembered that," Elwyn assured me gravely.

It is enough to mention that I was "off sick" for the next five days and Elwyn managed without me.

Mr. Justice Thesiger sent our client down for two years.

CHAPTER 38

AN EYE FOR A TOOTH

On 7ᵗʰ May 1974, in the aftermath of the Patty Hearst kidnapping, the United Kingdom's release of the hijacker Leila Khaled, the hunger strikes of imprisoned members of the IRA and Greece's deportation of convicted terrorists to Libya, Michael gave the Fourth Sir Winston Churchill Memorial Lecture at the Law Society to the Friends of the Bar-Ilan University. The talk was headed, "An Eye for a Tooth." In it, he tried to come to practical terms with the critical problems of the times, aiming to provide a basis for thought and examination. The theme was one which remains topical: terrorism. In his words, "Terrorism is crime in crisis: in chaos." During the opening of the talk, he described the difficulties of making the punishment fit the crime and the role of the judiciary and the executive in maintaining a public perception of law and order. We join the audience as Michael talks about those who protest against legally imposed punishment.

'Now while I have expressed a view as to what I believe ordinary folk feel about the extent of punishment there is another section of the public which is more articulate in its reaction to both crime and punishment. I refer to the so-called "Do-Gooders" who protest vociferously and patently when wrongdoers are punished, or when the incidentals of punishment are unpalatable to their liberal temperaments. These people, doubtless motivated by humanitarian considerations, protest at long sentences and express outrage at the forcible feeding of prisoners who refuse to eat. It is not so much their protest that concerns me: it is their deafening silence about the crimes committed by the prisoners in question. The voices of the famous protesters are not raised when the innocent are maimed or killed in the streets or in the air.

The protesters are not seen parading their condemnatory banners against terrorists: the most dangerous political dwarfs and cowards of our times.

No howling mob of protesters when real blood flowed past the Old Bailey. No traffic jams caused by "Do-Gooders" protesting about the massacre at Kiryat Shemona.

Although the Courts and the Executive must try to mirror all the people, and although it may be part of the judge's equipment to recognise

211

and try to understand all the threads of view which go to make up the fabric of society, I believe that they must set their minds against the dilution of principle simply because such dilution might seem to be temporarily popular. Certainly the quiet voice of tried good sense may be more effective and more penetrating than the shout of political protesters.'

He then went on to consider what it is like to live in an era of terrorism.

'In an age so liberally sprinkled with blessings it is a strident curse to be afflicted with indiscriminate terrorism.

'It appears in many guises: from the plunder of inanimate art treasures: to the kidnapping of an heiress in the name of justice to the starving and underprivileged; to the massacre of innocent pilgrims at Lod airport in the name of justice to the allegedly dispossessed: to the indiscriminate and discriminate violence inflicted by Catholics and Protestants on each other allegedly (at least in its now almost forgotten inception) in the name of God.

The attitude of the authorities to these outrages reveals marked differences of degree and kind. Kidnappers if caught may be subjected to the processes of the law and punished accordingly. In principle there is not difference in legal terms between such a case and one of domestic kidnapping for more or less private emotional reasons. The motive differs, of course: and this may reflect itself in the punishment meted out.

In regard to the bombing outrages arising out of the unity and extent of the United Kingdom there have been prosecutions where there has been evidence to justify it: and condign punishment where guilt has been proved. The judges, and, so far, the Executive too, have been resistant to fear, threats or pressures of any kind.

On the domestic scene the mass of the public, I believe, supports the law enforcement agencies to the hilt: and if a few flamboyant, publicity-seeking protesters think the forcible feeding of criminals is more outrageous than the crimes we can but sigh.

But where international terrorism is concerned a different and dangerous attitude seems to prevail. Principles are passed on like the traditional buck – everyone is afraid that it might stop with him. Nowhere is this illustrated more clearly than by international attitudes and reactions to Arab terrorists. I speak of this by way of illustration (albeit a vivid one) of the problem. It is not the only example: but it is one of the best publicised. For this audience it has a special significance.

Let us look at some random examples and consider them in context. Arab terrorists in Rome sought to plant a bomb on an aircraft bound for the Middle East. With distinguished cowardice or callous cruelty or both they selected two young English girls as the unsuspecting couriers of death. In the record-player they were given was an explosive booby-trap. The innocent and equally unsuspecting passengers and crew of the aircraft were not soldiers at war, not politicians and not statesmen. Many of them, indeed, might never have given as much as a second thought to the political predicament which was likely to be responsible for their deaths and the bereavement of their families. The plot miscarried. The Italian police made arrests.

Now it is a mistake to diagnose anything on the basis of too little information or simply on newspaper reports (which in the end are as reliable or not as the people who compile them), but it seems to me to be a fair comment that the anxiety to bring the case to a legal conclusion was hardly obvious. If the Italian authorities were fearful of reprisals, if the Courts imposed and the executive carried out sentences, that would have been a natural but (I submit) resistable reaction. It must have been with relief that the accused failed to answer to their bail and made good and safe their escape.

Leila Khaled on a flight to England was involved knowingly and by design in hi-jacking activity of a kind more likely than not to endanger the aircraft and its passengers. The plot misfired and Leila Khaled was captured at London Airport. It is idle to pretend that there was not great anxiety in some quarters here that if the law were to take its course there might be grave danger of reprisals by other terrorists.

Again it must have been a matter of relief (doubtless coupled with acute distaste) for those charged with the onerous duty of deciding what to do, to conclude that there were legal impediments to a successful prosecution: to find that a terrorist hijacker (whose criminal acts of con-spiracy were performed outside the jurisdiction) was after all liable only to expulsion from the UK, to relive the exploit in glory and encourage others to think that they, too, could act in a similar way in safety.

If this is the state of the law is it not time that it was changed? So that teeth can be seen in place of the sloppy gums of inaction.'

He went on to express his fears that a section of the public, seeing no reflection of its true feeling in the law where there is an abdication of responsibility to punish the wrongdoer, may take over the task. He said, "Terror breeds terror. Violence begets violence."

'Once it is seen that governments may be amenable to terror, then to terror they will be subjected and the name of justice will be abused and described as the patron of the exercise.

Let me translate into practical terms what I fear in this connection: suppose that terrorists of some persuasion or other commit some horrific crime in a European capital. As usual the victims are defenceless and innocent bystanders. Some are killed: many are injured. Diligent police work results in some of the terrorists being taken into custody and charged, inter alia, with murder. Their associates elsewhere (anxious to protect the murderers as well as to demonstrate their boast to new recruits that fear of capture need be no deterrent) threaten the government concerned with dire consequences if the accused are not set free. In the face of these threats the government is seen to weaken. "Hold your hands" they cry. "When the Courts have done, the Executive will intervene and arrange for free pardons, facilities for travel abroad to your champagne-parties-cum-press-conferences far away." A not unfamiliar pattern. But what of the outraged feelings of the public, the families of the victims, the people against whom the murders were perpetrated in political terms or political reasons? What if a *counter terror group*, itself embracing terror in the name of justice, promises (it is never a *threat* when you pretend to be on the side of law and order is it?) to inflict on the country of the capitulating government at least twice the harm threatened by the associates of the original terrorists they want to see caught, tried and punished?

And just to prove their determination seize hostages? What course is open in the face of a godless terror stalemate then?

Far from complaining that we do not even demand a tooth for a tooth, we may yet be forced to yield to those who would have *an eye for a tooth*. Here, alas, may be the logical end of it all, and double the terror is indeed an eye for a tooth.

214

A world lost to terror. The roots of such a disaster lie in the abnegation of the simple principles which I have described.'

He ended his speech with these words:

'If such an accursed end is to be avoided, Governments and all who are charged with the true duty of law enforcement will require the forthright courage of the great statesman in the memory of whose life and principles, Mr Chairman, ladies and gentlemen, I have tonight had the very great honour of speaking.'

CHAPTER 39

GO EAST, YOUNG MAN

1974. Everything seemed to happen at once. Michael became Head of Chambers at 2 Crown Office Row. There was nothing democratic about it. Members of Chambers seemed to expect him to take over from Peter Pain, the preceding Head, when he was appointed to the High Court. His parting gift to Michael was some personal advice, "If you don't have to do a case on a given day, stay at home or go shopping. Don't go near chambers. There will always be something for you to do."

There was so much to do that, in the end, Michael resorted to holding clinics for the other members to come to him with their woes or to run the eternal "something" past him.

Here I was, having just settled a case and Peter's words rang in my ears. I decided to follow his advice and to stay at home from Wednesday until the following Monday in a sort of hiding. Inevitably, as soon as I started to enjoy my first day of leisure, the telephone rang. Although Shirley's expression was a silent plea for me not to answer it, after half a dozen rings, it was unbearable.

My clerk was at the other end of the line. "Sir, could you go to Hong Kong tonight?"

Tonight? What was he thinking of? Hong Kong! Of course, whatever it was about, it was exciting. But, I would need vaccinations – hepatitis B – yellow fever – did you need malaria pills for the Far East? My imagination ran riot over all the tropical illnesses I could think of in the short term. I explained that I was unable to go without having all the jabs and, which was not quite a "no", whoever they wanted at short notice would have to have been properly immunised. I did not even ask what the case was about and I knew that, subject to what should be the mere formality of being called to the Hong Kong Bar, I would be allowed to practise in a system that was based on English common law. He said he would ring me back.

Within five minutes, the call came. "Can you leave on Saturday?"

I dared not look at Shirley.

"Yes." I still did not know why I was needed. All my clerk knew was it that was something to do with an injunction. I think I detected a feeling of relief in his voice as he said, "They'll send a car. You'll be travelling first class. You'll be there three or four days, maybe longer."

I was thrilled. I had long been fascinated by Oriental art and design and the very sound of "Hong Kong" was enchanting.

Saturday came and, with my sore, injected arm, I was ready to go. I had surprised myself by remembering that I had to take my wig and gown with me. A coffee and cream-coloured Rolls-Royce drew up outside the house at Burgess Hill, driven by a chauffeur in matching livery. Even as Shirley waved me goodbye, I was investigating the "toys" in the car as I luxuriated in its almost edible leather upholstery. Here were the wood-panelled cabinets, the renowned crystal decanters, the cut-glass tumblers. There were buttons to press and panels to slide.

I found an intercom switch to speak to the chauffeur.

"What's this?" I asked him. I had found a hatch-cover in the arm-rest.

"The telephone sir."

In a car? I pressed the button at the side. The lid slid back to reveal a coffee-and-cream telephone.

I had never seen a telephone in a car before.

"Can I phone my wife?" I hoped I didn't sound timid. Or too impressed.

"Just dial 092, sir. That will give you a line."

Seconds later, I called home. Shirley answered. "That was a quick ride to the airport," she said. "Where are you?"

"No, listen – I'm at Staples Corner on the North Circular Road!"

She was so excited. She phoned all the family to tell them that I had phoned her from a car!

I did not want the journey to end but eventually prised myself from the Rolls, only to be treated like a VIP from the moment I stepped on to the pavement at Heathrow. The flight was perfect and all the more relaxing as I had no details as to why I was wanted, had no papers and could not even work during the journey. The princely treatment lasted through the entire trip.

Kai Tak airport, together with the dramatic approach low over Hong Kong, was to me like the eighth wonder of the world. It looked as though we were flying down the high street with the wingtips almost touching the washing hanging from the balconies of the apartment houses. It was frightening and thrilling at the same time. I was met at the airport by a young English solicitor from Johnson, Stokes and Master, the biggest firm in Hong Kong. We chatted as we walked through to the car that was to take us to the Mandarin Hotel where I was to stay.

"I gather you want some sort of injunction," I asked him. I had gathered correctly. But what I had not foreseen was six bundles of around three hundred pages each.

"We want an *ex parte* injunction and a charging order on a Chinese bank[1] owned by Chang Ming Tien. He's a well-known financier out here."

"But, did you say six files … " Jet-lag suddenly began to loom.

"But it is *ex parte*," he said. The notion that the other side would not be attending was not very reassuring.

And there was another matter on which I felt I should come clean now that the work was becoming a reality. "Hong Kong law is the same as English, isn't it?" I knew that barristers from the Commonwealth were trained in the English legal system and took our Bar exams but it seemed prudent to be reassured before I made any silly mistake.

"Yes." Whew.

"We won't get it," the solicitor told me cheerfully, "but the client wants to give it a good try." We were against a moderately sized private banking corporation.

By now it was 7.30 a.m. There was the small matter of being called to the Hong Kong Bar before I could appear in court. That would involve explaining that I had special expertise that was not available locally. It was set to happen after I had breakfast and looked at the papers in the

[1]   Overseas Trust Bank.

hope that I might see something by luck that would be the clue to the whole matter. The papers were delivered and the one saving grace was that the listing was:- next day at 10.00 a.m. I felt slightly cheered by the prospect of having some preparation time.

"But the judge is going to take us if his case goes short today. He'll want to get you on at 5.00 p.m."

"Just a minute," I said, "I'll have to read at least half the correspondence to him. I'll be reading it myself for the first time!" The solicitor smiled. Of course.

And at 5.30, the case was called. Adrenaline took over from jet-lag. I had a grasp of what the case was about and what was wanted. I started to tell the Judge the story. He was frowning. After 20 minutes, he interrupted me. His voice was gruff and an Irish accent unmistakable.

"Mr Sherrard, I'm going to read my note and think about what you've told me so far. We'll adjourn for 15 minutes." This did not bode well, but he returned at the precise time appointed and he looked less stern. Fifteen minutes later, the same thing happened. And again. Each time, he seemed more affable. Finally, he said, "Thank you. We'll fix a time for tomorrow."

I was very tired. So much so, that his voice had begun to sound slurred.

I was stunned that, after starting late, the matter would go over to the next day. I asked him, "Would Your Lordship consider …"

Before I could ask him to consider anything, he leaned forward across the desk. Was I imagining that his wig was slightly askew?

No, I was not. "Mr Zherrard, what *exzhactly* do you want?"

There was an unmistakeable waft of something remarkably like whisky coming from the bench. Seize the moment.

"Order in terms."

"Abzholutely."

And I had my order!

I turned to my solicitor.

"Is this what he's like all the time?"

"Well, if he's under pressure, he might take a swig now and again. But not unless it's late in the day."

I had had a job to do and it was done, whether or not with the unexpected assistance of the bottle. I could now mooch around the town and be a tourist for a short time before being taken out for dinner by the senior partner. I asked him, "How did you get hold of me?" I had not meant it to sound curt so I went on, "I am so happy to be here. I've always wanted to come."

He said, "You settled a case last week and you were going to take some time off so we knew you were available. We have a firm in London that we use as our agent. I'd been on to them to say we needed a really tough, no-holds-barred QC for this. My agent said, 'We've just settled a case with a very nice but tough silk. He ran rings around our man.' That QC was you. And you did what we wanted. You got the order in terms. Now, you just wait and see the headlines tomorrow."

The newspapers had banner headlines, "Top silk freezes assets of Bank." There was not a mention of the helping hand of Black Label ...

I stayed for four days. This was only the opening shot of the battle and there were meetings to be attended between a couple of short sightseeing expeditions.

"We want you to come back," they said. That really was not on.

"I'm afraid my wife won't want me to go away again, so far and so soon. You have my skeleton argument. A local man can take over now."

"No, no! We want you. Bring your wife with you. Why not take a holiday en route – Thailand is very nice – we'll fix you up…"

It was too tempting. And so it was always to be with the East.

I accepted the case. Shirley and I had four or five exciting days in Thailand. Bangkok was under curfew. It made no difference to us. Given the choice of staying in or going out after 9.00 p.m. and getting shot, we found the hotel a perfectly comfortable place to spend the evening.

Then we returned to Hong Kong for the second round. This time I had an opponent. John Balcombe, QC. We had the same judge as at the first hearing. This time, he rose at 4.00 p.m. but there the day ended.

Later in the evening, back at the hotel, I learned that John was staying there too. He rang while Shirley and I were eating.

"Michael, something very serious has arisen. The police are involved. We may have to delay the start of the hearing tomorrow. Can you be at Deacons early?" I knew them as Hong Kong's second biggest firm of solicitors.

The next morning was Wednesday. I arrived at Deacons with Andrew Li, my junior, and Dennis Murphy, my second junior.

I asked Balcombe what had happened. I had hardly slept, I was so worried about what he had said. "A police matter?"

He explained, "My wife arrived at 4.00 p.m. yesterday. When we got to our suite, we found that the room-boy had discovered some loose wires around the outer door. He had called the manager who sent for the police. It seems that an enquiry agent from London has been arrested. Not to put too fine a point on it – he seems to have been bugging our bedroom."

I asked, "Who's behind it? What's going on?"

"Well," he said reluctantly, "we think it's your chap."

I hoped that it was not but could see why he would think so. I simply said, "We'll go before the judge and explain that an unexpected incident has occurred and ask for an adjournment until we can get to the bottom of this."

The judge said, "This is disgraceful. I will read the papers and adjourn until Monday. I think the parties should cool down in the interval."

The maladroit bugging was inexplicable. Hong Kong was the home of virtually invisible devices. You could buy them anywhere.

***

We now had a week to spare. John Balcombe did not waste any time. He went off to Penang for a few days. Now was to be the start of a more extended acquaintance with my second junior.

Dennis Murphy was an English barrister practising as a solicitor-advocate in Singapore. He was a partner in Murphy and Dunbar for some years then, in 1973, Dunbar bought him out on condition that he did not work as a solicitor in Singapore for twelve months. Dennis reasoned to himself, "OK: I'll go back to being a barrister," and took himself off to Hong Kong where he set up his own Chambers.

Dennis' life was conducted in accordance with the strictest of principles where alcohol was concerned. He was a passionate opponent of anything to do with drinking.

During the week.

But, come Friday, as soon as he left work at the end of the day, he would begin the process of downing prodigious quantities of drink. He had a huge reputation for being able to consume what appeared to be gallons of all kinds of alcohol – beer, wine, spirits – without ever appearing to be drunk and without showing any signs of a hangover when the dry season began every Monday without fail. New Year's Day (in the European calendar) was a big event for Dennis. He used to send brandy to the convent, assuring the nuns that it was for purely medicinal purposes.

He was well-known in Hong Kong and Singapore. People would point him out on the street and remark on his drinking or, if seen during the week, his non-drinking habits. His wife was also a remarkable local character. Maggie Murphy owned two or three beauty parlours in Singapore. She was tall and carried her generous excess of weight in flamboyant style. She billowed around town dressed in colourful, flowing garments.

As John Balcombe set off on his jaunt, Dennis persuaded Shirley and me to go to Singapore and meet his wife and stay at their home. Shirley, still naïve in the shopping ways of the Far East, had "nothing to wear" for the sudden trip but Dennis assured her that his wife would make her ample wardrobe available. Ample was the key word: she must have been several sizes bigger than Shirley and a foot taller. There was a marquee-like quality to each of the voluminous garments on offer. It did not take long to correct the wardrobe deficiencies: the shops of Singapore had all that anyone could wish for.

**

Dennis' house was wonderful. It was built on stilts in the tropical style with shutters instead of glazed windows. The sea lapped at the edge of the great lawn to the rear of the building. Energetic reclamation of the shore-line now places the coast far enough away from the property boundary to accommodate the Pan-Island Expressway.

When we walked round the garden, we came across two or three people who were apparently living and sleeping in the grounds or in what had become an artist's studio below the house in what would otherwise have been the basement. A stranger might call out "Good morning." There was no obvious reason for him being there. Another might be painting earnestly at an easel without looking up. Others might walk past, absorbed in conversation ignoring everyone else. If you asked Dennis who they were, he would shrug and carry on with what he was talking about before.

Staying at his house meant making close and rather unpleasant acquaintance with the several aggressive whippets he kept as pets and who either felt it their hospitable duty to get into bed with the guests or were making some sort of territorial canine point.

The idiosyncrasies of the Murphy household were entirely acceptable to us.

**

Dennis Murphy took us to meet old Mr Wong, the head of a very well established family in the Far East. Its members live in Hong Kong and Singapore and have wide business and banking interests. He was the reigning monarch of the Singapore branch of the family. We were not told his age but his older daughter, Mabel Hudson, was in her early seventies when we were introduced.

He sat on a large rattan chair, which immediately reminded me of the throne arranged for Sophie Tucker at David Jacobs' party a few years previously. He held court, impeccably dressed in a cream linen suit. His dazzling white shirt had a starched, high wing collar. He gave no sign of being uncomfortable in the oppressive heat. There was something brittle, almost transparent about his skin, best described as being like fine rice-paper. The room was decorated with prize specimens of a remarkable collection of orchids hanging from containers, filling the air with a delicate perfume.

The ladies lined up to pay their respects to him. He shook their hands and bowed his head to each of them. The prettier ones were required to lean forward to receive or give a cuddle. Dennis steered Shirley towards him. "Say something nice about the flowers," Dennis told her. "Go on," I urged her.

Shirley followed a large lady who had received a decorous hand-shake. She said, "We think your orchids are the most beautiful we have ever seen." It was not hard to say: they were. Mr Wong smiled and said, "You are my most beautiful orchid."

She was trying to work out a polite reply as he continued, "Kiss me, please."

Having seen the form of her predecessors, she leaned forward to give him a polite peck on the cheek but he turned his face so that the kiss landed full on the lips. Obviously embarrassed, she started to apologise. He wagged his finger at her authoritatively, clearly indicating that she was not to say anything. "Put your tongue in," he demanded. But she opted for some difficulty with his accent so as to be able to back away, smiling and thanking him for something inarticulately uttered.

We managed to maintain a relationship with the daughter who would have me over for her famous Sunday lunches when I was in Singapore.

In 1992, Mabel telephoned me. She said, "Come for lunch on Sunday. The High Commissioner will be there as well."

I did not need tempting. The food and company were guaranteed to be good. And there was another English visitor: Steven Norris, the Minister of Transport. He came bounding over to me as was his way and explained that he had flown over from Kuala Lumpur to study the MRT[1].

"You've come all this way for that?" I asked.

"Of course not," he said. "But I've got a spot of bother at home. The press have sprung a ridiculous story about me and a dozen mistresses. The MRT is an important diversion." But he went on to describe the details of his intricate life, much to Mabel's interest and amusement. He was good company and found himself launched immediately into the best social life that Singapore could offer: a place in the Stewards' Box at the races.

---

[1] Mass Rapid Transit rail system: operations commenced in 1987.

As another part of our introduction to Singapore, Dennis took us to meet Mrs Leah Nissim. Then about 80 years of age, she was a daughter of Sir Manasseh Meyer[1], a great entrepreneur and philanthropist of Singapore, after whom Meyer Road is named. In 1878 he built, largely at his own expense, the Synagogue in Waterloo Road.

Mrs Nissim had inherited her lovely house from her father who had also built a private synagogue, Chased-El, in the gardens. "You are welcome to come to our services," she said, as servants offered us tea and English fruit cake. As we usually only attended synagogue services on the high holy days, we did not take up the offer but we were delighted to accept her invitation to Friday night dinner, our first oriental shabbas.

We were pleasantly astonished that Jewish European cooking was the order of the day, slightly adapted to local customs. We were seated at a long table with several other guests. Two Chinese servants, each with two or three long, coarse hairs hanging from their otherwise smooth chins, their hair bound back in a long plait, and dressed in their traditional clothes, waited on the party, bowing and offering traditional Jewish dishes that we were accustomed to seeing in Europe.

An ornate blue-patterned porcelain dish in the Chinese style was filled with chopped liver. It was offered with the words: "Mrs Nissim wi' be pleased you ha' cho' li'ah, sir."

A tureen of soup followed. "Mrs Nissim wi' be pleased you ha' chi'en soup krepla'[2], sir. And lockshen, sir – you wan' lockshen?"

At the end of the traditional meal, as we made our farewells, Mrs Nissim assured us that she hoped to see us again and that her doors were always open to us.

***

Some months later, it was Yom Kippur. Michael was working in Singapore. He went to the service at the Waterloo Road Synagogue.

The service was conducted by a rabbi in a large, wood-panelled hall with a white marble floor and a ladies' gallery at the rear enclosed by

---

[1]   Sir Manasseh Meyer (1846-1930).

[2]   Kreplach: Won Ton

a wrought iron grille with the letter 'M' intertwined at intervals. Great copper-covered fans paddled the steamy air in the crowded room. I was dismayed to see the male congregants prostrate themselves from time to time on rattan mats flung to the ground by Indian servants immediately before they were needed. When their masters scrambled to their feet, the servants whisked up the mats and returned to their places to stand alert until the next time.

However, I was relieved to see that the religious ceremony was otherwise similar to those held in England: rapid, uncoordinated reading from prayer books and enthusiastic, tone-deaf singing. Many tunes were decidedly unfamiliar, even taking account of the wide variety of keys in which they were sung. The scrolls being taken from the ark to the dais formed a reassuring reminder of the English routine, even though accompanied by more prostrating. The reading of the law was very much what I was used to. I began to feel that the strangeness of the surroundings was of less importance than the familiar trappings of the service.

Then I heard a call from the dais.

"Who needs a blessing?"

A hand shot up from one of the large crowd of men.

"I do!"

"How much will you pay?"

"Three hundred dollars."

"Not enough!"

"Four hundred?"

"No!!"

I could not believe what I was hearing. I was listening to an auction for a call to the reading of the law. It was a way of intimidating the congregation into making large donations for the support of the poor. The charitable function was understandable but I was appalled. I decided to leave the service, feeling the particular loneliness that comes with being a long way from home at a time of year traditionally spent with family or close friends. I wondered how I would break the fast, thinking without much relish of the local custom of eating dates and sweets.

Then I remembered Mrs Nissim's invitation from the first visit to Singapore. I went to the private synagogue where a solemn and decorous service was under way in a room crowded by others who had no doubt been similarly unimpressed by the commercial exploitation of the religious service in Waterloo Road. A message reached me that I was invited to break the fast with Mrs Nissim and her family. I was doubly grateful for the invitation and a return to her comforting hospitality.

***

When we returned from the first trip to Singapore, it seemed that the solicitors had been busy. The case was settled. Could John Balcombe have settled it because I was out of the country? He could have carried on working by phone from Penang.

My client had settled for umpteen million dollars. He came to the hotel and showed me the cheque.

I made a few calculations and said, "This is better than a very good settlement. You are getting more than if you had won on every point. How did you manage it?"

He explained that he and Mr Chang, the banker, had thrashed out the agreement by themselves. My client said, "Does a few thousand dollars here or there create any problems?"

I said, "There has been a lot of bad blood. It wouldn't do any harm if I tell John Balcombe about the excess and that we will accept a substitute cheque for the appropriate amount."

"OK," he sighed. "You can ring Balcombe."

I did. I said to John, "In this funniest of all funny cases, your client has drawn a cheque for HK\$300,000-400,000 more than we seek in the claim. We'll take the correct figure on a new cheque."

He said, "Can I ring you back? It does look as though you may be right."

Later, he called me back. "There is no mistake. The cheque is right."

This was my first case in Hong Kong. I had yet to learn the nuances. I said to my client, "What goes on here?"

He was highly amused. He explained. "When you get to know Hong Kong a little better, you will know that it simply does not happen for the owner of a bank to make a simple arithmetical error. It's not the money he loses. It's the matter of face."

***

Whilst digesting my first lesson in saving face in Hong Kong and thinking about accelerating the return ticket, a lucky thing happened. Hong Kong is a funny place, not like London where your clerk sends you off on a moment's notice to deal with a matter in court and casually mentions that you should stay there for the day as there are a couple of matters that need your expertise. Reputation is everything in Hong Kong and, overnight – or, at any rate, since my original stunning unopposed victory – I had gained a reputation for success. This was likely to be in severe jeopardy after the bugging business which was yet to be resolved. That appeared to me to be the sort of set-back that would damage my newly-acquired status.

Whilst working with Dennis Murphy to tie up the loose ends in the banking case, a call came in from an important local firm of solicitors, P C Woo and Co. The caller happened to be a Steward of the Jockey Club against whom I was about to be instructed. He had taken no part in the disciplinary proceedings which led to the call. He asked, "When are you leaving Hong Kong? Can you stay another ten days?"

"Probably not," I answered. I knew I would have to co-ordinate with Chambers and, as I was now required for a different case, I would have to go through the process of admission to the Hong Kong Bar again. However, as was to become the norm, I was admitted to the Bar without too much in the way of red tape. In Singapore it was to be simpler: the Attorney-General's Chambers dealt with applications. The court was not concerned with complexity, only with the client's choice of leading counsel.

***

The Jockey Clubs of the Far East are outstandingly efficient and they generate great wealth. I learnt that the Hong Kong Jockey Club was the king of them all. It was without doubt the most prestigious, powerful and influential non-governmental body. It was no accident that the government and the Jockey Club were between them masters of high

228

quality horse-racing and fund-raising. The Jockey Club Stewards had a tight hold on the disciplinary functions: they were in effect the executive cabinet of the Club. They had the power to create the rules and enforce them. But, in the absence of an empowering rule, what they were not allowed to do was to say, "There's an owner here who, regardless of his knowledge of any wrongdoing, shall be disqualified."

Mr Ho Man Fat, my client, was the wealthy proprietor of a widely-read Chinese language newspaper and a passionate owner of horses. His was a memorable face to encounter, albeit often hidden by a well-tilted hat. The nick-name given to him by the press was Mr Ug Li. He had been disqualified together with his jockey and trainer (neither of whom appealed the decision) for being a party to cheating. The horse had been spared the same treatment and, fortunately for it, the even worse sanction of being shot.

Mr Ho Man Fat felt such a sense of personal grievance that he was determined to challenge the decision: the owner cannot be a victim and culprit at the same time. He was treated as if he was a party to the wrong-doing when there was not a shred of evidence that he had anything to do with it. His wealth and influence would be irrevocably damaged if his disqualification was allowed to stand. I looked at the brief. My initial reaction was that it would be difficult to succeed against the Jockey Club but it was worth a try. In fact, I took the view that the Stewards of the Jockey Club had misdirected themselves because they were disqualifying him not for anything he had done or encouraged but because his trainer and jockey had misbehaved. Notwithstanding that there would be reluctance to overturn the decision of the Jockey Club Stewards, I was prepared to argue that the Court should accept that it had the discretion to review the decision and put matters right.

This turned out to be my first encounter with Charles Ching[1], a very well-known and respected local silk. He was to be an important adversary in my professional life. He was bright and devoted to the law. He always acted for the Jockey Club. Most of the judges, even if up to the mark, were cowed by him.

---

[1] Charles Ching (1935-2000). QC, 1974. Chairman of the Hong Kong Bar Association 1975 -76. Appointed to the Court of Final Appeal in 1997 when the connection with the Privy Council was broken.

When we met, he said, "The Jockey Club has never been reviewed."

I said, "Well, here I am to see if it can be."

He assured me that he would give me a good run round the track. He might well do: I knew nothing about horse-racing.

Came the day of the hearing and I was opening my case with child-like simplicity. The judge seemed to be particularly sympathetic to my basic explanations, designed to help me as much as the court. He said, "Do you, like Mr Ching, know about the arcane workings of the Jockey Club?"

I said, "To tell you the truth, I've never been in a case with a horse anywhere near it."

The judge said, "Then please go slowly. I am not familiar with the interstices of the law of gaming in Hong Kong and I need to follow carefully what this is about." He, too, was a newcomer.

Charles Ching was not happy about the judge having no judicial knowledge to apply to the case. The judge was regarded as a great ally for my client. I put a stop to murmurings about an application for a change of judge. I told Charles, "Any attempt to remove the judge from this case about which he knows nothing and should know nothing will meet with protest in open court." That seemed to do the trick.

I argued that, in the absence of evidence of conspiracy, it was wrong to draw an inference that the owner was involved.

Charles Ching's case was equally simple: the Stewards of the Jockey Club knew best. He invited the judge to throw the case out, neck and crop. He said there was nothing further to discuss.

We argued for three days. I won! I believe it was the first time any litigant had succeeded in a case against the Jockey Club.

The headlines were, "Top Silk Breaks the Jockey Club." I am not certain if the Hong Kong press knew of any other adjective than 'top' to describe the QC on the winning side.

Every time we saw each other over the years, Mr Ho Man Fat would raise his hat to me.

I did masses of work against Charles Ching after the Jockey Club case. And I beat him once or twice ...

***

Years later, we were having dinner at our hotel in Singapore when one of our hosts piped up: "What was that business about the bugging of the Mandarin Hotel?"

I told them the story. How it was so clumsy and maladroit, it was designed to be discovered. After all, in Singapore and Hong Kong, you could eavesdrop to your heart's content and no-one would ever be the wiser.

"So who did it?" I was pressed.

"I don't know," was the honest answer.

Our host said, "I know."

Dreading hearing my client's name, I could not stop myself asking, "Who? And how do you know?"

He said, "Actually, I was acting for a third party to the transaction. My client didn't want to be cut out, so he used an enquiry agent from London, hence the rather obvious device." The third party was a Malaysian.

I said, "We owe an apology to Mr Chang and our client." It was something of an understatement.

CHAPTER 40

PLAYING THE RECORDER

Any judge has the power to deprive people of their liberty if the law so prescribes for the offence. A Recorder holds part-time judicial office and is empowered to preside over jury trials and pass sentences in common with other judges trying criminal cases. The reality of passing sentence is a very different thing from a casual chat with a colleague over lunch about how best to deal with the villains of the day.

People of calibre are needed to carry judicial responsibility. In the 1970's, the process was put in motion by the person, high in the legal ranks, who tapped a shoulder of calibre and suggested casually that the owner thereof might like to apply.

The appointment placed you straight on the bench – education for judicial office is a recent concept. The usual approach having been made, you rather slipped into the Assistant Recorder role and would then be thrown in at the deep end.

My first day on the Bench was as a Deputy High Court Judge. A phone call came in fairly early in the morning: the listed judge had been taken ill in the night. I was supposed to be going to Desmond Franks' swearing-in as a County Court Judge but that had to be set aside. Not without trepidation, I went to the Law Courts. I thought it was going to be rather grand, going through the judges' entrance. In the event, I had overdramatised my situation: I was nothing more than a body turning up for work and being told where the factory floor was. There was no sense of occasion. Any remaining sense of elation dissipated rapidly when I saw what my case was to be. A family matter. An elderly husband was seeking an injunction preventing his rather more youthful wife from committing acts of violence on his somewhat frail person. Even as I sat on the bench, I was racking my brain for any legal information that might be useful, but there was absolutely nothing there. It had been years since I had done any family work. I was mightily relieved to learn that Bobby Johnson, later Mr Justice Johnson, was the very experienced counsel representing the husband.

The usher asked if the witness should be called. At that point, I realised that I was more nervous than I had been in any case in which I had appeared as an advocate. My mouth was absolutely dry. I dreaded what sort of sound might come out if I uttered a word. A nod was the order of the day.

The husband needed to be taken letter by letter through the oath. Was that acceptable to His Lordship? Another nod indicated that it was. Bobby Johnson made his submissions and requested that the previously drafted order should be made. Again, the judicial nod sufficed. Without me saying a word, justice had been done.

I would never allow myself to be in that position again. I immediately set about updating my knowledge of family law with the inevitable result that the knowledge was never to be used at any other stage of my career. That was my first and last matrimonial case as a Deputy High Court Judge.

At the mid-day adjournment, I was passing through the courtyard in my robes in a solemn judicial procession of one. Martin Poleden's son, Daniel, was walking through, oblivious to the grandeur of the occasion. Martin is more than a life-long friend: he was born in the same street as me, on the same day but, luckily for our mothers, not quite at the same time otherwise the orange-haired Welsh midwife who delivered both of us might have had to make a difficult choice which patient to attend.

"Hallo, Michael," Daniel called. I had to decide quickly whether to offend the son of a lifelong friend or break all protocol. A compromise was needed. A curt nod and a barely perceptible curl of a finger to be interpreted as, "Shhh ... later.."

On 23rd September 1974 I received the letter from Hume Boggis-Rolfe, Clerk to the Crown and secretary to the Lord Chancellor, that my formal appointment as a Recorder was to run from 1st October. On 27th September 1974, I was sworn in as a Recorder at the Old Bailey by Mr Justice Caulfield[1]. After I had taken the oath, he leaned forward to give me important words of wisdom which I was keen to receive. He said, "Remember, if you need to pee, you just rise – you don't have to ask the judge."

Useful as that was, I felt that perhaps an opportunity had been missed for giving some sentencing guidelines or other practical points in run-

---

1 Mr Justice Bernard Caulfield (1914-1994). In 1987, he described Mrs (now Lady) Archer as "fragrant" in a libel case brought by her husbnad.

ning a major trial although I had been feeling my way as an Assistant Recorder for some time and had tried both civil and criminal cases. In fact, it was to be years before training became the norm for judges.

As an Assistant Recorder at the Old Bailey the previous year, I had had the opportunity to use the provisions of recent legislation[1] to order a psychology lecturer to pay £300 compensation to a victim whom he had assaulted by smashing him in the face with a beer glass. Fortunately, the wound he had inflicted was not life-threatening, but that was a matter of luck: he was within millimetres of being blinded. I saw no reason why the public should pay the compensation to which the victim was entitled.

Now I came to my first case at the Old Bailey as a Recorder. Two Afro-Caribbean men were charged with causing grievous bodily harm to four or five bookmakers' managers while robbing them of their shop takings. They had planned the operation carefully, tracking the movements of their victims who travelled regularly by train to a bank in South London that took night-safe money. The robbery was made easier because the station was not manned after 6.00 p.m. so there would be no-one around to call the police. When they caught sight of their prey, they charged down the platform at them, brandishing huge axes with blades eight inches square. They were whooping and shrieking out words from a song, words that were to be their downfall. They threatened to beat the victims to a pulp unless they handed over the money. One was so terrified, he had a heart attack and nearly died. Another was badly injured when one of the assailants struck his head with the flat of an axe. It was an horrific, brutal and premeditated assault.

The defence was simple: mistaken identity. But the words the men had been shrieking identified them: people from the flats below theirs knew them as thugs going about chanting the words as they menaced local people.

I thought it was a shocking case and the jury did too. The defendants sank like stones. The guilty verdict came back very quickly leaving me with the task of giving appropriate sentences to these thugs. Thinking about guidelines on sentencing and bearing in mind that there was not a single mitigating factor for either man, I had in mind that ten to twelve

[1] Criminal Justice Act 1972.

years would be appropriate. "But," I told myself, "this is your first case as a Recorder. You could be appealed if you pitch it too high."

"I will deal with sentence at 2.00 o'clock," I announced and set off to mull over the problem at lunch.

The judges lunch at one long table in the dining room at the Old Bailey. There are no subsidiary tables. There is typed list indicating where each of them will sit. They remain robed and do not remove their wigs. All are guests of the Lord Mayor and, of course, must be correctly attired. I found a table and was very soon joined by Mr Justice George Waller. I told him that I had this awful case.

"Sentence?" George said.

"Yes."

"What have you got in mind?"

"Ten years for the younger fellow, twelve for the older."

"Yes," he said thoughtfully. "Worth every minute."

As I was thinking that this was what I would call a good, tough judge, he continued, "But I wouldn't do it if I were you, because there's a danger that you'll run out of time. What if a worse case comes up? How much longer will you give for that? Perhaps seven to eight years each."

It seemed a sensible approach. At 2.00 o'clock. I passed sentence. They shouted something at me. It was unintelligible but conveyed the impression of being very unpleasant. The clerk of the court helpfully explained that the men had uttered a threat to my life. Their friends in the public gallery seemed to think that the sentiments expressed were a good idea. For a couple of months, the police kept a visible presence outside our house. After a while and a good few more sentences which were equally ill received, I decided that the family and friends of the guilty had a job to do by uttering threats as I had in giving them cause to do so. The police went back to their regular business and our house became anonymous again.

The axe-wielding thugs went through the process of an appeal against the length of the sentence. It failed. The Court of Appeal considered the transcript of the judgment and said: "We would add just this. If the learned Recorder would have passed sentence of ten and twelve years, we would not have interfered."

***

Not everyone required a swingeing sentence. A graceful guilty plea and heartfelt mitigation often gave some leeway on leniency. But there is a style of mitigation adopted so often by so few on behalf of so many: the defendant, who has admitted to or been found guilty of a crime which deserves imprisonment, should not be sent to prison because his girlfriend is about to have a baby or he has miraculously been offered his first job in several years, starting tomorrow – if permitted to do so – enabling him to contribute to society rather than taking from it. I learnt from a Northern judge who summed up the ennui of these probably truthful but otherwise trite points by saying, "The offer of a job is better than 12 pregnant girlfriends."

***

A young defence barrister made an impassioned plea, beginning somewhat inaccurately with the words, "On my knees, I beg you not to send him to prison ..." The plea seemed endless. I picked up my *Archbold*[1] and found the relevant section. I interrupted him.

"You have spent as much time as is appropriate on your explanation. Have you not looked at *Archbold*?"

"I haven't got one," the young barrister said.

How could he appear in court without *Archbold*? Without a clue about protocol he said, "Can I borrow yours?"

I said, "I'm going to put the case back." It sounded as if I was putting him in detention. "Go to the library. Look up why I cannot do the thing you are asking me not to do."

He stood his ground. "I've got a *Cross on Sentencing*," he persevered. A useful paperback but hardly the equipment required for a practising criminal barrister. "It's all I could afford."

---

[1] The criminal lawyer's bible: *Archbold: Criminal Evidence, Pleading and Practice* is published annually by Sweet and Maxwell

236

I remembered the hardship for pupils and the years of debt for young barristers struggling to make their way in the early years. But that was no excuse for not being prepared for his case. I expected him to look it up or ask somebody. Any member of the Bar would have helped him if he could not get to a library: he would have saved everyone a lot of time if he had found out that the law did not provide for the custodial sentence he was asking me not to impose.

CHAPTER 41

JOHN STONEHOUSE

John Stonehouse[1] was Postmaster General in Harold Wilson's Labour Government (1964-70). When Labour lost power and he returned to the backbenches as an opposition MP, he took to supplementing his income through various fraudulent business activities which eventually came under the scrutiny of the Department for Trade and Industry. Early in 1974, faced with exposure and ruin, both in finances and of reputation, he fled to America where he faked his death, leaving his clothing on a Miami beach and a suicide note for his grieving wife and daughter.

Very much alive, wearing a second set of clothes and using one of several new identities he had created for himself, he made his way to Melbourne where, as Donald Clive Mildoon, he set up home with Sheila Buckley, his secretary.

On Christmas Eve 1974, someone reported to the police that the English-sounding neighbour looked suspiciously like Lord Lucan. By then, Stonehouse was using the identity of John Markham, a deceased former resident of his constituency.

When the police arrived on his doorstep, Stonehouse admitted immediately that his new identity was false but the investigating officers were disappointed that they had not stumbled onto the solution of the Lucan mystery. For the next six months, the Australians puzzled over what to do about their unwelcome guest: how to deport a serving MP. Eventually, he returned to England to face trial for fraud, having failed in his attempts to secure asylum in Sweden or Mauritius. He conducted his own defence at his trial in 1976, at the time the longest fraud trial in English legal history. He was sentenced to seven years for fraud, theft and deception but only served three. He was released early on health grounds. Three years later, he had a heart attack and died whilst taking part in a television programme.

Ian Hay-Davidson was the managing partner of the accounting firm of Arthur Andersen. Within a fortnight of Stonehouse's Miami disappearance, Ian and I were appointed by the Secretary of State to inquire

---

[1] John Stonehouse (1926-1988).

into London Capital Group Ltd[1], a business in which Stonehouse had been deeply involved. He had arranged to change its name from that of a charity, the British Bangladesh Trust. At the time that we were asked to conduct the inquiry, I was about to leave for Singapore to prosecute a complicated six-week company fraud. The purpose of the Stonehouse investigation was to see if there was any impropriety in the way that the charity's funds had been used in the light of the complex transfers of money between the companies with which Stonehouse was associated and the route taken by very large sums into his personal bank accounts and those of the various personae that he adopted. The six weeks of the Singapore trial could be used to assemble the Stonehouse material so that we could make a start on the investigation on my return.

The Singapore case was under way when the immigration police in Melbourne discovered Stonehouse was alive and well and living on their manor. This came about because of the world-wide hunt for Lord Lucan who had disappeared after the death of his children's nanny in 1974. In December 1974, the Melbourne police were alerted to the presence of a tall, aristocratic and mysterious Englishman who had recently arrived in the suburb of Christchurch. When they knocked at the door of Stonehouse's apartment, he said, "It's all right, I'm putting my hands up."

"What is your name?" the police asked.

"I'm John Markham," he said. Then, "No I'm not. I'm John Stonehouse."

The police were confused about this. The Markham and Stonehouse names meant nothing to them. They reported back to Interpol, "We're looking for Lord Lucan but we've found this bloke who says he's Markham or Stonehouse. Does that mean anything to you?" The massive scale of his pre-"suicide" fraudulent activities had by then come to light. Stonehouse was most certainly of interest.

Now that he had turned up, Ian and I agreed to undertake the enquiry on the basis that the Government indemnified us against the libel actions that might be brought against us if Stonehouse were to feel that his hitherto good name were to have been impugned. Ian and his team of a dozen or so subordinates spent the remainder of the six weeks sift-

[1] Report published 1977.

ing through thousands of documents and following a paper trail through dozens of bank accounts.

Now that he had turned up, we could meet Stonehouse and see what he had to say about his activities. I realized that I was conveniently situated: Melbourne, where the Stonehouse interviews were to take place, was much nearer to Singapore than London. The Singapore trial finished and our enquiry group made our way to Australia. We made contact with Stonehouse's solicitor, a former police officer. He said, "You do realise that you've got no right to compel him to give evidence.

I said, "I imagine your man realises that we can't force him. But knowing the sort of chap he is, I should think that he would want to."

The solicitor said, "Well, I've advised him. You need to know that he says he's John Markham. There is no John Stonehouse to be interviewed. You'll have to call him Markham."

Whatever name he was using, the person we knew as John Stonehouse agreed to give evidence. He was sworn in.

I asked him, "Can you remember who you were in a former existence?"

"John Stonehouse," he replied.

"Does he admit to having taken the same oath?" I asked.

Markham, on Stonehouse's behalf, agreed that he did.

The days went by. He was in an impossible corner from which there was no escape. However, he behaved as though he were graciously offering a lesser mortal the opportunity for a rare encounter with a person of undoubtedly higher rank. He was always immaculately dressed and seemed to have a new, well-cut suit for each of our meetings.

"Perhaps you would like to offer an explanation," I suggested at one point.

He went into a long, rambling monologue. Nearing what seemed to be the conclusion of his speech, he said in declamatory style, "I will say to the end of my days, be they long or short ..."

Eventually, I stopped him.

"Forgive me. I have listened very hard and I have to say that you have really reminded of John Stonehouse on the hustings."

"Don't be under any misapprehension about him," he said. "I feel very close to John Stonehouse. We are very sympathetic to one another."

"That's fair," I said. "Would you like to let him know the likely sentence he would get?"

At our last meeting he said, "May I thank you for the fairness and good humour with which you have conducted this investigation?" He then swept out, imaginary courtiers trailing after him.

Stonehouse gave his evidence to us in the High Court of Melbourne. We were invited to use the court because they had recording equipment which meant that we did not need to have a shorthand writer.

At the end of the fortnight, he said that he was going back and the Government said that they would be sending police to accompany him. A bit of a waste of taxpayers' money as he was going voluntarily but who knows if he might have felt the urge to go on another swimming expedition whilst in transit somewhere around the world.

At that point, I regarded the English criminal process as being in train. I therefore advised that we should not continue the investigation at that time because there would be a clash with the probable Old Bailey trial. Witnesses would be criticised because they would have had a rehearsal. We therefore suspended the enquiry in Australia and Stonehouse returned to defend himself on charges of fraud. He ended up with the seven-year sentence he richly deserved.

Mr Justice Eveleigh told me long after the trial that he had made a slight mistake in giving Stonehouse the option of the transcript or the Melbourne tape recording going to the jury.

Very few people could love the sound of their own voice more than Stonehouse. He thought that the sound of his voice would be better than the sight of words on a dry, written document. As he was able to persuade himself of the truth of what he said, so he thought that the jury would be swayed by his oratory. The jury was interested and more able to spot the difference between truth and fantasy than the accused. When they got to the bit in our dialogue about the hustings, the jury fell about with laughter. It was probably the most amusement that the Old Bailey had seen before or would be likely to see again. Their opinion of his credibility was reflected in the guilty verdict. He went off to Wormwood Scrubs to serve his sentence and I resumed the inquiry by visiting him there in circumstances which were something less than the Victorian elegance of the Melbourne courtroom.

For the remainder of the inquiry, Ian and I were given the use of an office at the Hilton Hotel at Shepherd's Bush where we reviewed the evidence taken after the daily visit to Wormwood Scrubs. Stonehouse, whose latest identity was a number rather than a name, maintained his air of arrogant grandeur throughout our day-long meetings which were interrupted by a short break for lunch.

The Governor was delighted to have something different going on and offered us the hospitality of taking lunch in the officers' mess, an open plan room leading off the kitchen.

We were served by a prisoner who wore a white busby jacket over his prison garb and draped a prison-issue tea-cloth over one arm as if it were an elegant napkin, ready to be flourished. His daily opening gambit, translated initially with some difficulty from the strongest of Cockney accents, was, "Have you got a reservation, sir?"

I would reply, "I'm afraid not." This would earn a slight frown and the sound of sucking through his teeth.

"How many are you, sir?" he would then ask, before taking us to the same table, holding back our chairs to seat us, then offering us details of the menu.

"Today, sir, our special is Poy Wormwood Scrubs: minced meat with mashed white p'tito and a touch of HP sauce. Alternatively, we've Poy of the Shepherd, Shepherd's Poy."

There were several other variations on the same theme. Having translated "pie", the rest followed naturally. It always added up to a choice of Shepherd's Pie and nothing else.

We would finish the afternoon session with Stonehouse, get back to the hotel at about five then work for a couple of hours before going back to deal with whatever had come in during the day at chambers.

I had a message from my clerk one day, asking me to come back to chambers as soon as I had finished at the prison. The Head of British Rail Police was coming in from Liverpool Street and needed to see me as matter of urgency. I managed to be there for the meeting hastily arranged for 6.00 p.m. that day. He wanted some advice but started by asking me if I was enjoying my visits to the Scrubs.

"Yes, it's OK," I said. "How do you know I've been going there? I didn't think it was public knowledge."

"Do you remember, you prosecuted one of our people a few months ago? He was a chef who used to cook for the Queen's train. In his regular work, he ran a Pullman car swindle. He brought his own ingredients, cooked the meals and kept the takings. We were a bit slow off the mark in noticing what he was up to but eventually we noticed that there was never any money to pay in at the end of his working day."

Now that he had reminded me, I remembered the case.

"Yes, that's right," I said. "But I don't remember the defendant."

"He's the chef at Wormwood Scrubs now. He's rather good. We're interviewing him about others involved in the scam. You wouldn't have recognised him but he told our investigating officer that the bloke who put him inside is there every day, something to do with Stonehouse."

I could only imagine razor blades flavouring the shepherd's pie from now on. "Is it safe for me to lunch in the officers' mess, do you think?" I asked him.

"Oh, yes," he assured me, unconvincingly. "Perhaps don't have the soup."

The next day, as I was passing the kitchen , I could not resist looking to see which one he was. By now, I remembered every detail of the case – the Queen's train – the four-year sentence. In the event, I had no difficulty in recognising him, although somewhat differently dressed from the last time I had seen him in the dock. Now, he wore a chef's hat and white apron supplementing the prison uniform. He saw me and gave me a deep bow. I hoped that I was right to take this as meaning there were no hard feelings.

243

The weeks of interviewing Stonehouse resulted in our report. We concluded that, notwithstanding the criminality of most of his financial dealings and placed on record that, to Stonehouse, truth was a moving target, there was no impropriety in any use of trust funds.

Before the report was published, the Attorney-General, Sam Silkin, invited us to attend a meeting at the House of Commons to discuss its conclusions. We were led to a tiny, windowless room lit by a feeble, yellow light casting dark shadows onto the marginally less dark, dingy panelled walls. The Attorney-General was perched on the only seat, a shabby arm-chair with springs bulging below the seat, framed by the wings of a large, battered screen. He looked as if he had been scaled down to a miniature size as the rest of us crowded into the confined space with no room to sit. The Director of Public Prosecutions was there as were the Solicitor-General and his Parliamentary Private Secretary. The full legal panoply of state was squashed into the stuffy room.

I told the Attorney-General that the report was highly critical of the wrong-doing of which Stonehouse had been convicted but that, on the Trust matters, he was in the clear. One of the principal matters for us to investigate was to resolve, if we could, whether the British Bangladesh Trust had been abused, misappropriated or whatever. We thought that he had not actually robbed the charity.

"That's about the size of it right now," I said and concluded the report details by saying, "but we would have to resume the inquiry in order to change the report if further evidence arose." In a traditional court-room ending, I said, "Is there anything else I could do to help?" To which, there is not supposed to be an answer.

Through the shadows, I could see his face brighten up. "Well, yes. Could you put the kettle on? It's behind the screen. A cup of tea would be just what the doctor ordered."

The Stonehouse affair ended as the kettle boiled.

A curious side issue concerned a damning account of the activities of two people who had been complicit in the Stonehouse affair. When I was in Hong Kong at one stage of the preparation of the final report, *Private Eye* managed to get hold of the information that, as far as I knew, was in the one copy on my desk in Chambers. A courier with a plausible story had turned up to collect the copy and a junior clerk had handed it over. We were absolutely blazing but the one thing we couldn't do was to say, "No – you've got it wrong." In the end, we didn't use it. We had no evidence. But it made a good story for the magazine.

CHAPTER 42

NORMANSFIELD

Normansfield Hospital[1] was founded in 1868 by John Langdon-Down[2] as a Private Home for the "care, education and treatment of those of good social position who present any degree of mental deficiency". After Langdon-Down's death, his sons, and then his grandson, continued to run the hospital which became part of the NHS in 1951. In 1970, the family era ended and Dr Terence Lawlor, a psychiatrist, was appointed to run the hospital. Under what was perceived to be his authoritarian and incompetent rule, senior personnel resigned, buildings fell into disrepair and patients lived in squalor and degradation. He was suspended in 1976 in the middle of a nurses' strike, unprecedented in the National Health Service.

In February 1977, Michael was asked by David Ennals, the Secretary of State for Social Services, to chair a committee whose members were Thomas Fisher SRN RNMS, Dr Hector Fowlie Mb ChB, FCRP Psych, the Hon John Scarlett CBE and Mrs Alys Woolley: "To enquire into patient care and staff morale at Normansfield Hospital, Teddington, and in particular into complaints made by staff at the hospital and others; to enquire into the causes and effect of unrest at the hospital and the action taken to deal with the situation; and to make recommendations." This became known as the Normansfield Inquiry.

The report highlighted a failure of the senior medical, nursing and administrative staff at the hospital to co-operate with each other. Hostility between Dr Lawlor and virtually all the other nursing, paramedical and ancillary staff was the main cause of the strike. Dr Lawlor was over-critical of the nurses and ran an intolerant, abusive and tyrannical regime. He was not checked by his medical colleagues as none of them wanted to work with him nor even cover for his holidays. There were other contributing factors such as the very low standard of nursing care, low morale, poor administration and poor working conditions. The report concluded that "the strike was avoidable but no-one sought to avoid it. Normansfield itself has considerable potential and should not be closed."

[1]   www.hamptonwick.org/normansfield_hospital.htm
[2]   John Langdon-Down (1828-1896), original researcher into Down's syndrome.

There was understandable pressure for a public inquiry. David Ennals, Secretary of State for Health, knew me from the days of the Challenor Inquiry: his role had been Counsel for Liberty, an interested party. He had had more recent contact with me because of my work on the Stonehouse report. He decided that I was the man for the new job in hand. He telephoned to ask if I would be interested in conducting an inquiry into what was then the national scandal of Normansfield Hospital. Elwyn-Jones was called in to persuade me. Both said that the Committee was expected to sit for about six weeks although there would be further time needed to complete and publish the final report.

At the time I accepted the invitation, I was beginning a three week commitment as a Recorder at the Old Bailey and I was already three days into trying a case. Six weeks was a long time to allocate out of a busy practice in addition to the Recorder days. I needed another conversation with Elwyn. I could only realistically undertake the Committee work if I was released from my Recorder's stint.

"Don't worry about that," he said, his Welsh accent gently stretching the vowels. "We are so grateful to you for undertaking this task. Do you mind if I write to thank you?"

I knew that he would forget to write. But he did not forget to release me from sitting as a Recorder. But it soon became obvious that the estimated six weeks were not even going to scratch the surface of the problem. It was to be nearly two years before I went back. I explained, in the introduction to the Report, how it came about that so much time had been needed:

"Despite every fair and reasonable economy we could devise, and despite a sometimes ruthless pruning of the documentation, coupled with a willingness to sit in open session for long hours, we were engaged for 124 days hearing the evidence, we visited the hospital on several occasions, we examined no less that 11,000 documents and records, heard 145 witnesses and read the statements of many others. There were 14,856 pages of transcribed evidence[1]."

By accepting the offer to chair a Committee of Inquiry, Michael was given the privilege and power of administering the oath. He prepared an

[1]   cmnd. 7357, 1978, p. 3, para 7.

outline of how he would conduct the inquiry based on the general infor-
mation that had been given to him. He announced that the preliminary
sessions would be occupied with those who wanted to be heard putting
themselves forward. They did so in large numbers, many of them being
represented by lawyers to deal with the diverse areas associated with
treatment of mental illness, not only from Normansfield. As it turned
out, the Committee convened day after day, week after week until seven-
teen long months had elapsed. At first, proceedings were conducted at
Church House, Westminster. After several months, they were rehoused in
the Government Press Office in St James.

I kept my practice together and coped with Chambers' management
by arriving at least once a week at Chambers at about 7.30 a.m. and
working for an hour or so. I would return after the Committee's business
then work late. I saw light of day by walking briskly along the Embank-
ment to and from Chambers.

We took oral evidence and heard of the dismaying experience of seeing the pitiful conditions in which the patients, profoundly physically
and mentally disabled, had been left to fend for themselves despite being
utterly incapable of doing so. The harrowing experience of the inquiry
was only alleviated by the good things that came out of it, including the
camaraderie that developed between the Committee members and the
friendships that were formed. I still have regular contact with Hector
Fowlie, the psychiatrist from Dundee. Another of the people involved
was Duncan Watson, a most remarkable solicitor, who was later knighted. He had been blind from birth. He acted for the Treasury team. Philip
Otton QC[1] and John Toulmin represented the Treasury Solicitor. They
were, effectively, the prosecution.

Although conditions at the hospital had been bad, the strike was a
collective act of barbarity. The result of patients being left to their own
devices during the course of that day was that they lived in filth, eating
excrement and harming themselves. They were denied care, medication
and the respect that one would hope that civilised beings would accord
to those in need.

It was hard to imagine how the strikers were able to live with themselves. I asked the shop-steward, "What did you do when the strike be-

---

[1] Since then, a Lord Justice of Appeal, now retired.

gan?" I am still haunted by his reply. "I pulled the sheet and blankets over my head," he said.

Brian Rix, who was later knighted for his charitable work for the mentally ill and who was to become a key member of the hospital's successful fund-raising committee, highlighted the difficulties that staff had to contend with as well as parents and relatives of the patients. His daughter, Shelley[1], had lived at Normansfield since early childhood. She was then a young adult. "Who will look after her when my wife and I are gone?" he wanted to know, as did other parents in the same situation. Normansfield had been his and their hope for the answer to the question.

Time and again, people asked the same question, or described how morale had disintegrated so that people whose jobs were to care had now become indifferent to the outcome of any drop in standard. Almost every day had its share of reflective sadness and the intensity of the hearings took its toll of all of us. Not least of our ordeal was in witnessing the distress of parents and family or sometimes just good friends of patients. There were a number of occasions when relatives would say something to the effect that they were getting on in years and were tormented by the fear that there may be nobody left to care for or visit their loved ones.

It was hard and emotionally draining to deal with these issues over so many months. I would regularly hold at least a half-hour session with the Committee members when we dealt with general matters, rather than the horrifying evidence. The Committee was able to have some respite when I went through written legal submissions. For example, a question arose as to the state of mind of the supervisor who was at the root of many of Normansfield's problems. I had to rule on whether it was in the public interest for it to be known what was said about him. I could then release the Committee for a short time and, having ruled, would circulate the ruling to them before we went back to hearing the witnesses and counsel's submissions.

Apart from the relatively short breaks at Chambers before and after the Committee sessions, work on the inquiry spilled over at home, going through back transcripts, and preparing the report in draft after draft.

---

[1]   Shelley Rix had Downs Syndrome. Born in 1952, she was an in-patient from the age of 7. She died in 2005.

During seventeen months of unmitigatingly depressing evidence, the Committee became drained. It was so wearing that there began to be adverse effects on the members' family lives. In particular, Hector's wife, Christine, was becoming worn down by the impact on their home life. I spoke to her several times to cheer her up but there was nothing I could do to improve the demands of the timetable. Although ultimately rewarded with an OBE, Hector had no choice but to go back to Scotland on Friday, exhausted, and then return to London on the Sunday, ready for the hearing on the Monday. For all of us, even if our journeys were not so long, it was as if there was no life outside the Committee. For our families, it was as if we were not part of their lives. It was a thoroughly miserable time of unremitting commitment to the task in hand.

Eventually I went to see David Ennals. I wanted to moderate the scope of the inquiry because it was extending beyond the specific local events concerning one hospital. I had to go to him to discuss changing the terms of reference which had been put to me.

He was in hospital himself, having had some minor surgery. To support the system, he was in an NHS ward with nothing more than the standard curtain on rails around his bed to establish any degree of what one might be allowed to call privacy. With all the less exalted members of the ward highly interested in the governmental comings and goings, I pleaded my case at the cramped bedside, but came away with nothing.

"I'm very sorry," he said, "but I made the appointment in the public interest. Whilst utterly sympathetic to the problems you face, I simply could not justify changing the terms of reference."

His Permanent Private Secretary hovered at the far side of the Ministerial NHS plywood bedside cabinet, wringing his hands in classic Sir Humphrey mode, but quite unable to make any recommendation in my favour. The remit of the Normansfield inquiry would be as wide as needed to cope with the available evidence[1].

---

1   In the opening paragraph to his Foreword to the Report, David Ennals was warm in his acknowledgement of the difficulties the Committee encountered. He said, "I am grateful to Mr Michael Sherrard QC and to the members of the Committee of Inquiry for the conscientious manner in which they have performed an exacting public duty: for accepting the exceptional disruption of their professional and private lives that it must have entailed; and for producing a clear, thorough and forthright report

On a different occasion as the hearing was drawing to an end, another Sir Humphrey arrived at the St James' offices allocated to the Committee. He wanted to – and did – take me to lunch at Overtons.

It appeared from his thinly veiled remarks about each member of the Committee that I was going to be involved in recommending gongs. When the hints demanded an answer I said, "I'd like to recommend the VC for everyone!" In fact, two of the Committee received OBEs.

***

One event livened the dark days of the Inquiry. Grandma's birthday.

My aunt called to remind me that my much-loved maternal grandmother was soon to celebrate her 100th birthday. She said, "She's looking forward like nobody's business to the Royal Telegram."

"She won't get one," I said. Grandma was one of the wave of Jewish immigrants to England around the turn of the century. Somerset House had no record of her birth and there was no way that she could prove her age so as to get the longed-for Royal communication.

"But you're a QC," my aunt insisted. "You can arrange it."

"I really don't think there is any way it can be done for ladies from Austria with no evidence of their date of birth."

My aunt was not persuaded by this logic. "Michael, you *must* do it! Let the Palace know."

At this time, we were in the new offices in St James. The walk to and from Chambers took me along Pall Mall, past the St James' Palace Post Office. I noticed that it carried a Royal Coat of Arms above the doorway.

---

on the circumstances at Normansfield Hospital in the period before and leading up to a strike at the Hospital in May 1976." In a letter to me, also published with the Report, he said, "I know that you and I are at one in the need to put new heart into Normansfield Hospital as speedily as possible in the interests of the patients there. I know that the Chairmen and their Authorities totally share this aim." On 30th June 1978, I wrote, "We are delighted to learn of your decision to appoint a senior and experienced "task force" to run the hospital." The hospital was transformed: under enlightened management with the benefit of skilled and caring staff, a significant number of patients became fit to take their place in the community. Normansfield Hospital closed in 1997. The main building awaits development. The grounds contain new houses and the theatre has been restored as a thriving arts centre.

After my aunt's call, the idea occurred to me that the telegram form was very likely to have that insignia printed on it. I went inside and asked if that were the case and, to my delight, it was.

I completed a form with the words 'Warmest congratulations and every good wish on your hundredth birthday, Elizabeth and Philip.' I handed it to the post-mistress and told her I would like the telegram to arrive on Tuesday. She read the words and looked up at me with a quizzical expression. I simply nodded. After a moment, she smiled and said, "It'll get there."

It did.

My aunt called me on the Tuesday. "I knew you'd be able to do it," she said.

The Ravenscroft Nursing Home arranged a party for my grandmother. The family were all there. I made a speech. My aunt said, "Shall I reply for you?"

"Certainly not," said my grandmother. "I can manage my own speech."

And she did.

Six months later, in the natural course of events, she died.

Not long ago, my aunt, who had then reached the age of 91, said to me, "You know, I've still got grandma's telegram from the Palace."

"I didn't know," I answered. "But if you still have it, you will see that it's from St James', not Buckingham Palace."

"They have palaces everywhere!" My aunt rebuked my ignorance. "They send the telegrams from wherever they are on the day."

CHAPTER 42

THE CALL TO THE BENCH

Another miserable day with the Normansfield Committee. Another long journey home. Dan Hollis QC, Middle Temple Bencher, telephoned the Sherrard household.

Shirley took the call a few moments before I came through the front door. So she knew before me. I took the receiver from her. Dan said, "Good evening, Master."

There is only one meaning for that title. Only Benchers are addressed as Master. Even so, I was not sure. I said, "What do you mean?" Then, somewhat lamely, "Nobody's asked me."

"We don't."

I've used the trick myself several times when informing a new Bencher of his title.

"I hope you'll enjoy it," Dan said, understating the prospect of what my feelings would be for becoming an officer of the Inn.

The call takes place at High Table. The Bench lines up behind the Treasurer in the corridor leading to Hall. The Porter strikes the wooden staff on the floor to signify to the diners in Hall that they should rise to receive the formal procession of the Bench as it makes its way to High Table along the gangway between lines of pupils in their short-sleeved gowns and barristers in their formal robes, the candles flickering on the tables. The new Benchers wait aside as the Benchers stand at their places. The newcomers will be seated in the four places at the end of the High Table. The catering manager announces them.

"Master Treasurer, I present Michael Sherrard one of Her Majesty's Counsel."

He turns to the new Bencher: "Mr Sherrard, by invitation of Master Treasurer and the Masters of the Bench, you are invited to take your place at the High Table." The new Bencher then shakes hands with Master Treasurer and goes to the place which will remain his on all formal dining occasions until the next new batch is called. When all four are called, the porter's staff strikes the floor again, Grace is said and everyone takes their seats. Dining commences. The most junior of the Bench-

ers is of most recent call. He will in due course become Master Junior when the Treasurer proposes the loyal toast: "Master Junior..."

At the time of my call, the new Benchers and other Masters of the Bench would go into the Parliament Chamber where, in a private gathering, the new members responded individually to a toast to their health. The quality of the speeches was variable but a combination of discretion and the rules of confidentiality forbid me from mentioning either the mistakes Benchers made or any of the marvellous speeches we heard over the years. Good or bad, they are for the ears of the select few: unless you were on the inside, you will never hear them. The rules of purdah have now been changed: the toasts and speeches are made in public.

But I can say this of the days gone by. The speeches were not without risk. Very senior judges were there who might hear someone tell a bawdy or inappropriate story which, in what I can call my day, would have automatically black-balled them from the High Court. Then as now, it is, literally, a question of poor judgment on display. Of course, good judgment will be reported to the right ears.

I remember Ralph Kilner-Brown sitting next to me on an occasion when a new Bencher's response to the toast prompted him to say, "That's quality. Must mention him where it counts." That is how it was done.

Of the three others who were elected with me, one was an eminent barrister, Sir Wilfred Bourne, Clerk of the Crown. I was to learn that he was known to everyone as John. Another was my predecessor as Treasurer, Ronald Waterhouse. As the most junior Bencher, my place was laid at the end of the High Table. On retiring to the Parliament Chamber for dessert, I found that it was to be my privilege to ring the bell to signify preparedness for coffee to be served.

Call to the Bench was always a special occasion. There was standing room only in the Parliament Chamber. Lord Dillon looked much put out that he had to stand. The Treasurer referred to "John" Bourne as "John" as he introduced him. Bourne was daunting at the best of times. His response was chilling. With a grim expression on his face, looking through rather than at his audience, he said in a flat, almost menacing tone, "I am known as John but my name is Wilfred ... I hope you will call me Wilfred." The Benchers acknowledged this cold statement with a selection of slight coughs and some shuffling movement. He continued, without expression, "I agree to preserve the business of the Inn." As this was not a speech, I hope that I will be forgiven for reporting what was said.

I could see that Lord Dillon was furious. This great honour was being treated, if not with contempt, with frigid indifference. If I had recited *Little Bo-Peep* – with feeling – it would have been greeted with acclaim. What was I to do to return some warmth to this great occasion?

I did it with a few imitations – Tom Denning, Sir Gerald Dodson – if there was quirk of accent or mannerism, the Parliament Chamber occupants heard it that evening. The words, of course, I will not tell. It made quite an impact! My acceptance made clear my heartfelt delight and my welcome could not have been warmer, even from the very magisterial Lord Justice Sachs and his intimidating father-in-law, Lord Goddard[1].

Lord Justice Sachs came to me after my speech, put his arm around my shoulder and said, "My dear Michael, you must call me Eric."

Of course, I could never call him anything from that day on. I noticed at lunch that all the benchers around me must have had the same invitation. No remark at any time thereafter included his – or any – name.

***

After I was told that I had been elected to the Bench, I developed an instant and extraordinary addiction to the Inn. For me, it was like falling in love with the girl next door: not quite love at first sight but love as soon as I noticed she was there. I had had little to do with the Inn up to that time because of the strange circumstances of paper dining whilst I was university and during my pupillage. I had attended only two formal dinners prior to my call to the Bench but I used the library and lunched there from time to time. After I became a Bencher, I would have done anything possible for Middle Temple. I was to immerse myself in the Inn and become devoted to its role in perpetuating the profession.

---

[1] Lord Justice Goddard, as Mr Justice Goddard, was the trial judge in 1953 when Derek Bentley was convicted of murdering a police officer. The murder conviction was quashed by the Court of Appeal in 1998. Lord Bingham, the Lord Chief Justice, sitting with Lord Justice Kennedy and Mr Justice Collins, said the summing-up at his trial "was such as to deny the appellant that fair trial which is the birthright of every British citizen". The jury had been misdirected on the standard and burden of proof required for conviction and the summing-up had put unfair pressure on the jury to convict.

Within days of being called to the Bench, I was asked to become part of a small committee which had the aim of furthering the interest of students in the role of the Inn. London-based students dined only to comply with the Inn's requirement. Without having completed the designated number of dinners, it was not possible to be called to the Bar. Enjoyment was not an item on the agenda. Oxbridge and other out-of-town students were coming to dine in term on Friday and Saturday. They all had to log in to show they had eaten enough dinners. A number of them realized this was a total waste of time and money: the food was not very good and they were highly unlikely to encounter a barrister or a judge, particularly at the weekends. Their central question was: "What is the point of dining?"

It was suggested that if a group of students met at McDonalds, they could do better in progressing legal discussions. Even if dining had been the main educational function in the 17th century, it was not working now. Unless someone did something to show that people would benefit from the dinners as part of the learning process, the entire requirement of dining would be counter-productive.

The Treasurer said to me, "If we can crack this problem somehow, we'll avoid an attack on the Inn's traditions. I agree that we must show that dining is for the benefit of students, not just for keeping the Inn alive. May I leave this with you?"

Although put as a question, I had been given a task. I said, "I'm honoured."

I was yet to learn that, after dining in Hall as a Bencher a dozen or so times, you realise you are dining with the same people every time because you were called together. With all due respect to your gang of four, you can be bored – or boring. You get to know the minutiae of each other's lives. Although talking about interesting cases, the requirement at the other end of Hall, was considered to be bad form, it might have introduced new elements into the conversations. Although mixed dining was eventually to take place at High Table, the first step was the implementation of the idea of mixed dining in Hall, put forward by two young barristers, one of whom was Joseph Smouha[1]. I found time to ask about

[1]   Joseph Smouha took silk in 2003.

what the other Inns were doing to encourage student interest and saw that they had events involving barristers taking seats in student messes. They also encouraged activities such as revels which were not necessarily educational but focused attention on the Inn. I thought this was the right approach.

We eventually recommended that mixed dining should take place to enable newcomers to the Bar to spend time with benchers and barristers. This made me unpopular with some of the senior people: it seemed that certain individuals could not or would not be bothered with students. Against the background of grumblings of disapproval, I said, "You'll have to vote against my Committee's report." This would have been difficult for them to do as it would have been a vote against encouraging the interest of the Inn's new members. It turned out that the senior people, the judges and benchers, were nervous about their ability to deal with close encounters with students. The truth, uttered by several people in only slightly varying terms was: "I won't know the answer to their questions." Some had been out of practice for 10 to 20 years. They believed that grass-roots stuff was no longer in their ambit.

I phoned Joe Smouha.

"I have a feeling that we are looking at the wrong target. The people we want to come and talk to the young are barristers who are going through the mill and who are at a relatively early stage at the Bar. They will able to give fresh answers to questions about chambers and pupillage." As pupillage was compulsory by then, how to secure it was the main student concern.

Even though I had realized that young barristers would be the cornerstone of the plan for mixed dining, it dawned on me that, if you tried to get them to come and dine, you would interfere with their practice-building. I well remembered overnight case preparation, being newly-married and not coming home that evening to read the kids a story or fitting in an extra case to meet the demands of the clerk. How could we find a way of attracting the junior barristers? And overcoming the reluctance of senior barristers? And dealing with the diffidence of judges, so long removed from the cut and thrust of their early careers?

The problem was how to persuade the spectrum of members to participate in the Inn's tradition of dining and learning. The answer was to attract people at different stages of their career: to let it be known that if you wanted success at the Bar or judicial office, you would do very well to let yourself be known to the more senior members. The judges and Benchers would be able to take a relaxed view of potential candidates for election to the Bench and have a social framework for reference for high office. The faces of young barristers would become known to a wider circle than in the courts. The word would get around that the door to the Establishment could be opened through connections at the Inn.

One of the recent Treasurers was concerned about the idea of having junior barristers playing a key role in mixed dining and how it would help the Bench to recognize whether they displayed any particular talents which might be useful in their future careers. He said, "How will we know who these people are who dine with the students? They all look the same to me."

I explained that he could talk to them from time to time, picking them out by the fact, which he must have noticed, even if he had forgotten from his own experience, that barristers have sleeves on their gowns and students do not.

I said, "I will introduce the importance of dining by having a large, attractive book on display at the entrance to Hall. Each barrister dining as a member of Hall will record his participation by signing it." This permanent record would be taken seriously as an indication that barristers who found time to do this had made a valuable contribution to the work of the Inn. They would be entertained at a drinks party when they were at the stage of taking pupils and would be assured of getting to know 'the governors'. The attendance book was the way we got this going.

It hadn't crossed my mind that a wholly unexpected side effect would be a revolution in the quality and shape of the Hall Committee, membership of which became an important step on the upward rungs of the career ladder. The Hall Committee has become very influential. When I became Treasurer, I made its Chairman a full member of the Executive. This was a little reactionary for traditionalists for whom power had to be restricted to those at the top. More than once, I heard protests that "You can't let the tail wag the dog!!!"

Tails and wagging were some way down the line. For the time being, mixed dining was approved by the Bench. I think I did more for myself vis-à-vis the Inn through this programme. I suspect this was ultimately behind my invitation to become Treasurer.

***

The tradition of the Inn is that at least one Bencher dines or lunches at the High Table. Students from outside London were encouraged – and they came by the coach-load – to come up for the weekend to make an inroad into compulsory dining. Shirley and I used to dine frequently on Saturday nights and regularly had Sunday lunch in Hall. It made up for the paper dining of my pupillage days. However, I had difficulty with saying the Christian Grace on account of my Jewish faith. No problem ever arose because there was always someone of the appropriate faith who was able to give religious thanks for the food so the tradition was properly maintained.

Over the years it was a matter of interest as to how Jewish Treasurers overcame the Grace problem. There were two situations: Lord Reading[1] and his son[2] were Treasurers of the Inn. They appeared to have taken the view that it would not be appropriate to read the Grace but, as it was a great part of the tradition of the Inn, they would invite the next senior non-Jew to read the Grace. Sir Cyril Salmon, who became Treasurer after the war, took the view that being Jewish was totally irrelevant: the Treasurer was a figurehead of tradition. He had no difficulty with reading the Grace and was known for saying, "It's not me, Cyril Salmon. It's the Treasurer." Ewen Montagu[3], better known as the author of *The Man Who Never Was,* said Grace when he was Treasurer. This may have been because, as a judge, he was known to have missed the sound of his own voice in the cut and thrust of cross-examination and would interrupt

---

[1]   The 1st Marquess of Reading, Rufus Daniel Rufus Isaacs (1860-1935), Viceroy and Governor General of India 1921-1925.
[2]   Gerald Rufus Isaacs, 2nd Marquess of Reading (1889-1960).
[3]   The Hon. Ewen Montagu, QC, OBE, DL (1901-1985). In World War II, together with his fellow intelligence officer, Sir Archibald Cholmondley, he helped to save the lives of thousands of Allied personnel through their plan, 'Operation Mincemeat', in which the Germans were deceived about Allied invasion plans of occupied territory. The book was an account of the operation. It was also made into a film in 1956 in which Montagu took a small part, belittling his film character, played by Clifton Webb.

counsel frequently. This was an opportunity for him speak up without risk of criticism.

I had given my mind to the problem of the Grace but not discussed it with anybody. My first official dining act was to be Duty Bencher at Sunday lunch. I would be Master Junior. I thought it would be – and it was – a pleasant occasion. But five minutes before lunch, I discovered that Shirley and I were to be alone at High Table. Other Benchers would be lunching in the less formal atmosphere of the Parliament Chamber. I broke the news to Shirley. We imagined ourselves as two miniature figures perched, on display, at High Table. It was a dismaying prospect.

The Senior Registrar of the Family Division took pity on me in the minute before we started our procession of two.

"Michael, are you going to say the Grace?"

I said, truthfully, "I'm taken by surprise ..." It was my naïveté as a new Bencher that I had not realised that the Sunday stint meant that there would be no understudy who could deal with the Grace for me.

"Would you welcome it," he said, "if I as Senior Bencher came in and read the Grace for you?"

Would I? Arms out – I would have hugged him if there were a protocol for it – "Would you?" I asked.

We made our entrance, the Grace was said for me and no-one took any notice of the fact that it was a substitute rather than me. My personal thanks were not only for the meal but for having been spared from resolving a moral dilemma.

***

Shirley and I were to dine with a fellow Bencher, Charles Whitby and his guest, Mr B, in Hall one Saturday evening. As we were chatting before dinner, Lord and Lady Diplock unexpectedly arrived. Shirley was slightly acquainted with Lord Diplock as she had sat next to him at another Hall dinner. It turned out, as one thing in their conversation led to another, that Diplock had had an unfulfilled ambition to be a jockey. Horses were more than a hobby to him "Do you ride?" he asked Shirley. How little he knew of the moraes of North-West London.

They had come from a grand function and were resplendent in full evening dress. Staff hastily laid two more places for them.

Lord Diplock, as the senior Bencher, sat at the head of High Table. I sat to his left, facing Mr B. What passed for conversation consisted mainly of a speech by his Lordship, triggered by the portrait of Charles I, dominating Hall. Lady Diplock's diamonds sparkled as she nodded her head in appreciation of her husband's monologue. As he progressed through a series of dates, I lost hope that he would finish before midnight.

Neither Lord nor Lady Diplock could, or did, look at Mr B after having apparently sized him up as being not quite suitable to sit with them. The subject of churches developed between courses, not so much as a topic of conversation but on an anecdotal basis by Lord Diplock. He ignored Mr B throughout: he just was not there and could be excluded by the making of the long speech. This also had the effect of excluding all the others, apart from Lady Diplock.

I could feel myself waiting for a break in the speech to try to get Mr B into some form of conversation. But Diplock's knowledge of churches seemed to be limitless. Barely drawing breath, he continued smoothly through the ages. Eventually, Mr B interrupted him. Undeterred by the little less than majesty of the speaker, he said, "Well, Lord Diplock, that's interesting but utterly incorrect."

"Oh, Really?" Lord Diplock seemed to have noticed something unpleasant at the far end of the Hall. "I'll bear that in mind," he said coldly.

"No," Mr B pressed on. "You are quite wrong. It does not have the historical implication you suggest."

"I assure you that I am right."

"Do you have any authority for your views?" Mr B was quite insistent.

Diplock did not deign to hear.

Mr B pressed him. "I was asking for your source."

Diplock Signed. "Yes. Of course. The Oxford History of England."

Mr B was indignant. "That's no authority!"

Lady Diplock frowned loyally.

Diplock said, "The Oxford History of England should be a good enough authority, even for you."

Mr B said, "You are quite right. It is good enough. But what you have said is not in it."

Diplock was outraged. "I assure you that it is."

"And I assure you that it is not. I should know. I wrote it."

We retired to the Smoking Room. Coffee was served in silence. Lady Diplock said, "Well, Kenneth, we should be getting away for an early night." They both nodded and went off to be escorted home. It was not considered safe for them to be unaccompanied even for the couple of hundred yards that they had to walk within the secure boundaries of Middle Temple.

Charles and Michael became closer as friends and colleagues after surviving the experience of that evening.

CHAPTER 44

A SEX SCANDAL

Michael had the interesting task of defending Joyce McKinney, the Miss Wyoming of 1972. In November 1977, she was committed to trial at the Old Bailey where it was expected that she would face charges of kidnap and what can only be described as the rape of Kirk Anderson, a Mormon missionary and her ex-lover. The press could never decide whether he was a fortunate or unfortunate victim. In explaining why she, helped by her friend Keith May, had managed to lure Anderson to a remote country cottage, manacle him to a bed and force him to make love to her, she said, to the joy of reporters, "I loved Kirk so much, I would have skied down Mount Everest with a carnation up my nose."

Mr Anderson had requested a posting overseas after Joyce had, in modern terms, stalked him relentlessly. She was utterly infatuated with him and followed him wherever he went. His plan to escape her attentions by going abroad was thwarted. She hired a private detective who found him in London in 1977. Dragging Keith May in tow, a man who was under the sort of spell that a former Miss Wyoming was capable of generating, she pursued Anderson. Keith May helped her, hoping to ingratiate himself by his loyalty. Together, they stopped Anderson on a London street. They threatened him with replica guns, forced him into a car and drove him a rented cottage, where during three days of captivity, Joyce subjected him to repeated sexual assaults. The press was fascinated by the victim's evidence of how the kidnappers had spreadeagled him to the bed, tying his arms and legs with padlocks, chains and rope. The gist of newspaper reports was that, in evidence, Mr Kirk described how Miss McKinney had torn his pyjamas from his body and chained him so tightly that he could not move. He complained that she proceeded to have intercourse with him. "I did not want it to happen," he said. "I was very upset.'

One can only imagine the magistrates suspending disbelief as she explained confidentially, but ultimately to the world at large, "Kirk has to be tied up to have an orgasm. I co-operated because I loved him and wanted to help him. Sexual bondage turns him on because he doesn't have to feel guilty. The thought of being powerless before a woman seems to excite him."

They granted bail. At consultation prior to the hearing, I could do little more than advise her to keep her mouth shut for the duration of the trial at least.

But by the time of the trial, listed before Mr Justice Bernard Caulfield in May 1978, she and Keith May had jumped bail, disguised as nuns. They flew out from Heathrow, returning to America. Nobody from the press phoned me to tell me in advance that she was going over the top. We arrived at the Old Bailey, all ready to go. I heard it when Bernard heard it. He said, "I gather we shall not have the pleasure of meeting Miss McKinney." And that was that. We will never know what the jury would have made of her defence.

CHAPTER 45

RHODESIA

In 1965, Rhodesia, now Zimbabwe, was under the leadership of Ian Smith[1]. He made a unilateral declaration of independence to which the United Nations responded the following year by imposing the sanction of an international embargo on exporting oil to the former British colony. Although this was brought promptly into English law, the effect of the ban was watered down not only by the activities of South Africa and Mozambique but more so by British oil companies. The 1978 Bingham Inquiry[2], ordered by David Owen, the Foreign Secretary to the Labour Government, found that civil servants in Whitehall had known from the outset that the sanctions policies were being broken through covert transactions through the Shell and BP offices in neighbouring countries.

Michael advised two consecutive Attorneys-General in the 1970s about obtaining evidence to prove that the oil companies had broken the sanctions. The Labour Government [3] hoped to prosecute BP and Shell for sanction-busting. The Tories in opposition between 1974 and 1979 were keener to deal with the problem than when they were in office from 1979.

Sam Silkin was the Attorney-General in the 1974-1979 Labour Government. In opposition, he had raised questions in the House about the Tory Government's lack of progress in the Rhodesia matter. It seemed as if it was more of a concern for the opposition, whichever party that happened to be. However, in October 1978, he summoned me to tea at the House of Commons to talk about the matter generally. The meeting took place in a small, dark room principally decorated by cobwebs. I was offered a chair with springs bursting from the seat. The only practical alternative was to stand. There was not even room to pace about during our discussion. Although the Attorney-General seemed oblivious to the surroundings, we were in truth in something of a large cupboard generously stocked with precariously piled boxes from which clouds of

---

[1]   Ian Smith, 1919-2007.
[2]   The Inquiry was carried out by Thomas Henry Bingham, Baron Bingham of Cornhill, KG (2005), PC (1933-), Lord Chief Justice 1996-2000.
[3]   House of Commons Public Administration 1st Report: 27 January 2005: 2004-2005.

dust billowed with the slightest movement near them. There was a lot of coughing.

An ancient electric kettle trailing an alarmingly frayed cable was the only indication that there might be any refreshment during the course of the meeting. The task of boiling the kettle was delegated to me, perhaps following the tradition set by our meeting about the Stonehouse report, with a nod of the Attorney-General's head in its direction and "You make the tea, Michael" as an order, not a request. The water it disgorged on to the Government-issue tea-bags had a murky appearance, closely related to the oil we had been discussing.

Sam Silkin was very keen to prosecute. The problem was that successive governments had different attitudes. Silkin was under more pressure than his predecessors because his tenure of office was more in question. This government had the slimmest majority. However, he had enormous stamina and appeared to be ready to commit all necessary resources. He instructed me to advise on the legal issues, principally on the evidence that was needed for a successful prosecution.

My junior in this engagement was Tony Grabiner[1]. At the weekends, we worked at the country cottage Shirley and I had bought in 1975. It was supposed to be a quiet haven where we could concentrate without too many interruptions and talk in confidence without risk of being overheard. If being attached at the back rather than the sides makes a house semi-detached, my cottage was semi-detached. The rear-attached property was occupied by a chap who was in a very prominent position in the GCHQ at Cheltenham. After some years of living in the village, we used to joke that it was a nest of retired agents and we half-suspected that our cottage had been well and truly bugged. If that was so, whoever was carrying out the surveillance would have had the quickest access to the advice Tony and I were going to give the Attorney-General. As the only unusual feature was the party telephone line, we chose the cottage to do our work. This was a sensitive matter and it was useful to have a place to meet where we thought there was no chance of our conversations being overheard. I had done some groundwork by going to see Tom Bingham at Fountain Court. He had written about sanctions-busting and was particularly knowledgeable. We were able to ascertain that a record had

[1] Now Lord Anthony Grabiner QC

266

been made which illustrated how prohibited goods, principally petrol and oil, got to South Africa. An observer from the British High Commission went on train-spotting duty. Camouflaged in a classic beige raincoat and armed with mosquito repellent and a folding camping-chair, he would sit reasonably well concealed by foliage along the railway near the place where a side-track branched away. Points would divert the train to the illegal route, carrying the prohibited fuels. The observer's personal record contained his notes of the engine numbers, time of day and position of the track.

While Tony and I were doing this work at the cottage, he would come early on a Sunday. On one occasion he brought along a girlfriend who was a passionate gardener. She persuaded Shirley, without much difficulty, to let her take part in licking our garden into shape while the case against the sanctions-busters was being considered behind bugged doors. The young lady was also an avid theatre-goer. She had theatre tickets at one time for *Amadeus*. Shirley and Tony had both seen it so they went off to dinner at a mutual friend's house and I accompanied the stunning girl-friend to the play. Actually, it was rather an embarrassing exercise: I could see heads turning to stare at my lovely companion. I could almost read their minds: what's a stunning creature like that doing with *him*? No sooner had the thought come into my head than I noticed a familiar face turning to watch her as she led me across the theatre foyer. He noticed me and I realised, with a sinking heart that, it was one of my clients, someone who had important and useful contacts. Not someone that I should hurry past with a smile and a nod. He made his way purposefully towards me, obviously expecting to be introduced to my lovely friend. But how could I introduce her? I could not remember her name. Later I learned – it's always later, isn't it? – that he told at least three people that he had caught me out with a 'dolly bird'. I don't imagine that he thought for a moment of the incongruity of having a secret assignation at the National Theatre.

The girl-friend made a marvellous job of the garden.

Tony and I met several times but before we could complete our advice, the Government changed. Michael Havers QC became Attorney-General. He was not at all interested in progressing the matter. He did not seem to remember that he had asked questions in the Commons as to why the preceding Government were not prosecuting.

The pressure, as seemed to be the pattern, came from the opposition. Although questions were being asked now by Labour, neither Tony nor I had been brought in to the Commons to sit in the advisory box. The Attorney-General's staff had changed. Michael Havers did not know who had been advising. He gave answers off the top of his head. Eventually, we were able to let him know how far we had progressed with our advice and that what was needed now was disclosure of documents. The Foreign Office served notices on BP and Shell to produce all the relevant documents. Acting on the advice of the maestro, Bob Alexander[1], their compliance was meticulous. We thought they would say no order should be made, instead of which, they co-operated so fully, they drowned us. They sent three or four Pickfords' pantechnicons with every piece of paper they had ever had on Rhodesia. The task of sifting through them was impossible: it would have taken years. We treated it as if it was a paper filibuster.

In the House, Michael Havers made a statement to the effect that the Government was not minded to proceed because key witnesses had died, retired or had dispersed around the world without leaving a contact address. The Opposition ridiculed the decision and found the idea of a squad of aged employees who could no longer be tried was laughable: and they laughed accordingly!

We did not hear what happened to the contents of the lorries. We could only conjecture as to whether they were returned to sender or consigned to an archive somewhere or other.

It was left to the Bingham Report to rap the oil companies over the knuckles. It really came to nothing in the end because while there were plenty of inferences to be drawn, there was precious little material available to us for the purpose of bringing home a case which would have established criminal activity beyond reasonable doubt.

---

[1] Lord Alexander of Weedon QC (1936-2005).

CHAPTER 46

JADE

Michael's mother loved jade. She introduced him to its beauties when, for his sixteenth birthday, she took him to Bond Street and bought him a beautiful piece of green, imperial jade which was to form the first item in his collection. His interest in works of art and historical artefacts has extended hugely since then. A large part of his collection is focussed on the Far East, enhanced by his contact with artists and galleries in Singapore and Hong Kong.

I had been to Singapore several times when I met Professor Chen, an artist of distinction. He was known for his especially fine finger-painting technique. Using his finger and nail, he created figures and shapes of exquisitely detailed perfection that others could not hope to emulate with a full panoply of brushes.

His studio had the great advantage of being in an ordinary shop with a long window admitting full light. It was packed full of his work with the main picture being displayed for sale on an easel in the main area. He worked at the rear of the shop in an area separated by a curtain on a rail. If the Professor was not creating one of his works of art, he would be sitting in something similar to a deckchair, always ready to talk about his paintings to visitors even when they had only come to look.

He was happy to show me the paintings on display and to talk to me with the help of his grand-daughter who was there to interpret for him.

On one of the visits, he asked me, out of the blue, "What you like about Chinese art?" This, of course, is the granddaughter's translation.

"I'm more interested in things than in paintings."

I was sitting facing him near the door of the studio. His back was to the street. Our transaction was shielded from the public eye.

The Professor sat in the deckchair, almost reclining. I was not a little alarmed and tried to look away when, looking at me, he put his hand into the waistband of the trousers, struggled, and, to my relief rather than embarrassment – what was I trying to preserve – my modesty? dignity? – he eventually produced a disc attached to a pink cord, not unlike lawyer's tape. The cord was pinned into his trousers at the waist by a safety

Professor Chen's jade, photograph by John Goldman

pin. The Chinese are great collectors, the elderly would wear a band of their treasures around their waist. What he was producing was the best of his possessions. In Chinese, he said, "Look at this."

Now I could look. It was the most exquisite piece of jade.

Collectors or people with a mutual interest have more than a sense of appreciation of a thing of beauty. The viewer wants more than to see the quality. There is a desire to share in the power of the object itself. They would always want to handle it.

Suppose you have, as I do, a really fine 200-year old piece of porcelain: a vase. The dealer takes it out of the showcase. You ask the dealer, "Can I hold it?"

The answer in the Orient is, "No – you can't. But you can pick it up and put it back."

Throughout the whole of the Far East, if you are dealing with someone in the trade or a serious collector, one puts it down, the other picks it up, looks, puts it down. And when you think about it, that is so clever. It is to prevent any question of responsibility for damage or breakage, apportioning blame in a clumsy transfer.

He could see that I was interested. He put the jade down on the table at his side. Although it had been next to the Professor's skin for goodness knows how long, as I put out my hand to touch it, I was instantly aware of its luscious coolness against the skin. It had a mysterious, soothing sweep of ancient colour. I knew that it fulfilled all the reputation that jade has: this would place problems into perspective and give a sense of enduring well-being.

I picked it up. I put it down. The exquisite chill of the jade remained on my hands and the beauty of its design stayed in my mind as I watched him take it back.

I could barely speak. I wanted that piece of jade. But I managed to say, "It's lovely. How much do you want for it?"

He tucked it back into the trousers, and settled himself into the chair, arms folded across the concealing waistband.

He laughed and told me, through the grand-daughter, that it was not for sale.

I had been building my collection of jade, some of which came from a Mr Tan whose gallery was nothing more than a room in his apartment piled from floor to ceiling with neatly stacked boxes, each exquisitely covered in dark, embossed silks and brocades . The exteriors hid the contents of an Aladdin's cave. The multitude of boxes were stored in a perfect filing system: he knew exactly where to find each object that he sought, even though there was no over label. We bought some lovely pieces from him.

But nothing like Professor Chen's piece of jade.

I coveted it. There is no other word to express how much I wanted it once I had seen it.

I began to feel ashamed of myself, wanting it so much. Each time I returned to Singapore, I visited him. Each time my offer to buy it was refused. I tried on several occasions to persuade him to part with it. My requests had to be translated into Chinese and his responses were then translated into English for me. They were always, "Tell him I'll leave it to him in my will."

In November 1979, I was in Singapore to defend a stockbroker who had been charged with insider dealing. He came to see me after his acquittal. He was carrying a velvet-covered box.

He said, "Professor Chen is my godfather. He told me not to tell you that he had recommended you to defend me: he didn't want to put you under any special obligation because of our relationship. He decided that he should not wait to die for you to have this."

There, in the box, was what immediately became and remains one of my most prized possessions. Professor Chen's piece of jade.

CHAPTER 47

A WIDOW'S WEB

Indonesia's national oil and gas company, Pertamina had a decade or so of phenomenal growth from the mid-1960s, funded largely by European and North American investment, not all of which made its way into the company's coffers: corruption was a significant feature in dealing with Pertamina. When the Indonesian Government prohibited foreign borrowing in the mid-1970s, the company became unable to service its loans. An investigation then began into the deficit in its accounts, generally believed to have been caused by corrupt payments or bribes. This led the Government to believe that it had a rightful claim to the contents of the Singapore bank account of one Lieutenant-General Achmad Tahir, the former assistant to the Director of Pertamina. Tahir, effectively a civil servant, could only have amassed the millions of dollars in the account if he had been accepting bribes. The account appeared to contain what remained after Tahir had set up shelter companies using capital derived from rewards for assistance that he was in a position to offer. This included the selection of the German company, Siemens, as the successful bidder in a 1972 tender for building a Pertamina steel mill.

In early 1979, I was in Singapore. I had finished a consultation at my solicitor's offices and was making my way down towards the lobby. An Indian man joined me in the lift. He looked worried and harassed. He noticed my European appearance and asked me without any ado, "Would you know where I can find Mr Michael Sherrard QC?" This was my first meeting with Siva Selvadurai, a Singapore solicitor, a delightful man who was to become a great friend. We were to travel the world together in the course of our work and I would be at his deathbed too few years later. For the time being, all I said was, "That's me."

"I need your help," he said.

He told me that the Singapore branch of the Japanese Bank Sumitomo was holding on deposit vast sums of money in the account of one Lieutenant-General Achmad Tahir, who had died a day or so earlier in Jakarta. Siva explained that Mr Tahir had held high office in Pertamina and had used the Sumitomo account to conceal and hold the proceeds of corrupt dealings with Siemens. Mrs Tahir, a former Indonesian beauty queen, was in Switzerland when she was told of her husband's death.

Instead of flying to Jakarta for the funeral, she had made her way straight to Singapore where she tried to empty the account.

This was fascinating stuff. Siva enlightened me further over a cup of coffee.

The manager of the bank had declined to hand over the fund. As a result of the enquiries made in Jakarta, several parties had been informed of the background. One party in particular, the Indonesian Government, Siva's client, was busying itself to ensure that no payment should be made out of the Tahir account until other interested, or potentially interested, parties had been protected.

A complicating factor was that the Indonesian legal system was based on Roman law, bequeathed by the Dutch colonisation. Indonesian law governed the background to the transactions that brought the money to Sumitomo in Singapore where the English common law applied. Singapore had no interest, legal or otherwise, in the Indonesian project or the Tahirs. The Singapore courts simply, if that is the word to apply to anything to do with Pertamina, formed the arena in which the different legal systems and various parties could fight it out. A Roman-Dutch lawyer would shortly be instructed in Amsterdam to act as an expert but for the time being, the freezing of the Tahir account was entirely within my area of expertise.

Siva had said he wanted me to advise urgently. Within thirty minutes of our meeting, we were on our way to the High Court to apply for an order that would freeze the Sumitomo account funds until the rights of others had been ascertained. The technical word for the process is "interpleader". This set into action the complex series of applications and appeals in which I was to be involved for several years. On the way to the court, I explained the process.

"Pending evidence coming up to scratch," I explained, "the account will be frozen. The money will be kept in the bank and the parties can formalize their individual claims. The bank will pay out as soon as it knows who has the legal entitlement. Once the Indonesian Government has agreed, we can go full steam ahead."

We did not know then how slow that build-up of steam would be. Indeed, some of the best brains at the English Bar flowed into and ebbed from the Pertamina litigation. As the years passed, they grew older, their hair turned grey, they took judicial appointments or handed over their role to those who had more time to spare. All counsel were brought in for their special expertise in international fraud or heavy commercial matters. The list of eminent silks included Robert Gatehouse, Nicholas Coleman, Colin Ross-Munro and Gordon Pollock (many years down the line and then only for one day). Mark Saville lasted even less: he flew out for one day for an application but went home without completing his submissions when the judge took another matter. Michael Thomas, a former Attorney-General of Hong Kong, was one of the silks who acted for the widow at one time. I believe that I would have become embroiled in Pertamina even if Siva would not have found me that day. Mrs Tahir's solicitor in Singapore was the eminent Joe Grimberg. He had briefed me several times and, if I had not been instructed for the other side, I might well have found myself with a shorter involvement in the case. Mrs Tahir was to change counsel as often as they changed socks. On the assumption that the pattern of change was inevitable, I might have found myself with more time to spare over the following twelve years.

The court issued the formal interpleader summons: all interested parties were then on notice that battle had commenced for release of the Tahir funds.

The return date came.

I remember opening the case with a turn of phrase that I so enjoyed: "At the time of her husband's death, Mrs Tahir was in Switzerland. In her great grief, she arranged to fly, not to Jakarta where his remains rested but to Singapore where his funds lay. Armed with large but empty suitcases, she decided against packing them with the clothes he had left in Singapore but to use them instead to carry as many millions as she could stuff into them whilst en route to Jakarta. I daresay that is what he would have wanted."

Mr Justice Sinnathuray was assigned to the case. He ordered the account to be frozen. Poor chap: he was to be dealing with the case for most of the years to come. Only at the trial in 1992 was there a change of judge, but by then I was no longer involved. In the intervening years, however, there was much to be done involving regular and frequent trips to Singapore and to the Roman-Dutch lawyer, Wilhelm de Seriere, in Amsterdam. On one occasion, when I was working in Hong Kong, I suddenly had to go to New York because a crucial party was about to succumb to a settlement which Siva and I were to negotiate. Once in New York, we spent six days, locked in negotiations, until eventually, the other side agreed. I flew home. Three days later, Siva was on the phone. "I miss you. We have to go back to New York. The other party reneged – they sold their rights to someone ..."

This was the sort of complicating factor, apart from the widow's rapid disaffection with counsel, that was to add years to the case. Back to New York I went, then back to Singapore. Round the world twice in a week. At least, in opposite directions.

The travelling would have been impossible to handle had I not had regular work in the East. I had to fly to Jakarta several times at short notice but I could, at least, go home in the evening. Home was Singapore.

After twelve years of applications and appeals against judgments, the trial was fixed. I was desperately concerned that it should take place on this fixed date because I had a programme stretching two or three years ahead, including one to which I was absolutely committed, the defence of the Vice Chairman of the Hong Kong listing exchange, a solicitor in some difficulty. A week before the fixed date of the Pertamina case, the widow changed counsel again.

And Siva was replaced.

And I learned that officials within my client's bureaucracy had reneged on a court order – they could not see the reason for it – for disclosure of crucial documents. Perhaps there were too many cobwebs on the files. Perhaps someone had become lazy. The failure to comply with the order served no purpose unless someone somewhere thought the case would settle at the last minute. The disregard for the court order placed me in an intolerable professional position. Whatever the reason for it, I could not continue. In due course, I learned that the widow did not succeed[1]. Pertamina recovered US $21 million from the Tahir account. Perhaps that is a happy ending.

***

---

[1] *Pertamina v Kartika Ratna Tahir* (1993) 1 SLR 735

The legal argument on which the application to freeze the funds was made was based on the Court disapproving the long-established Court of Appeal decision in *Lister & Co v Stubbs*[1] which appeared to allow the holder of ill-gotten gains to benefit from the wrong-doing of those who had originally obtained them. The argument was accepted by the Court and later clarified further by the Privy Council, in *Attorney-General for Hong Kong v Reid*[2] when a bribe or secret commission is offered or accepted by a fiduciary in money or in kind, the legal estate in the property thereby conveyed to the fiduciary rests in the beneficiary. Equity, however, insists that it is unconscionable for a fiduciary to obtain and retain a benefit in breach of duty. As soon as the bribe or secret commission is received it should be paid to the person suffering from the breach of duty. Equity treats as done that which ought to be done. As soon as the bribe or secret commission is received, the fiduciary holds the money or property on constructive trust. Translated back out of legalese: the Pertamina bribes consisted of money that should originally have been paid to the Indonesian Government and had, in effect, been received by one of its officials on its behalf.

[1]   (1890) 45 ChD 1
[2]   [1994] 1 AC 324.

CHAPTER 48

GRAY DAYS

There was a time in Singapore that was like a gold rush. People were using gold as a currency which generated a profit in much the same way that the activities of a business benefit the shareholders. Gilbert Gray QC ("Gilly")and Michael were instructed in double harness for two appellants, who had been convicted in a "bucketing" fraud.

"Bucketing" is the term of the art for dealing in gold bullion. In something approaching a gambling concept, members of the public would go to a "bucket shop" where, at a front counter, they would buy shares in gold bullion from firms and companies which dealt with the price of gold on a world basis.

Our clients were charged with fraud by taking criminal disadvantage of members of the public who came in to buy shares in gold. The front office of Gilly's client's shop was the purchase counter. The back office was a hive of activity, business being conducted on telephones. The customers were given the impression that there was huge dealing and very significant profits being made. They could hear the "busyness" and this encouraged them to buy more share certificates. One chap stood at the counter and dealt with investors who were only too willing to part with their money because it was apparent that they were dealing with a thriving organisation.

But all there was was a bank of telephone recorders in the back of the shop: much noise to be heard but nothing to be seen. The tape-recorded evidence was what brought them down.

Gilly's client was the active villain, the ringleader. Mine was the solicitor. The trial judge convicted them both and gave out tough sentences. Gilly's client: six years, mine: three.

Gilly is one of the great advocates of my generation. He can take his listeners, whether a jury or an after-dinner audience, from tears to laughter and back again and keep them spellbound every inch of the way. The appeal judge was impervious to the nuances of advocacy. In the whole twelve days that we were there, he never uttered a word. Not even, "We'll adjourn now." He left in silence at 4.00 p.m. precisely, even if one or other of us was in mid-sentence, until we got the knack of finishing on the dot. At 10.00 a.m. the next day, he caught the eye of whoever was currently on his feet, nodded, and we were off again. It is a tribute to Gilly's skills as an advocate that, after an impressively persuasive argument, the judge was seen – clearly seen – to lift an eyebrow. Gilly reacted immediately: "I'm going to treat that as a concession."

During the course of the appeal, Gilly challenged the prosecutor's submission that the court should rely on a precedent set by an English case. He said, "The English authority is only persuasive. The case does not bind you."

I got to my feet. I thought that I could step in and play the heavy here, having a wealth of local knowledge.

"Wishing only to correct my learned friend," I said, "Insofar as the judgment of Lord Diplock is concerned: this has been acknowledged and approved by this court. It is not simply persuasive. And is therefore binding."

Gilly turned to me, his great eyebrows drawn down low, managing to look almost like a bull about to charge. He said, "Ee ba goom – tha's nowt to do wi' thee!"

The judge, unable or unwilling to break the silence that he had hitherto maintained, leaned forward and shaped his mouth into something that would have allowed the word "What!!" to escape. Gilly saved him the trouble by repeating, with emphasis, "Nowt to do wi' thee!"

Which was true. It was nothing to do with my case. Nowt at all.

***

My bloke's appeal succeeded.

CHAPTER 49

LUXEMBOURG

In the spring of 1979 the Lord Chancellor, Lord Elwyn-Jones, wrote to Michael and Shirley to invite them to join a delegation of members of the British judiciary to Luxembourg for a few study days. Michael was included because of his role as a Recorder. The party was to be led by Lord Justice ("Spider") Cumming-Bruce. It promised to be an interesting weekend, albeit not quite as instructive as might have been intended. The other members of the party included Rose Heilbron[1], Lord Justice John May, Judge Douglas Grant, Lewis McCreary, a couple of High Court Judges, one from Scotland, and Lord Brightman, a senior Chancery Judge in the Court of Appeal. Jean-Pierre Warner was the Advocate-General who had succeeded Gordon Slynn at Luxembourg. The object was to find out what went on at the European Court although, as Exchange Control[2] was still in effect, not too much spending would be involved.

Spider was a fellow Bencher of Middle Temple. He turned out to be an engaging host as well as a capable leader of the group.

The central part of our visit was to see the operation of the European Court. At the end of it, the Lord Chancellor expected a short report, summarising our impressions and opinions. The duty of compiling the report fell to Spider Cumming-Bruce and we each helped by giving him a short comment. Mine was to be: "A little like the court of appeal on a dull day."

We had known from the outset that the visit would include receptions and working lunches so it would be all work. I believe it was Spider's idea that we should reciprocate the hospitality that he expected would be lavished on our group. In our role of legal ambassadors, we invited our hosts, the judges of Luxembourg, to relinquish their duties on our last night and to become our guests. They accepted our invitation and helped by choosing the restaurant, a tavern on the outskirts of town.

---

[1] Rose Heilbron (1914-2005), first woman to be appointed KC, first woman Recorder, first woman judge to sit at the Old Bailey.
[2] Exchange controls were abolished in 1979.

On our last working day, our group met at lunch-time on the terrace of the Court. We had coffee and sandwiches, having been plied with gallons of wine and endless amounts of food the previous evening. Spider and John May came up to me. Spider said hesitantly, "Michael, we have a – a problem ..." His voice tailed away.

"Can I help?" I asked, realising that they would not have confessed to me without expecting me to have some part in resolving it. He was strangely diffident.

"Michael, do you have one of those – ah – credit card things?"

"Yes," I told them, "I practise in the Far East. It's an essential part of my equipment. You have others to do the spending for you."

They nodded solemnly. "You see, we are to host tonight's party. We appear not to have organized how to pay for it."

"Do you want me to put it on Amex?"

"Yes!" They were delighted. The problem was solved. "It will be sorted out in London and you will be repaid in sterling."

We turned back to our coffee and sandwiches with the rest of the party, continued into the afternoon's court visit and then prepared for the evening.

We all made our way by taxis and a couple of cars, in which some of the party had made the cross-Channel journey, to the tavern. It was a delightful place, with wood-panelled walls and colourful plants arranged in the window alcoves. It was very different from the formal surroundings of earlier in the day. The patron provided us with a large room with a very long refectory table. The British contingent was about to repay the lavish hospitality with as much style as we could muster. If wine could outflow that which had been offered to us on previous days, it would. The food and venue were definitely to the taste of the erstwhile hosts who now, in the role of guests, took their seats along one side of the table as we sat facing them. We all began to enjoy one another's company and had a marvellous evening.

The conversation was lively, scarcely interrupted by the vast quantities of excellent food and wine. Spider presided over one end of the table. Arthur Prest, the full-time Recorder at Manchester, acted as host

281

at the other end. I was to take care of the bill and Spider asked me to sit near him.

"When the time comes," he said, "I'll give you the nod."

The party showed little or no sign of slackening, even at 1.30 a.m. and the rapidly approaching prospect for the British visitors of the early start for the flight back to Heathrow. As the party showed no sign of ending of its own accord, Spider whispered to me that calling for the bill would be a way of bringing it to an end.

I signalled to the waiter. "Bill, please!" A few yards of bill arrived. I passed my credit card over my shoulder and turned back to continue the conversation at the table. Almost at once, I felt a discreet touch on my shoulder. I turned to the waiter and saw a youthful incarnation of Hercule Poirot. He bent forward and whispered words that sounded remarkably like, "Very sorry, m'sieur – we do not accept credit cards. We only take cash."

Spider sensed something was wrong. He leaned towards me. "Do we have a problem?"

"Yes."

"What exactly is it?"

"We jurists seem to have forgotten to ask the prior consent of the Patron to pay the bill by credit card." He sighed deeply and sat back in his chair gazing at the ceiling. The waiter stood back, realising that something else was going to have to be done.

"Let me think now," said Spider, taking a very long minute to do his thinking. "I have a solution," he said with a comforting smile. "You go and have a word with the Patron and deal with it."

"Me?" But he had turned to face his European counterpart and was back in genial host mode. I was on my own.

I gave a genial smile of my own to my opposite number and went off to the patron. I asked if we could do something … perhaps give him a cheque the next day.

"I do not think so." He looked up over the top of the little round glasses that sat somewhere near the end of his nose. He definitely did not think so.

I became aware that Arthur Prest was hovering at the curtain which hung in the doorway of the patron's office. He was concerned about the outcome of the conversation and anxious not to cause embarrassment.

"My dear Patron," he said sweetly, "we were not aware that you do not take credit cards."

"Don't worry," the patron said. "I will send the bill to the Court."

"No, no," said Arthur. "They are our guests!"

"Alas," said the patron unsympathetically. "In that case, you must speak to my son." He gestured to the young Poirot who had followed Arthur to the doorway of the office and now hovered patiently. The son was the waiter who had brought the bill.

Arthur said, "We'll discuss this in a minute." We left the room and talked in the corridor where our voices were masked by the innocent laughter of our party. He said, "I think we can rustle up the money from our side."

I was not in favour of this. "How can you do that without the guests seeing?"

"We'll crawl along the table. You pull their jackets or attract their attention and ask for their wallets and purses. I'll be right behind you … making a note of how much you have taken from each. We'll sort out the arithmetic later."

I arranged my face into what I hoped was a nonchalant expression which, had it been noticed by our guests, was belied by the curious gait that had to be adopted to bring me to face level with the English guests and enable me to tug at their pockets discreetly. I waddled along the line of chairs, almost on my knees, followed by Arthur. I dared not look at him. The guests seemed to follow my cue. We were, if not invisible, certainly not interesting to them.

Brightman was first. I bent behind the back of his chair and tapped his jacket pocket saying "We need to collect some cash. Can I have your wallet?" He was listening intently to a story being told by a senior Luxembourg judge. He turned slightly towards me, without taking his attention from the speaker.

"Could I have your wallet?"

"Wallet?" he murmured.

"Yes, please."

Still concentrating on the other side of the table, he discreetly handed me the wallet. Turning aside, I removed £25. I handed the wallet back to him out of sight. I whispered in his ear, "I've taken £25. Arthur's making a note." His chin moved towards his tie by a fraction of an inch, which I took to be an acknowledgement of my words. I whispered, "Thanks a lot." I smiled broadly at the facing Luxembourg judge and nodded sagely at whatever it was that Lord Brightman was agreeing with before moving along the British line, attracting the attention of my victims with a little tug at their clothing. I really believe that none of the guests noticed what was happening.

One after another, the British judiciary handed over their purses and wallets. Rose Heilbron gave me a commodious black handbag in which I had to search blindly for the purse whilst balanced dangerously on my bent knees. I managed to find it without overbalancing and continued along the line on my mission, giving each benefactor the whispered assurance that Arthur would be making a note. He followed me along the line, writing down each extracted amount.

When each contribution had been collected, we returned to the Patron and said that Judge Prest thought we had collected enough currency to clear the bill but we remained short of enough for a tip (richly deserved, said Arthur). The Patron said he was giving us the most favourable rate of exchange and, as a concession would accept a personal cheque from me to cover a tip. I wrote one for £150. "He can use it in England," said the shrewd father.

The bill having been settled, Spider could now concentrate on getting everyone home. The local people, who had arrived separately or in groups, now returned to the vehicles that had brought them. We waved them off and set about going back to the hotel ourselves. Transport was a slight problem. It had started to rain, it was the early hours of the morning and it seemed as though there was not a taxi on the planet. We arranged for the ladies and Arthur to go in Douglas' car, a station wagon, while the rest of us waited for the taxis that we were assured would come eventually. He was just about to drive away in what was now teeming rain when Lewis McCreary asked plaintively if there was room for one more. This was achieved by Shirley sitting on Arthur's Prest's lap.

The packed vehicle eventually moved off, leaving the remainder of our group sheltering as best we could. By 3.00 a.m., the last of the taxis came, and I was the last of all to step into the lobby of our hotel, the Holiday Inn. Instead of finding the place virtually deserted, there appeared to be another party in progress. The bar was open; there was great activity and much laughter. Spider and Brightman were locked in a fierce debate on the other side of the lobby. I gathered later that they were working on a price formula for the evening. One of them thought the Lord Chancellor should pick up the expense of the party. The other did not agree. I never found out precisely what the compromise was.

The official visit ended a few hours later. Some very bleary-eyed delegates boarded the plane back to London, although some others, including Douglas, extended the trip by taking a leisurely drive home.

Spider's report to the Lord Chancellor on our experience of the European Court was short and limited to legal business. He gave us to understand that our comments helped although his own description of one of the sessions, which never made it into print, was: "Despite the brilliance of the translation, I had to remove my headphones."

The report was, in the end, a tactful summary of the formal aspects of our brief visit to the Court and the limited oral advocacy which we had experienced.

CHAPTER 50

MAXWELL

Robert Maxwell[1], the media and publishing tycoon, had a short political career as Labour MP for Buckingham from 1964 to 1970. There was a disputed takeover bid for his Pergamon printing companies in 1969 but it came to nothing when it was discovered that the group's profits were inextricably linked with the assets of privately owned Maxwell family companies. This led to a Department of Trade and Industry Inquiry, chaired by Owen Stable QC. His 1973 Interim Report ended with the words[2]:

"We regret having to conclude that, notwithstanding Mr Maxwell's acknowledged abilities and energy, he is not in our opinion a person who can be relied on to exercise proper stewardship of a publicly quoted company."

That opinion did not stop Maxwell extending his media interests over the following years, using the Liechtenstein-based Maxwell Foundation. It acquired the Mirror Group Newspapers in 1984, together with what he appeared to regard as a useful source of petty cash: the Mirror Group's pension fund. He drowned after falling from his yacht in 1991: either a mystery or the obvious solution to his financial problems.

Bob Maxwell expected anyone who dealt with him to jump to his orders. At all times, he was the boss. Rumour had it that he once sacked someone for smoking in the Pergamon offices. When he realised that the smoker was a visitor, he handed over a wad of £10 notes as his apology but had it been one of his staff, the employee would have been out of the door before he had had the chance to stub the cigarette out. It was important to keep on the right side of him.

You can imagine that he was very displeased when he was required to attend the Inquiry being carried out by the Department of Trade and Industry. He regarded the request as a gross intrusion into his private life. He employed 'people' to look after these petty nuisances but, under the current legislation governing the way that companies operated, he

---

[1]   Ian Robert Maxwell (1922-1991) (né Jan Ludvick Hoch).

[2]   Department of Trade and Industry Website: Report concerning Maxwell Scientific International [Publications]; R Maxwell and Co; Pergamon Press Ltd.

could be compelled, as a director, to participate in the Inquiry and answer questions put to him. He thought this was an outrage. Morris Finer and I considered that the procedure to which he was to be subjected was, to give him credit, unfair.

Maxwell made it quite plain that he welcomed the opportunity to challenge the Inspectors' alleged rights and was adopting an *over-my-dead-body* approach to the requirement that he attend. At the meetings with the Department of Trade and Industry inspectors, Morris represented Maxwell and I represented Mr Clark, the chairman of Pergamon's board. Our needs were simple: we wanted the Inspectors to give us the opportunity to cross-examine any witness who gave evidence adverse to us. The Inspectors refused. We would only have the right to make submissions. Bob Maxwell took the stance that refusal to speak to the Inspectors was the order of the day. That resulted in him being committed for contempt.

We fetched up before the Vice-Chancellor, Mr Justice Plowman, then the Vice-Chancellor, and made a great to-do about natural justice[1]. The principal question was the rights and duties of Inspectors as opposed to those of a judge conducting a trial. Plowman found Maxwell in contempt for refusing to give evidence to the Inspectors but would take no action pending an appeal. We took the approach that there was a vendetta against us. The judge was equally robust. "You can't insist on cross-examining," he told us. "It's an investigation, not a trial."

Such a view brought us fairly promptly to the Court of Appeal constituted by Lord Denning, Lord Justice Sachs and Lord Justice Upjohn. I argued that the rules of natural justice applied to the investigation as much as to an actual trial. Denning said, "I will not let Mr Sherrard and Mr Finer turn [an investigation] into a contentious matter" and handed down what is now known as the Pergamon Press decision[2]. This, in short, was adverse to us although it resulted in Lord Denning laying down a sort of code for the conduct of Inspectors in future.

The night that judgment was given, I had been invited to a legal dinner. As the line of guests passed my table, I felt an arm around my shoul-

---

[1] *In Re Pergamon Press* [1971], Ch 388.
[2] *Maxwell v Department of Trade and Industry* [1974] 1QB 523.

der. It was Tom Denning. He grinned at me and said, "Well now, young Michael, I bet your chaps are going to spill the beans now."

There was no chance to answer that evening.

***

One of the features of Bob's directorship of Pergamon Press was the fact that the company headquarters were in the extensive grounds of his house in Oxfordshire. Headington Hill Hall, renamed "Pergamon" by Maxwell, had been a rotting hulk until he came on the scene. It was owned by the County Council. They rented it to him – he was therefore a council tenant – in return for him restoring it to its former splendour. The rent was reputed to be £4 or £5 a week. Although he talked about having a lease for life, he did not realise that it would be a relatively short one.

That is where he threw the great parties for which he was renowned. I tried to avoid socialising with clients: we were invited to numerous grand occasions and managed to refuse most. But once or twice there was no avoiding a Maxwell event. Those we went to were outrageously sumptuous. One feature was that the evening would be punctuated by award ceremonies. The music would stop, Maxwell and the ambassador of a foreign state would go up to the platform where the orchestra was seated and the ambassador would put a ribbon around his neck or pin a gong to his lapel to mark some spectacular event or other. We persuaded David and Iris Freeman to go with us to one of the parties. Maxwell bore down on us, his great chest billowing like a ship in full sail. "Don't think I don't realise who my friends are," he said, apparently to the world at large. He was wagging his finger and pointing at us as he passed our table.

***

Being invited to Maxwell social events was an indication that he liked you. This was a heavy burden to bear. Once, when Shirley and I had gone to Paris with our children for the weekend, Maxwell thought of something he wanted to discuss with me, as a friend. In order to contact me, he had to find my telephone number. From my entry in *Who's Who*, he found Shirley's maiden surname, Bagrit. Maxwell then contacted her uncle, Sir Leon Bagrit, who gave him the telephone number of his brother, Shirley's father. Maxwell managed to get my address from my father-in-law as he would get anything that he wanted – brute force,

288

probably – and turned up at the hotel with his wife, Betty, just as we were about to go out for lunch.

"We're taking you out to eat. I know a great place," he said. "It's not far from here. Let's go."

We had been hi-jacked! We had a pleasant enough meal and Bob was lively company. When the bill came, we were "Maxwelled", a process familiar, as we later learned, to quite a few of his impromptu dinner guests. The white paper lay on the table, with rather a lot of numbers because he was quite fond of wine and only the best would do. He patted every one of his pockets and told Betty to look in her bag but all to no avail. He had come out without his cards or cash. Of course, there was no problem. We had the wherewithal and he was suitably abashed. "This is so silly of me – it will be my turn next time." But the Maxwell process was that every time would be the next time.

He was a stickler for detail. He had even found out which flight we were on and had thoughtfully arranged to change the seating so that he and I sat together and Shirley and Betty were relegated to another part of the aircraft, as were our boys. "This is such a good idea," he said, "There are a few things I wanted to talk to you about." And talk he did.

***

He had no respect for the rules of solicitors instructing counsel. He had my contact details and used them whenever he felt like it. In 1990, there was a scandal when it was discovered that parts of a 'supergun' were being exported to Iraq from the UK by the Coventry-based engineering firm, Matrix Churchill, in breach of the then arms-supply embargo. At about the same time, a lorry was stopped en route to Greece, carrying the parts which would complete the assembly of such a gun. The *Daily Mirror* thought it would be a good story to pay for the defence of the lorry driver. They would distribute T-shirts with the slogan, "Thanks Cap'n Bob," on his release. The paper was set up with its matching headline and a picture of the driver in the shirt. But the *Sun* had a similar idea and word reached Maxwell that there was to be a competing headline with the slogan 'Thanks a lot, *Sun*'. They had even lifted 'his' picture.

That evening, Roy Greenslade, the editor of the *Daily Mirror* got a call from Bob. Typically, he launched straight into what he had to say.

"Have you heard?"

"Yes," Roy said. "You've done well." Roy thought it was good: a battle between the *Sun* and the *Mirror* was the stuff newspapers were made of.

That was not what Bob wanted to hear. He called me directly. As always, he neither needed nor gave any greeting or introduction. His accented, rasping voice was unmistakeable.

"I'm the victim here – tomorrow's *Sun* is carrying our photo but taking all the credit! "

This was too obscure for me although his outrage was clearly expressed. Impatiently, he told me what was going on and that the *Sun* had to be stopped.

"I will not be trifled with," he shouted. "I'm sending the editor over. Now!"

"But it's half past ten -"

"I'm going to sue them and I want it done now. *NOW!*"

There was nothing that could be done now, or *NOW!*

"They are going to print it anyway," I said. "They must have already gone to press."

But Roy came to see me, as per his orders. "You know Cap'n Bob," he said. "Tell me what we can do." He explained that Maxwell wanted me to go to Marylebone Magistrates' Court to obtain a summons for a private prosecution. It was 1.30 in the morning before he left, bearing the tidings back to Maxwell that there was nothing that the magistrates or any creature on the planet could do to stop the *Sun* going to press. I had the feeling that Maxwell's next step would be to make a takeover bid for the judicial system. What point was there in having courts if they wouldn't dispense justice?

***

Not long after the supergun story, Robert Maxwell sold Pergamon Press to Elsevier, another publishing giant, in part of a series of transactions to inject capital into other branches of his business empire. After he drowned in 1991, it was learned that his business empire was nothing more than a pack of cards: he had plundered the huge pension fund of the Daily Mirror to shore up the financial needs of his companies which were declared insolvent in 1992. His sons, Kevin[1] and Ian Maxwell, were acquitted of fraud in 1996 after an eight-month trial. The DTI report of 2001 on the collapse of the Maxwell companies described father and sons as acting "inexcusably."

[1]   Kevin Maxwell's first wife, Pandora, is the daughter of my old college friend, John Warnford-Davies.

CHAPTER 51

THE MISSING MILLIONS

Towards the end of November 1980, Michael was in Singapore in discussion with Mohideen Rubin, generally known simply as "Rubin", a very competent criminal lawyer[1] with whom he enjoyed working.

The telephone rang. Rubin took the call in my presence. It was from his friend, a Mr Pachimsawat, in Bangkok. Mr and Mrs P had recently been involved in a very serious lawsuit in Hong Kong. What was clear from Rubin's side of the conversation was that the decision had gone against them and they wanted advice as to an appeal. Rubin said he would do his best to help. As soon as the call ended, he said to me, off his own bat, "Do you think you'd be interested in doing this case?" He gave me an outline of their problem. The story was indeed fascinating and I was agreeably swept into the leading role for the clients. Rubin obtained a copy of the judgment of the Hong Kong court and the court documents together with the transcript of the fifteen day hearing that had taken place a few weeks earlier.

I will let the story speak largely for itself.

Mr and Mrs P were rich Thai citizens who enjoyed a luxurious lifestyle in Bangkok and on their frequent world-wide travels, during the course of which they liked to have ready access to cash. The tale begins in 1975 when they visited Hong Kong and decided to open a bank account. What could be simpler than keeping a few million dollars as a float in Hong Kong, a nest egg to use if they were running short of pocket money? They toyed with small accounts in the central branch of the Hong Kong and Shanghai Bank in Queens Road "HKSB" and the Bank of America "B.A." in Kowloon but soon decided that the HKSB was preferable. Mrs P made arrangements for the HKSB to take substantial sums on deposit. Between August 1975 and May 1977, the couple visited Hong Kong and placed the sum of US$2,329,000 in cash with the HKSB. They were required to sign numerous documents including provision of specimen signatures in relation to the holding and release of funds. They set up arrangements initially to collect correspondence from

[1] Mohideen Rubin was later to become a High Court Judge and eventually a senior Singaporean Diplomat.

the HKSB at the bank itself but after a time arranged a poste-restante address at a friend's home in Lock Road, Kowloon.

In August 1977, in the belief that it was acting on the instructions of the couple, the HKSB closed the account and transferred the whole of the accumulated funds to the B.A.

The original B.A. account had been opened with the comparatively small sum of HK$2000. The 1977 deposits boosted its contents to over HK$5 million, all of which was drawn out, in cash, by Mrs P, according to the B.A. but, according to Mrs P herself, it was another lady best referred to here as "Madam X" (as she was to be called in the course of the eventual trial). Madam X presented a passport in the married name of Mrs P to identify herself and signed the necessary documents. The likeness on the passport photograph must have been hard to discern: the Mrs P who withdrew the money wore large dark glasses and a headscarf. The money was paid over to her, placed in a large cardboard box which she carried, not without difficulty, out of the building. If Madam X was seen again, it would have been without the benefit of the scarf and glasses: she could have been just about any one of the numerous smartly-dressed women in Hong Kong. This is no more than conjecture, but there was also the possibility she could have been Japanese, like the girl-friend of an HKSB officer who was no longer employed by the bank at the time the fraud was discovered. That was 3 November 1977 when the real Mrs P called at the HKSB to deposit more money. She could not believe what she was told: the HKSB no longer held any of her funds. To her dismay, the HKSB assured her that they had relied on her written instructions to make the transfer to the B.A. She categorically denied having given any such instructions to transfer a single cent from the HKSB and certainly not to the B.A. She demanded to see the letters which had triggered the transfers.

A diary of transactions	
Aug 75	Ps put US$5000 in HKSB
	Ps put US$2000 in B.A.
May 76	Ps close B.A. account
3 May 76	Deposit US$193,184 HKSB
Aug–23 Sep 76	Deposit US$439,346 HKSB
22 Oct 76 – 2 May 77	Deposit US$607,791 and US$662,280
3 May 77	US$206,466 renewed

| 4/6 July 77 | Letters from Austin Avenue requesting HKSB to send HK$4 million to B.A. |
| 3 Aug 7 | Transfer to US$ savings A/C US$1,355,545 |

Seeing the letters sparked disbelief and anger: she could see at once that they were forgeries and denounced them accordingly.

Needless to say, there was considerable activity by police, lawyers and handwriting experts acting for all concerned. There was much face to be saved: the whole department at the bank was under suspicion, given that the bank held all the records containing Mrs P's signatures. None of this helped the Ps: they were several million dollars short and wanted their money from the HKSB where they had left it.

The HKSB's attitude was forthright and simple, namely that the Ps were parties to a massive fraud on the bank and that Mrs P had, herself, written the suspect letters, signing in her maiden name, Kamalee Sukosol. The bank agreed that the suspect signatures differed slightly from the originals but alleged that Mrs P had deliberately contrived those differences so as to make the signatures look like forgeries. .

The HKSB refused to pay and on 3 February 1978, Mr and Mrs P started formal proceedings by writ in the High Court of Hong Kong. In its defence, the bank persisted, until a late stage in the trial, in the allegation that Mrs P had disguised her signature slightly so as to be able to point to the features of difference in support of her denial that she had written at all! It also alleged that the revival and operation of the B.A. account was carried out by Mrs P herself, including the removal of the cardboard box of money. It is not clear whether Mrs P, whose style in accessories did not extend to cardboard boxes, was more offended by this allegation than that of fraud. It merits a mention that the B.A.'s offices are in the lobby of the Peninsula Hotel facing some of the world's most elegant shops. One can only imagine that, had Mrs P been involved, the money would have been carried off in nothing less than a Louis Vuitton bag, readily available across the way from the bank.

The staff at the B.A. who dealt with Madam X between 22 June 1977 and 17 August 1977 were called as witnesses. They not only failed to identify Mrs P as the person who acted in relation to the funds but, more importantly, described someone else. The description simply did not fit Mrs P.

Of the three hand-writing experts called, only one was of the opinion that Mrs P had signed her name at the B.A. But he made it clear that he had found this aspect of the case "extremely difficult". Both the Government Chemist and a third expert were firmly of the opinion that the "identifying expert" was wrong. The issue faded away when the identifying expert agreed that if Mrs P had not been in Hong Kong at all at the material time, she could not have been the woman who signed at the B.A.

Now then: a critical feature of the case was that between 16 July and 17 August 1977, Mr and Mrs P went off on an organised tour to Europe so that Mr P, a lover of golf, could watch the Open at Turnberry. Mrs P had last been in Hong Kong on 4 May 1977 and was not to return until November.

These were crucial dates. Mrs P's passport – a real passport, definitely not forged – supported the itinerary. Significantly, more than half the contents of the B.A. account were uplifted to the tune of HK$4million during this period. It is worth adding that full enquiries regarding telephone calls made during the European holiday and in Bangkok supported their case that they were in Europe when they said they were. Correspondence had mysteriously been sent, not to the authorised Lock Road address, but to an address in Austin Avenue, certainly not with Mrs P's knowledge or consent. The couple denied any knowledge of Austin Avenue and, when Shirley and I searched it out during the preparation for the appeal, it was a nondescript winding alley. A small apartment block with dozens of letter boxes seemed to be a convenience address of some sort. At the trial, there was no evidence to show that the Ps had taken part in any arrangements for it use. Indeed, the only point of the Austin Avenue address was to ensure that correspondence was sent there rather than to Lock Road.

There were many other instances of evidence supporting the Ps' case. But the HKSB remained firmly committed to its assertion that the removal of the funds and the attempt to claim them again amounted to fraud. Even so, nothing is certain in litigation. The HKSB needed to protect itself in the event that it were to lose the case. It brought the B.A. into the proceedings by way of a legal device known as a "Third Party Notice". The effect of this would be to pass on liability to the B.A. if the Ps succeeded in their claim.

The trial began before Mr Justice Bewley in the latter part of 1980.

In the normal course of events, the plaintiffs would start the case. However, allegations of fraud had been made. The onus of proof of fraud was on the HKSB and the Ps therefore had the benefit of the right of silence in that aspect of the case. Even so, the Ps decided to give evidence first. They had nothing to fear and were prepared to be subjected to cross-examination. It was not precisely clear what the bank was alleging which was supposed to have amounted to fraud by the plaintiffs themselves but the forensic phrase "up hill and down dale" fitted the cross-examinations to which they were subjected. They had no admissions to make and none was made. The HKSB called no live evidence.

Final speeches were made and judgment was given.

Mr Justice Bewley found against Mr and Mrs P. In his relatively long and detailed judgment, he made the finding that they were not telling the truth and were not victims of fraud.

I read his reasons over and over trying to find a record of any facts that might have supported his decision. It was strong on rhetoric but weak in substance. There was almost too much meat for an appeal.

"... for all [her] charm and polish I do not believe her story is true... Generally speaking, she gave her evidence with assurance, not to say panache. Only occasionally, during a long ordeal in the witness box did her charm and quick wit [fail]. Once she broke down in tears and this was not, I am sure, orchestrated for the benefit of the Court. I did give this due weight. Against this, there was something about her attitude which did not become a woman who had been cheated of $10 million. As pointed out by defence counsel, a feeling of outrage was missing from her demeanour. She seemed to be challenging the court to prove her wrong ...

Mr P was as bad a witness as his wife was a good one. Not only did he contradict her on a number of matters ... but he was also guilty of prevarication, repetition and plain stupidity ...

I cannot conceive how they could be in such apparent difficulty when describing other events which, if they are untainted with fraud, should form part of a simple, logical narrative. I conclude that their story is untrue. They have no reason to lie to the court unless they have attempted to defraud the defendant. For all these reasons, I find that their claim fails.

"For all these reasons ..." At best the judge was trying to find a reason to build up to the balance of probabilities without anything on which to base his judgment.

Against this background, I opened the appeal before three High Court judges in June 1981. The first few hours were tough going and I said that findings should not be accepted which could not survive being thoroughly tested. I made it clear in my submissions that the judgment was fundamentally flawed. By the end of the first day, the feeling was that we had made a serious but justified attack on it. I had essentially made it plain that it was riddled with misunderstandings and inconsistency. I had no difficulty in pointing out that the reasoning of the judge was faulty and his basic findings were not clear. And I brought home the point that there was massive speculation and theorising which could not satisfy even the civil standard of proof. The issues, rather than being found on the balance of probabilities, were treated by the judge as "competing possibilities" and I said so.

I took the appeal judges through the material papers and submitted that it was not clear as to what exactly the judge had found. However viewed, his findings did not survive scrutiny.

The case for the HKSB was robust. But it seemed plain that our criticisms were wholly justified. My opponent, Richard Yorke QC, was engaged in an uphill struggle.

On 11 August 1981, the Court of Appeal delivered its judgment. The first of the three Justices of Appeal to give judgment was Mr Justice Barker. He set out the principles which should have been applied.

"It is conceded by the defendants that the onus of proving that the plaintiffs were party to the fraud lies on them. It is a heavy onus ... 'in proportion as the crime is enormous, so ought the proof to be clear ...' It is difficult to imagine a more serious charge of fraud than the one levelled by the defendants against the plaintiffs in this case. The degree of probability therefore required to be established against them is in consequence very high. The question in this appeal is whether the defendants have achieved the requisite proof ... in arriving at [the conclusion that the plaintiffs had attempted to defraud the bank], he made a

number of mistakes, and also, at least on the face of it, failed to take into account certain factors. ... here was only one finding the judge could (and should) have made (but did not) which was that Mrs P was not and could not have been concerned with the forgeries ... [the judge had] not checked his impression on the whole subject of demeanour by a critical examination of the whole of the evidence ...As Mr Sherrard, in my judgment, correctly submitted, there is a difference between evaluating probabilities on the basis of a substratum of direct or substantive evidence, and speculating in a vacuum on a footing wholly unsupported by evidence or suggestion in the case... It is extremely difficult to extract from the judgment any findings of primary fact, save that there was a fraud and that the judge was satisfied that the plaintiffs had been lying. He did not find, as I think he was compelled to do find that the plaintiffs were not in Hong Kong when the B.A. forgeries were being perpetrated or that the woman who withdrew the money could not have been and was not Mrs P...

Next came Sir Alan Huggins, VP. He was concerned that there was no conclusive expert evidence attributing the handwriting fraud to the plaintiffs. *"I am by no means persuaded that the fraud could not have been committed by some person or persons independent of both the plaintiffs and the defendant ... in the absence of any admission by them either of involvement in the fraud or of any fact from which such involvement could properly be inferred, that contention cannot be sustained. There was no such admission and I think the judge's conclusion cannot be supported. I do not overlook the difficulty facing any party who alleges fraud but that difficulty is no justification for applying a lower standard of proof...In my view, the evidence was never more than would arouse suspicion against the plaintiffs ..."*

Finally, Mr Justice Zimmern gave his judgment. After analyzing the evidence and rejecting the basis on which the trial judge had been satisfied that the signatures had been forged by Mrs P, he picked up the points about Madam X. *"The important issue is whether Madam X was in fact Mrs P. [One expert] was not impressed that at the time of the B.A. episode Mrs P's passport showed that she was not in Hong Kong. There was more cogent evidence. Madam X had been well identified by officials of B.A. After all, she was the woman who had opened two accounts and signed documents before the B.A. officials. She had upon a day's notice withdrawn over five million dollars in cash and packed the notes in a cardboard box. She was seen off the B.A. premises by an official and escorted to a taxi. The bank official gave a vivid description of Madam X to the police which included her height, appearance, eyebrows, eyelids, mouth, fingernails. Yet Mrs P was in the witness box for a long time and no evidence was given on behalf of B.A. identifying her as Madam X. That speaks for itself that she was not and she could justifiably feel aggrieved that there was no such positive finding."*

Zimmern was in no doubt that a massive fraud had been perpetrated against the HKSB and described how the trial judge had whittled the suspects down to *"the [Plaintiffs] as prime suspects and rested his judgment on the ground that they had lied when, if innocent, they had no reason for lying."*

He went on to say:

"Mr Sherrard attacked the judgment on various grounds. First he said the bank case collapsed after it failed to prove that the instructions to transfer were signed by [Mrs P] or were autoforgeries and that Mrs P and Madam X were one and the same person. Second, that fraud must be distinctly alleged and as distinctly proved. That it was not possible for the learned judge to speculate on the case nor should he have allowed himself to be drawn into a consideration of the case based on competing theories whether it was more likely that "the staff of the Bank" on the one hand or the appellants on the other were the culprits... To me, the elimination of suspects one by one on probabilities or likelihood without a solid foundation of direct or circumstantial evidence and then point a finger of guilt at the plaintiffs is singularly unattractive and quite unacceptable .... I fail to understand [the judge's] reasoning and how the opening of the accounts could lead to a false trail and suspicions. Mr Yorke said the purpose was to test the various banks in Hong Kong to determine what sort of identification was required to open an account in preparation for an intended coup. Mr Sherrard retorted the Plaintiffs could have obtained the same information by attending at the banks and asking without opening an account – an intending robber does not leave behind his calling card on a reconnaissance.

... At the end of the day, the most that could be said was that the judge was suspicious of the plaintiffs but it has been well said before that all the suspicions in the world do not amount to a grain of evidence.

... The bank has fairly and squarely lost...

***

And interest at 15% followed ...

An afterthought: it does not pay for judges to be amateur detectives.

CHAPTER 52

SAN IMPERIAL

Privy Council Appeal No 20 of 1980

David Ng Pak Shing and Others   *Appellants*

v

Lee Ing Chee and others   *Respondents*

FROM

THE COURT OF APPEAL OF HONG KONG

JUDGMENT OF THE LORDS OF THE JUDICIAL COMMITTEE OF THE PRIVY COUNCIL, DELIVERED THE *20ᵗʰ April 1982*

Present at the Hearing:

LORD FRASER OF TULLYBELTON

LORD ELWYN-JONES

LORD RUSSELL OF KILLOWEN

LORD ROSKILL

LORD BRIDGE OF HARWICH

(Delivered by LORD FRASER OF TULLYBELTON)

This is an appeal from the Court of Appeal of Hong Kong pursuant to a 55 day trial in the High Court of Hong Kong ... In June 1976, CK San was arrested on charges of fraud[1]. He was then the beneficial owner of

---

[1]   The fraud was not connected to the San Imperial matter.

20,000,000 of the 48.2 million shares in the San Imperial[1] Corporation Limited. He went to Taiwan and failed to surrender to his Hong Kong bail. One of the appellants, Ives, is a solicitor in Hong Kong. He and two others, Ng (a stockbroker in Hong Kong) formed a syndicate to obtain a controlling interest in San Imperial which they say they did by acquiring C K San's shares through a third party. The plaintiffs [the respondents] are creditors of C K San (who is not a party to the appeal). In 1977, they sought to set aside the share transactions by obtaining charging orders nisi[2] over 15,000,000 shares in San Imperial which the appellants claim were owned by "the Syndicate" as nominees of C K San. The respondents allege that the transfer of the shares to the Syndicate was a sham and that C K San, who was indebted to them, remained the actual owner of the shares. The trial judge made the nisi order absolute. $2,813,300 had been paid into court to cover part of the transaction. The judge at first instance ordered that money to be paid over to one of the plaintiffs. Part of the appeal required the repayment of that money. The facts which give rise to these proceedings are complicated and it is by no means certain that they have been fully expiscated at the trial ... The trial judge did not believe that Ng found C K San by coincidence in Taiwan. He *"would have thought that C K San ... who was heavily in debt and a fugitive from justice, would have avoided going to public places"* ... The syndicate was concerned about dealing with C K San but Ives took legal opinion from counsel in London who advised by telex in January 1977: *"if the client's sole motive is the commercial one of buying the shares for himself"* as distinct from financing or assisting a fugitive, the client (purchaser) would not be accessory to the defence offered by C K San ... *[Thus] counsel's advice gave the green light for the Syndicate to proceed with the acquisition of the shares* which they then sold on at a profit to Coe, another appellant ...

The San Imperial case lasted for a record-breaking 55 days marked by vitriolic exchanges between counsel and unprecedented – because it was permitted by the judge – browbeating of witnesses. The purpose of the hearing was to decide whether an order should be made effective to

---

[1]   The title 'San Imperial' indicated an hotel company of the highest quality: 'San' is the honorific for respect; 'Imperial' refers to the Japanese throne.

[2]   A charging order is a court order to enforce a judgment. The order 'nisi' must be made absolute before the debt can be recovered.

transfer 15,000,000 shares allegedly owned by C K San to the Malaysian Bank Bumiputra to whom he was indebted. The shares had been sold on, via two third parties, to a syndicate consisting of two Chinese businessmen and a Hong Kong-based English solicitor. The syndicate, in turn, sold the shares on to an entrepreneur. The transactions involved huge sums of money. $2,813,300 had been paid into court by the defendants to cover part of the losses the bank alleged it had incurred. The court had to decide: was the transfer legitimate, as asserted by the syndicate in the first instance case; or was it a sham as alleged by the aggrieved bank which had been deprived of the shares by the transfer. The bank succeeded first time round in a hearing presided over by T L Yang. It had been essential for TL to cut a dash in the way he ran the case to impress those who needed to be impressed that he was the obvious, immensely competent choice who merited the role of Chief Justice.

Anyone in the law who visited Hong Kong knew about the marathon San Imperial case. The bank had sustained extensive losses when CK San jumped bail and decamped to Taiwan, taking his share certificates with him but leaving a large bank loan gathering interest. There was not much prospect of him coming back to sort out his financial problems. There was no extradition treaty between Hong Kong and Taiwan so it was a favourite refuge for fugitives from justice (or the miscarriage thereof). Villains even had a favourite hotel in Tapei!

The trial was a rare event of such public interest that it became a television special in Hong Kong. It was very unusual to have a commercial case reported so widely. Richard Yorke QC, a well-known silk from London, represented the bank. He was a colourful character who flew his own plane. He was very well-known in Hong Kong. I had been against him in several other cases. He led Charles Ching QC, the local man, a familiar adversary to me.

At the trial, the judge barred no holds. Tempers became so frayed during the hearing that old friends fell out as the rancour extended beyond the court and the robing room. The bank's team taunted and insulted their opponents at every opportunity, even out of court. The time came when the two opposing legal teams refused to sit in the same cabin of the aircraft on the journey to London for the Privy Council hearing.

Counsel set about the Syndicate, treating them like dirt. T L let them get away with it. The Privy Council picked up on this:

"... [Ives] was made to appear deceitful by being cross-examined on a question of law, in spite of a protest by his counsel, on which his opinion ought never have been asked. In the case of Ng, he was subjected to abuse (one 'question' consisted of the statement "Mr Ng, you are the most dreadful and awful liar") which in spite of another protest by his counsel was not withdrawn by the cross-examiner nor checked by the Court."

There is no record of any oral intervention by T L but I was told that he engaged in a dismissive, irritable wave of his hand to make it clear that counsel's objections were more of an irrelevance than a legitimate complaint.

T L Yang handed down what was intended to be an appeal-proof judgment. Omitting the defects in procedure, but perhaps allowing his decisions to be clouded by his personal distaste for the syndicate dealing with a fugitive from justice, he stated that he had seen and heard the witnesses and found the defendants were all untruthful. He found the evidence for this to be overwhelming. The syndicate was forensically slaughtered. The shares were steered back to the Bumiputra Bank and the rest of the story could begin. An appeal was inevitable whichever way the case had gone. Not only had there been a huge amount of money involved but also reputations were at stake.

Michael was in Hong Kong on another case at the time the trial came to an end. As he walked along Connaught Road to meet a friend for lunch in the Hong Kong Club, Mr Ives stopped him and introduced himself.

I had never met him but he knew me. He told me he was a party to "the banking litigation." I knew a little about the case. "We were going to bring you out," he said. "Now we're at the appeal stage and I can tell you this: we don't want advice on whether to do so. We are determined to appeal. We'll go to the Privy Council if we have to. Will you lead for us? We'll add Henry Litton QC[1] to the team." Henry was the doyen of the Hong Kong Bar. It would be a delight to work with him.

---

[1]   The Hon. Mr Denis Henry Litton, Chairman of the Hong Kong Bar Association 1971-72, 1977-79, 1983-1984. Subsequently (and currently) a judge in the Hong Kong Court of Final Appeal (to which all final appeals now lie).

"And you can have Robert Tang[1] as your junior." Robert was an outstanding young barrister.

I was frank with him. "Fifty-five days at first instance certainly does not encourage me. Even on the brief summary you have given me, I have to say that I am not optimistic." But Ives was insistent.

I said, "In any event, it all depends on whether I am available. But you need to know that, notwithstanding what you've told me, as a matter of principle, I would definitely advise you on the prospects of success."

So I agreed to look at the transcripts and did so over the next few weeks. It was certain that the syndicate would take the case to appeal . The idea was for me to lead the team. I had a meeting with them at an early stage in the preparation of the appeal. I could not see why lawyers of this calibre required a leader from London. I asked them, "Do you two chaps really need me for this case?"

"Oh yes," Henry Litton answered for them both. "Because the syndicate is so unpopular and you are so popular, we thought your name should appear early. This has been so acrimonious." Bearing in mind my personal experience of Yorke and Ching, I could see how this had come about but it was hardly a logical basis for choosing a leader.

In the many meetings which followed, there was not too much feedback from the two Chinese clients: they spoke no English. Ives was by necessity the only client who could communicate directly with me but the Chinese nodded intensely as their solicitors muttered some sort of translation to them. I managed to get across to them that I thought we would be very lucky to get to first base in the Court of Appeal because TL had prefaced his judgment by saying he had relied on his impression of the credibility and demeanour of the witnesses. He had found them untruthful: liars, no less. They shook their heads in disagreement and made it known to me, through the solicitors, that they had at all times dealt with the shares on a strictly business basis. We learnt that James Coe had even gone to the trouble to take counsel's advice in London on the probity of his part in the transaction. The view of John Vinelott, Coe's counsel for the appeal, was that, regardless of the findings against

---

[1]   Robert Tang QC, now a Judge of the Court of First Instance of the High Court, Hong Kong.

the syndicate, there was insufficient evidence that he had acted other-wise than in good faith.

Our main difficulty vis-a-vis the syndicate was that there seemed no sensible way of re-opening the merits. The Court of Appeal would not, save in very exceptional cases, retry a case of this kind without over-ruling the judge's view, he having seen and heard the witnesses in a long case. The clients remained undeterred by the gloomy view I had of their prospects on appeal. Fifty-five days of trial should have been good enough for the judge to make up his mind about which witnesses he believed. Moreover, a further appeal to the Privy Council would face the same impediment of the convention of concurrent findings of fact being found at trial and appeal. If the judgment was upheld, that would have meant there had been concurrent findings of fact.

"Yes, Michael. But we want to have a go," was the considered re-sponse.

I advised that our only real hope was that we should try to get the three Appeal Judges to dissent from one another.

"How are you going to do that?"

"T L has given six examples of the untruthfulness of two members of the syndicate. I think that he has made the mistake of making the find-ings conflict. If I can show – and I think I can – that these findings are inconsistent, we have a chance."

And that was the chance on which I worked at the Court of Appeal.

**

The Appeal was to be heard by Sir Geoffrey Briggs, Chief Justice and Judges of Appeal Huggins and Pickering. The parties and their legal teams assembled in Hong Kong in readiness.

It was a pleasant relief to hear from John Vinelott, a chancery silk, known to me only because he was exceptionally tall. He had represented Coe the first time around. He phoned me when he arrived. Until then I had been virtually trapped in my room. After the standard greetings and complaints about the tiring flight, John asked how long I thought the ap-peal would last.

"It's not going to last another 55 days," I told him. But we agreed that it was going to be at least two or three weeks.

"Ah," he said. Then: "In strictest confidence, I will tell you that I have been appointed to the High Court but I have asked for it not to be gazetted until I get home." He went on, "The Lord Chancellor eventually agreed that I should leave at once for Hong Kong."

"Congratulations! Are you going to say that you came all this way to tell me you can't do the case?"

"No, I told the Lord Chancellor I'd read the papers and was fully prepared. I told him I would have to deliver it even if I couldn't do the case myself. He was very good about it. He said, 'You can't bargain with judicial appointments but we'll say that this one hasn't begun yet – just come back as soon as you can.'"

"That won't be very soon in any event," I said. Vinelott was 'tail-end Charlie'. Although the case was important to his client, Coe, the involvement was only in the final transaction and, chronologically, his story had to be told last of all.

"Ah, but as you are the overall leader, you could carry the burden of the case without me. But I would need you to let me go first."

Go first! In Hong Kong, everything is about saving face and hierarchy. There would be a lot of face for my clients to lose if Coe's case were heard out of the established pecking order. I had to devise a modus vivendi that would help John and at the same time be acceptable to the court and to my clients.

"I'll have to say that you have compelling personal reasons for your part of the case to go first." To my clients, I insisted that there was no harm in it. Coe needed some persuading as well, as it was convention that those making the appeal would get the last word: in his case, he would now have to rely solely on counsel's first words. Eventually, he said, "If Sherrard succeeds, I succeed."

In less than three days, Vinelott delivered a brilliant introductory outline, using the names of the parties so frequently that, when it came to my turn, the characters were well known to those of the judicial audience who had remained awake throughout the proceedings. Having laid the ground for all who followed him, he asked for, and was granted, leave to return to London. The announcement of his judicial appointment followed pretty much as his plane touched down at Heathrow. He was, in fact, on his way to becoming the Senior and much respected Chancery Judge.

The rest of the appeal continued. For several of the remaining twelve days, I set about arguing the defects in the findings of fact. The Court of Appeal dealt with the matter as I had predicted: "We can't retry the facts that have been found."

I was, of course, slapped down by Richard Yorke. "I have never heard such nonsense," was one of his politer comments on my advocacy.

They reserved the judgment for a week. Huggins spoke first. "The learned judge was wrong about points 4, 5 and 6 on credibility but right about points 1, 2 and 3 ..."

Then Pickering, reversing the order on credibility: "... Mr Sherrard has criticised the judge's finding of fact, relying on the credibility of the witnesses. But he is not entitled to claim that inference in the Court of Appeal ... the appeal is dismissed. The Court will not interfere with adverse findings of fact."

Sir Geoffrey appeared to have slept all through the appeal. However, he recovered consciousness long enough to agree with both dissenting judgments given by his colleagues.

***

Although we lost, the judgment contained all the seeds of the eventual victory before the Privy Council. Although there was not a glimmer that they thought we could succeed at the final appeal, we were approached by the bank's legal team as soon as they knew we had our sights on London. They took a pragmatic approach. The gist of their proposal was: "You can't get anywhere at the Privy Council. Can we settle with a financial package and call it a day?"

***

Michael's people seemed to regard the Hong Kong Court of Appeal's decision as little more than a step towards victory. Nothing was going to stop them going on with the case.

The meeting after the hearing was about the practicality of going to a 'real' appeal in London. I said, "We'll be slaughtered. There are transcripts of fifty-five days of evidence essentially on issues of fact – the Privy Council won't let this through. We're stuck on credibility. Let's cut our losses and run."

This less than encouraging speech was greeted by a clamour from the clients, some in translation: "Please don't drop our case. We have confidence in you. We have confidence in the Privy Council. Please!"

The fact of their confidence was not relevant to the likely outcome. But, they were insistent and there was the glimmer of hope arising from the strange judgment of the Hong Kong First Instance Court of Appeal.

The 55 days of animosity at first instance and 15 days of ill-feeling during the Hong Kong appeal rumbled on. The clients and the Hong Kong lawyers from both sides were at daggers drawn at Kai Tak airport. Unfortunately for all concerned, or perhaps as an additional feature of local spite, their respective travel agents had booked them on the same flight. Although they asked to be, and were, seated apart on the plane, some bitter remarks were made in the airport lounge within the hearing of our clients so that we knew that the approach of our opponents was that the appeal was considered to be an abuse of the process. Translated from legalese, our clients were left in no doubt of the Malaysian bank's certainty that we would lose.

The clients and lawyers arrived on the Sunday. We took a suite of rooms at the Howard Hotel at the side of the Temple. There were seven of us, including Henry Litton, Robert Knight and the team of solicitors. The options for the case were limited.

I said, "We've got to bludgeon them into hearing this case and not being bound by the first court's finding of facts. I'm morally certain that T L Yang got it wrong."

For some time we debated how to get the Privy Council back to the stage of primary evidence. We decided on a strategy. If it did not succeed, that would be the end of the story. We took bets on how long it would be before one of the Law Lords said, "You can't do that!" One of us thought that we could last until the afternoon.

***

309

The Privy Council is the highest court of appeal for Commonwealth countries and Crown territories. In a vast, panelled room, in Downing Street, five Law Lords sit as the supreme judicial panel at a huge half-circle table stretching the breadth of the far side of the Chamber. The opposing teams of lawyers sit at tables on either side of the long room. Counsel's podium is opposite the mid-point of the great table, facing the judges and separated by several yards from his support team which is too far away to offer any help whatsoever. The judges sit in lounge suits but counsel are in full-bottomed wigs and all the traditional costume of silk. You can only hear what the judges are saying if you lift the flap of the wig.

***

You can, of course, hear what your opponent says as you are assembling your papers before the hearing starts. Mesmerised by his own prospects, Richard Yorke, who had patronised me in our previous encounters, took advantage of the opportunity for yet another sneer. Studying his hands in what he considered to be an elegant gesture, he asked them, or so it appeared, "What magic illusions have you got for us this time?"

Lord Fraser of Tullybelton (obviously and irresistibly called Bellybutton – but he must have thought of that before he took the title) took the chair. It was his first time. He was very pleased with himself and it showed in his beaming smile and general bonhomie in a place that was more accustomed to grimly set jaws, pallid skin and weary, drooping eyes. He regarded his position as a great honour. One can only imagine that, behind the scenes, it must have been fascinating to have worked in the company of Elwyn-Jones, Roskill, Bridge and Russell on complex points of law.

At 11.30 a.m. I moved to the lectern. My heart was thumping in my chest. I told myself, "Don't have a heart attack now, whatever you do." But I got into my stride and all was well. At 3.30 p.m., the bet was won.

I had been on my feet for about three hours. Lord Bridge interrupted me. He said, "Mr Sherrard, as you have progressed through this fascinating story, my mind keeps going back to the principles of appellate advocacy. I have to say – which I am sure will be no surprise to you – you seem to have to overcome two hurdles. First, the judge had ample opportunity to observe the demeanour of the witnesses, which he found wanting. Second, there are findings of fact which cannot be overturned. Don't you think you are contravening the concurrent findings of fact rule?" I was prepared for this intervention.

"My Lord, this case took fifty-five days at first instance, then fifteen days on appeal. I recognise that there are problems. But would it be too much, in the interests of justice, to allow me five hours to put my case? I am confident that will be sufficient for your Lordships. If at the end of that time your Lordships think I do not have a case, I will sit down. If you think I have ..." This was a moment to let the words tail away.

They went into a little huddle then Lord Fraser leaned forward. "That seems fair enough," he said. "Carry on, Mr Sherrard."

Imagine my joy on seeing the stony glare on the face of each of the opposition and hearing, even through my wig flaps, Charles Ching sucking air through his teeth as he had done every time he had lost against me in the past. Very luckily, we did not break into hostilities in the robing room, although I did hear one of the opponents say, "Well, I think we could safely book our flights home for Monday."

At the end of the first day, we left Downing Street on foot but soon found that we had to slow our pace. We had caught up with Lord Bridge and felt it best to maintain a respectful distance. He had not noticed us, weighed down as he was with two huge green bags which could only contain the papers from our case. This meant that he was going to read the documents. We were being taken seriously, even while I was short of my five hour target.

Next day, as I stood at the lonely podium, he greeted me with the words, "I spent the whole of last night reading the papers." He was grinning from ear to ear. "I suppose you're going to say that there were incorrect findings of fact and there were no concurring judgments." I restrained the thought that he was granting the appeal with those words. Just as well. He leaned forward and said, "But we must listen to the case. We are going to entertain the appeal."

I was on my feet for four or five days. It sounds a long time but there was a lot to say. Lord Roskill later told Bob Alexander that it was the best opening speech he had ever heard.

Then they called on Richard Yorke who, I think, made a rather silly mistake. He decided to criticise me and my style of advocacy, in much the same way that had impressed the wakeful members of the Hong Kong Court of Appeal, although leading to unfortunately different findings. I believe that the Privy Council had come to like me by then and that his three-day critique of my speech might better have been applied to involving himself in the matters which were of concern to the court. He was trying to cover his back because much of the damage to his clients' case had come from the unrestrained mismanagement of his and his junior's cross-examination of the syndicate witnesses.

Another silk followed him. He spoke in haste and requested leave to return to Hong Kong where another, apparently more pressing, matter awaited him. Lord Fraser said, "Go," not even looking at him. His absence was excellent news for me as he would not now be able to reply to any questions that might arise. Although he was allowed to leave early that day, I was not. I found myself locked into the building. Although after some hours I had resigned myself, in that pre-mobile-telephone era, to a hungry night in an uncomfortable chair, I eventually managed to make a lady security guard hear my mortifyingly silly calls for help. She was persuaded by my advocacy, so recently criticised, to letting me free. No-one had noticed that I was missing!

By the twentieth day, I had started my closing submissions. We adjourned at 4.00 p.m. on the Thursday, to return at 10.00 a.m. next day. At the appointed time, four judges entered and took their seats at the table. There was no sign of Eustace Roskill.

Lord Fraser said, "Mr Sherrard, we are very sorry to tell you – and we are very aware of the distress that this will cause to all the parties – but Lord Roskill was taken to hospital last night. He has double pneumonia. It appears that we will have to abandon the appeal and start again before a new court after Christmas." The real problem was that Roskill, whose pen had been busy throughout the hearing, had drawn the short straw to write the judgment. He was the only one of the panel that was indispensable. We could have limped on with any combination of four, provided that Roskill was included.

There was a way around the problem. I said, "Would you give me the chance to curtail my speech? I believe that your Lordships – including Lord Roskill – have heard all that needs to be said in this matter."

As the opposition were still being overjoyed by the assumption that my clients would now have to give in as they would be defeated by the costs of another hearing, Lord Fraser consulted with his colleagues. They agreed to the proposition.

....

Months later, after our appeal had been allowed, I met Elwyn-Jones in Middle Temple.

"I'm not talking out of school," he said. "In fact, I promised the others I would tell you what had happened."

And this was the story that Elwyn told me.

Eustace Roskill was in hospital for Christmas. When he came out, he was going to recuperate in Madeira where he would write the judgment so as to be able to catch up on time. Lord Fraser was very anxious about the delay in handing down the judgment and, on a bitterly cold night, set off in person to collect the transcripts from Lord Roskill's car, parked in the Temple, so as to take over the job. But in doing so, he managed to slip on a patch of ice on the pavement. He fractured his scapula and had to go off to hospital for emergency treatment. Some hours later, when he was arranged in bed with his arm in a sling and dosed up with pain-killers, he said to his wife, "And I still have to write the judgment. I'll do it with a Dictaphone. Could you get the porter to fetch the papers? It's rather a lot – fifty-five volumes of transcripts."

Lady Fraser went to the car with the porter. A few minutes later, she came back to ask where the car actually was. She had been given the right place but the car had gone. Complete with the papers. It turned up two weeks later in Shoreditch in a sorry state, but with its cargo intact. Lord Fraser could complete the task! Just as well, really. We'd decided before Christmas that you would win!"

***

The Hong Kong clients were overjoyed. Nine months after the judgment was delivered, I was in Hong Kong on another matter when I received a message at the hotel. The Syndicate wanted to entertain the legal team to dinner. They fixed a date.

At the end of the dinner, Mel Ives got to his feet.

"Michael, this is not a formal note of thanks. But the team is very grateful. You must have wondered all those months ago why I said that we could go to the Privy Council. You must have thought the Court of Appeal in Hong Kong could have given us what we needed.

"I will explain why not going to the Privy Council was never an option. Mr Ng, the "dreadful liar", is a very religious man. He went to Lantau Island to visit a monastery where a large figure of Buddha stands in the grounds. You ask the Buddha a question and take a scroll which bears the reply. The scroll interprets what is ailing you.

"The question asked by Mr Ng was, 'Can we win this case?'

"The answer on the scroll was written in Chinese. A very rough translation is, '*You must not fret for you will not get your help from three worthies but you will be the beneficiary of the wisdom of five.*'

"The five judges of the Privy Council – helped along by you – gave him what had been predicted."

***

The story does not quite end here. There was a little matter of over several hundred thousand dollars that had been overpaid to the bank. The cheque that was made out to our clients was over a million dollars. I explained that it had to be returned so that a replacement could be provided. But back it came in the same amount: it was a question of face. The director of the bank could not be seen to have made a mistake in his calculations. If the Bumiputra Bank said an amount was correct, it was.

CHAPTER 53

A BOUT OF ILL HEALTH

In August 1982, Michael and Shirley went to Capri for a holiday. He had spent the preceding months paying no attention to a health problem that was not showing any signs of going away on its own. They returned to London in September for him to begin a stint at the Old Bailey, sitting as a Recorder. Four days into an armed robbery trial, the annoying symptoms turned into a haemorrhage that could not be ignored. On the fifth day scheduled for the hearing, Michael went to see Sir James Miskin, the Recorder of London at the Old Bailey.

"I saw a specialist on my way in this morning," I told him. "He wants me in the hospital this evening. O master of all solutions: what would you have me do? Die in your service?"

"I'm not going to let you discharge the jury," he said. "You look fine to me." The implication was that I would look fine to them as well. "I suggest you just leave the building now. "I'll get another judge," he said. "I'll explain there is a problem." But what he did not explain and what I never told him was that I was suffering from cancer.

My armed robbery started again with Dan Hollis QC as the new judge and I went off to The Garden Hospital to start a week of pre-surgical procedures mainly involving a process of spring-cleaning of my intestines by not being allowed to eat anything.

Day by day, I was thinner and thinner, and definitely cleaner and cleaner.

My medication consisted of two small tablets, taken daily. It was explained to me that their effectiveness was owed to the space programme. Thereafter, they were called "astronaut pills". I asked my specialist whether, if they were ineffective, I would shuttle off this mortal coil. He stolidly assured me that their efficacy of maintaining bodily functions in space had translated into their effective use in more conventional therapeutic situations.

Shirley and I had a number of decisions to make in the face of this life-threatening event. First, I made up my mind that if I survived, I would not want to take judicial office, a matter which we had occasionally discussed. Secondly, we decided that nobody was to be told what had happened to me. We knew from the experience of those less reticent that health problems lead to one's professional funeral being arranged by well-meaning friends.

My mother was not aware of my having cancer. We had the cover story for her. I did not want to worry her and I believed that modest deception was the best way. Sadly, she was to suffer a major heart attack three months later. She died in January 1983. I was comforted somewhat that she had not known that my life was at risk.

I told my clerks I was going into hospital but they did not know why. Shirley decided that the best smoke-screen was a partial truth: she invented a recurrence of the previous year's unpleasant encounter with haemorrhoids. "Poor Michael," she said, "two years of surgery on the trot!"

I had a resection of the colon on September 21· 1982. I lost a tremendous amount of weight and had a cadaverous appearance. I kept out of the way. People in Hong Kong, practically my second home at the time, thought I was in England and vice versa. In between the two was Singapore: my convalescence included some paperwork whilst in hospital and a conference at home in the middle of October with some clients from Singapore who came over especially to see me. Soon after that, I went into town and dropped into Middle Temple. I daresay I was not looking in the best of health. I met Spider Cumming-Bruce. He glanced at me as we were about to pass one another near the Library. A moment's scrutiny was enough.

"You've had a spot of bother," he said.

"Yes," I answered.

He nodded. "Stick at it!" he said, exercising the maximum amount of compassion that convention permitted.

Spider was not the only one who thought I looked a wreck. Whilst I was recuperating, Wililiam Chan, my first Hong Kong pupil, came to see me. He insisted on taking us to a local restaurant. I wore a black raincoat and a trilby hat and felt rather smart. He took a photograph of me. I regarded it as being of someone else for a time as the camera cannot lie – someone green and gaunt, at death's door. Hardly the picture of someone who had actually recovered from an illness. I have it framed in my study.

When our window-cleaner saw it, he said, "Christ almighty – what's the matter with 'im, then?" It was rather unfair to have looked so ill, especially as I had been lucky enough not to have needed chemotherapy.

I had to go for regular check-ups for a while. After a few weeks, I began to look as well as I felt, although I took four months off work all together – apart from consultations with my clients and paperwork, which I regarded as therapeutic. My complete recovery was marked by resuming work in Hong Kong in early December: dealing with the long-running cases of Carrian and San Imperial were part of my rehabilitation process. The journey was my main concern but I handled it as if there had never been anything wrong.

I went to the hospital for a "signing-off" check-up. I had developed a regular line of banter with the surgeon. He would start the consultation by saying, "How are you?" and I would answer, "You know better than I do – you tell me."

To the nursing staff, my usual greeting was, "How's business?" And they would say, "We were full yesterday – we're full today." That sort of thing.

"Any casualties?" was another opening gambit intended to be funny in a hospital with no A and E department. At the last visit, I had an unexpected answer.

"We've got a chap who's in bad shape," the nurse told me. "He's had the same as you – a colon resection. He thinks he's going to die. Why don't you go and cheer him up?"

I was casually dressed for comfort: this included wearing a black fedora hat and a white polo-necked sweater rather than a shirt. I was not sure that I was dressed smartly enough to visit a stranger. I hesitated.

"Go on," the nurse urged me. "I know you'll do him good."

I decided that he would have to take me as I was. The nurse took me to his room and left me as I knocked at the door. A weak voice invited me in.

"Good morning," I said and stopped short. I could see that he was crying. "What's the trouble?" I said.

"Oh, father," he said, "I've got cancer."

317

I could see he was very ill if he did not recognise his own dad.

He continued, "I don't believe I will recover. I have three daughters, father. How will my wife manage? How will they manage?"

"What do you do?" I asked.

"I'm a professional rugby football referee," he managed to tell me, between racking sobs.

"Listen to me," I said. "You're not going to die. Believe me – I've had the same as you, and I'm still here."

"What faith are you?" he asked.

"I'm Jewish."

"I didn't know there was a Jewish chaplain here!"

I caught sight of myself in the mirror. I could see that I was a chaplain. My polo-necked sweater was, to the untrained eye, a dog-collar. Father Sherrard had spoken.

"This is my travelling outfit," I explained. "I've just got back from Hong Kong." I had his interest and he had stopped crying. Between recovering sniffs and much blowing of the nose, I assured him that I was well and he could get better. I advised him to use his strength to do just that rather than planning for the worst.

"I don't believe you," he said. But I could see that he wanted it to be true. "Do you have a purple scar running from here to here?" I drew a line across my abdomen and challenged him. "Because so do I," I said.

He lowered the waist of his pyjamas. The identical scar to mine was displayed.

"Yes," I said, "except that mine's not so purple – it's getting old now."

He shook his head in disbelief. "Very well. It's truth or dare. I'm going to strip off." And I did – partially. A relatively modest drop of the trousers and there was my more mature scar on display. He peered at it in amazement.

"And you flew to Hong Kong?"

"Yes. I'm working again. And you ought to be as well."

Trousers were pulled up, pyjamas straightened. He sat up in bed, no more sign of tears. It was as if I had turned on an electric light bulb in his head.

"I'm not going to die," he said. "I'm not going to die! I can't thank you enough. Will you see me again?" But I was too busy at work to go back and he was discharged within a couple of days.

There might have been better advocacy than this in my life, but this was certainly the most rewarding. He just wanted someone to tell him that he could get better so that he could have confidence in his ability to get well again.

The one thing I realised quickly and then again and again over the years was that I never knew his name. To me he has always been "the rugger bugger."

The only real consequence of the surgery is that I am permanently lop-sided. My tie makes a perfect plumb-line and my body tilts to the left.

***

In early 1983, Sir Denys Roberts telephoned me from the airport when he arrived in London on a visit. "Are you serving drinks?" was his request for an invitation

I had been put under pressure by him before 1982 to take an appointment. There had been talk in Hong Kong about setting up a new court system to cope with and modernise commercial crime in all its aspects.

I had been involved in a long-running case for many months in Hong Kong. It had given me a taste of what it would be like to be part of the regular life there. There was much to recommend it but there was also an oppressive aspect of living as if in a goldfish bowl, constantly under the scrutiny of the small club-like group of closely linked members. I was enjoying life at the Bar so much, the thought of having to give up the cut and thrust was unattractive and as a tourist or even a regular working visitor I was free.

He arrived by taxi and with very little ado set about discussing the benefits of an appointment. Before my illness, I had been reluctant to consider an offer. Now, I was certain. A permanent judicial appointment was not for me. So, our meeting became purely social and I remained free to continue my career at the Bar.

CHAPTER 54

SUMMERTIMES

Shirley and Michael spent two or three summer weeks at the same hotel on Capri for several years. The year of 1983 was a good year. Michael had recovered his health and the holiday was strictly for enjoyment and relaxation. The hotel's terrace overlooked the bay and its bar and lunch tables were a meeting place rather than containing small areas of privacy. The tables were close enough together for conversations to be overheard. The atmosphere was informal and people were used to other guests joining in their discussions and, if necessary, taking sides in their arguments.

We first met the Gelbarts while we sat on the hotel terrace one lunchtime. Our acquaintance there varied over the years as some people died off or stopped coming for less compelling reasons. Newcomers always filled the available space. We were talking about American humour with an American lawyer. I said that I did not think that, as nations, we laughed at the same things but that the funniest film I had ever seen was *Tootsie* with Dustin Hoffman.

I felt someone tapping my shoulder. Larry Gelbart introduced himself to me saying, "Sir, you're my new best friend – I wrote *Tootsie*." He pointed to a nearby table. "That's my wife, Pat, over there," he said. She came to join us.

We struck up an immediate rapport. It was fascinating for me to piece together his life story from his anecdotes. I learned that when Larry was a schoolboy, his dad was a barber in Hollywood. One of the customers at about the time Larry was sixteen was the comedian, Jerry Thomas. Larry's father asked who wrote his gags. He said Larry could do it better. And he did. Jerry signed him up to write jokes for him. It was not long before word spread about him and he was writing gags for Bob Hope and Sid Caesar amongst others. I had seen a piece of his craftsmanship in action without having realised that I was listening to a script.

Jack Benny was invited to appear on the Parkinson show. He got in touch with Larry. "What do I say," he asked, "to keep up my pretence of being mean?"

Larry advised, "Get him to ask if you are life insured. He's bound to ask if you would mind telling for how much."

The question was engineered. The Gelbart-drafted response was, "I would mind, but I tell you this – when I go, they go." Watching it in London, I was one of many thousands of people who thought that Jack Benny was too funny for words, when all the time, the words were Larry's!

He has the fastest, sharpest wit of anyone I have ever met. The most casual remark is likely to lead to an achingly funny, spontaneous reply, as I realised the next time we met. I'll tell you the story even though putting a joke on paper usually kills it off. Shirley and I were going out for dinner later that day. Leaving the hotel was a risky business. It was surrounded by narrow alleyways which the sun scarcely penetrated and which had become hazardous walkways because of the prodigious amount of dog-mess littering the ground. No-one ever cleared it away. We bumped into Larry as we prepared to tread carefully through what we told him was, for obvious reasons, called Turd Avenue. Larry instantly described the location as "au bord de la merde." I knew then that I was in the presence of a master.

He told us how to encourage and praise people in show business. The method is that after the performance, at the back-stage visit, it is essential to show that the performance was thoroughly enjoyed. Lines from the script must be recited: this shows a degree of enjoyment so great that the words have impressed themselves into your memory. The technique was adapted from Noel Coward. "I stand on the edge of the wings," Larry explained. "I'm tall enough to see across to the actors. I mouth the word, 'wonderful'. Noel would actually say, 'Wonderful is not the word.'"

His advice remains with us to this day: to use the system whenever a camera points at you at social functions. "At weddings, parties and bar-mitzvahs, when the camera comes around, you'll be seen, mouthing the word 'wonderful'. The host will be happy forever."

Larry originally came to live in London as an exile from the McCarthy era. Although the witch-hunt ended in the late 1950s, he and his wife stayed in their Hampstead house for some years. Eventually, they sold it and moved back to the States.

Larry phoned me before they left.

"Do you need a plain-paper fax machine?"

"I do," I said. Thermal paper was an absolute pain.

"If you can use it, I'd like you to have mine," Larry said. "In the States, we have one in each room. If I don't see you, I'll get the agent to send it round."

A few days later, a splendid BT-labelled machine arrived.

Larry called before I had a chance to thank him.

"How are you getting along with the fax-machine?" he asked.

"Fine," I said. I was about to launch into suitable expressions of gratitude when he said, "That's a shame. BT want it back – unless you feel you can handle stolen property."

We went back to thermal paper for some time after the departure of the Gelbart offering.

***

On another trip to Capri on our usual holiday break, I was cooling off in the pool and a tall American joined me. I had seen him over the past three days since he had arrived but we had not yet spoken. The silence was now broken.

"Good morning," he said. "My name's Wald – Mel Wald. Am I right in thinking you're a barrister?"

I only had time to nod before he carried on.

"I've been watching you reading the same book that I've just finished. May I pick your brains?"

"Well," was as far as I got.

He continued, "I'm Standing Counsel to the Bank of America in San Francisco. I'm on my way to London to see one of our cases. It's been going for four or five weeks but I'm taking a break here for a few days before I get stuck into it. Are you by any chance familiar with a guy called Andy Bateson? He's a QC. In London," he added, with emphasis to show that this was impressive.

This did call for an answer which I was allowed to give. "Yes, I know him very well. He happens to be Chairman of the Estates Committee of my Inn. I'm on the Committee myself. The odd thing is, I was supposed to phone Andy with some information about one of the Inn's buildings and I only remembered to do so when we were at the airport, waiting for our flight."

"We haven't used him before but I've formed a very high opinion of him," Wald said.

I told him, "I should think they'll make him a judge some day."

"We sort of had to use him," Wald told me. "We wanted another guy, Malcolm something-or-other but we didn't get very far because he was in some long case abroad and couldn't fit ours into his timetable. It was a real pity because he'd been recommended very highly by the New York branch of the Bank of America."

I knew this would have been a good recommendation as I had worked for them myself in the past. We carried on chatting, moving away from the pressures of Wald's work to general small talk. After a time, he said, "By the way, you haven't told me your name."

"Michael Sherrard."

"Michael?"

"Yes."

"Were you doing a case in Singapore recently?"

"I do a bit of work out there. My last case was three or four months ago."

He pondered this. "Now I remember! – It wasn't 'Malcolm' – it was 'Michael'. This is extraordinary. It was you that I was trying to book!"

"You're in better hands," I reassured him. "You needn't worry."

He asked, "Do you know who introduced you to me?"

I had no idea.

"Do you know John Beachey of Coward Chance?"

I certainly did know him. "Yes," I said. "The last gaming licence case I did was with a man called Bob Alexander who was with me, representing the Playboy Club of Park Lane. It was fighting off alleged irregularities in gambling. We were trying to save their licence. John Beachey instructed us. Bob and I were taking it in turns but to all intents and purposes, we both lost. That was the last case I did with John."

"There's no end to the coincidences!" Wald was thoroughly enjoying the unfolding of the links between us. These would not have been uncommon between English barristers or, no doubt, between American lawyers but were unusual across the Atlantic. "John Beachey is instructing me for the Bank of America!" He started to climb out of the pool, saying my name and shaking his head as though he made an astonishing discovery.

"Michael Sherrard! I can't believe this," he said and continued, "I'm going to phone him about this right now before I forget the details."

Twenty minutes later, he was back. He had interrupted a 'not-to-be-interrupted' call that was going on when his call came through. In a further stretching of the list of coincidences, John Beachey had been on the telephone to Mel Wald's secretary, trying – unsuccessfully as she did not know where her boss was – to get hold of him to tell him that an offer had been made to settle the Bank of America case and he was needed urgently in London. Urgent meant as soon as he could book a flight so there was time for him to invite us to have lunch with him, which we accepted. He brought Shirley a beautiful bunch of – ah – lilies ...

***

These are holiday high spots. Generally, I was not good at holidays. There was never enough time to take them and when I arrived, I would either fall ill or hurt myself. Shirley began to think that I did it deliberately.

In the early days of our marriage, we went to Italy with an old friend, Freddy. We drove to a modest hotel in San Remo on the Italian Riviera. In accordance with my practice, I selected one of the many bugs that sought me out as a good host for infection. I developed a high fever and could not bear any light. Shirley and Freddy were so worried about me, they decided to call an emergency doctor. The hotel staff found someone who could and would make a house call. Freddy waited on the steps for the doctor. The candidate arrived. An enormous, Pavarotti-like character, improbably perched on a tiny motor scooter. Freddy brought him to the room where I lay shivering with fever and wearing dark glasses. The doctor stood in the doorway, transfixed by the dark glasses, His opening speech was, "Ist er ein schauspieler[1]?" That was the nearest we came to a diagnosis. He touched my forehead briefly, took a handful of something like aspirin out of his pocket and stamped out of the building, muttering in disgust. The aspirin brought the fever down but I spent the remaining few days of the holiday in bed, recovering from whatever had made me ill. Freddy and Shirley drove the car back from Italy through France as I lay sleeping on the back seat. When we reached Le Touquet, they decided to put me out into the sun for a couple of hours so that my mother would not be too shocked at my near-death pallor. But I tripped on the edge of the chair and twisted my knee. I was not quite home on crutches but I had a pretty impressive limp. And I remained as pale as could be.

And so it was with most of my holidays: I seemed to need to be at work to keep up my resistance to infection or to avoid accidents.

In Cornwall, I managed to survive drowning by water polo. The recovery period was rather an intrusion into the holiday. I needed more attention than our children and Shirley was under a lot of pressure. Pamela Thompson, a neighbour in the village where we had rented a holiday cottage came to see if she could help. She offered to take care of the boys so Shirley could look after me. She would not let us be grateful. As far as she was concerned, she was doing something she wanted to do. We have stayed the best of friends with her over the years. She was, and is, such fun and is now sprightly as ever, in her nineties.

Mrs Thompson introduced us to Colin Gill, a jolly priest, not unlike Friar Tuck in build. His church was St Magnus Martyr in the City of London. He observed events and memorised information. He was a friend of John Betjeman at Magdalen College, Oxford.

We were having dinner with him at a Cypriot restaurant run by an Irish woman and her husband in Percy Street, London. As Colin devoured what appeared to be a whole duck, he talked about Betjeman. When there was nothing left but the bones, he wiped his hands dry, then took his wallet from his pocket. I was preparing to argue that there was no question of him footing the bill when he unfolded a piece of paper that certainly was not money.

---

[1]   An actor.

"This is what John tacked on my door when we were at college," he said. He read it out.

"Guggery guggery nunc,
Your room is infested with junk.
Plush and maroonery,
Too much buffoonery,
Please pack it all up in a trunk."

If this, as Colin Gill said, is an original work of John Betjeman's, remember that you read it here first.

CHAPTER 55

CARRIAN

The story of the Carrian Group's spectacular rise and fall is a story of corruption and bribery permeating banking, business and legal circles. Hong Kong's Independent Commission against Corruption ("ICAC") has some interesting statistics on Carrian[1]:

Longest case	17 years
Longest bail period	13 years
Highest bail amount	HK$50 million in cash and HK$2 million in sureties
Highest prosecution costs	HK$210 million
Longest extradition process	7 years
Greatest number of investigators commended	10 persons
Problem loans involved	HK$6.6 billion
Exhibit documents	4 million pages
Witnesses interviewed	450 persons
Investigators involved	44 persons
Investigating hours logged	102,292 hours
Countries visited for investigation purpose	Malaysia, Singapore, UK, France, USA, Switzerland, Australia, Germany

The Chairman of the Carrian Group was George Tan. He came to Hong Kong in 1972 to work on an engineering project. At that time, he was 37 years of age. By 1978, he was very well established and had set up over 200 companies to engage in a variety of businesses throughout the Far East, Australia, New Zealand and the USA under the umbrella of Carrian Holdings Ltd. The businesses flourished at what would later be described as an alarming rate. The holding company was listed on the Hong Kong Stock Exchange and, as its property dealings increased, so did its share prices.

1   www.icac.org.hk .

By November 1980, Carrian Group shares peaked at HK$17.90 after declaring massive profits on two high-profile property deals for which George Tan announced that no bank loan had been sought. Within two years, the property market was in decline and Carrian had cash flow problems. The share price fell. Banks, hitherto queuing to lend money, now applied for Carrian to be put into liquidation but it remained in business until January 1983 when the Stock Exchange suspended trading in its shares. The Bank Bumiputra of Malaysia had ploughed millions of dollars into Carrian, most of which had disappeared into a black hole of debt.

Carrian's activities had, in the meantime, caused not a little interest at Hong Kong Government level which had instigated an ICAC enquiry resulting in George Tan being arrested several times over the coming years and charged with a series of offences relating to conspiracy to defraud and bribery. The first arrest was in 1983, after which Carrian was liquidated in the biggest corporate collapse to date in Hong Kong. These charges were dropped because of legal complications but more charges followed. At the end of December 1985, a further 43 charges of conspiracy to defraud and bribery were brought, involving HK$5 billion; George Tan was remanded in custody.

George Tan was a tycoon, even by Hong Kong standards. Although he was known to be a shy man who avoided personal publicity where possible, the press enjoyed reporting that he was a big spender who worked in luxurious offices, drove expensive cars and had a fine house. When the Group was functioning – before the troubles – bank managers were vying to do business with him. They wanted to lend him money to increase Carrian's buying power even more. George seemed to have the Midas touch in business. Because he was doing so well, there was competition to be in the magic circle. When Carrian began to experience difficulties, the bank managers came to pay him another visit, trying to lend him money to finance the way out of trouble. But Carrian was too far down the route to insolvency.

I was brought in to lead for George Tan early in 1986. My role was to deal with committal proceedings in the local magistrates' court in Hollywood Road. Someone with a sense of humour had named the court the "Old Bailey" many years before and the name had stuck. I met George Tan in the cells.

"I was been told I can get bail," was his precursor to telling me what he wanted.

"Was you been told?" I repeated.

"I was," he assured me. I could see that there might be some communication difficulties. I did not realise that we would have professional dealings over many months, during which we would come to understand better the niceties of each other's turn of phrase.

It would be quite a knack to get him out of custody. It was thought that it would take $50 million if bail were to be granted at all.

The prosecutor opposing bail was an aggressive New Zealander by the name of Warwick Reid. He had made a name for himself and become what he would call 'big' in the Department of Criminal Justice.

I asked him to agree bail.

He laughed at me. "No way. Your man will be out of Hong Kong like a flash."

"I don't think so," I persevered. It was well known, and I knew that George Tan was hugely superstitious. He had been told by a seer forecasting the future and comforting those in trouble that he would not survive if he ever left Hong Kong. And he never did. He had the resources to get on the plane and go but he was terrified of leaving under any pretext whatsoever. I would learn that his wife begged him to leave. It would have been so easy: a motorboat from Aberdeen harbour and a drive to South East China or Taiwan where a man could easily disappear and live out his days without being persecuted by the authorities.

"Well, I've information to the contrary," Reid said. And that was the end of negotiations between us. We both attended the court where the defendant was in the dock. Reid spoke first.

"I'm here to oppose bail," he said angrily. It sounded like "bile", which suited the expression on his face rather better. He was justified in his own mind in thinking that George Tan would go over the top. He went on, "There'd be no assurances that he wouldn't leave the Colony. History shows that people who've been given bail when the stakes are so high, have absconded."

The magistrate must have been aware of the almost overwhelming press interest in the case and did not appear to be swayed by the prejudicial publicity generated so far. He said, "This is not proper." He appeared to be minded to accept my application.

Reid was annoyed that his advocacy had not had the required immediate effect. He leaned with his left elbow on the lectern and stabbed the forefinger of his right hand towards the magistrate.

"Won't you people ever learn?" he thundered. "I can give you names of five people in Taiwan" – he reeled off a list of names – "to whom he could run as quick as you like. How can you seriously contemplate bail?"

The magistrate, one of "you people", listened to Reid's speech. He said, "I can't make a decision based on mere conjecture prefaced by "Won't you ever learn.""

Reid looked as though he was ready to explode. He was going to look like that and worse as the day went on.

"That's why I say, *why won't you people ever learn!*" He was almost shouting. "There's every risk. Here's another one ready to do a runner! I'm going to complain to the Criminal Justice Department about you."

The magistrate said, "I really do not know how to deal with this submission."

My tack was to drop references to the merits of permitting my client to retain his freedom and respond to Reid's style.

"Sir, it is absolutely disgraceful that you have been treated with contempt by Mr Reid. "*Won't you ever learn?*" How dare he! How dare he! It is a disgrace that he should seek to intimidate you. It is unprofessional and arrogant. What you have been subjected to is a gross contempt of court. The respect to which the judiciary is entitled has been flouted by the prosecution. You have done nothing for which a complaint can be made."

The magistrate knew how to deal with that submission. He set bail at HK$50,000, the equivalent then of US$5,000.

I thought that Reid would die. He spluttered and coughed until he managed to catch enough breath to say, "That will be appealed." It sounded like "appalled." "Today," he added vehemently.

I told him that I had got it the first time.

Later that day, Reid managed to get us before a red judge: Judge Gerald de Basto. I was in a real jam. I knew bail should be $5 million at the very least and 10 times that was the more realistic figure. On the other hand, the judge would have been concerned that a man of important social status should not be kept behind bars for the duration even if the prosecution case was clearly articulated. Because the magistrate had granted bail, the judge was more likely to uphold bail in principle but would have been struggling to fix a more appropriate sum but one that George Tan could raise so that he would not appeal on principle.

I supported his line of reasoning entirely but, in the end, it was HK$50 million. Of course, the opposition was "very satisfied." The figure was too much for any surety to risk, given the prosecution's view of the likelihood of Mr Tan absconding.

I asked the judge, "Will you give us a little time?"

The judge replied, "I think you will need a lot of time."

"Well, until 4.00 o'clock?" I asked.

The judge looked at me as though I had taken leave of my senses. "Do you really want me to stay?" he asked. He had come down in favour of a figure that he believed was beyond reach.

During the lunch break, whilst on $50,000 bail, George Tan introduced me, without a trace of irony or a hint of explanation, to his very rich lady friend, coincidentally named Carrie Ann. George assured us that she would sign a bail bond. Given the amount of money involved, I was concerned that, even if she would sign the bond, she would not be able show that she had the assets to meet it. Soon after our meeting, I returned to the court, leaving George and Carrie Ann to deal with the paperwork.

At 3.45 we were called and the judge came back. At that time, I thought I was throwing in my hand. But George's friend appeared at the back of the court, modestly dressed, with no overt sign of the degree of wealth that would be needed to fulfil the very large financial commitment. With some trepidation, as I did not know to what extent she would be able to help, I said, "The surety is here. Is the bond ready to be signed?"

The surety piped up, "I can manage it," when asked if she could guarantee the unimaginably huge sum.

He got bail and remained free for the next thirteen years.

I do not know who was more surprised that George had managed to obtain a surety for such a vast amount of money, the prosecutor or I. I do remember that I remained impassive while Reid looked as though his shirt had shrunk two sizes, leaving his head and neck boiling with rage above his rather grubby, strangling collar.

Reid was to have a story of his own. A couple of years later, he was convicted of massive corruption involving appeals[1] and, on the same principles that applied in the Pertamina case, had to account to the Hong Kong Government for his ill-gotten gains.

***

It was difficult to stay away from home for the ten consecutive months that were needed for the committal stage of George Tan's case, even in the splendid luxury of the Mandarin Hotel. There is something quite artificial about living in an hotel. Fortunately, George's property interests seemed to have survived the company difficulties. He arranged for me to be given the use of a beautiful penthouse in one of the tallest apartment blocks in Hong Kong. It overlooked the Happy Valley racetrack on one side and the football and athletics grounds on the other. We had a marvellous view of the aircraft flying in to land on the route that took them in a direct line down the High Street. George invited me to use the apartment after I had been staying at the Mandarin for about six weeks with my son, Nick, who was helping me as a forensic accountant.

---

[1] *Attorney-General for Hong Kong v Reid* [1994] 1 AC 324. The corrupt monies received by Reid had to be repaid to the Hong Kong Government: as soon as a bribe or secret commission is received, the fiduciary holds the money on constructive trust. I.e. Reid was effectively holding his ill-gotten gains on behalf of the State in whose official capacity he had been acting. Lord Templeman said, 'Bribery is an evil practice which threatens the foundations of any civilised society'.

As soon as I saw it, I told Shirley that she should come out sooner than we had planned and indeed she did so. Money was no object in furnishing the apartment: George seemed to have retained extensive personal resources. I chose wonderful antique furniture including the most beautiful blackwood cupboard, graceful in design and a work of art in its own right. The apartment came complete with a car and driver at Shirley's disposal all the time. I could watch the racing from my study. We could place bets instead of playing bridge.

The day that we moved in, two men came over from the Mandarin bringing two huge hampers of food. The manager had sent them with the message that he knew from experience that I would not have remembered to bring in any provisions. Reading between the lines, I suspect that he thought I would have been hotel-institutionalised after six weeks and would have expected food to have appeared by magic. His note said, "Here's enough to keep you going." It was enough food to feed a small family for a week or more!

It would have been just like playing house if Shirley could have made the state-of-the-art German cooker work but the manual was in Chinese and it was few days before someone could unscramble the instructions which had been through German to Chinese and now needed to come into English. There was another slight domestic difficulty that Shirley managed to overcome: the apartment came complete with a Filipina servant who was only able to express herself in the body language of terror, who spoke no English and was impervious to any form of sign or gesture that might have replaced words. She seemed to hold the office of housekeeping staff. I believe that the problem was overcome by leaving her to keep the apartment tidy without being seen by us.

On the social front, we were given provincial membership of the Jockey Club. Although this was an honour, it was a perk we did not need: we were always being invited as guests. This meant that there was always something going on at weekends. However, there was no real break for a holiday during those ten months. Bank Holidays are not extended as they are in England. The courts close only for the actual Bank Holidays and weekends, even over Christmas. We could not go back to England for the four days of a Christmas that extended into a weekend – or for the two actual days of the holiday so, when I was working in the East through the winter, we would go to Penang or Singapore for a short break. Only once in the years that I was working in the East did we manage to get a whole ten days off over Christmas. The manager of our hotel at the time asked me if I would accept, as a gift, ten days in any suite of my choice in the hotel. Shirley and I agreed without too much discussion that we would accept the very kind gesture.

In another very long trial, the hotel management moved us every month to another suite. Each one seemed more luxurious than the last. The move was carried out by the hotel staff. One morning we would be in one suite, that evening in another and we would not have had to move a single item ourselves. Once, when we went to Macao for the day, we came back to another suite on a different floor as a complete surprise: we had not been told in advance.

There is no such thing as an easy case and the work I did abroad was often made harder by having to overcome initial jet-lag or being in strange surroundings. But something about being in an hotel or, as during the Carrian committal, a luxury apartment, gave the work something of a holiday air.

Comfortably settled in the penthouse, there was something almost unreal about going off to work every day. But work it was. The committal proceedings started and crawled on and on. The prosecutor, Harry Ognall QC (later Mr Justice Ognall) had been brought out from England. Eventually, as the case dragged on, he made only guest appearances, leaving the day-to-day drudgery to his weary juniors, of whom he had several. Sometimes a junior would tell me, "Ognall's coming this afternoon." I would ask, "How long is he staying?" Invariably the answer would be: "Leaving tomorrow." I would announce immediately before the court rose for lunch, "I am advised that we will be having a guest appearance from Mr Ognall this afternoon."

There were several leaders from London. We became an expat club, lunching and dining together. Yes, it was more like a holiday than work. For others, it became something like a permanent job as the case went on for twelve years or more after my part had finished.

The trial judge was Dennis Barker, a man whose potential career as a concert pianist was put aside in favour of the Bar and who had made his way up to the Court of Appeal in Hong Kong where he had granted my appeal in the Pachimsawat case. He was brought back to the lower court as the authorities thought – rightly – that a wealth of experience was needed for such a complex matter. But that did not take account of his alcohol habit, the hangovers, the days off with injuries after he had fallen flat on his face, the terrible and frequent loss of dignity. He made such a mess of things. And apart from the acquittals that should not have happened, there were suicides and even a murder: one of the witnesses, an accountant, was killed in the Regent Hotel in Kowloon, strangled by the cord of his bathrobe. The parts of his dismembered body were eventually found in a banana plantation, to the great interest of the press, the particular fascination being with the hotel porter who had lugged the suitcases containing the body parts to the taxi. "Bloody heavy cases and I didn't even get a tip!"

The very strong opinion, always uttered in my presence: "George Tan murdered him." I was sure he hadn't.

I was in George Tan's case for about three years then passed him on to other counsel who were more locally based and could deal with the day-to-day running of what seemed to be endless hearings and applications. By the end of the total thirteen-year run, Anthony Scrivener QC was leading George's defence. After a final plea of guilty, George was sentenced in September 1996 to three years in prison. The first time he heard the clang of the prison gates was in March 1996 when his bail was revoked.

***

HANSARD Debate 20 July 1994

FOREIGN AND COMMONWEALTH AFFAIRS

Hong Kong

Mr. Cohen : To ask the Secretary of State for Foreign and Commonwealth Affairs, pursuant to his answer of 14 June, Official Report columns 400-1, which other officials of the Hong Kong Government, including officials of the Law Officers' Department such as Crown prosecuting counsel, visited Malaysia in connection with the affair generally known as Carrian; on what dates; and on how many occasions, and for what purpose in relation to the Carrian investigation Mr. Warwick Reid visited Malaysia.

Mr. Heathcoat-Amory : There are very few, if any, visits to Malaysia by members of the Attorney-General's chambers in connection with the Carrian case. Full details could be obtained only at disproportionate cost.

***

Mr. Cohen : To ask the Secretary of State for Foreign and Commonwealth Affairs what was the name of the Hong Kong official who granted immunity from prosecution to Mr. Ibrahim Jaafar; and what was the relationship between that official and Mr. Warwick Reid.

Column 230

Mr. Heathcoat-Amory : The immunity was granted by the then Director of Public Prosecutions in Hong Kong in consultation with the Hong Kong Attorney-General. The letter offering immunity was signed by Mr. Reid in his capacity as head of the commercial crimes unit of the prosecutions division of the Attorney-General's chambers.

Mr. Cohen : To ask the Secretary of State for Foreign and Commonwealth Affairs, pursuant to his answer of 21 June, Official Report column 99, why Mr. Warwick Reid was dismissed from his post in January 1990 ; whether Mr. Reid was prosecuted; what process of law was used to obtain the return of Mr. Warwick Reid from the Philippines to Hong Kong ; and which Government requested, and which Government executed, that legal process.

Mr. Heathcoat-Amory: Mr. Reid was dismissed from his post in the Attorney-General's chambers when it was discovered that he had breached the conditions of his bail by absconding from Hong Kong. On his return to Hong Kong he was prosecuted, and convicted, for an offence of having in his control pecuniary resources or property disproportionate to his official emoluments contrary to section 10 of the Prevention of Bribery Ordinance. Mr. Reid was deported from the Philippines when he was found to have entered that country on a forged travel document and was repatriated to Hong Kong as his last known place of residence in accordance with procedures in the Philippines.

CHAPTER 56

HOW CAN THE EGGS

Lee Kuan Yew[1] was the Prime Minister of Singapore from the date of independence, 3 June 1959, to 28 November 1990. He continued to exert considerable political influence after handing over power to his son, who in turn ceded the reins of office to another son. Joshua Ben (J B) Jeyaretnam[2] was the first and only opposition member of the Singapore Parliament in the first sixteen years of independence although, in 1984, a second opposition member was elected. The Prime Minister appeared to take a dim view of being opposed and of his opponents: to him, they seemed to be hand in glove with the communists and, which was almost as bad, he considered Jeyaretnam's speeches to be rambling and boring and that, by being elected, he had kept a better candidate out of office. If an opposition had to be tolerated, Lee would have preferred a single dissenting voice and someone more worthy. And preferably remaining in the singular. To have to tolerate two opponents in the otherwise complete cabal of agreement was a ridiculous waste of resources.

In a country where litigation was a major industry, with 2,000 solicitor-advocates in a population of some 4.5 million in the mid-1980s, Lee was actively involved in pursuing cases to maintain his good name as a matter of principle, although he reported giving all the damages he won to charitable causes.

In Singapore, there is only one qualification for the right of advocacy in its courts: everyone is a solicitor and advocate, regulated by the Law Society. A barrister could come out from England and be admitted to the Law Society because he was the client's choice, unlike Hong Kong where special expertise had to be shown.

The first time I was taken out to Singapore, I was to lead David Marshall, a former pupil of Morris Finer. He was the First Minister of Singapore in 1955 but resigned in 1956 after he failed to conclude negotiations to achieve Singapore's independence. He had founded the Worker's Party of Singapore but eventually ceded leadership of the party to J B Jeyaret-

1   Lee Kuan Yew (1923-).
2   Joshua B. Jeyaretnam (1926-2008).

nam, a lawyer who had held the office of Registrar of the Supreme Court before he went into politics. David returned to the Bar where he developed a deserved reputation as a brilliant advocate. He secured acquittals in the sixty capital murder trials in which he defended. Lee Kuan Yew interpreted David's success as an indictment of the jury system which he set about abolishing after he came to power in 1964. David was kept at arm's length by being brought into the diplomatic service, where he served as Singapore's ambassador to France, Portugal and Switzerland, far enough away from home, so as not to annoy the regime.

A feature of Jeyaretman's opposition style was that he would not only make critical statements about the Government but would direct much of the content again Lee Kuan Yew personally. Lee would promptly sue him for libel, usually successfully. It might be uncharitable to press home the point that by then there were no jury trials in Singapore and the appointment of judges was in the gift of the office of the Prime Minister.

As far back as 1976, Jeyaretnam had made allegations of nepotism against the Prime Minister, claiming that he had procured the grant of favours to the family firm of solicitors, Lee and Lee. Lee's wife and brothers were partners and, for reasons which, at the time I started working in Singapore, I had not fully appreciated, they were very keen to get me to take work from them. Soon after I had begun to build a name for myself in Singapore, I was invited to their offices and was greeted by Mrs Lee, the senior partner in active practice. She offered to bring me a cup of tea herself. This was an indication of great honour: the more usual form would have been for her assistant to ask the question and for a yet more junior person to carry out the task. It was a sign of how seriously they wanted me to be encouraged to accept instructions from them.

In the nepotism libel case, Lee Kuan Yew was represented by Bob Alexander QC. John Mortimer QC, doomed to fail, was for Jeyaretnam. John later wrote a scathing attack on Singapore society in the New Statesman. He presented the state of everyday life in the city state as oppressive to the menial workers. He said they were treated like coolies. Amongst other iniquities, he had observed their activities on the "pedang" (Singaporean for "lawns") at the cricket club. It is just across the street from the law courts. While the judges were in the air-conditioned court, the workers spent the day heaving huge lawn-rollers in preparation for the next cricket match, sweating and puffing in the stifling tropical heat. He did not get it quite right but the story was so much better than the truth. It turned out that he was made *persona non grata* shortly after the article was published, a matter of little consequence to him as, by then he had retired from practice at the Bar. It is said that in Singapore there is freedom of speech but no freedom after speech.

Jeyaretnam took his role as the political opposition seriously. He was always at crossed swords with the government. Although that was his job, Lee Kuan Yew did not quite see it that way. In 1984 Jeyaretnam was acquitted of charges relating to his party's accounts but found guilty after the retrial which followed the government's successful appeal against the acquittal. He was sentenced to three months' imprisonment, commuted to one month, fined and, as a consequence of his conviction, disbarred[1].

As if things were not bad enough for him, events took yet another serious turn in 1986. I was in Singapore, prosecuting a complex fraud, when Jeyaretnam was prosecuted for breach of parliamentary privilege on two counts. One charge was on the grounds that he had made an unsubstantiated allegation in Parliament concerning the wrongful arrest of a member of the public, and the other for allegedly failing to declare his pecuniary interest in a matter raised by him in Parliament. A Select Committee was appointed to deal with the matter. The Prime Minister returned to his legal roots as a trained barrister and personally undertook the game of chess that was the prosecution case. His junior, Glenn Knight, was given the title "the Black Knight" by Leo Price QC, another regular working visitor to the Far East. Lee's mission was to prevent anyone accusing him of corruption from achieving credence. Jeyaretnam was fair game: he was to be annihilated as a parliamentary opponent, as a threat to the Prime Minister's unassailable reputation and even as a lawyer.

It was Knight's task to be the principal mouthpiece, to carry out the cross-examination. But he made the mistake of trying to hoodwink Lee during the case. He was frequently absent from the hearing. Although he

---

[1] The Privy Council found in 1986 that J B Jeyaretnam had "suffered grievous injustice ... having been fined, imprisoned and publicly disgraced for offences of which [he is] not guilty ... [and] deprived of his seat in Parliament and disqualified for a year from practising his profession..."

340

gave the excuse that he was suffering from a series of virulent colds, he was not on a sickbed but abroad, running his private luxury hotel business in Batan, off the coast of Indonesia. He managed to give the impression of being available in all but his presence, thereby justifying his fees, by having all calls transferred to his telephone abroad. The actual reason for his absence was discovered and led to his eventual prosecution and conviction for perjury. He sent messages asking me to write a reference for his plea in mitigation. I was able to say that he had behaved properly in the cases which I knew about, had not given or asked for favours within the profession and, as far as I could detect, had prosecuted fairly. I said that his absence from the Bar would be a great loss. I finished by saying that anyone who had been Mr Lee's barrister scarcely needed a reference and that I would be prepared to attend court to say so. The sentence of one day's imprisonment resulted in his career in Singapore coming to an abrupt end.

Lee Kuan Yew decided that the public could best be educated as to the fairness of the political system, with the added bonus of being seen by his loyal subjects, by having the proceedings of the Committee televised. And so it was, relentlessly, day after day. Although I was very much occupied with my own work, I recorded it and was able to watch it after my days in court. It was like watching David standing up to Goliath, seeing Jeyaretnam defend himself. I saw him being crushed. Although he bore himself with dignity throughout his ordeal by trial, his difficulties were compounded by the fact that Eddie Barker, the Chairman of Committee of Privileges, was Lee Kuan Yew's brother-in-law and a former partner in the Lee firm. Eddie was a thoroughly jolly, imperturbable character and, on the occasions that I was invited to his home, an excellent host. But he was in the thrall of the Prime Minister.

Jeyaretnam struggled on. It was painful, seeing him under pressure which was obviously intolerable to him. Things looked as though they might become brighter for him at one point when he urged the Prosecution to call the Attorney-General: it looked as though new evidence would come to light. However, he could not find the words to explain to the satisfaction of the Chairman why he was needed. Lee was magnanimous. He assured the Chairman that justice had to be seen to be done. "Let him question the Attorney-General, if that is what he wants."

But when his moment of glory came, instead of making the Attorney-General squirm under the fire of questions, Jeyaretnam became tongue-tied. This happened again and again. Just as you thought he was about to ask a question, there might be a gasp or a strangling sound. Nothing more. Lee Kuan Yew would lean against the bench, smiling. After a suitable length of silence and paper-shuffling, he would ask, "No questions, Mr Jeyaretnam?"

The Chairman would take his cue. "Come on. You must have questions!"

No doubt he did. But he couldn't get the words out, poor chap.

Lee Kuan Yew fed more generosity to the Chair. "We should not pressurise him. He's representing himself. This is Singapore. We have a fair process. We should adjourn until 2.00 p.m." And the Chair echoed, " … adjourn until 2.00 p.m."

After the adjournment, the Attorney-General resumed his place at the witness table and spent a few moments examining his perfectly manicured hands. Jeyaretnam at last found his voice. "We were good friends when we were at University?" he asked. His tone was pleading.

"I knew you," was the curt response.

"Very well, I think," Jeyaretnam countered, the note of pleading increasing.

"I knew you. What is it you want me to say?" The tone was icy.

"We were very close," Jeyaretnam wheedled.

"I do not know what you mean by 'close'." The Attorney-General looked pointedly at his watch.

"You were my best man in London!" Jeyaretnam put down his trump card.

It was now time for the immaculate cuffs to be straightened. The Attorney-General said, "Yes. I knew you." The unsaid words, "but I had rather not" hovered in the air as Jeyaretnam could think of nothing else to ask, to make the point that he had not got round to.

And then there was the Chief Justice who attended on subpoena to face a silent Jeyaretnam.

In the absence of any questions, Eddie Barker said: "This is disgraceful. You can't go on like this. You have summoned the highest judicial officer for what? To look at him?"

Lee Kuan Yew rose to his feet. Addressing the wider audience, exuding calm and bonhomie he said, "Mr Jeyaretnam is nervous. It's understandable. Let him take time to consider coolly what questions he wants to ask and whether he wants to ask them."

The case adjourned for the day but no questions were forthcoming when the hearing resumed. Jeyaretnam's tongue remained tied.

The Committee fined him $1,000 on each of the two matters. And another $1,000 for making comments in Parliament during the proceedings. And in the matter of five letters which he had sent to his constituents on the conduct of the hearing, complaining that the Executive had interfered with the Subordinate Court judiciary, each letter resulted in a $5,000 fine. It was Parliament's view that they presented a distorted report of the proceedings. Of course, the Government was not happy about anything but a correct account of the way it went about its business, which was how it came about that Jeyaretnam was fined a further $10,000 for publishing another distorted report in his Party's newspaper, about the last sitting of the Committee in December 1986.

I said to the taxi-driver on the way back to the hotel from court, "Have you been listening to the best of Jeyaretnam?" He said that he had. There was no need to specify the trial: the whole of Singapore watched it at home, in cafes, in shop windows: wherever there was a screen, people kept up to date with it. Everyone was an expert. "What do you think?" I asked the driver.

"I'm surprised that the Prime Minister can do this," he answered. "Is that called fairness?" It was a good question and, in the suspicious atmosphere of the time, brave of him to ask. He sighed and shrugged as I pondered a safe answer to give him.

"I am Chinese," he went on. "In my country we have a saying." He recited some words in his local dialect then translated them into English. "How can the eggs against the stone?"

For J B Jeyaretnam, the eggs did indeed meet the stone. He was crushed; he lost his parliamentary seat. In his mitigation, his bravado came across as arrogance yet fear permeated his words.

***

Some years later, I went to Macao for a short visit. I had been told there was a beautiful chapel in a cavern on the rocky hill above the beach. For quite some time, I wandered around the twisting, turning ways but I could not find it. After a while, I realised that there would not be enough time to conduct the search on my own. Hot and bothered, I decided to take a taxi. En route, we came to the luxury hotel which been converted from an ancient monk's retreat and whose grounds contained the chapel. I decided to break the journey by going in for a well-earned cold drink after my long walk. As I went past the swimming pool, a man on a sun lounger called me over.

"Long time since I've seen you, Mr Sherrard," he said. It was J B Jeyaretnam. It took me a moment to recognize him.

"Not so long since I've seen you," I said. "I thought you were badly treated." I was talking about the televised trial but, as he was always badly treated, it could have been about any one of his collisions with the Lee regime.

"Oh, I'll be back," he said cheerfully. Then, "Do you know my son?" A young man stood up and came over to shake hands.

"He had the highest marks in the law final," his father told me proudly.

I hoped that his name would not stand in the way of a successful career in Singapore.

CHAPTER 57

HEYSEL

In May 1985, Shirley and Michael went to Italy to celebrate their thirty-third wedding anniversary.

On 30 May we were in Venice having coffee on the Giudecca. It was the morning after the European Cup Final, an event of which we were dimly aware. We have never been football fans and football could not have been further from our thoughts that day. We were enjoying watching the world go by and marvelling at being able to spend some time simply relaxing. We were sitting near an American couple. The man was reading an English newspaper. Shirley made out the headline, "Heysel Final Football Disaster." I asked the American if he would mind letting us have a look at the paper as it was clear that something awful had happened.

He handed it over and we read about the previous day's events. We learned that English fans, Liverpool supporters, had chased the Italian supporters of the opposing team, Juventus, with such ferocity that, in the surge of people trying to escape the violence, a retaining wall of the stadium collapsed, killing the people within. We thought how terrible it was that English supporters should have behaved in that way. According to the reports, the police found that some had been carrying flags wrapped around sturdy bamboo poles, others had done the same with iron bars. They went along the roads chanting and provoking the Italian supporters, chasing after them, threatening and attacking them. The words "Going equipped" came to mind.

We were shocked and ashamed by what we read. We felt that we had to apologise to the Americans, in case they thought that the English fans' behaviour was in any way representative of our country. The Americans were charming and after a short time of chatting and moving on to the splendours of Venice and a discussion about their interesting trip, our minds went away from what happened at Heysel. After a time, we left to continue our own journey. We were going by train from Venice to Garda later that day and our arrangements needed to be completed.

We went back to the hotel to find the normally charming, helpful staff had become surly and had developed serious difficulties with English overnight. We managed to find the departure time of our train by translating our own way through the railway timetable as the concierge was unable to help us. He also forgot to send someone up for our luggage, nor could he find anyone to help us get a taxi. We sorted ourselves out and eventually reached the station where our smattering of Italian was not enough to find out which platform we needed. Finally, we were able to find a porter who spoke some English. He pointed to the platform where the train was standing but hurried off when I asked him to take our luggage.

Between the two of us, we hoisted the cases on board the train which almost immediately started to move off. Through the open window of the access door, we could hear laughter and shouting. We could see a group of people with their arms pointing at the train shouting in Italian, which we could not understand, and English, which we could.

"English thugs! Killing our boys! English thugs!"

Some were laughing because the porter had put us on the wrong train. It was an hour before the first stop en route to Trieste and over an hour before we could turn back. There was a similar degree of help at the station at Jesolo but this time we were aware of what was going on. This was the first of the days in which Italy was a no-go area for British tourists, no matter how removed from the savagery that characterised the Heysel disaster. We had no choice as we were simply there. It did not occur to either of us that I would be part of the case that followed.

We returned to London after another couple of days. With dismay, we had followed more detailed reports of what had happened.

There was a message for me from Helen Garlick in the DPP's chambers. I called her back and she asked if she could come to see me urgently. We arranged a meeting later that day. When she arrived, she launched straight into, "Do you know about the Heysel Stadium affair?"

"Strangely enough, I do," I said. I told her how Shirley and I heard about it in Venice and how we had followed it through as more details were published.

She came straight to the point.

"The Belgian Government proposes to seek the extradition of the main English suspects." I knew that the DPP would act for a foreign government in extradition proceedings. She went on, "The DPP is acting for the Belgian Government. Who would you like to lead?"

I guessed that, with the large number of potential defendants, I would need two juniors. I asked for Robert Rhodes[1], who had recently joined chambers, and Daniel Janner[2], another very bright junior. He was to be involved in much of the basic preparation. I was concerned about whether it would be good for him to be locked into the committal proceedings for two or three months. It was something that he was delighted to do and, in the end, it did him no harm.

The whole awful thing had been recorded. For much of November 1985, we watched the videos over and over. Once we had identified somebody charging along with an iron bar, we were able to find out from the Liverpool police who it was. We spent hours and hours and hours running the video and rewinding it, pin-pointing someone at the scene who was actually or potentially misbehaving. By the time the DPP's office had delivered my formal instructions, the video had imprinted itself on my mind. It was the stuff of nightmares but it had enabled us to identify who was to be arrested. There were more than a dozen defendants. The Belgian Government sought their extradition.

There were some legal complexities. I was asked to advise in relation to a proposed charge of conspiracy. I took the view that if someone is caught with an iron bar inside a hollowed out bamboo pole or wrapped in a flag and there are other people with iron bars behaving in the same way, there was probably enough material to charge conspiracy. However, they could not be extradited for conspiracy because it was not extraditable. Any conspiracy must have been hatched in England – before they went to Belgium. It would therefore have been an English offence, making a viable case for arrest and trial in England. The alternative was to use the video material and, no doubt, the evidence of witnesses at the event to support charges in Belgium where they had committed the substantive offences. The latter course was to be adopted.

Throughout the next year, we continued to prepare the case for extradition. In Belgium, in parallel proceedings, a lady magistrate was appointed to liaise with me and whoever else she thought appropriate. We

[1] Robert Rhodes, QC 1989.
[2] Daniel Janner, QC 2002.

travelled to Brussels several times for consultations. On one of the journeys, in those pre-Eurostar days, we ran out of time to get from the court to the airport for the return journey. Someone made our problem known to the police who were remarkably helpful, escorting us along the motorway on the wrong side of the road, sirens blaring, lights flashing, all the way to the airport. We arrived with five minutes to spare. They drove us straight onto the airfield, to the steps of the aircraft, no formalities.

Apart from legal technicalities, there was the logistical difficulty that the hearing could only take place in a spacious courtroom because of the large number of people involved. It was quite a problem getting a court to try it. There were a huge number of witnesses. Finally, Highbury Magistrates Court was selected for the extradition hearing in early February 1987.

My diary at that time was tight, to say the least. I was involved with another major case in London, representing Gerald Ronson in the DTI inspection of the Guinness transaction. On 2 February 1987 I went to see the Guinness inspectors at 10.00 a.m. before going to a Heysel consultation at 2.00 p.m. Later that afternoon, I was back at another Guinness meeting. The next day, I opened the Heysel case to David Hopkin, the Metropolitan Stipendiary Magistrate, and for the remainder of the month, I was at Highbury.

The defendants were represented mainly by local barristers instructed by Liverpool solicitors. Anna Worrell QC and David Harris, later in silk and now a senior circuit judge, were strictly professional as were most of the other members of the defence team. Unfortunately, there were several other barristers who, from time to time, appeared not far distant in vocal style and volume from those whom they represented: a sort of legal version of a football mob with much of the same disregard for normal social rules, let alone standards of advocacy. They barracked and interrupted and raised every conceivable objection, sometimes singly and sometimes, with more noisy effect, in groups. After a short time, David Hopkin got their measure. He was not standing for any nonsense, no matter from the advocates. But he did not see or hear one of them on the first day, swaggering in at the head of a group, playing to the audience from Liverpool and saying with a nod towards me and my juniors, "There you are. I told you. They've brought in the Jews. Three of them... "

I tried personally at one stage of the case to let one of the defendants out. A young man who was planning to become a Catholic priest was with the Liverpool people when the police started making arrests. He had been pulled in. "You're with them. Now you're coming with us," was what the police said to him. He could easily have been trying to help rather than being involved in the mayhem. I had taken the view that this chap was the only one on the merits who should not be extradited but David Hopkin had pronounced the view: "That will come out in the wash."

The application for extradition was successful. The defendants were committed to prison, awaiting deportation. They appealed to the Divisional Court, consisting of Lord Justice "Tasker" Watkins[1]. and Lord Justice Mann. Benet Hytner QC was representing the defendant who did not seem to fit the pattern of the others.

In the wash at the Divisional Court, when I was replying to the defendants' submissions, Tasker asked, "Why were you taking the view that this particular defendant was to be considered separately?"

I explained, "Because we were relying on amateur films, his participation may easily have been misunderstood. It may have been that he was running to give assistance to injured people, to help them out." But the point was equivocal and I did not press it. I believe that, in the end, he was acquitted.

As things stood, the Divisional Court overturned the magistrate's decision. Tasker pronounced, in his strong Welsh accent, that there would be no extradition. During the course of his brief reasons, he said words to the effect that he was sick and tired of extradition cases being poorly prepared. I did not need prompting on meticulous preparation, as my juniors had learned at the start. The criticism was wholly unjustified. In any event, the Divisional Court's ruling was flawed.

I went straight to the Attorney-General. I said, "We've got a political hot potato here." This was a matter which had to go to the House of Lords for resolution. The defendants, in the meantime, were on bail granted by the Divisional Court.

---

[1]   Sir Tasker Watkins (1918-2007), VC, GBE, DL, LLD

In the House of Lords, Lord Bridge explained Tasker's criticism. "Lord Justice Watkins with his usual frankness has clarified that his Lordship had been thinking of a different set of circumstances." This was, effectively, a public withdrawal of the Divisional Court's criticism.

Our appeal was allowed. They were extradited. Some were acquitted. One defendant committed suicide.

***

There is an iconic photograph that illustrates the havoc of that dreadful day: the picture of the thousands of odd shoes left by the fleeing survivors, among the debris, streaks of colour illuminating stark tragedy.

***

POST-SCRIPT

The battleground was in an area designated by the Belgian organizers as neutral territory.

There has never been an official enquiry into the causes of the disaster.

Despite the havoc, the match between Liverpool and Juventus was played after a delayed start. Juventus won 1-0.

CHAPTER 58

HIGH SPEED TRAVEL

On 15 April 1986, the United States bombed two major cities in Libya as a warning against Libya's alleged involvement in the support for international terrorism.

I was working in Singapore for most of March and April, heavily involved with the Pertamina case. Its international ramifications meant that, before coming back to London, I had to go to Sydney and New York with a short stop-over in Singapore on the way. As I was to be in New York for a few days, Shirley and I planned to meet and have a short holiday. However, the trip came up within a couple of weeks of the American bombing raids on Libya. Public concern had not yet abated about the risks of terrorist attacks on aircraft and there were particular concerns stirred up in the press about travel between the United States and Europe.

As I was on my flight from Singapore to meet Shirley in New York, she was preparing to leave from Heathrow. Unfortunately, as she was the only passenger brave enough to make the journey, her flight was cancelled but that had not stopped the airline processing her luggage: she was in London and her bags were locked into a system from which they could only be retrieved in New York. She was committed to coming, albeit the next day. I made good use of her late arrival: for once, I could admit to jet-lag and was able to sleep through the unplanned separation.

As was often the way with the demands of my practice, the trip to New York combined holiday and work. I had been instructed in a matter involving the loss of gold bullion: ingots had been disappearing at a prodigious rate from a local manufacturing jeweller whose insurers were based in London. This would be a good chance to visit the locus in quo.

Shirley and I were taken over the workshop. We were greeted by the remarkable sight of twenty or so orthodox Jews, sitting in a walk-in safe, wearing full Hasidic regalia including tsitsis and talesim, ready for the prayer-break that was about to take place. Their eyes were firmly averted from the sight of the female visitor. The place was an Aladdin's cave, filled with gold of every description and at every stage of being manufactured into jewellery: gold blocks, liquid gold, sheet gold, shimmering in the slightest movement of air. It was almost a shock to the system for

Shirley to be given a great sheet of gold to handle – an extraordinary sensation. She did not want to give it back! Not that there was much chance of keeping it: all entrants were searched on entry and departure, although that had not stopped the losses. Even so, it would have been a pity for Shirley to have been 'collared' for someone else's criminal activity.

We left, gold-free, and carried on with our shortened holiday. On our last day, we were shopping in Fifth Avenue and saw an improvised notice in the British Airways shop. It read, "Free flights to the UK" and appeared to be BA's response to the demands of English hoteliers who were making one hell of a fuss about the lack of American tourists. The free flights were to encourage travelers to be bolder about air travel. It is a curious thing but people are often prepared to take what they perceive to be risks if the opportunity offered is free or inexpensive.

I said, "Why don't we see whether Concorde is flying? It would give us an extra half-day here. We could make up some of our lost day."

Shirley considered this for a moment then said, "All right, we'll do it!" We went into the shop and saw a girl at an improvised reception desk. Her name tag identified her as Mary Lamb. While she was taking a phone call, Shirley said, "It would be nice if she married Larry Lamb." Larry Lamb was a well-known actor.

After Mary greeted us, Shirley could not let go of the name connection.

"You're not married to Larry Lamb, are you?" she asked. We waited to have the joke recognized but Mary answered, deadpan, "Not after today. Our divorce comes through this afternoon."

This was not at all the answer that we had expected. If a joke falls flat, you just let it go. I explained that we wanted to be part of BA's offer.

"We want to go back for free but we've already got first class tickets. So we wondered, is Concorde flying?" We knew that it should be but did not know if it would be subject to the sort of timetable changes that Shirley had suffered.

"Oh no," Mary said. "That simply cannot be done." We accepted her decision gracefully and went on our way, leaving our contact details for her to confirm our booked flight.

At 3.30 p.m. we arrived back at the hotel to find a message from Mary Lamb. "Celebrating divorce! Allowed 1300 flight on Concorde."

We arrived at the airport and had all the special treatment that was offered to Concorde passengers. All was arranged most beautifully, although there was a considerable number of vacant seats on the flight.

After we took off, it occurred to us that we were a good target.

CHAPTER 59

IS GUINNESS GOOD FOR YOU?

Guinness left an aftertaste that has lingered on. The European Court of Human Rights press release highlights the matters that continue to rankle.

> *On 19 September 2000 in the case of Lyons, Ronson and Parnes v the United Kingdom, the European Court of Human Rights held unanimously that there had been a violation of Article 6(1) of the European Convention on Human Rights as regards the use made by the prosecution at the applicants' trial of statements which they had been compelled under statute to give to inspectors appointed by the Department of Trade and Industry... The evidence related to City of London takeover practices and had been disclosed to other defendants who had faced separate criminal proceedings arising out of the Guinness bid ... The applicants maintained that the material which the Inspectors obtained from them under compulsory powers was provided directly to the Department of Trade and Industry and then passed directly to the Office of the Director of Public Prosecutions in furtherance of carefully worked-out arrangements ... this strategy was kept hidden from them so as to ensure their continued co-operation with the inspectors and in order to postpone, intentionally, the intervention of the police, the benefit of pre-trial safeguards and the formal preferment of criminal charges...*

The story? The value of the winning Guinness takeover bid for United Distillers plc in 1986 was £2.6 billion. It depended largely on corporate investors supporting the Guinness share price. In return, they received success fees. Even to men used to dealing in millions, the fees were recognisable as being at a significant level. Now, the fairness of the City in having true information available to those who trade in the market is that there is nothing kept from them which might affect their judgment. Inevitably, if you take the success fees into account, you would realise that they reduce the real value of the Guinness shares. There is no way to explain the inexplicable but matters do not exist in a vacuum. The success fees had to be paid from somewhere. There is a shareholding that can be sold but on top of that is the success fee. The authori-

ties' concern was, at root, whether what had happened amounted to an attack on the reliability of information about Guinness shares. It might have persuaded people to go on to the market. The propriety of success fees was to be more than questionable: they were likely to distort that particular market. It was the value of Guinness' marketworthiness that was at stake. While Guinness shares were high, United Distillers could be acquired.

The Department of Trade and Industry inquired into the process. The company directors who were involved were required by law to co-operate with the investigation. The alternative was a hefty fine and six months in prison.

The names of those who took part in the inquiry were well known in the City. Among them were Ernest Saunders, Chairman of Guinness, and Gerald Ronson, Chairman of the Heron Group of companies. They were to be joined in criminal proceedings by Anthony Parnes, the stockbroker who introduced the scheme to Ronson, and Sir Jack Lyons[1], a financier. Other well-known people from the world of finance were involved. Thomas Ward, Roger Seelig, Lord Spens, David Mayhew: stockbrokers, businessmen and bankers.

In 1990, the first four were to stand trial on charges arising from the share support operation and the success fees for three of them. Gerald Ronson: £5.8 million (although he had repaid it). Anthony Parnes and Jack Lyons: around the £3million mark

We were not to know that David Donaldson QC and his fellow Inspector, Ian Watt, were informing the police of the content of what the interviewees were saying under the compulsion of the current Companies' Act. The statements should have been strictly confidential. They were part of a report which was not to become a public document until November 1997. Not a syllable, whether of notes, drafts or proposed final form should have been disclosed until the report was published. It appeared that there was an unprecedented arrangement between the so-called independent Inspectors and the police party waiting to board the vessel. It infringed the rights of the subjects of the inquiry not to incriminate themselves and breached every principle of natural justice.

---

1   Isidore Jack Lyons (1916-2008)

It was ironic that shortly after being instructed for what would turn out to be the defence, I was offered the Guinness prosecution brief by the Serious Fraud Office. I could have taken it if my client, Gerald Ronson, were to be called as a witness for the prosecution but that was not to be.

The trial of the Guinness Four, Saunders, Ronson, Parnes and Lyons, took place at Southwark Crown Court. At the cost of £7.5 million to the public purse, it was the most expensive to date in the English courts. It lasted for 112 days. The jury deliberated for five days and returned on 27th August 1990, with verdicts of guilty: Saunders, Ronson and Lyons were convicted of conspiracy, theft and false accounting; Parnes, was found guilty of theft and false accounting.

In mitigating for Ronson, I took the view that it was possible to distinguish him from the others. He had twice been Businessman of the Year and could fulfil an outstanding contribution to society through his renowned charitable work if he remained at liberty.

Sentences were passed.

Saunders had not been the best of witnesses and made things worse for himself than they might otherwise have been. Five years. Parnes, the messenger: eighteen months. The ill-informed Gerald Ronson: two years. Lyons was spared prison by his poor health.

Pending the appeal, I did my level best to secure bail for my client if only so that he could sort out essential business matters in the short term. I damn nearly got him bail but we did not know even until after the appeal about the police deal with the Inspectors and the improper use of material withdrawn from the DTI Investigation. It was like swimming through treacle. Gerald was stuck with the consequences of having relied on bad financial advice and being gullible and easy-going.

The others? They had trials that fizzled out or did not happen. Seelig, for example, behaved so erratically that his trial was stopped because, in the judge's diagnosis, Seelig was about to succumb to an imminent nervous breakdown, making him unfit to defend himself. Charges against Mayhew were dropped.

The next stage for the Guinness Four was the Court of Appeal: May 1991 before Lord Justice Neale, Mr. Justice Ogden and Mr. Justice Owen. The judges were not concerned with evidence concerning what turned out to be Saunders' depression rather than a mis-diagnosis of incipient Alzheimer's disease. They were only concerned with his previous good character. His sentence was reduced to two and a half years. The convictions were upheld.

On 22 December 1994, the Home Secretary referred the cases of the Four to the Court of Appeal on the grounds that disclosure of important material had not been made available to the defendants at the time of the trial. This might have aided the defence and affected the outcome. The aim, for the defendants, was to secure a new trial in which they hoped to be exonerated.

The appeal was heard between 16 and 26 October 1995. The Lord Chief Justice, Peter Taylor, presided over the Court of Appeal, joined by Mr Justice MacPherson and Mr Justice Potter. Now the whole story was known to the defence, it came pouring out. The Chief was appalled at the Inspectors' behaviour: "It is absolutely scandalous!" he said, "How could an Inspector abuse his independence by feeding information outside?" He was sympathetic to the defence's main principle: that reports should remain confidential. Of my final speech, he said: "This is pure poetry."

Victor Mishcon, my instructing solicitor, wrote me a note which said, "The Sun shall not set today." But it did. The appeal failed.

So then there was Europe, by which time I was no longer involved. Saunders went to Europe first. Ronson, Parnes and Lyons followed. In 2000 the European Court of Human Rights "held unanimously that there had been a violation of Article 6(1) of the European Convention on Human Rights as regards the use made by the prosecution at the applicants' trial of statements which they had been compelled under statute to give to inspectors appointed by the Department of Trade and Industry…."

If I have personal feelings about the outcome, it is fair to say that it rankles that, as we now know, the Department of Trade Inspectors deliberately withheld from the prosecution the decision of the panel that approved a similar take-over process. They withheld the information and we only knew of the omission after the trial and the appeals were over. They withheld information that indicated there was nothing wrong with success fees.

Finally, the European Court delivered its dictat: the trials were unfair. The defendants had been denied a fair trial by being compelled to provide potentially self-incriminatory information to Department of Trade and Industry inspectors which was then used as primary evidence against them. This breached their right to silence. But what effect did that have? Ronson's hopes had been dashed in the Court of Appeal. Peter Taylor's manifest disgust with the Inspectors' conduct and his comment on my final speech had led to the fleeting hope that the sentence might be quashed. But this was a case of all for one and one for all: previous good character was not enough.

***

POSTSCRIPT 1

Hansard debate 04 06 97

... The inspectors have not yet completed the Guinness report, but it is expected shortly. That is not my fault. It should be noted that the inspectors have been constrained – I will not use the word hampered – by the judicial procedures. They were guided by the need to ensure that while court proceedings were in train they were not open to accusations of harassing witnesses and pursuing matters that were before the court. I am sure that that is a cause of frustration to DTI inspectors and former Ministers ... Everyone in Scotland and elsewhere who has taken an interest in the Guinness affair wants to see that report concluded as soon as possible. I am advised that it is expected shortly.

When the report is received, it will be given due consideration. It is the usual practice to publish reports into public companies, but a decision on whether to publish this one or any other such inspection can be made only after careful scrutiny of the signed report ...

As for the Guinness inspection, inspectors were appointed in November 1986. They submitted their interim report in November 1988. By that time, Ernest Saunders had been arrested. The first Guinness trial started in January 1990 and convictions were obtained in August 1990. In March 1991, the inspectors were directed to limit their work while the criminal proceedings against other defendants were in train. They resumed their work in March 1993. In March 1994, the inspectors went to court to certify Thomas Ward's failure to attend for interview. Ward was sentenced to six months' imprisonment for contempt. He is currently in the United States and contempt is not an extraditable offence.

Following the evidence gathering part of the inspection, the inspectors have spent most of the remaining time writing their report and, significantly, applying the fairness procedures. That process is commonly referred to as Maxwellisation and involves inspectors' putting the substance of their criticisms to those whom they are minded to criticise in their final report ...

The process takes time and it is sometimes open to abuse. It involves trying to balance the need to produce a quick report as efficiently as possible against the need to apply fairness by offering those likely to be criticised an opportunity to seek to dissuade the inspectors from their critical opinions.

I do not believe that any of the parties in the relevant cases have been denied that fairness. The delays in the publication of the report are, however, one reason why we want such powers to be used sparingly in the future.

***

POSTSCRIPT 2

From the judgment of *R v Lyons and others (on appeal from the Court of Appeal, Criminal Division [2002] EWCA Crim 2860*

Lord Bingham of Cornhill, Lord Hoffmann, Lord Hutton, Lord Hobhouse of Woodborough, Lord Millett

Their Lordships, although bound by the judgment of the European Court, trumped it by the time factor: the Human Rights Act did not come into force until after the trial.

"It is not the treaty but the statute which forms part of English law. And English courts will not (unless the statute expressly so provides) be bound to give effect to interpretations of the treaty by an international court, even though the United Kingdom is bound by international law to do so. Of course there is a strong presumption in favour of interpreting English law (whether common law or statute) in a way which does not place the United Kingdom in breach of an international obligation."

CHAPTER 60

TWO WANGS

On Michael's second trip to Singapore, back in the 1970s, he was taken to a ramshackle back street in Chinatown, far off the tourist route. It was Sago Lane. The houses, all of some six storeys in height, were of considerable age. The ground floors were taken up with shops, many of them selling flowers. This was not, as it appeared to be, a district for florists.

Allen Yau took me to the death houses of Sago Lane. He explained that what we were seeing was a form of social engineering.

"When old people, near death, have to be looked after," he said, "this is where they come when they have outlived their relatives and their only illness is their age. The hospitals have no treatment for that. The newcomers are usually reasonably well. They are taken to the top floor. As they weaken and their care needs increase, they gradually move down, floor by floor. When they come to the first floor, they die."

Allen did not comment whether this was cause or effect.

He also told me that the shops sold flowers and paper trinkets to accompany the late residents of Sago Lane through their funeral rites. Professional mourners were engaged, either as a charity exercise or because of religious superstition, to maintain the tradition that every good Chinese, anywhere in the world, is entitled to a respectful death. I could hear mourners keening in one of the houses as we walked by. They would sit there, crying and wailing, through the day and night until the funeral, praying that the deceased should be admitted to heaven. Allen described the route.

He said, "What determines the standard of the afterlife is the degree of luxury directly proportional to their standing in their actual existence. But that can be changed by rice-paper models which represent their hopes and ambitions."

I understood that, in this way, the Chinese poor could have their dreams made tangible in heaven as they take their paper aeroplanes, houses, boats and other paraphernalia with them to the grave.

I took visitors to Sago Lane several times. It was a fascinating experience, not at all macabre. It was encouraging to see a society take over the

360

role of the family to help its aged members. In years to come, I was to wonder about the fate of those whose bodies are not discovered.

Which brings me to Hong Kong.

When Teddy Wang disappeared, it was easy to imagine the Chinese superstition that his soul – eventually – would hover outside heaven, with no clue to his standing in life.

Hearing the news of Nina Wang's death on 4 April 2007 brought Nina and Teddy back to mind. They[1] had moved from being very rich childhood sweethearts in Shanghai to being the richest couple in Hong Kong. Nina, together with her penchant for wearing her hair in schoolgirl pigtails, brought her personal fortune to their marriage and was closely involved with her husband in the management of the huge conglomerate founded by Teddy's family, Chinachem. At the time of her death, in 2007, Nina Wang was the richest woman in Asia and the world's 35th richest person. Some of her wealth may have accrued from her notoriously parsimonious ways, not the least of which was her habit of buying her clothes from thrift shops and bargain basements.

During their lives, they were at high risk of kidnapping. The agreement they had with each other was that they would not give way to threats nor would they pay any ransom. They took all sorts of precautions to ensure their personal safety but, in spite of their care, in April 1983, Teddy Wang's car was hi-jacked and he was kidnapped. For a time, Nina stuck to the bargain and did not pay the ransom that was demanded by the kidnappers. But when Teddy's ear was posted to her, with the threat that this was the first sequence in the process of dismembering him, she took an executive decision and paid the money demanded.

Teddy was convinced that he would have been found and released without any payment having been made. He was absolutely furious that Nina had dipped into the petty cash for what he saw as a hard earned HK$11 million to secure his release.

I represented them in a case which involved a joint building venture where they were accused of operating a fraudulent business through a complex system of overcharging. Certainly, their building interests were unusual: vast properties would be constructed, never to be inhabited then

---

[1]   Nina Wang, née Kung Yung Sum (1937-2007); Teddy Wang (1933 – ?).

later demolished for redevelopment and the process would start again. Their case came and went. Strange, yes. Fraudulent, no.

Some years later, in 1990, Teddy Wang made a new will leaving his entire estate to his wife. Within a month, he was kidnapped again. This time, Nina tried to obey her orders. She was 50% successful. She paid only half the HK$68 million demanded. That was not enough. Teddy Wang was never seen again. It was rumoured that he had been killed and his body dumped in Hong Kong Harbour. Nina coped with her worry and grief by greater involvement in the business. She devised the title "Chairlady" to describe her new role in Chinachem. He was declared dead in 1999.

The boats that could have accompanied his soul to heaven must have been made out of the rain-forests of paper used in the litigation that followed. In November 2002, after a 170 day hearing, the High Court of Hong Kong declared the HK$128 million will a forgery and made Teddy's father the beneficiary of an earlier will. Nina's first appeal failed and she was charged with forgery in early 2005. She soldiered on to the Court of Final Appeal and the criminal charges were dropped when that appeal succeeded in September of that year. She died on 3 April 2007 and a new battle is under way over the authenticity of her will, the most recent of which (October 2006) leaves her personal fortune to a property investor with whom she had been acquainted since the early 1990s and whose hobby is said to be *feng shui*.

Feng shui is the practice of enhancing health and prosperity through the architectural design of living and working space. Its underlying philosophy is that the arrangement of furniture and objects in the chosen space will assist personal well-being. Dates and numbers are also involved. It is nothing to do with mysterious disappearances and convenient dates. It is all about harmony.

CHAPTER 61

BACK TO BACK IN THE EAST:
SUPERSTITION AND REALITY

There is an irresistible urge never to leave the Far East without making firm plans to return. It is a drug that cannot be ignored. The judges may be a shade more idiosyncratic than at home and the trials may take longer but at the end of the working day, the sky is always clearer and at night the different constellations are bright and fascinating. If there could only be one word to sum up what it was like for Michael to work in the East, he says, "Fun."

But although it was fun, the trips were so frequent that it is true to say that his feet barely touched the ground for years. And the consequence was that the journey could sometimes take its toll.

In the mid-1980s, I had work to do in Singapore but a hitherto tolerable or, at any rate, tolerated back problem flared up so badly on the flight that I was brought off the plane in a wheel-chair. I was going to be in difficulty with preparing the case and appearing in court. As soon as we arrived at the Shangri-la, Shirley telephoned our friend, Christine Sipiére, and told her about my problem. Christine asked, "Do you know about Chi Kung?"

We did not. She explained that this was a way of relieving my pain and straightening my back, although the first would have been enough. It was a system that could be described as similar to Tai Chi but the similarity stopped with the gestures. Chi is the life energy which is within everyone, promoting healing from within. Some forms of illness, such as pain, are seen as resulting from a reduction or mal-alignment of the patient's Chi. The movements of Chi Kung direct the energy forces from the master to the patient, promoting the healing process.

Xiao Li was the Chi Kung master. He would hold sessions in a theatre to train students in the art. Seeing the treatment carried out was as fascinating for the public as the effects were miraculous on his clientéle. Christine described my predicament and made arrangements for me to meet him.

Getting there was one of the most excruciatingly painful experiences of my life but we managed somehow to get to his flat which was off the

East Coast Road. He saw me in a large room with a desk and chairs at one end. On the facing wall, about twelve feet away from the desk, was a fireplace surrounded by a carved mantelpiece. He could see that I was rigid with pain and did not suggest that I sit in a chair. My main concern, as he carried out his examination by walking around me, looking at me, was how I was going to manage to get down the stairs again. I scarcely noticed what he looked like and answered his questions in monosyllables. The pain? "Bad." How long it had been there? "Weeks." Did it wake me at night? "Yes." Was it getting worse? "Yes." In fact, it could not possibly have got worse. It was the worst it had ever been.

He looked at me for a few moments, moved back to the level of the desk, then asked me to stand by the mantelpiece and look at the painting above it. The dull agony of my back had translated to acute pain from having climbed the stairs to the office. Moving those few feet was as much as I could bear. Standing was painful and standing straight was impossible. With pain the overriding feature, he told me not to worry. I could hear his voice from behind me. His position at the desk might have been a mile away. He said nothing else. There was absolute quiet.

In the silence, I began to feel myself being drawn gently backwards. From an agonising forward stoop, I was upright, I was leaning backwards, further and further. I realised that I was angled 45° to the floor. I heard myself say, "I'm falling."

"Don't worry," he said. "I'm here for you."

Indeed he was. There behind me, not touching me, but holding me with gestures from his hands. There was an almost palpable current between us, supporting me. I was leaning backwards into nothingness and I was safe.

I walked out of his apartment, pain-free. After that, I saw him for different ailments. I had the greatest respect for his methods.

***

Some years later, in the early 1990s, I was in Hong Kong, defending Charles Sin, a solicitor and Vice-Chairman of the Listing Committee of the Hong Kong Stock Exchange, in a corruption case which, with its various adjournments and interim applications, was to last in the region of seventeen months. He and six others were on trial for fraud, bribery and corruption. The nub of the matter was a suspiciously large allocation of free shares. Ten of the jury were Chinese. The case was conducted in English. Their understanding must have improved quite a lot by the end.

It was very hard fought. The Government was riding high on its success with Mr. Ronald Li, the Chairman, who had been convicted of corruption in relation to the share dealings of the Listing Committee. There were six or seven defendants in this trial, including Li's son (a solicitor and an advisor to the Committee). My client was one of the group being tried as being accessories to the Chairman's fixing of the listing.

Michael Kalisher QC was prosecuting. Like me, he had come from London. He had two very competent juniors, one of whom was Mary Sin.

The hearing was spread over such a long period of time, with so many defendants, leaders, juniors and solicitors, we were given permission to adapt the courtroom to our needs. We were virtually living there for the duration. The defendants acquired their own areas where they could make themselves relatively comfortable and keep with them the belongings they would need for the day. There was no formality limiting them to the confines of the dock which came to be allocated as the junior Li's territory. My client was in the left-hand row of seats. As the Vice-Chairman, he considered this position to be suitable to his status.

Mary sat to my left. During lengthy evidence from the current occupant of the witness box, she tapped my arm and whispered something that sounded like "The defendant is pointing his umbrella at Michael Kalisher's back."

And that is precisely what she had said.

There was nothing strange under the circumstances about the man having an umbrella, or any other item of personal equipment, with him in court. People came equipped for the vagaries of the weather: on leaving or arriving, it would have served to protect him as much from the blazing sun as from any monsoon downpour. I turned to see what she had noticed. The fact that Li was handling a furled umbrella at all had sparked her interest, although no-one but she seemed to have seen what was going on. He was manipulating it, pointing it menacingly at Michael K's back. Although the notion that it could cause any harm was ridiculous, he behaved as if the effect would be painful, notwithstanding that the ferrule was about fifteen feet away.

Mary said, "He's going to use the umbrella to give bad and painful joss to Mr Kalisher." This was nonsense. I rather pooh-poohed the suggestion. I hoped that I did not sound too patronizing when I asked, "What exactly is the umbrella going to do?"

All the while, Michael K was examining a witness-in-chief. He was between the witness and the whole of the defence audience, including Li. Only Mary, Li and I seemed to have any idea that any sort of drama was building up.

Mary said, "We'll see. Funny things happen out here."

I thought: silly woman. I could see the umbrella pointing but I thought her suggestion that it could cause any harm was bizarre rubbish.

When Michael K was half an hour into the examination-in-chief, he stopped talking and suddenly, as if stabbed by a dart, grabbed his back. He uttered a dreadful sound – a combination of a groan and a sharp intake of breath.

The judge immediately asked, "Mr Kalisher, are you all right?"

He was not all right. He could neither speak nor move, his spasm of pain was so great.

The other junior, with Australian sang-froid, appeared to take no notice of his leader's predicament. Mary looked at me. A lift of her eyebrow was the nearest she came to making any comment about being right after all.

The judge said, "It's ten to four. Let's adjourn until tomorrow. We will find some medical help."

Michael K was in such pain, he could not bear to be touched. There was no helping him even to sit. While someone went off to find a doctor in the building, he found his voice.

He said, "Mary is talking some rubbish about the evil eye. The rest of you. Stop gawking. I've never had pain like this before." The pain was incapacitating, something vague by way of eventual diagnosis relating to his cervical vertebrae. He was housebound for several days and the hearing, which had adjourned on a Wednesday, did not resume until

366

the following Monday. He was much better then but not free of pain. He refused the judge's offer to permit him to remain seated to continue the examination-in-chief: he was more comfortable standing and, in any case, it is less commanding to be seated whilst asking questions.

We got through the morning. Just before the lunchbreak, Mary said: "Li is doing it again."

I was not convinced that he had done anything in the beginning. "Barrister's back" is often acquired after years of carrying a heavy bag around, twisting the spine to one side as I knew only too well.

"So what's he doing?"

"He's got the umbrella again. Now he's aiming the metal ferrule at Michael's lower back."

This was ridiculous. I was getting short tempered. "Well, what's going to happen?"

We were seated on green leather tip-up seats. On the seat between us, Mary had her handbag. She reached towards it and took out a small mirror as she said, "I'm going to reverse the vibes."

I watched her manipulate the mirror so that it picked up the reflection of the umbrella. This was too much.

"Mary," I said, "your job is to take a note. Keep your mind on what you have to do."

"But I'm giving him some of his own medicine," she said, not making the required move to pick up her pen.

"Bollocks," I thought.

"Mary, the note. Please," I said.

"Wait and see," was her reply.

I do not know if Mr Li noticed the light flashing from the mirror. But within half an hour I saw him become very pale and stagger backwards. The umbrella fell to the ground as he tugged at his collar as if trying to find a way to give himself more air to breathe.

He called his solicitor over. A message came back. "Mr Li is feeling unwell. He is not fit to carry on."

Mary could not resist pressing home her point. Replacing the mirror in the bag, she said, "I told you so."

We looked towards Mr Li. He was deathly pale and sweating profusely. He lay down on the bench in the dock. His solicitor reported: "He's running a very high temperature and is not fit to continue."

He was taken to hospital and a rumour quickly reached the court that it could be meningitis. I said, "That can't be right. He was all right when we started."

We never did find out what was wrong with him but he was kept in hospital for three days. To the jury's delight, we adjourned until he returned, the umbrella nowhere in sight. By then, I think he'd gone off the idea of using it except to keep him dry.

The end of the story? The jury retired for five days. We didn't know where they were, nor was there any need for us to know. But while we were waiting for the verdict, we had to be on call twenty-four hours a day. As the court was not sitting, there was a government-inspired economy in effect: air-conditioning was turned off. It was like a Turkish bath indoors.

We sat outside, sometimes on the lawn. We must have been an odd sight, with our tropical-weight gowns scattered about us like portable shadows. After the first day, we took it in turns to go to the Shangri-La restaurant, just two and half minutes away. We went in shifts: a couple of leaders, a couple of juniors. We didn't dare go further. It was slightly more attractive than baking in the sun or boiling indoors.

All defendants were acquitted. There was, however, the matter of Li senior who was serving a three-year sentence passed at his earlier trial. He was now to have a further sentence passed on him for the offence to which he had pleaded guilty in the current trial.

George Carman QC was flown out specially to mitigate for him. Having hurried from London overnight, he came with his heavy robes, wearing waist-coat, morning coat – the whole shebang. The rest of us were in our summer, lightweight gear as befitted the tropics. He said, "I feel like a lump of butter melting in a very hot dish." He gave every appearance of having understated the case: he was streaming with perspiration and obviously uncomfortable.

George had a rudimentary knowledge of the case. In a very short hearing, the judge disposed of the outstanding sentence by ordering that the balance of it be served concurrently with the sentence he was already serving.

I had a lovely time with George. He introduced me to his son, Dominic, who was editing a high-class glossy magazine that was devoted to legal matters in Hong Kong. We had dinner at the café at the Mandarin where he brought me up-to-date with the London gossip.

***

Some months later, I was in the same court in another case (this time a civil matter) with Michael Ogden QC and Peter Scott QC who had also come out from London. Peter was sitting in the same seat where Michael Kalisher had been. He suddenly felt a sharp pain in his back. The judge, Michael Kempster, a senior judge in Hong Kong, agreed to rise so that medical treatment could be sought. Shirley was in the courtroom that day. She went to get the doctor.

There was no doubt that Peter had severe pain. However, this time, there was a history of an old back problem. And there were no umbrellas. And Mary Sin wasn't there. And there was probably no coincidence in him having been in Michael Kalisher's seat: I am sure that many dozens of people must have sat there between the two events …

***

The next time that I flew out to Hong Kong, my client insisted on meeting me at the airport and accompanying me to the Mandarin Hotel. I knew perfectly well how to get there and was accustomed to taking a taxi but he wanted to meet me as a matter of respect and I understood that the courtesy could not be refused. I had not been prepared for the client's attention to be extended so far as to ensuring that the accommodation, which was always perfect, would be acceptable. However, when we arrived at the hotel, the assistant manager came to greet us and the three of us trooped off to the suite which had been reserved for me. At the doorway, before the key had been put in the lock, my client tugged at my arm, pulling me away. He was in a state of some agitation.

"Don't go in! Don't go in!" He was obviously genuinely alarmed. "You can't have this room! You can't go in!

369

The assistant manager was not in the least surprised. He would probably have had this problem with any oriental guest. The suite was probably reserved for Americans and Europeans. As an Englishman, I was not expected to mind a room with the number 1444 which, in Chinese/Cantonese equates in translation to 'death'. "I'll get the keys for 2020," he said.

***

Superstition governs the way that many lawyers go about their business in the Far East. Omens and auguries can affect the outcome of a case and rituals have to be followed to preserve the omens of luck. One of my instructing solicitors in Singapore was so consumed by the protocols of his obsession with superstitious beliefs, he forgot the hard basics of the law and became a danger to himself and his clients. Legal precedents meant less to him than ensuring that he had the appropriate green socks to wear to court, something that may not have assisted him as much as he would have hoped in the techniques of cross-examination or making a closing speech.

***

A matter needed to be closed: the question of being Head of Chambers. A career in which the only real breaks were achieved by sitting on an aeroplane was one which gave limited time to manage the increasing responsibilities of 2 Crown Office Row.

I had been thinking about the demands of my work over those of Chambers. I had been Head of Chambers for about seventeen years. Recently, it had come to the point that there were barely enough hours in the day to manage my practice let alone deal with the increasing commitment required by Chambers which continued regardless of whether I was in England, abroad or traveling between one and the other. I felt that it was time to hand over the title to a suitable incumbent. And there was Michael Burton QC.

There was little need for attention to detail: being Head of Chambers was an honourable title but one that could be passed on, at that time, without any reference to democratic procedures. It was mine for the giving. As the title had been given to me by Peter Pain, now it was time for me to pass it on. The idea had been developing for some time. When Michael came into my room in chambers one afternoon after I returned

370

from one of several trips to the Far East in 1991, I decided it was time to pop the question. Except that it was a statement.

"Michael," I said, "I've decided to stand down as Head of Chambers and that you should take over."

He was taken completely by surprise. "You don't mean it!" he said. But I did.

"We'll talk about it tomorrow," he said. But he didn't refuse.

"There's nothing to talk about," I said. "Congratulations. I know you'll do a great job."

"Tomorrow," he said. And when you think about it, that is quite ambiguous. There had to be some certainty here.

So I telephoned *The Times* and managed to have an announcement inserted for publication the following day. "Michael Burton QC has taken over from Michael Sherrard QC as Head of Chambers of 2 Crown Office Row."

He came in to see me the next morning and said, "Look, Michael, I've been thinking about what you said and I don't think – "

But there was nothing to think about. I showed him the advertisement. "Congratulations," I said again. And this time it was a *fait accompli*.

CHAPTER 62

THE TASTE OF OSLO

Michael John Hunt was one of three people arrested in 1991, in the UK's largest tax fraud to date. A fourth man, the billionaire philanthropist, Octav Botnar, fled to Switzerland where he remained out of reach of UK authorities[1]. Michael Hunt had been Managing Director of Nissan UK[2] for 17 years and at the time of his downfall, owned 13.5% of the company, founded by Botnar, then valued at £1 billion. It was alleged that Hunt and Botnar had fraudulently evaded taxes of over £200 million by setting up sham companies and questionable charitable trusts overseas.

Peter Rook QC[3], Angela Morris and others were prosecuting. They wanted to take evidence from a man who would not come to England. However, he agreed to make a deposition before a Norwegian judge in Oslo pursuant to legislation governing criminal fraud at international level.

Twelve of us flew from London to Oslo. We arrived to find a nice clean city, not too densely populated and altogether rather a pleasant place.

The court was to sit early: at 8.30 a.m., the sort of time that an English court would entertain only in a dire emergency. We arrived at the modern but rather drab, bare building and made our way to the courtroom on the ground floor. A large abstract painting in striking red, green and blue tones was fixed to the wall behind the public gallery. The Bench was raised slightly on a platform at the end of which sat a young woman with a word-processor.

The lawyers' benches were at right angles to the Bench and facing each other. The witness box was in the middle of the room.

A number of officials and interested parties gathered, waiting for the proceedings to begin. Among them was a tall, attractive lady in a bright red denim suit, a gray and white check band around her waist, and much modern jewellery, including the longest row of grey pearls that I have ever seen. She was chatting to some people at the side of the Court and

---

[1]   Octav Botnar (1913-1998), died in exile in France.
[2]   Formerly Datsun UK, set up by Octav Botnar.
[3]   Peter Rook QC is now an Old Bailey Judge.

then at exactly 8.30 a.m. she revealed herself as the judge! She said, "OK," and walked onto the Bench, took her seat, spoke a few words in Norwegian and then changed to perfect English. She asked us to introduce ourselves. We did so. She enquired whether we had any objection to her as the judge. I replied for all of us, "On the contrary!"

She simpered and wagged her finger at me. The hearing began.

The whole session should have lasted about two hours and it would have done had there not been constant arguments among the Norwegians as to whether the translation into English could be improved and whether the recorder had taken down the definitive version.

There were also some delays as the judge managed her private life during the hearing, taking calls from her son – in English! – on the telephone, the single object on the Bench. This was a surprising facility, not to be seen in England. We could hear every word of the lively discussions about whether he could use her car that evening. There was no sign of the Court closing for the day even at the hallowed time of 4.00 p.m.

We were all quite tired after our early start and the long journey. At about 5.00 p.m. Peter Rook sent me a note. "You are senior. Can you ask her how late she intends to sit?" He was starving. Everyone was except, apparently, the judge.

"Madam," I said, "May I ask how long you propose to sit?" She said airily, "Until midnight, if necessary." We were all taken aback, particularly as dinner had been booked for us at a highly recommended restaurant in the centre of town. I said that I hoped we could avoid a sitting of such length. So we pressed on.

At 6.20 p.m., the judge asked whether she could slip away for ten minutes. I tried to imagine an English judge asking counsel for permission to do anything.

I replied, "Of course: it is up to you."

She left the courtroom leaving us with vocal stomachs. She returned within the promised time, carrying a large hand of bananas from which she proceeded to break and pass one banana to each of us in the well of the Court. "I thought you might need something to eat," she said, adding, "I can sit as long as is needed." And, as if she had not realised that we knew from her side of the telephone conversations, "I have given my son my car for the evening."

Mine was the last banana.

"We are most grateful for your generous gesture," I said. It was one of my most heartfelt speeches. She replied with a half-smile and we went straight back to business, having eaten our sole sustenance of the day.

At 8.30 p.m., after the deposition was read in Norwegian, the witness and his lawyer put on their coats and prepared to leave. I asked them to wait while the English translation was approved and any necessary amendments made to the Norwegian. The lawyer, grim and tired, retorted that there was no way he or his client was going to wait for "the English". This led to some acrimony, whereupon they walked out of the room. The judge sat smiling, unmoved. She knew what she was doing. It turned out that she had been left with the key to the locked main door, the rest of the building being deserted. The two of them could not leave.

And indeed, they returned, somewhat embarrassed. The lawyer was angrier than before but his client, who had a better sense of humour or a greater ability to withstand the pangs of hunger, took off his coat, walked to the witness box and asked for the English version to be read to him. So it was. The English lawyers were happy with the translation. Our work was done. The key was handed over to an official, the front door was duly unlocked and we left, making our separate ways through a darkened Oslo, to D'Artagnan, the highly recommended restaurant. We were just in time before they gave up hope that we would ever arrive.

The Norwegian evidence never surfaced in the trial which took place in 1993 before Mr Justice Gatehouse in a specially commissioned courtroom prepared for us in Chancery Lane. It was the only way that there was enough space for the massive amount of papers the case had generated. In earlier days, Bob Gatehouse and I had been pitted against one another in Hong Kong more often than I can remember.

The opening took three days. The defence was that there was a fraud but carried out by other parties, largely in Japan. There was powerful evidence to support the Japanese links.

Support for the essence of the defence began to emerge when the first witness, a Viennese man, readily admitted that the people he had dealt with were not our defendants but two witnesses from Tokyo whom he identified by reference to a photograph which I was in the happy position of being able to produce. He had met them in Vienna where the photograph was taken. The judge was visibly surprised by these admissions and reacted facially.

As the evidence progressed, it became more and more obvious that Bob Gatehouse was not happy about it. Subtle signs became obvious. My client spoke to me during the mid-morning break. He was very upset. "The judge is behaving disgracefully," he said. "The jury can see he is not believing a word of our case."

I said, "Be patient. We don't want to get on the wrong side of the judge so early in the trial. He'll come round." I was wrong about that.

The client was not happy with the waiting game. "I want you to object," he insisted. The senior solicitor could not persuade him otherwise. The client was not satisfied with this approach. "Object," he said. "It's what I want."

I asked that the jury should remain out of court when the judge returned. He walked slowly to his seat, looking at me in a puzzled way. He sat down, raised his eyebrows as the question.

I explained that I had asked to speak to him out of desperation and without any intention of causing offence. I said something along the following lines:

"Your Lordship and I know each other well enough for you to recognize my style of cross-examination. *It is a poor thing but mine own.* It may not be a style that Your Lordship appreciates. I regret to say that Mr Hunt considers the jury may have been upset by the impression that you may have conveyed to it of your own apparent incredulity and disapproval. The jury may think that it is the witness who has caused this when all along, it is I. My client is upset that the jury may read into your Lordship's facial reactions disapproval of our case."

He replied at once, smiling broadly. It was thoroughly disarming.

"Mr Sherrard, you know I do not disapprove of your style of cross-examination. It is very good of you to express your client's objection in the way that you have. I will explain to the jury that no inference is to be drawn from any of my movements or expressions which I shall do my best to control." He then asked Mr Hunt to stand.

"I apologise if I have allowed my facial display to indicate that I have formed an adverse view of your case. If you have any further concerns in this respect, please instruct Mr Sherrard to object again."

He had the jury brought back and he said, "You may have wondered about my reaction to the evidence given so far. I have not formed any view that should influence you. Judges have all sorts of reasons for facial expressions, as do all of you. Now, shall we get on?"

My heart had been in my mouth. Never in all my years at the Bar until now had I had a client with the stomach to say, "Sock it to him." The judge remained impassive after that.

In the end, several months later, the jury thought the evidence was stacked up against him. Although he was acquitted on half the indictment, he was sentenced to eight years for the guilty half.

CHAPTER 63

SPARE THE ROD

Extract from the Singapore Criminal Procedure Code:

"… any person who commits an act of vandalism … shall be guilty of an offence and shall be liable to a fine not exceeding $2000 or to a jail term not exceeding three months, and shall also subject to Section 231 of the Criminal Procedure Code be punished with caning with not less than three strokes and not more than eight strokes …"

The severe punishment for vandalism had its origins in the Vietnam conflict. Singapore had been a haven for lucky escapees from, and protesters against, the war. They abused Singaporean hospitality by daubing anti-American slogans on all sorts of available walls and surfaces. The law was promulgated for the express purpose of bringing to an end the graffiti epidemic.

Michael Fay, a 17-year-old American schoolboy, fell foul of the law in September 1993 by spraying aerosol cans of paint at motor cars in the carparks of high-rise buildings in Singapore. One belonged to an individual who was about take up his appointment as a High Court judge. The damage to the vehicle was estimated at $50.

Fay pleaded guilty. The trial judge determined that, although the law provided that caning would not be imposed where the vandalism consisted of writing, drawing or making marks on surfaces with "delible" substances such as chalk or crayon, paint came under the category of indelible substances. He sentenced Fay to four months in prison, six strokes of the cane and fined him $3,500 because there had been more than one offence. Fay's solicitor announced that he would appeal and bail was set in the amount of $75,000.

International press coverage condemned the notion of flogging as barbaric. The Americans were enraged at the prospect of corporal punishment being carried out on one of their citizens. The boy's father, estranged from his mother, came from the United States to Singapore to add to the voices of protest. President Clinton instructed his ambassador to assist in promoting clemency. His message was that it was very important that an appeal be pressed with all vigour.

The solicitor who represented Fay at first instance rang me in England to instruct me in the appeal. "I honestly can't face trying to do this in front of Pung How," he said.

Yong Pung How, the Chief Justice, had the power to increase the sentence, even to double it. This power had the collateral effect of shortening the list of appeals considerably.

I suggested that consideration might be given to abandoning the appeal. The boy had pleaded guilty to crimes for which specific penalties had been laid down – malicious damage and graffiti were taken seriously in Singapore. The fact that he was terrified of the flogging and dreaded the prospect of prison might be an encouragement to the Chief Justice to be as harsh as the law permitted rather than turn to anything that might be considered lenient.

The solicitor urged me to take the brief. "See if you can persuade him to reduce the sentence on the basis of his frankness."

I reminded him that he had tried that at the hearing. I suggested that he ran the appeal himself and say at the start that he was abandoning it in order to rely directly on the clemency of the President of Singapore, Ong Teng Cheung.

"But President Clinton told the American ambassador that he had to get someone with the most experience in the courts here. He asked me to get you. I really need you to help me – I'm afraid I took the liberty of telling the ambassador you would do it," he said.

The prospects of success seemed so remote that I considered it was disproportionate to use me. But, after some more discussion from which I understood that my presence had been requested at the highest level, I agreed to take the case.

So, out I went.

After my arrival, on the eve of the hearing I went to the Cricket Club where I was likely to – and did – meet a group of silks who were over for a large commercial case. My visit coincided with that of Lord Bingham. The silks told me that he was surprised I had been prepared to do the case. He had asked them, "Is it really worth his while coming all this way for graffiti?" I explained that there was a serious principle at stake without elaborating on President Clinton's particular interest in the matter.

On the day of the hearing, it was almost impossible to get anywhere near the courthouse. It was surrounded by press and sightseers. The father and the boy arrived. Michael Fay was a strapping lad, over 6 feet tall. When I went to greet him, he started to cry. This would not impress Pung How.

"You're not going to weep in court," I told him briskly. "Get it over and done with now."

Whilst preparing for the case, I realised there was a glimmer of a possibility of success. Michael Fay had not written anything on the cars but the nature of the charge implied that he had. His activities had been confined to spraying horizontal lines. The worst feature was that the target had been a judge's car.

Given the American interest in the outcome, I thought it unlikely that there would be an increase the sentence. But I decided it was worth winkling the 'defence' point into my argument although it was essentially what should have been put forward rather than the guilty plea. The idea was for the court to end the political embarrassment the sentence had caused by finding that the boy had pleaded guilty to the wrong charge. A lot of face could be saved if it occurred to Yong Pung How that it was his idea in the first place. This was much to aim for.

Any hope of that sort of result was dashed the moment the Chief Justice came into court, his features compacted into a grimace that was somewhere between hate and fury. With every word I uttered, the contortion increased.

I started as gently as I could on the theme that this was not a matter of passing interest. "Perhaps this should have been noticed before: this relates to the origin of the law. There are no words to offend..."

It would not have mattered what I said. He would have interrupted if I had said "Good morning." He said through gritted teeth, "Yes, yes. I know the point you have in mind. It wasn't taken before. The objection is not in time."

I followed the more traditional tack: how ashamed he was; how great his fear ...

Pung How was not impressed.

"Appeal dismissed."

But he had not increased the sentence.

My next task was to visit the US ambassador. I helped him draft a letter to the President, appealing for clemency. President Ong, as a gesture of goodwill to the United States, reduced the sentence from six to four strokes.

The boy collapsed after the first lash but the punishment was carried out fairly: the next stroke of the whip was delayed until he had recovered.

CHAPTER 64

EAST ENDERS

So many cases and characters of the Far East clamour for mention. Most must be left outside these pages. But surely not the three merry widows?

Ada, Mabel and Florrie were the three widows of a Malaysian millionaire. In fact, Ada was the lawful widow, Mabel was the First Mistress and Florrie was the Junior Mistress. Whilst the husband was dying at the Hong Kong hospital where he was being treated for cancer, they devised a working truce in the interests of their common cause: they had discovered, to their mutual shock, that, although he had left something in his will to each and their offspring, he had been disloyal to them. There was another woman. They suspected that she might have rights to their husband's estate under local law, unless they took appropriate steps.

I was able to advise them that the local law allowed for rectification of a will where someone had been disinherited for whom provision had legally to be made. I explained that, as long as provision had been made, it was the fact of the provision rather than the amount.

They met to discuss a plan of action over supper at the Mandarin Grill. Ada, as befitted her senior status, began the conversation.

"Ladies, we have a problem. I did not know about Mabel or Florrie. Mabel did not know about Florrie." According to convention, she ignored the evidence that had come to light about the fourth woman because it was not acceptable to insult their husband's reputation. She continued as if there were a hypothetical situation. "What if there is another widow? Another child? Why should we or our children suffer if there is anyone else?"

They went to a solicitor's office and bought an official will form. They copied the original will which was in their possession, updated it and got the solicitor to deliver it to their errant husband in hospital. It now said, "In the event that any wife other than the three referred to above should make herself known as applying to benefit under this will, provided that she proves to the satisfaction of the court that she has been wrongfully omitted from my will, I leave to her and each of her offspring the sum of Singapore $200."

The husband signed the will and without much further ado, he died.

Another widow turned up and was very disappointed to find that she had been provided for. She went to see a solicitor. "Remember the will," he told her as he tried to explain that all that was required was provision for her, not any particular amount. She had a credible case but would have had an uphill task against the wording of the will. She settled for Singapore $2000.

***

And then there was the fragile, ageing client whose appeal was heard in the typhoon season.

The Hong Kong Jockey Club had been the victim of a fraud. Someone – not my client, as I managed to persuade the Court of Appeal – had forged a ticket after a race to ensure that someone – again, not my client – could claim a large amount of winnings. Everyone arrived at court soaked to the skin and many got even wetter inside as the building was unable to stand up to the onslaught: it was damp in any event and leaking prodigiously. Outside, the rain was inescapable and the wind was blowing umbrellas inside out. I felt so sorry for my client, brought into court from the prison transport. She had been remanded in Tai Tan Gap , a prison Shirley had recently visited with a friend who was a magistrate. The client was late for the hearing because there had been a landslide. A tree had come down and the police van could not get through. The ride had been a terrifying experience, particularly so for a lady of advanced years. She stood in the prisoner's dock, her straggling grey hair tied back, shivering and stooped in her wet prison outfit. The court permitted her be seated, as she was so gaunt and frail. She looked wretched and commanded pity.

The appeal was allowed and she was taken away by her family who invited Shirley and me to lunch the next day at the very expensive Sharks Fin Restaurant. We arrived at the appointed time. Whilst we were waiting in the reception area to be taken to our table, a good-looking woman seated in one of the alcoves was waving to us. We didn't know her but we nodded politely as we waited for the maitre d' d'hôtel to attend to us. After a moment, she came over to greet us, saying, "Don't you remember me?"

She had dark, glossy hair, was well-dressed, beautifully manicured and made-up.

Yes. A morning at the hairdresser and beautician, we could not believe the transformation. The sickly wraith was a picture of health and had turned the clock back twenty years overnight. She insisted on buying us the most beautiful tablecloth as a gift. The perfect taste with which it was chosen was hers but it remains unused in our house. Perhaps waiting to be transformed into something simpler.

***

Another group of ladies figured prominently in a Court of Appeal case in Hong Kong.

I was involved in much litigation concerning rubber companies. As the use of synthetic materials increased, the rubber companies began disposing of their assets. They rapidly became cash rich under conditions which led to all sorts of financial shenanigans ranging from sharp practice to breaches of contract to outright fraud. In one of these cases, I was instructed to get an order which was to do with the winding-up of companies and the proper mechanism of avoiding someone's claims for certain funds. This was dry, practical law. No cut-and-thrust of cross-examination, just plodding through mountains of paper, piecing together the relevant evidence. But there was something about the case that struck me as odd. All the companies involved – and there were several – had charming names: Po-Lin, Bo-Peep, Sweet-Heart and so on.

I asked my instructing solicitor what I should say if one of the Appeal Judges were to ask if there was any significance to these names. The client cheerfully explained.

"Each of these lovely names is because I named the companies after the Mama-San most recently visited." He smiled. "So-Mei-Lin," he started to give the example but he went off into a reverie of remembrance of the lovely So-Mei-Lin, whose immortality was now to be curtailed as the activities of the eponymous trading company were being wound up. So it was when he was prompted on any other name. Each colourful butterfly, every tenderly offered title of love carried memories that transported the client away from concentrating on the work that had to be done. The client was a generous man. His parting gift to each transient friend was title to the company which bore their name (or nick-name). All they had to do was wind up the company and take the cash.

CHAPTER 65

CALLING TIME AT THE BAR

There comes a time in a man's life when he begins to think, if not of wind-
ing down, of changing direction. The wind of change came from Gray's
Inn in 1993, having originated in America and routed via Australia.
George Hampel, a judge of the Supreme Court of Victoria, was invited
by Michael Hill QC, a very active Bencher of Gray's Inn, to demonstrate
a system of advocacy training that he had modified for use in the English
courts. Until the Hampel system was adopted, advocacy was more often
acknowledged to be dire than stirring. Or interesting. Or persuasive.
The natural advocate is a rare breed. More often such skills as were
currently displayed in court had been acquired by accident and the ac-
cumulation of experience, not necessarily what clients on the learning
curve may have had in mind. Judges themselves had learned in the same
ad hoc way and, even if infuriated by bungling words from newcomers,
would have remembered being in the same position themselves at the
start of their careers. For three or four years, the Inns of Court School of
Law had been providing advocacy training in its Bar Vocational Course
and, at the time, the Bar Council was stirring from its educational leth-
argy, considering whether it should demand a compulsory course in ad-
vocacy. The nine hours training that it was intending to impose were
unlikely to make a Marshall Hall[1] out of any student.

My career had started with no training except for a kind word on the
hoof from an experienced colleague. I learned by mistakes designed to
enrage judges and alarm clients. Nothing had changed significantly for
newcomers in my forty or so years at the Bar. The procedure was more
akin to slapstick than high drama. The new graduates stumbled along
in much the same fashion as their predecessors. I had been arguing for
some time that advocacy could not be learned by osmosis. It had to be
taught and it was time for the Inns themselves to take a more active
part in training new recruits to the Bar. So, ideas such as those George
Hampel was presenting were likely to be of great interest. I went to one
of his training programmes where the system was to be demonstrated
through role-playing of examination-in-chief and cross-examination of

---

[1] Sir Edward Marshall Hall KC (1858-1927), a criminal defence barrister, renowned for his theatrical style of oratory and advocacy skills.

a witness in a criminal trial. A pupil had agreed to be the witness and barristers were to be the guinea-pig advocates to learn the method which essentially involved an instant criticism of any error, followed by a demonstration of how to correct it. I was seated with my notebook and pen, getting ready to take what I hoped would be a few useful notes when George Hampel pounced.

"Here is Michael Sherrard, a well-known advocate who has been known to express views on the standards of others. Will you show us how you would go about examination in chief of the witness?"

Perhaps he saw the look of alarm on my face. Even in fun, it was difficult to imagine taking someone through evidence-in-chief without any preparation. As I hesitated, George said, "I'll tell you what, you can cross-examine him. You'll be more spontaneous if you're not trying to make up the story as well." I felt not unlike my first day in court. I said, "I really don't think I can do this with half the Court of Appeal sitting at the back taking particular interest in me."

George said, "Why?"

I said, "Because I'm nervous!"

There was a murmur of approval from the back of the hall, any one of whom could have been appointed as the next to make a fool of himself. I heard: "Yes. Me too. Let's adjourn for a month." And various other comments that indicated no-one relished the thought of being on display and subject to criticism.

Inevitably, George manoeuvred me onto the platform. I asked my questions and was called to order. "Do it this way. Say that." I heard what was wanted. I started to do it and get it right.

That meant the others had to be willing to perform and many of them did, one after the other. Although there was more to learn from hearing mistakes corrected, our lot would have been easier if the pupil had been a better witness. As it was, he was absolutely terrible, so bad that it may have played a part in George changing his role.

In the new scenario, he was subjected to a further round of cross-examination. I watched his performance. Now, far from being demolished, fumbling and mumbling as he had been at the first demonstration, he was now holding up well. For a start, he had become audible and was using appropriate judicial language.

I put my hand up. "George, can I interrupt?" Which obviously meant that I had interrupted.

George said, "I suppose you'd better get it off your chest." So I asked the pupil, "Could you tell us what has happened? Why couldn't you answer my questions like you're answering these? Your language, your answers: you have been trained as a witness. How do you explain that?"

He said that he not been trained before and was as intimidated as I had been at the outset but had learned from the critiques applied to the role-playing trainers.

That opened the door for me. It confirmed my view that it could not be right that pupils were not trained in advocacy before going into court. This system was something that could be of fundamental importance to the future of the Bar and I was going to try to do something to make it part of our student training programme.

In the weeks around the training session I had begun to think that, simply by the passage of time, my career at the Bar was likely to draw to an end. If retirement was to be anything like a holiday, I had certain misgivings: although many of my holidays had passed without mishaps, my usual experience was setting off with high hopes and returning with various wounds or fevers that would not have happened if I had stuck with what I enjoyed best: work. But a change of career that could combine my passion for advocacy with education for the incoming members of the Bar was a fascinating proposition. I started to sketch out a workable system, based on what George had shown us, for training students in advocacy. This, in turn, would depend on the goodwill of the established members of the Bar and, in particular, their willingness to be trained as trainers. The aim was not to discourage natural, creative talent nor to produce "clone" advocates but to ensure that every beginner was competent to go into court with fundamental professional skills without dilution of individuality.

Having seen the Hampel method in action, I was convinced that it was the way forward. As a Bencher, I had a platform within the Inn to put forward my ideas for the Middle Temple School of Advocacy. More importantly, I had known for some time that I would have the power to establish the school. A year or so previously, on our way into a meeting of Parliament, the governing body of the Inn, Benet Hytner QC, a fellow Bencher, came over and congratulated me.

I asked, "Why?"

He clapped me on the shoulder. It is the Bar's way of indicating that something important is going to happen to you. "You're being put up as Third Man to be Treasurer in three years' time."

"Really?" I was amazed. "No one's told me," I said. But they had also forgotten to tell the current Third Man so perhaps that is part of the tradition as well.

In Middle Temple's jargon, this was nothing to do with a Grahame Greene novel. It is the Inn's way of planning three years or more ahead for the appointment of Treasurer, its highest office. There is always a pool of likely and willing candidates to be Treasurer. In the normal way, three persons are involved in the appointment and election of likely Treasurers. They become a triumvirate consisting of the Treasurer, the Deputy Treasurer and the Third Man but the Third Man needs to be identified a year or two before he moves into that most unofficial of roles. Even more in the shadows is the Fourth Man …

The progression towards high office is that, before the end of the Treasurer's year of office, the next candidate, always the Deputy Treasurer, will seek to be elected. His opponent will be the current Third Man who, by convention, is always defeated but then moves into the position of Deputy Treasurer at which time, a new Third Man is brought in. On the 1 January of every year, the Deputy Treasurer becomes Treasurer, taking over from his outgoing predecessor. The Third Man has time to put his practice affairs in order in the years leading up to high office. Invariably, being Treasurer is virtually a full-time role and, if he is not retired from practice or planning to do so, he will probably need a sabbatical from his main career, even though he can call on the Deputy Treasurer to ask for his assistance. The merry-go-round runs perpetually. There is always a Third Man in the wings waiting to be elected, knowing that the body politic has approved him as future Treasurer. It also gives him the opportunity to learn the ropes and he is reassured by knowing, as he comes to do in time, that the Treasurer has taken soundings from other Benchers as to whether they have ambitions: that is the beginning of the chicken and egg situation.

In my case, in the casual, after-lunch way that so often brings home matters of importance, the Treasurer of the day had asked me as we were leaving the High Table, "Do you fancy being Treasurer?"

This meant that it was almost mine for the asking, in three or four years time at most. But, convention requires a relatively guarded answer. Under the portrait of Queen Elizabeth I, I was thinking, "Oh, yes!" But by the time we had reached Charles I, I heard myself delivering a more measured response, consistent with someone more senior than me being considered a better proposition.

"It all depends. If I have to work as hard as you, I don't think so. " At which point I thought I detected a hint of a frown. I managed to change the emphasis " But, yes," I said. "I would put myself up." Which meant, I would not object to being put up. So, I was not completely surprised when Ben Hytner congratulated me. The wheels were now in motion and, as they were turning, I could now press home my ideas for the greater involvement of the Inn in advocacy training, although I had not realised that it would become a total involvement until I handed over office to Barry Mortimer QC in 2004, then continuing on an "as-needed basis".

The next Parliament convened to consider the business of governing the Inn. After my first experience of the Hampel style of training, my concerns about the future of advocacy had been reinforced by an article by Frances Gibb in *The Times* about the inadequacies of training for pupils. The Bar Council's proposition that nine hours advocacy training in the twelve months of pupillage was sufficient did not accord with my concept. My plan, which came to fruition, was for a two-week course, dedicated to advocacy. I had not really discussed my ideas but when it came to 'any other business', I was ready to state my case.

To the Benchers packed into the Parliament Chamber, I said, "I don't know if other members have detected a growing undercurrent of concern about the inadequacies of advocacy training. If you ask me what is the remedy, I would have to say that the Inn should provide the necessary training. Somebody should be willing to undertake the responsibility of investigating the position, looking at it from the Inn's point of view, covering both finance and the mechanics of running a training programme. It will be not only for the students but for the good of us all. I have formed the view that we should put this on proper footing: have a timetable, a prospectus and, above all, train the trainers so that we have consistency of methods and standards."

Lord Wilberforce, descended from William Wilberforce, the slave-trade abolitionist, had come to this particular Parliament. He said, "I think this is of great importance for the Bar. The only people who can put it right are the barristers. Master Sherrard said that they have to be trained and that is true."

His voice carried terrific influence. He went on, "I don't see why we should postpone this discussion. I'm going to move, when Master Sherrard has finished what he was saying when I interrupted, let's do this now."

I said, within the privilege of Parliament, "I'm rather committed to some cases but if they can be disposed of, if I'm given *carte blanche* for eighteen months, I'll get it up and running – and I wish me the best of luck." And I sat down.

So that was the birth of Middle Temple Advocacy. I was stuck with it. I had needed a kick in the pants to get it off the ground but in the end, I had done the kicking myself.

Having given it some publicity round the Inn, I had more than two hundred enthusiastic offers to help from some very senior people, including High Court judges. But most of them expressed the desire to be left to their own devices when it came to how they taught: it required not a little advocacy skill to persuade them to accept the idea that they needed to be trained as trainers. They hoped there would be an open endeavour to see how much we all had in common. But I was adamant: we could not have a situation where there were different methods. This was a particular area of work: ethics, written skills and disciplinary aspects could come out of a book but the art of advocacy could not.

We started the show. I devised a course and a curriculum of lectures and was given offices and a budget. We had a title: Middle Temple Advocacy "MTA". I was made its Director and managed to carry out the wide range of responsibilities with the invaluable assistance of the most competent of administrators, Christa Richmond. As well as its prime teaching function, the ethos of MTA became part of the demolition process for breaking down the barriers that separated the ranks of a hierarchical profession.

I was appointed as Director of MTA in 1994. This meant that I would close my practice as I now had a job to do and only two years to go to the start of my year as Treasurer. No time for going to court, consulting with clients or travelling round the world – except on MTA business. It was easy to refuse new instructions but very tricky to manage the completion of my current overseas work. Gradually, I completed my work or, where necessary, put it into competent hands so that I could concentrate fully on my duties in the Inn. Although I retired officially and had a farewell party at 2 Crown Office Row, there was no time for any regrets about the end of an era. The new one had already started.

Our potential trainers were in line for four hours training at the Inn over the period of a month. Many of them were experienced practitioners who had made an art form of the leading question: they had to unravel their experience and their intellectual knitting and be able to criticise leading and demonstrate how not to lead. They were greatly encouraged in their re-learning endeavours by taking the alternative of a weekend at Cumberland Lodge, the beautiful house in Windsor Great Park which, by permission of the Queen, hosts Middle Temple's educational gatherings. Not the least of the pleasures was for a group of them to meet her Majesty, the Queen Mother, after church on the Sunday of the course weekend. Until the death of Her Majesty in 2002, this was also to become a high point for the students who came to the courses at Cumberland Lodge.

The trainers remained committed to the two-week compulsory training without which pupillage could not be completed. Lincoln's Inn and Inner Temple took up the same method but Gray's Inn, the smallest of the Inns, did not have the resources to run their own programme. Michael Hill was quite emotional about it. "We just can't do this at Gray's," he said. "You are greatly admired for this. We would look second rate."

But the Bar is all about co-operation and helping each other. I assured him that he could do the same thing. We would give Gray's our materials and their people could come to us for training. It took a little while for their Parliament to see it was possible. The day was carried eventually and Gray's Inn still is entitled to the credit for getting the ball rolling.

Running MTA was a demanding business. In the first four years, for example, we had 940 two hour workshops. That covered a lot of people. They had 436 hours of lectures and over 300 full court days. To me, that sounded like training.

The system? The trainers have a sheet with six headings denoting the stages of the training exercise. These are: the headline, naming the fault; playback, in which the mistake is re-enacted or read back by the trainer from his notes; remedy, which is where the trainer explains what has to be done; demonstration, in which the trainer shows how it should be done; and then the replay, where the student picks up the pieces and – with skill, not luck – gets it right the second time around. Because the work is done in groups, the first one usually has the hardest time and the others often learn from his mistakes.

In addition to it being personally rewarding, there were lessons for us all to learn from our experiences. One young Canadian girl, in England on a scholarship, was making heavy weather of an application for an ex parte injunction. In spite of the heaviest hints, she did not produce a document that would have supported her case. We had created a battery-chicken-farmer to be her client. He was designed for his counsel to find him repellent and to harden the heart of the judge. But he was about to be prevented from running his lawful business because his neighbour was going to build a fence, albeit on her own land, that would stop the delivery lorries from being able to turn after visiting his farm. The judge knew that the neighbour had written a vitriolic, threatening and insulting letter showing that, even though battery farmers are ethically deplored, some neighbours are even worse. Time and again, the girl did not take the hint that she should show the letter to the judge. Eventually, I intervened. I reminded her that the judge is only human. It is a serious matter to interfere with a person's right to deal with his own property as he wishes but the rights of others have to be respected.

"You should consider showing the judge the neighbour's letter. It is poison in the well of any case she might have. It will give him the chance to justify granting the injunction." I told her to try again.

And again she did not show the letter.

The judge took a helping hand.

"Miss X," he said. "I see that you have another document that you have not yet shown to me. Does that assist your case?"

She looked at the letter and with some relief said, "Oh, it does, My Lord. It shows that she even put poison in his well."

Ah, the use of language! I should have been more precise in recommending English idioms to someone on whom the nuances were clearly lost.

It really is never too late to learn.

Middle Temple Advocacy has gone from strength to strength. In 2004, after ten years, I handed over the Directorship to Barry Mortimer, GBS, QC, recently returned to England after retiring from judicial office in Hong Kong. In part, it was the years catching up with me but there was also the problem that, because MTA was more like play than work, perhaps I enjoyed it too much. At leisure, my health has too often let me down and some annoying neurological symptoms were eventually diagnosed as Parkinson's. This is a condition that affects mobility and causes a functional tremor in the hand. In my case, the right hand. And being a right-handed person, this was more than annoying. It was disabling. At first, I had the idea of learning to write with my left hand but that is rather difficult. In the end, I went for mind over matter and with some hard work, I have managed to make my right-handed writing a slightly wobbly version of what I can recognise as my own. I can only recommend to other sufferers from Parkinson's to battle on and retrain. It's something that you can do without but you have to live with. I don't like the walking stick very much, so I'm in perpetual training to do without it. And mostly I do.

Whatever the state of my health, it's only the body that is not in the best of working order. Whenever the Inn was short of trainers for the next couple of years, I would be there, headlining, remedying and, with any luck, getting a replay which meant that, after all, an advocate, if not born, had been made.

With Christa Richmond (first on left) and students of
Middle Temple Advocacy, 1997

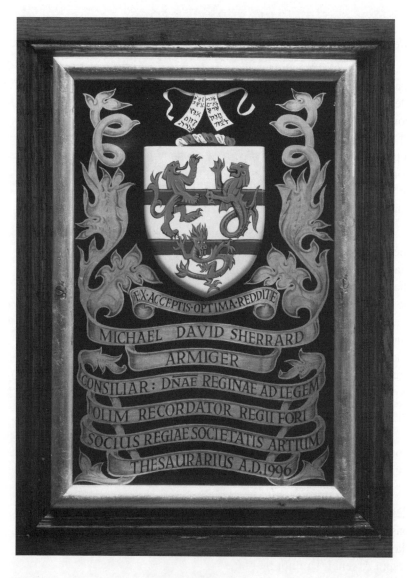

Sherrard coat of arms, photograph by Richard Hill, courtesy of Middle Temple

CHAPTER 66

TREASURER'S TROVE

Meanwhile ...

The role of Treasurer is that of the most senior officer in the Inn. It was a total takeover of my life for 1996 with much of the Third Man and Deputy Treasurer years being occupied with preparation for what was to come whilst coping with the demands of Middle Temple Advocacy. Part of the honour of being Treasurer is the right to Heraldic arms, a wooden representation of which is mounted on one of the oak panels lining the corridors and Hall. The coat of arms is handed down from father to son. In my case, the tradition started with me. As the first Sherrard to have a coat of arms, one had to be designed.

I went to see the Richmond Herald. I hoped that elements of the career that had brought me to this great honour could be shown by an association of symbols of England, Singapore and Hong Kong. My idea was that the arms should include the rose of England and Singapore could be represented by the orchid. I particularly wanted the red bauhinia to feature in the design. It is a Hong Kong flower whose delicate beauty and brilliant colour reflect the paradoxes of the Hong Kong society that I knew and loved. I explained this to Richmond Herald. He took his notes and did not question my suggestions. He was less happy with the proposition of Charles Whitby, one of the two Readers attached to me as Treasurer.

Before our visit to the College of Heralds, Charles asked me, "Are you going to organise getting your arms? I've got to do mine but I'm a bit ginger about walking into the College of Heralds. Let's go together."

He had good reason to be apprehensive. He was pretty sure that the design he had in mind would not be acceptable. He wanted the only true passion of his life to be the feature of his arms. No lions or dragons or flags or stripes. He said, "If they won't let me have something to represent Arsenal, I'm not having anything." He was adamant about it. He told Patrick Dickinson, Richmond Herald, right at the beginning: "This is key for me."

Patrick was concerned. He said, "I don't think it's heraldic. Garter King of Arms is not at all likely to approve." Charles was stubborn, "If he doesn't, I won't bother."

I could imagine the empty, white-painted square in the oak panelling. There are one or two scattered about Hall. They are often thought to be a sign of disgrace but they actually mean a variation of some sort on the Whitby situation: the space is for the arms to which you are entitled. If you have none, the space remains.

But Richmond Herald was more imaginative. "Let me think about it," he said. And he thought Arsenal, weapons, guns … So that is how the cannon came in – right at the top of the shield. The Gunners, after all, have a place in history outside the football field. It made Charles very happy. He got what he wanted and did not have to compromise.

While the design for my coat of arms was progressing, I was in Hong Kong, either tying up the loose ends of my last couple of cases or bringing Middle Temple Advocacy training to the Far East. A letter came for me from Richmond Herald. We knew it contained the long-awaited sketch. Shirley telephoned me and described the design. I listened to her, trying to put out of my mind that Charles had wanted Arsenal and, one way or another, he was going to get it. For me, my respectable symbols of the traditions of West and East had come out rather differently from my expectations. The design Shirley described was a figure of a knight in armour carrying an enormous sword, backed in a sort of tango by a creature out of Alice in Wonderland. The accompanying note said, "We have incorporated the Gryphon with tail and the arms of the King of Bohemia." Not much evidence of orchids, English roses or any other flower. I was cheered by the thought that I still had choices and this was not one of them. I set aside the notion of the white space on the wall and waited for Shirley to speak to Richmond Herald. The upshot was that he was as sorry as could be. "I hope I haven't got it wrong," he said. "I haven't been very well. I realised I hadn't done the sketch for Michael's arms and rather hurried it through. I couldn't understand what he meant by "bohinia" so I thought I must have heard it wrong. Which is why you have Bohemia."

In the nicest possible way, Shirley said "I think you've got it wrong." I was due back in London in a few days and we agreed to review the design on my return. Since first considering the heraldic form, I had, before going to Hong Kong, been to a dinner where I had been seated next to Richard Charteris, the Bishop of London (one of the best we've ever had), an Honorary Bencher: a big, lively man. He had told me that the reason that priests and barristers wear bands is to represent the two tablets that God delivered to Moses. "So you see," he explained, "they actually represent the ten commandments. What could be more appropriate for lawyers and priests?"

I now had the chance to change my mind about the design without looking as though I had been dithering about what I wanted. I had by then decided that the flower thing was a bit wishy-washy. I chose, instead of flowers, physical symbols. I introduced the red lion rampant of Kings College – Reggie the Lion. Running across the horizon of the shield is a blue and white ribbon, a river representing the roots of my religion in Israel. At the top of the arms is a pair of barrister's bands with Hebrew text, the first letters of each of the commandments on each band. My coat of arms signifies my loyalties to the law and to Judaism. Mine is one of several shields that bear a Hebrew inscription.

My arms caused more interest in the Inn than many of the others. The shield turned out to be a focal point. One way or another, I got what I wanted. Once the sketch was approved, it became part of the scroll, the actual arms document, a treasured possession. It is a great honour for me that my coat of arms should stand in Middle Temple along with those of Edmund Burke, William Congreve, William Cowper, Charles Dickens, Francis Drake, John Evelyn, Henry Fielding, Sir Martin Frobisher, Sir John Hawkins, Thomas More, Richard Sheridan, William Makepeace Thackeray. They certainly did more outside the Inn than I ever did, but we are there together. It's still hard for me to believe.

The ceremony of becoming Treasurer was one I had witnessed many times since being elected to the Bench. There was something almost regal about heading the procession into Hall, accompanied by an enormous feeling of goodwill that radiated from my friends and colleagues. By now, the Inn was the rival for my affections but Shirley did not try to win me back: she joined me in my love and admiration for the remarkable institution into whose history I had stumbled.

Apart from the splendid trappings of the role, which included generally being regarded as the host for all Inn functions, my word was law. There was also a great deal of business to be done. It was my delight to call people to the Bar and Bench, each time remembering my own experience. In addition, I was Chairman of all Committees and conducted the proceedings of Parliament. Entertaining visiting dignitaries or representing the Inn in away matches was a social pleasure, none greater than that of attending the Lord Mayor's annual banquet. At home, I presided over all dinners and made speeches on all the more formal occasions. I worked in very close co-operation with the Treasurers of the other Inns, well aware that there could be the sort of tension that had to be warded off when Middle Temple Advocacy's programme (at whose helm I remained throughout my time as Treasurer) overtook that of Gray's. There was the element of diplomacy that coursed through the year of office which seemed to go past all too quickly. The Inns have mutual amity days once every five or six years and it was my job to ensure that they were – and they were – amicable.

My room in the Inn was the Treasury office which is just off the main corridor behind Hall. The bar was always fully replenished so I could always offer guests a drink. Even if there were hundreds of them, and there sometimes seemed to be, and even if they were all parched with thirst, there was little chance of Middle Temple's Treasurer's supplies running low.

One of the functions I attended in my official capacity of Treasurer was a dinner at the Banqueting Suite in Whitehall. The Leader of Her Majesty's Opposition, Tony Blair, was the guest of honour. He was better known to me as a pupil in, and former member of, my Chambers at 2 Crown Office Row. After the dinner, he got to his feet to speak. It was a good speech, well delivered. It went down well. I was impressed. In an avuncular way, I was proud of him. After he finished, instead of returning to his table, he came towards mine. "How lovely to see you!" he said.

He turned to the room and said, "This is the chap who gave me my first break. I couldn't pass him by." He then took me across the floor to the High Table to greet the chairman, Eldred Tabachnik QC, and for me to renew acquaintance with Cherie Booth. This was a kind gesture and one which gave and was intended to give honour to me. Without indicating that she was talking about the coming election, Cherie said, "We're going to win, Michael. There will be some wonderful years ahead." Politically, she was correct from the Blair perspective. And she was right about the wonderful years ahead: for my part I was, even as we spoke, in the course of a particularly remarkable one.

There was a sombre part of the role of Treasurer. It was my duty to deal with the death of members. I had personal responsibility for ensuring that the widows, or widowers, were accompanied by the Porter with the Long Gavel to be seated at the highest position in our side of Temple Church, the other side being the spiritual home of Inner Temple. I attended the funerals and read the lesson. My relationship with the Master of Temple Church was very co-operative and, throughout the religious ceremonies, my role remained secular.

CHAPTER 67

END OF PART 1

Michael was enormously proud and flattered to receive the honour of a CBE. A letter came six weeks before the Investiture of Wednesday, 29 October 2003.

Downing St. The Prime Minister. "I am minded to recommend to Her Majesty that you be awarded ... For services to the legal profession".

You know this is confidential. You don't breathe a word for six weeks. At first, you can barely breathe with the excitement. The last time I had experienced that almost overwhelming sense of joy in my professional career was when I was appointed to silk. Or perhaps when I was called to the Middle Temple Bench. Or elected Treasurer. There have been so many landmarks but this was unique. The award could only have been made on the recommendations of the highest in the profession.

I was taken completely by surprise. I knew nothing before opening the letter.

Some weeks pass while you make sure your tails are pressed, your shirt appropriately starched. Your hair cut not too near the date. You then receive a letter saying the announcement will be in the Birthday Honours. The next thing you get is an appeal for money and the information that you can have your children married in St Paul's for free.

For services to the profession ...

I believe those services were not so much for the past but for the future. Middle Temple Advocacy will send out young lawyers who can speak their part and promote justice. The other Inns have their programmes on a par with Middle's but that of Middle Temple was my special project. Handing over the reins to Barry Mortimer was a moment of great pride, tempered with a little sadness, most of which dispersed when I received a call from Christa Richmond within days, requesting my services to assist with training: they were short of help. Now, I was being rewarded for something that had been hard work and was recognised as being of immense value to the profession but – was it fair to be rewarded at such a high level for something that had been so much fun? I decided that I was unbelievably lucky.

With grandchildren, Kate and James Sherrard, outside Buckingham Palace,
October 2003

And definitely over-excited on the day. The ceremony is organised with precision. Not a detail is overlooked about where you have to be, when to turn, what to do. It's a pity there is no one to remind you about braces when you dress. That it is not until you are walking on the appointed routes through Buckingham Palace that you realise that, unless you hold your waistband with one hand, artfully arranged to be sub-Napoleonic in position, you will probably end up on charges of treason for dropping your trousers in front of the Queen. They did not fall. I left the Palace properly attired, as I had arrived, but this time with the insignia of CBE.

My family, friends and professional colleagues were all delighted for me. The Inn then took a remarkable step. It commissioned a portrait of me. You can see from my smile, captured by the artist Zohar, that I can barely contain my own delight that I should have had such an honour

Sketch of portrait (2003) by Israel Zohar, photograph by John Goldman, courtesy of Middle Temple. As shown on the book jacket

bestowed on me. It was presented to the Inn at a special ceremony: yet another honour.

***

I took my former co-pupil, now Judge Nina Lowry, to lunch at the Inn. I showed her the portrait. She stood there with tears in her eyes. "Oh, Michael," she said, "Have you come so far?"

And, frankly, I had.

Time to move on.

Index

Brittan, Leon 129

Broadcasts for BBC 48

Brownlie, Ian 145-6

Buckman, Irene 142-5, 162, 206

    pupil, becoming 144

Burton, Michael

    Head of Chambers (Crown Office Row), becoming 370-1

Buzzard, John 67-72

CBE, receiving 400-1

Caborn-Waterfield, Michael, *see* Dandy Kim

Capstick, Brian 51, 191, 195

Carrian Group 328-37

    Hansard report 336-7

    statistics 328

    Tan, George (Chairman), case involving

        bail application 328-33

        committal stage, stays in Hong Kong apartment 333-4

        events during 335-6

        hands over case 336

        length of 336

        outcome of 336

        prosecutor opposing bail (Warwick Reid) 330-3, 336-7

Cartoons in court, draws 137-41

Caswell, J D 9

Challenor, Detective Sergeant Harold 105-12

    brick planting case 106-110

    other half of brick, case on 110

    post-script on 111-12

    public inquiry 111

Chambers, *see* Crown Office Row; Hare Court

Chan, William 145, 316

Civil work 26, 42, 147

Clerides, Glafcos 13, 168, 175-7

    President of Cyprus 176

Clinton-Davies, Stanley (Baron Clinton-Davies) 14, 57, 88, 105-7, 110

    Lord George-Brown case, instructing solicitor in 201, 204

Coat of Arms 394, 395-7

Concorde, flight on 352-3

Cork, Kenneth 158, 161

    acting for 186-8

Cradock, Frank 113-17

    'arrest' of 113

Crespi, James Caesar 199

Criminal Bar Association 201fn

Croome-Johnson, David 159, 164, 166

Crown Office Row

    chambers members 51, 398

talk to Law Society, theme of 211-15

Thesiger, Mr Justice 207-10

Training, *see* **Education and training**

Treasurer (Middle Temple), *see* **Middle Temple**

Tullybelton, Lord Fraser of 301, 310

University, King's College London 11-15

    academics 12

    fellow students 13-14

    law degree 14-15

Vinelott, John 305-8

Violent crimes

    cases involving 87-90

Wang, Teddy and Nina 361-2

War, 2nd World 5-6, 7, 11, 17

Whitby, Charles 260-2, 395-6

Wig and gown

    first uses of 20, 27

Wilberforce, Lord 389

Williams, Glanville L 12, 152

Wilson, Harold 203-5

Winn Committee 142, 148-9

    effect of being on 149-50

    final report 149

    invitation to be on 148, 149

    members 149fn

Winn, Rodger 147-9

Winston Churchill Memorial Lecture, Fourth 211-15

Wormwood Scrubs

    lunches in 242-3

Yorke, Richard 297, 299

    San Imperial appeal, acting for bank in 303, 305, 308, 310, 12

Zohar, Israel 402